State 6, Tues, Sec 1
Instr. J. Como

380
54 C

Quiz 1	Oct 19	85	Chap 2-3
2	Nov 16	100	Chap 4 (part)
3	Dec 14	80	chap 4-5
4	Jan 25	86	Chap 6-7-8

Final Thursday, Feb 10, 1955

GUILLET'S

Kinematics of Machines

GUILLET'S KINEMATICS OF MACHINES

Fifth Edition by AUSTIN H. CHURCH

KINEMATICS AND MACHINE DESIGN

By LOUIS J. BRADFORD and the Late

GEORGE L. GUILLET

GUILLET'S
Kinematics of Machines

Fifth Edition by

AUSTIN H. CHURCH
Professor of Mechanical Engineering
New York University

JOHN WILEY & SONS, INC., NEW YORK
CHAPMAN & HALL, LIMITED, LONDON

SECOND PRINTING, MARCH, 1952

PRINTED IN THE UNITED STATES OF AMERICA

Preface
To the Fifth Edition

In revising this book an attempt has been made to maintain the conciseness and clarity achieved by Professor Guillet. It is a difficult task to work on a textbook which has attained a widespread reputation for its "teachability," for the danger is always present that this more or less intangible quality may be lost in the process.

The chapter on velocity and acceleration in plane motion has been largely rewritten, particularly the material on the image methods, as it is believed that this portion could be expanded for better understanding. At the end of this chapter an article on Coriolis' acceleration has been added. This may be omitted for shorter courses, but it is needed to solve acceleration problems for many types of common mechanisms that can be handled in no other way.

The gearing chapter has also been largely revamped to shift the emphasis of gear kinematics to the currently used generating principle of producing gear teeth, which has largely replaced the use of formed milling cutters. In this connection I should like to express my appreciation to Mr. Allan H. Candee, of the Gleason Works, for the many excellent suggestions and help given in the revision of this chapter.

In addition, the following changes may be noted: revision of the articles on simple harmonic motion, and the scale determination for the velocity and acceleration curves in Chapter 2; the addition of the tabulation method for locating instant centers in Chapter 3; revised proof of Klein's construction, and the inversions of the slider-crank mechanism in Chapter 5; introduction of the pressure angle of cams, selection of cam motion, applications of cams, and the method of manufacture in Chapter 6; emphasis on the tabulation method for epicyclic gear trains, and the addition of an article on epicyclic gear trains with no member fixed in Chapter 9. Some of the drafting-room problems have been removed and new ones added. Uniform and consistent symbols have been adopted. To keep the length of the book approximately the same, certain portions of Chapter 6 on circular arc cams and Chapter 10 on pulleys and sprockets were removed.

It is hoped that these changes will make *Kinematics of Machines* clearer and more interesting to the student. The reviser would welcome any suggestions that may occur to the users of this book.

Austin H. Church

October, 1950

Contents

1 General Considerations

1·1 Kinematics of machines is that portion of the study of machines that deals with the motions of the parts of which they are composed.

In general, the design of a machine must be carried out in four stages: first, the purpose for which the machine is to be used must be considered, and the necessary motions must be studied; second, some device must be selected that will produce the required motions; third, the forces acting in the members must be calculated; and finally, a choice of materials must be made and the parts properly proportioned to withstand the forces determined above. The final form is necessarily influenced by many factors whose consideration is outside the province of this book. As far as possible, we shall confine our attention to the study of motions in machinery. The four stages just mentioned, comprising the subject of machine design, are, however, interdependent to such an extent that an entirely separate consideration of any one of them would be useless from the standpoint of practical design. Thus, theoretical forms derived from kinematic considerations alone must nearly always be modified on application to real machines, for the reason that other factors, such as strength, wearing qualities, and ease of production, must be taken into account.

1·2 A machine is a combination of parts of resistant materials having definite motions and capable of transmitting or transforming energy. A machine must always be supplied with energy from an external source. Its usefulness consists in its ability to alter the energy supplied to render it available for the accomplishment of a desired service.

An internal-combustion engine transforms the pressure energy of the gas into mechanical work which is delivered to the crankshaft. This machine, therefore, transforms one kind of energy into another.

A transmission gear may be used to connect two shafts which are required to rotate at different rates. Its function is to alter the mechanical work supplied to it, with regard to the speed of rotation and twisting moment, the result being to put the energy into a form more suitable for some specific purpose.

Resistant materials are those that do not easily become distorted or change their physical form when forces are applied.

1·3 A mechanism is a combination of pieces of resistant materials whose parts have constrained relative motion. A machine is composed of one or more mechanisms. When we speak of a mechanism, we think of a device that will produce certain mechanical movements, and we set aside the question of whether it is capable of doing useful work. A mechanism may or may not be able to transmit an appreciable amount of energy; a machine must do so. The latter is, therefore, a practical development of the former.

A working model of any machine, the works of a watch, and the moving parts of an engineering instrument are all termed mechanisms because the energy transmitted is very small, just enough to overcome friction, and the motions produced are the important consideration.

A structure is a combination of pieces of resistant material capable of carrying loads or transmitting forces, but having no relative motion of its parts.

A machine frame may be built of several metal parts rigidly fastened together so as to allow no movement to take place between different sections. It is, therefore, a structure. Other examples are bridges and buildings.

The sectional view of the jeep engine, shown in Fig. 1·1, contains illustrations of practically all the definitions covered in this chapter and many of the mechanisms considered in this text.

1·4 A link is a part of a machine or mechanism connecting other parts which have motion relative to it. A link may serve as a support, to guide other links, to transmit motion, or to function in all three ways.

Thus, in a steam engine (Fig. 1·5), the connecting rod, crank, crosshead, and frame are links, since each functions in at least one of these ways. A single link may be composed of several pieces of material, provided that the several portions are so

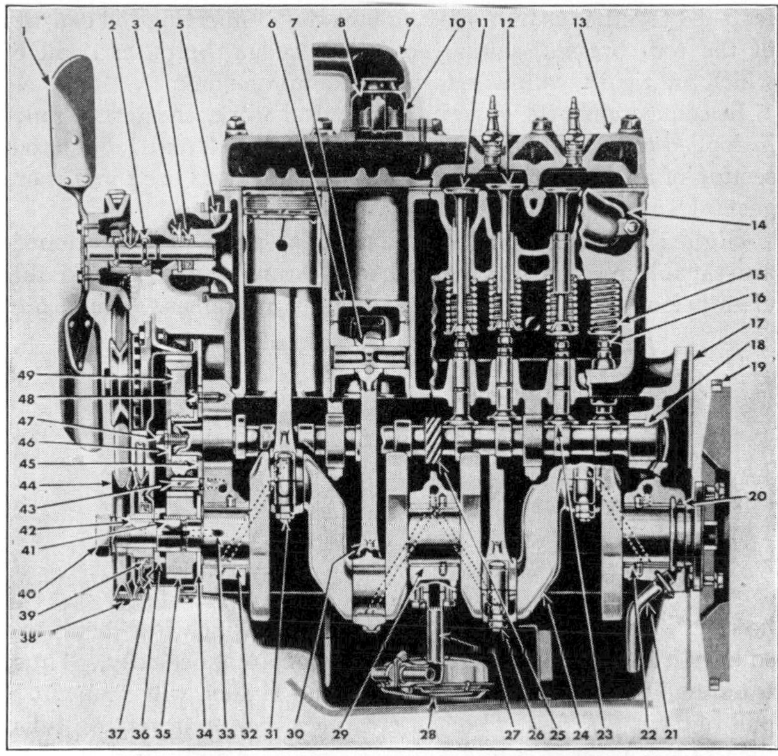

Willys-Overland Motors, Inc.

FIG. 1·1 Sectional View of Jeep Engine.

1—Fan assembly
2—Water-pump bearing and shaft assembly
3—Water-pump seal washer
4—Water-pump seal assembly
5—Water-pump impeller
6—Piston
7—Wrist pin
8—Thermostat assembly
9—Water-outlet elbow
10—Thermostat retainer
11—Exhaust valve
12—Intake valve
13—Cylinder head
14—Exhaust manifold assembly
15—Valve spring
16—Valve-tappet self-locking adjusting screw
17—Engine plate—Rear
18—Camshaft
19—Flywheel ring gear
20—Crankshaft packing—rear end
21—Crankshaft bearing rear drain pipe
22—Crankshaft bearing rear—lower
23—Valve tappet
24—Crankshaft
25—Oil pump and distributor drive gear
26—Connecting-rod cap bolt
27—Oil-float support
28—Oil-float assembly
29—Crankshaft bearing center—lower
30—Connecting-rod assembly—no. 2
31—Connecting-rod bolt nut
32—Crankshaft bearing—front lower
33—Crankshaft oil passages
34—Crankshaft thrust washer
35—Crankshaft gear
36—Crankshaft-gear spacer
37—Timing-gear cover assembly
38—Fan and generator-drive belt
39—Crankshaft oil seal
40—Crankshaft nut
41—Crankshaft-gear key
42—Fan and governor-drive pulley key
43—Timing-gear oil jet
44—Fan-, generator-, and governor-drive pulley
45—Camshaft thrust plate
46—Camshaft-gear retaining washer
47—Camshaft-gear retaining screw
48—Camshaft-gear thrust-plate retaining screw
49—Camshaft gear

fastened together as to move as a unit; the connecting rod consists of the rod, brasses, shims, adjusting wedge, bolts, etc., all of which are rigidly connected and make up one link.

In connection with general mechanical work, the term "link" is applied to a slotted bar, as shown in Figs. 1·2 and 1·3, or to a section of an ordinary chain. In kinematics it is used in a more general way, as noted previously.

Rigid links, such as the steam-engine parts just mentioned, are capable of transmitting either a thrust or a pull. To this class belong most of the metal parts of machines. There are,

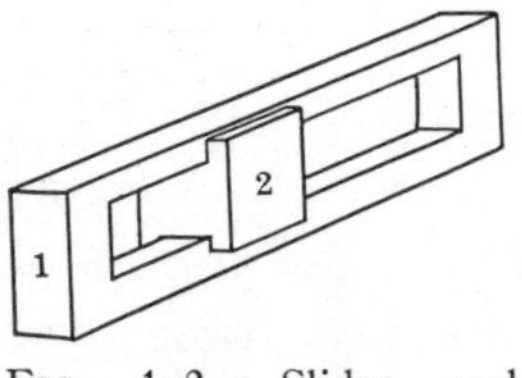

FIG. 1·2 Slider and Straight Guide.

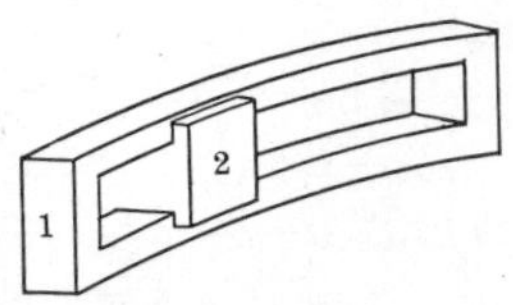

FIG. 1·3 Slider and Curved Guide.

however, many examples of **flexible** links, which in general are so constituted as to offer resistance in one manner only. Thus, **tension** links, such as ropes, belts, and chains, will transmit a pull but not a thrust, whereas **compression** or **pressure** links, such as the water in a hydraulic accumulator and pump system, or the oil in a hydraulic-braking system on a car, are capable of carrying only a thrust.

When a number of links are connected to one another in such a way as to allow motion to take place in the combination, it is called a **kinematic chain.** A kinematic chain is not necessarily a mechanism; it becomes one when so constructed as to allow constrained relative motion among its parts.

1·5 Pairs of elements Links may make contact with one another in various ways. Contact may take place over a surface, along a line, or at a point. Those portions of two links making contact are known as a pair of elements. **Sliding pairs** are those in which there is relative motion of the points of contact (see 1 and 2 in Figs. 1·2 and 1·3).

When two bodies are so connected that one is constrained to rotate about a fixed axis passing through the other, the contact surfaces are known as a **turning pair.** The pin joints of Figs. 1·4 and 1·5 belong to this class. Turning pairs in practical machines generally have sliding contact, and it would therefore seem that they might be classified as sliding pairs. Theoretically, however, a turning pair requires line contact only (i.e., along the axis of rotation), so that no sliding action is kinematically necessary.

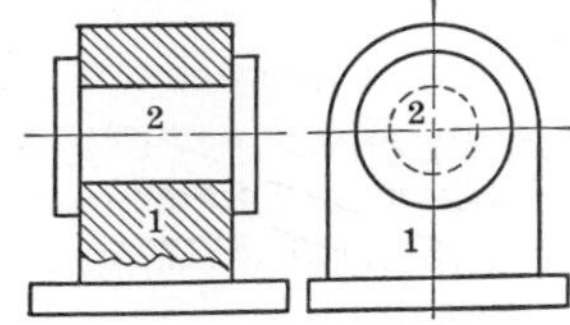

FIG. 1·4 Pin Joint.

Rolling pairs are those in which there is no relative motion of the points of contact. Ball bearings and roller bearings contain examples of this kind of pairing. In Fig. 1·11 is shown a section of a tapered roller bearing in which rolling pairs are formed by the contact points of rollers and races.

Lower pairing is obtained when two links are in contact over finite surfaces, the two elements of the pair being geometrically similar. A revolving shaft fitted with plain bearings, a threaded bolt and nut, an engine crosshead and its guides—these all are illustrations of lower pairing (see Figs. 1·4 and 1·5). This is the most common form of pairing in machinery, because it has the practical advantage of large wearing surfaces.

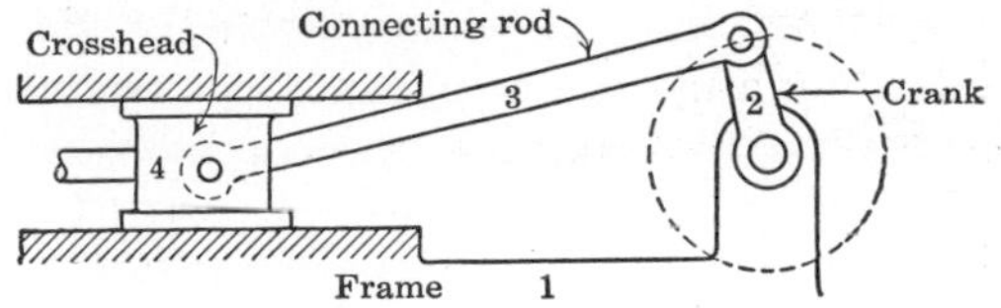

FIG. 1·5 Direct-Acting Engine Mechanism.

Higher pairing exists when two links make contact along a line or at a point. Here the contact surfaces are not similar in form. Higher pairing is found in gears, the teeth making contact at points or along lines, and also in ball and roller bearings, the rollers and balls making line and point contact, respectively, with the races. Higher pairs with rolling contact have small friction losses.

It should be noted that in practical machines, since the materials employed possess a little elasticity, some distortion of the contact surfaces takes place when pressure is applied. Thus, when line or point contact should occur, actually we always have some surface contact. This condition, combined with the use of lubricants, makes it possible to use sliding pairs with line or point contact in cases where the sliding velocity is low.

Alteration from higher to lower pairing can be accomplished without any change in the motion of the original links. Figure

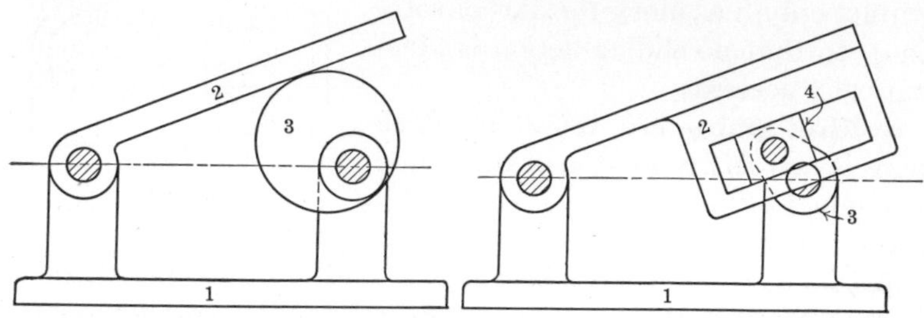

(*a*) Cam mechanism with higher pairing.

(*b*) Mechanism with lower pairing derived from that of part *a*.

FIG. 1·6.

1·6*a* shows a circular cam driving an oscillating follower with line contact. Figure 1·6*b* is an equivalent mechanism with lower pairing. The motions of links, denoted by the same numbers, are identical in the two mechanisms. Figure 1·7*a* shows the mechanism used to drive the valves of a duplex steam pump, higher pairing again being in evidence between one pair of links.

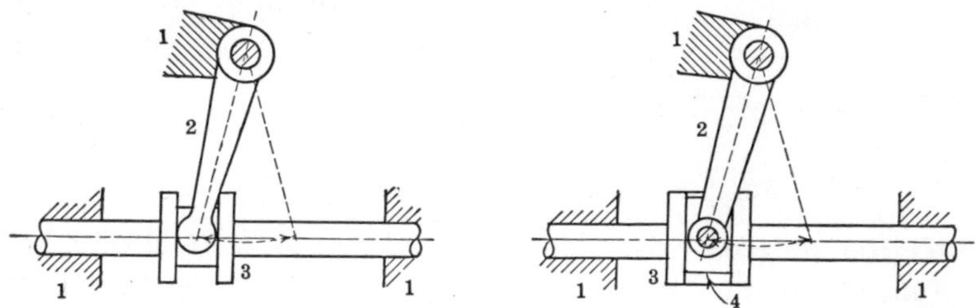

(*a*) Valve motion of steam pump with higher pairing.

(*b*) Valve motion of steam pump with lower pairing only.

FIG. 1·7.

Figure 1·7*b* shows this mechanism changed to one with lower pairing only.

In both the cases just mentioned, lower pairing has been brought about by the addition of one link. This is the method that must usually be adopted.

1·6 Link types Links forming parts of machines move in such a variety of ways that no general classification with regard to motion is possible. The following are three types in common use:

A **crank** is a link in the form of a rod or bar, which executes complete rotations about a fixed center (see 2, Fig. 1·8).

A **lever** is a link in the form of a rod or bar which oscillates through an angle, reversing its sense of rotation at certain intervals (see 4, Fig. 1·8).

A **slider** is a link in the form of a rod, block, or slotted bar, which slides over the surface of a second link. It may move in a straight line, as does the crosshead of the steam engine of Fig. 1·5, or it may move in a curve, as does the block in Fig. 1·3.

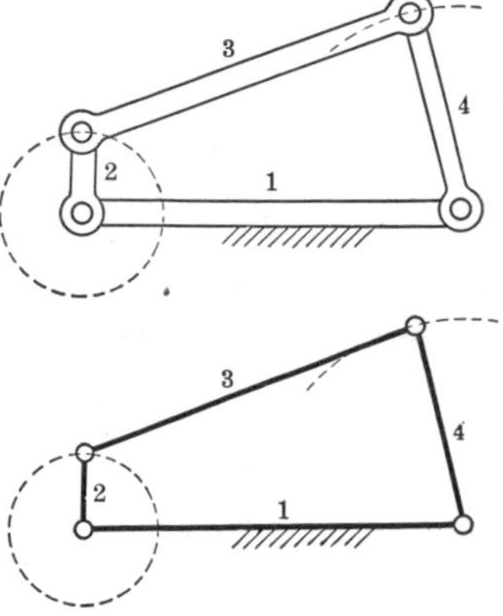

FIG. 1·8 Four-Bar Linkage.

1·7 Motion can be defined as a change of position. Motion is always a relative term; that is, we cannot conceive of any motion of a body except by reference to another body. It is usual to regard the earth as a fixed body, and we therefore speak of the **absolute motion** of a body when we mean its motion relative to the earth. We apply the term **relative motion** to the movement of one body relative to another moving body, the earth again being considered as stationary. Strictly speaking, we have relative motion in both cases, and the afore-mentioned designations are only a conventional means of distinguishing them.

Constrained motion A body is said to have constrained motion when it is so guided by contact with other bodies, or by external forces, that any point on it is obliged to move in a definite path. Any link in a mechanism has constrained motion.

Partial constraint exists when the movement of a body is only restrained in certain directions, or so as to take place within certain boundaries. For example, considering the kinematic chain shown in Fig. 1·9, consisting of five links with turning pairs, it is evident that the links 3 and 4 are only partially constrained, since a point, such as A, may move anywhere on a surface whose boundaries are fixed by the lengths of the links. If, however, we add to the chain another link, such as 6, with pin joints, then constraint becomes complete, since any point on any link we

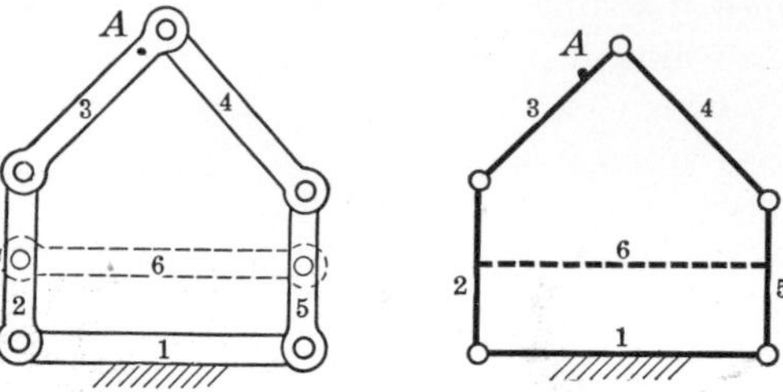

FIG. 1·9 Compound Mechanism.

may select will have a definite path of motion. The chain is now a mechanism.

The following common classes of kinematic chains have complete constraint, provided the pairs are so formed as to maintain contact:

1. Chains containing four links, each link bearing elements of two lower pairs. Figures 1·5, 1·6*b*, 1·7*b*, and 1·8 illustrate this class.

2. Chains with three links, each link containing elements of two pairs, higher pairing being used between two links and lower pairing for the other two connections. Figures 1·6*a* and 1·7*a* show two of these mechanisms.

These chains are known as **simple mechanisms.**

There are many mechanisms known as **compound mechanisms,** which have more than four links and in which certain of the links contain elements of more than two pairs. Figure 1·9, when link 6 has been added, illustrates a mechanism of this kind. A compound mechanism is frequently a combination of two or more simple mechanisms.

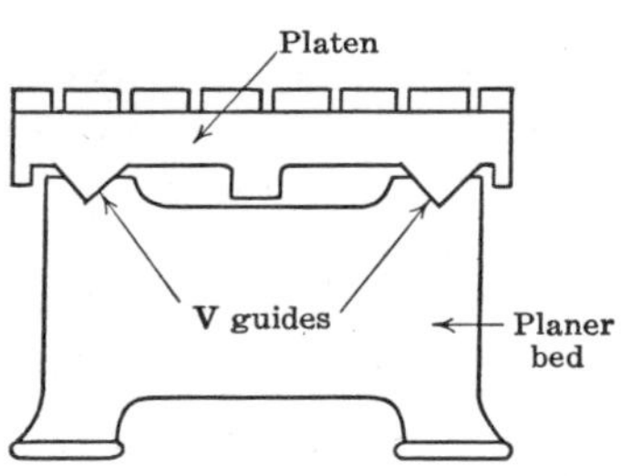

FIG. 1·10 Constraining Motion by Gravity.

In many mechanisms constraint is not effected entirely by the form of the links, the action of gravity, spring pressure, centrifugal force, etc., being utilized. For example, the platen of a planer is held in contact and alignment with the bed by gravity, which prevents the V-shaped guides on its lower side from coming out of engagement with the corresponding grooves on the top of the bed (see Fig. 1·10). Also, in many cam mechanisms the follower is kept in contact with the cam by means of a spring.

1·8 Inversion of a mechanism In any mechanism we have one link that is "fixed," that is, at rest relative to the earth, or to the body on which it is mounted. Exactly the same system of links may often be rendered suitable for a different purpose if the link originally fixed is allowed to move, while some other link is held stationary. Thus, in Fig. 1·5, the ordinary engine mechanism, 1 is the fixed link. By fixing the crank 2 and allowing 1 to move, we obtain a device that is used as a quick-return motion in certain machine tools. The latter mechanism is called an **inversion** of the former one.

It is important to note that **the inversion of a mechanism does not in any way alter the relative motion of the links that compose it.** In Fig. 1·5, for example, no matter which link is fixed, the motion of 2 relative to 1 is that of rotation, and 4 always slides in a straight line on 1.

1·9 Classification of motions Most motions that occur in mechanisms fall into one of the following classes:

(a) Plane motion of a body is obtained when all points in it move in parallel or coincident planes.

When studying plane motion, we disregard the thickness of the links perpendicular to the plane of motion and speak of the center of rotation, instant center, etc., instead of the axis of rotation, instant axis, etc., which are the correct terms for the real bodies. This somewhat simplifies the treatment and does not detract from the value of the information obtained, since all points in any perpendicular to the plane of motion move in an identical manner. Plane motion is common to all mechanisms shown in Figs. 1·2 to 1·10. Our diagrams may be simplified by drawing lines to represent links, thus obtaining what are called "skeleton diagrams." In Fig. 1·9 is shown the projection of a mechanism, also a skeleton diagram.

Rectilinear motion is a form of plane motion in which all points in the body considered move in parallel straight lines (see 4, Fig. 1·5).

(b) Helical motion is executed when a body rotates about an axis and at the same time moves parallel with the same axis, the two motions bearing a fixed ratio to each other. The motion of a nut on a threaded bolt is a very common example. Any point on a body with this form of motion describes a curve called a **helix.** The contact surfaces in helical motion are called a **screw pair.**

(c) Spherical motion A body is said to have spherical motion when moving in such a way that any point in it remains at a constant distance from a fixed point. Any point on the body, therefore, moves on the surface of a sphere. Figure 1·11 shows

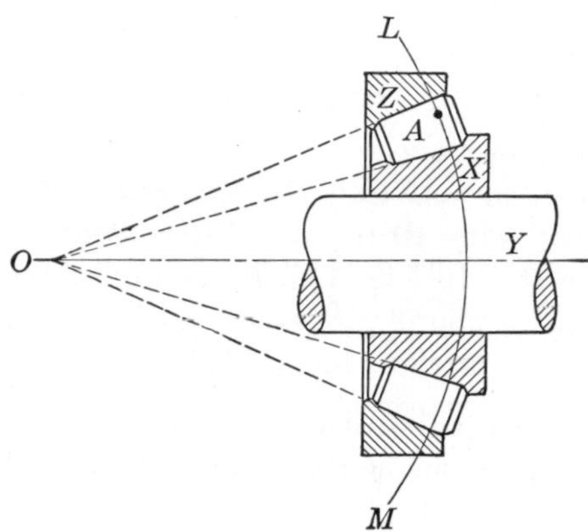

FIG. 1·11 Example of Spherical Motion.

a cross section of a tapered roller bearing. Generally the inner race X revolves with the shaft Y, and the outer race Z is stationary. Any point, such as A, on one of the rollers moves on the surface of a sphere LAM, whose center is at the point O; hence the rollers have spherical motion. Other examples are found in certain ball bearings, in bevel gears, and in universal joints.

1·10 Determination of the motion of a body The motion of a body is studied by consideration of the motion of certain points on it. The number of points to be considered depends on whether the body can move in any manner, or whether its motion is limited to some special type, as, for example, plane motion and helical motion.

In general, to determine the motion of a body completely, we must know the motion of three noncollinear points on it. This can easily be demonstrated as follows: If we take any body and fix three points on it, it is evident that no motion is possible unless these points lie in a straight line. Likewise, if we move each of the three points along a definite path in space, any other point on the body will also follow a definite path, and constraint is complete.

When a body has **plane motion,** by the same reasoning it may be seen that it is only necessary to control the motion of two points in order to secure complete constraint.

When the motion is **rectilinear,** the motion of one point determines that of any other in the body, since all points on it have exactly the same motion.

QUESTIONS

1·1 Define the terms "machine" and "mechanism." Give one example of each.

1·2 Distinguish between a structure and a mechanism.

1·3 What is a link? What is meant by (*a*) a rigid link, (*b*) a flexible link, (*c*) a pressure link, (*d*) a tension link?

1·4 Define (*a*) pair of elements, (*b*) sliding pair, (*c*) turning pair, (*d*) rolling pair.

1·5 Explain why lower pairing is generally more desirable than higher pairing with sliding contact.

1·6 Distinguish between higher and lower pairing, and give an example of each.

1·7 Give an example of how a linkage with higher pairing can be changed to one with lower pairing, and point out the nature of the alteration required.

1·8 What is a crank, a lever, a slider? Sketch mechanisms containing examples of each.

1·9 Explain what is meant by partial and complete constraint. To what extent is unconstrained motion possible?

1·10 Name three classes of kinematic chains in which the motion of the links is completely constrained.

1·11 What is (*a*) a simple chain, (*b*) a compound chain?

1·12 What is done when a mechanism is inverted? Illustrate. How does the act of inversion affect (*a*) the relative motion, (*b*) the absolute motion of the parts?

1·13 Define (*a*) motion, (*b*) plane motion, (*c*) rectilinear motion, (*d*) helical motion, (*e*) spherical motion. Give an example of each of the four varieties of motion just mentioned.

1·14 In order to determine completely the motion of a body, how many points on it must be considered, (*a*) in general, (*b*) when it has plane motion, (*c*) when it has rectilinear motion?

1·15 Mention two methods employed for securing closure of a mechanism by external forces, and illustrate each one.

2 Displacement, Velocity, and Acceleration

2·1 Definitions The **displacement** of a body is its change of position with reference to a fixed point. Both direction and distance are necessarily stated in order to define completely the displacement of a point or body.

Velocity is the rate of change of position or displacement of a body. A body may change its position by translation through space or by angular movement. Thus it may have **linear** or **angular** velocity.

Linear velocity is the rate of linear displacement of a point or body along its path of motion. It includes two factors: namely, speed and direction of motion. Linear velocity is often measured in feet per second, or in miles per hour, though other units are found more suitable in special cases. A linear velocity can always be represented graphically by a vector, the direction showing the direction of movement and the length representing the magnitude of the velocity.

Angular velocity is the rate of change of angular position of a body or line. In order to state it completely, the sense of rotation should be given. Angular velocity is commonly measured by the angle turned through per unit of time. The angle may be expressed in radians, degrees, revolutions, etc. Thus, "radians per second" and "revolutions per minute" are often used as units.

2·2 Relation between angular and linear velocity Let B, Fig. 2·1, represent a point on a body which is rotating about O. O is therefore a fixed point, and B is moving, at the instant considered, in a direction perpendicular to the line OB, its linear velocity being **v** fps as indicated on the diagram.

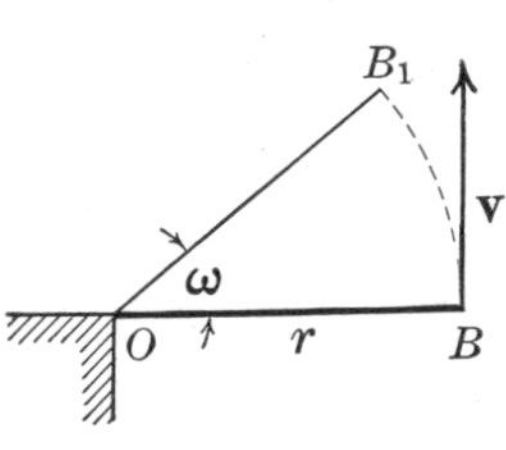

Fig. 2·1.

Assuming that B continues to move at the same speed, after an interval of one second it will have reached the position B_1, the arc BB_1 having a length equal to $\mathbf{v}$, by definition. The angle $\boldsymbol{\omega}$ turned through by line OB during the same interval is measured in radians by

$$\frac{\text{Arc } BB_1}{OB} = \frac{\mathbf{v}}{r}$$

Therefore,

$$\boldsymbol{\omega} = \frac{\mathbf{v}}{r} \quad \text{or} \quad \mathbf{v} = \boldsymbol{\omega} r \tag{2·1}$$

where $\boldsymbol{\omega}$ = angular velocity of the body in radians per unit of time. We may, therefore, state the following law:

The linear velocity of a point on a moving body is equal to the angular velocity of the body multiplied by the distance of the point from the center of rotation.

2·3 Acceleration is the rate of change of velocity with respect to time. Since velocity may be either angular or linear, we likewise have both angular and linear acceleration.

Linear acceleration is the rate of change of linear velocity. If a moving body or point has a linear velocity at a certain instant of 10 fps, and a second later the velocity has become 18 fps, we have a change of linear velocity of 8 fps in the one-second interval. Thus, the acceleration for the interval considered is 8 fps^2. Note that this value is only an **average** acceleration for the given one-second period and does not tell us how the acceleration may have varied during the interval. More information would be necessary in order to get the acceleration existing at a particular instant. Linear acceleration, like linear velocity, can always be represented graphically by a vector which shows the magnitude and direction.

Angular acceleration is the rate of change of the angular velocity. When the angular velocity is measured in radians per second, our corresponding unit of angular acceleration will be "radians per second per second"; or, if in revolutions per minute, it may be either "revolutions per minute per minute" or "revolutions per minute per second."

For **linear motion,** the relationships among displacement $\mathbf{s}$, velocity $\mathbf{v}$, and acceleration $\mathbf{a}$ may be expressed mathematically as follows:

$$\mathbf{v} = \frac{d\mathbf{s}}{dt}, \qquad \mathbf{a} = \frac{d\mathbf{v}}{dt} = \frac{d^2\mathbf{s}}{dt^2} \tag{2·2}$$

Here $\mathbf{v}$ is the instantaneous velocity, or velocity at a certain instant, and $d\mathbf{s}/dt$ expresses the rate of change of the displacement. Similarly, $\mathbf{a}$ is the instantaneous acceleration and $d\mathbf{v}/dt$, or $d^2\mathbf{s}/dt^2$, the corresponding rate of change of velocity.

When angular motion is dealt with, the displacement is $\boldsymbol{\theta}$, the velocity $\boldsymbol{\omega}$ and the acceleration $\boldsymbol{\alpha}$. Then by definition: $\boldsymbol{\omega} = d\boldsymbol{\theta}/dt$, $\boldsymbol{\alpha} = d\boldsymbol{\omega}/dt = d^2\boldsymbol{\theta}/dt^2$.

When the motion of a particle or body starts with an initial velocity $\mathbf{v}_0$ or $\boldsymbol{\omega}_0$ and is uniformly accelerated to a velocity $\mathbf{v}$ or $\boldsymbol{\omega}$ in time t:

$$\mathbf{s} = \mathbf{v}_0 t + \tfrac{1}{2}\mathbf{a}t^2 \quad \text{or} \quad \boldsymbol{\theta} = \boldsymbol{\omega}_0 t + \tfrac{1}{2}\boldsymbol{\alpha}t^2 \tag{2·3}$$

$$\mathbf{v} = \mathbf{v}_0 + \mathbf{a}t \quad \text{or} \quad \boldsymbol{\omega} = \boldsymbol{\omega}_0 + \boldsymbol{\alpha}t \tag{2·4}$$

$$\mathbf{v}^2 = \mathbf{v}^2{}_0 + 2\mathbf{as} \quad \text{or} \quad \boldsymbol{\omega}^2 = \boldsymbol{\omega}^2{}_0 + 2\boldsymbol{\alpha\theta} \tag{2·5}$$

If the initial velocity, $\mathbf{v}_0$ or $\boldsymbol{\omega}_0$, is zero, that is, the body or particle starts from rest, these equations become

$$\mathbf{s} = \tfrac{1}{2}\mathbf{a}t^2 \quad \text{or} \quad \boldsymbol{\theta} = \tfrac{1}{2}\boldsymbol{\alpha}t^2 \tag{2·6}$$

$$\mathbf{v} = \mathbf{a}t \quad \text{or} \quad \boldsymbol{\omega} = \boldsymbol{\alpha}t \tag{2·7}$$

$$\mathbf{v}^2 = 2\mathbf{as} \quad \text{or} \quad \boldsymbol{\omega}^2 = 2\boldsymbol{\alpha\theta} \tag{2·8}$$

2·4 Normal and tangential acceleration The velocity of a moving point may change in two ways: (*a*) its linear **speed** along its path may increase or decrease; or (*b*) the **direction** of its motion may change.

(*a*) The rate of change of speed in the direction of motion is the **tangential acceleration,** since this involves an acceleration acting along the path of motion.

(*b*) The change in the direction of the motion is due to the **normal** or **centripetal acceleration,** which acts in a direction normal to the direction of the path of motion. We may therefore define these terms as follows:

The **tangential acceleration** is the linear acceleration in the direction of motion at the instant considered and is measured by the rate of change of speed along its path.

The **normal** or **centripetal acceleration** is that acceleration which causes the direction of motion of a body to change. It acts along a line perpendicular to the path of motion and toward the center of curvature of this path.

For example, suppose a point A (Fig. 2·2) is traveling along the curved path XY. O is the center of curvature of XY at the point A. Assume that the linear velocity of A is increasing. Then A at the instant considered has a tangential acceleration represented by the tangent **AB** to the path of motion. The value of this acceleration is $d\mathbf{v}/dt$, where $\mathbf{v}$ and t represent velocity and time, respectively. A also has a normal acceleration acting along AO and represented by a line **AC**. Calculation of the value of the normal acceleration is considered in the next article. The resultant acceleration of A is evidently represented by the diagonal **AD** of the parallelogram $ABDC$.

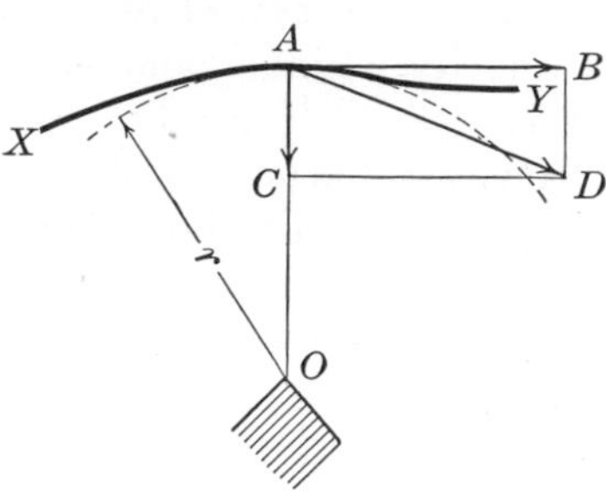

Fig. 2·2.

2·5 Value of the normal acceleration This acceleration may be expressed in terms of the velocity of the point and the radius to the center of curvature of its path. In Fig. 2·3 a point moves along a curved path XY. Let A represent the position it occupies at a certain instant, its velocity then being equal to $\mathbf{v}$. After a short interval of time Δt, the point has moved to position

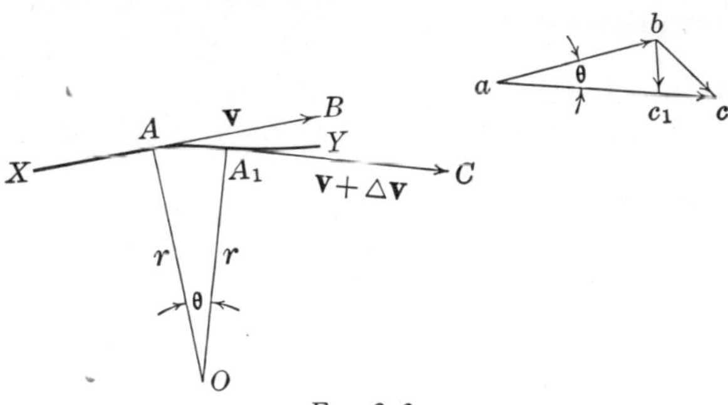

Fig. 2·3.

A_1, and its velocity is now $\mathbf{v} + \Delta\mathbf{v}$. Let lines **AB** and $\mathbf{A_1C}$ represent $\mathbf{v}$ and $\mathbf{v} + \Delta\mathbf{v}$, respectively. These lines are tangents to the curve XY at A and A_1. The center of curvature of the small portion AA_1 of XY is O, and the radius of curvature $r = OA = OA_1$.

The change in velocity is found graphically as follows: Draw a velocity triangle *abc* in which **ab** is equal and parallel to **AB**, and **ac** is equal and parallel to $\mathbf{A_1C}$, these two sides thus representing the initial and final velocities for the small time interval Δt. The third side of the triangle **bc** represents the total change in velocity. Find a point c_1 on **ac** such that $\mathbf{ac_1} = \mathbf{ab}$, representing **v**.

If we assume now that $\boldsymbol{\theta}$ has an infinitesimal value, $\mathbf{bc_1}$ becomes sensibly parallel to both AO and A_1O and represents the change in normal velocity, while $\mathbf{c_1c}$ measures the change in tangential velocity. The angle $bac(= \boldsymbol{\theta}) = \boldsymbol{\omega}\, dt$, where $\boldsymbol{\omega}$ is the angular velocity about the center of curvature. The normal acceleration is calculated from $\mathbf{bc_1}$. From the figure,

$$\mathbf{bc_1} = \mathbf{ab}\,\boldsymbol{\theta} = \mathbf{ab}\,\boldsymbol{\omega}\, dt = \mathbf{v}\,\boldsymbol{\omega}\, dt$$

$$\text{Now, the normal acceleration} = \frac{\text{change in normal velocity}}{dt}$$

$$\mathbf{a}^n = \frac{\mathbf{bc_1}}{dt} = \frac{\mathbf{v}\,\boldsymbol{\omega}\, dt}{dt} = \mathbf{v}\boldsymbol{\omega} = \frac{\mathbf{v}^2}{r} \quad \text{or} \quad \boldsymbol{\omega}^2 r \qquad (2\cdot9)$$

For a point revolving about a fixed center, the normal acceleration has the same value in terms of the velocity and radius, because only instantaneous conditions were considered in deriving the afore-mentioned formula.

2·6 Relation between tangential acceleration and angular acceleration These two quantities bear the same relationship to each other as do linear velocity and angular velocity. For, since $\mathbf{v} = \boldsymbol{\omega} r$, differentiating both sides of the equation gives

$$\frac{d\mathbf{v}}{dt} = \frac{d\boldsymbol{\omega}}{dt} r$$

or

$$\mathbf{a}^t = \boldsymbol{\alpha} r \qquad (2\cdot10)$$

The tangential acceleration of a point on a moving body is equal to the angular acceleration of the body multiplied by the distance from the point to the center of rotation.

Example The flywheel for a metal shearing machine is 4 ft in diameter and rotates at a normal speed of 180 rpm. During the shearing period, which lasts 2 sec, the flywheel speed is reduced to a final value of 150 rpm. Assuming constant angular deceleration, determine the normal and tangential acceleration of a point on the rim at the instant when the speed is 160 rpm.

Solution The angular velocity in radians per second corresponding to 160 rpm equals

$$\omega = \frac{160 \times 2\pi}{60} = 16.74$$

The normal acceleration of a point on the rim equals

$$\mathbf{a}^n = \omega^2 r = (16.74)^2 \times 2 = 562 \text{ fps}^2$$

Since the wheel speed changes from 180 to 150 rpm in 2 sec, with constant acceleration, the value of this acceleration is

$$\frac{150 - 180}{2} = -15 \text{ rpm per sec}$$

which equals

$$-\frac{15 \times 2\pi}{60} \quad \text{or} \quad -1.57 \text{ rad per sec}^2$$

Therefore, the tangential acceleration of a point on the rim is

$$\mathbf{a}^t = \alpha r = -1.57 \times 2 = -3.14 \text{ fps}^2$$

The negative sign indicates a deceleration.

2·7 Simple harmonic motion When a point A (Fig. 2·4) moves in a circle with uniform velocity about a fixed point O, B, the projection of A on any diameter such as XY, moves with simple harmonic motion.

The **period** is the time required for a complete revolution of the generating line OA (Fig. 2·4).

The **amplitude** is equal to the length of the generating radius, OA or r (Fig. 2·4).

The **phase** is the angular position of the generating line at any instant with respect to a reference line, or θ (Fig. 2·4).

The mechanism shown in Fig. 2·5, commonly called a "Scotch yoke," gives simple harmonic motion to the link 3 when the crank 2 rotates with uniform velocity.

2·8 Displacement, velocity, and acceleration for SHM Suppose OA (Fig. 2·4) starts from an initial position OX and rotates counterclockwise. Let $\boldsymbol{\omega}$ equal its constant angular velocity. Then, after a period of time t, the angle turned through will be $\boldsymbol{\omega} t = \boldsymbol{\theta}$, and the displacement of B from its mean position at O will be

$$\mathbf{s} = OB = OA \cos \boldsymbol{\theta} = r \cos \boldsymbol{\omega} t \tag{2·11}$$

It may be observed that the sign of the displacement $\mathbf{s}$ will be positive or negative, depending on the value of $\boldsymbol{\theta}$, or $\boldsymbol{\omega} t$. Reference to equation 2·11 shows that a positive value of $\mathbf{s}$ occurs when point A is in the first or fourth quadrant; hence a positive value

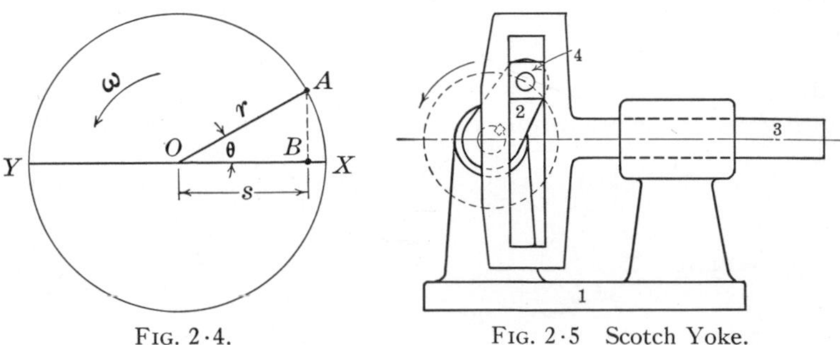

FIG. 2·4.   FIG. 2·5 Scotch Yoke.

of $\mathbf{s}$ indicates a displacement to the right of the midpoint O, and a negative value is to the left of the midpoint.

The velocity of point B may be found by differentiating the displacement with respect to time:

$$\mathbf{v} = \frac{d\mathbf{s}}{dt} = \frac{d(r \cos \boldsymbol{\omega} t)}{dt} = -\frac{r(\sin \boldsymbol{\omega} t)\, d(\boldsymbol{\omega} t)}{dt} = -r\boldsymbol{\omega} \sin \boldsymbol{\omega} t \tag{2·12}$$

Again the sign of the velocity $\mathbf{v}$ will be positive or negative, depending on the value of $\boldsymbol{\theta}$. Reference to Fig. 2·6 and equation 2·12 shows that a negative value of $\mathbf{v}$ occurs when point A is in the first or second quadrant, and the direction of the velocity of B is then toward the left. Hence, a negative value of $\mathbf{v}$, obtained from equation 2·12, indicates the velocity is towards the left, whereas a positive value indicates the velocity is towards the right.

The velocity expression may be illustrated by vectors, as shown in Fig. 2·6, where the constant velocity of point A equals $r\boldsymbol{\omega}$ and is represented by the vector **AC**. The component of this velocity parallel to the reference diameter XY is **AD**. It represents the velocity of point B along the path XY and, as may be seen from the figure, equals $r\omega \sin \omega t$.

The acceleration of point B may be found by differentiating the velocity equation 2·12 with respect to time:

$$\mathbf{a} = \frac{d\mathbf{v}}{dt} = \frac{d(-r\omega \sin \omega t)}{dt} = \frac{-r\omega(\cos \omega t)\, d(\omega t)}{dt} = -r\omega^2 \cos \omega t \tag{2·13}$$

The significance of the sign in this case is that a negative acceleration means that the increase of speed is occurring toward the left, whereas a plus acceleration indicates it is occurring to the right.

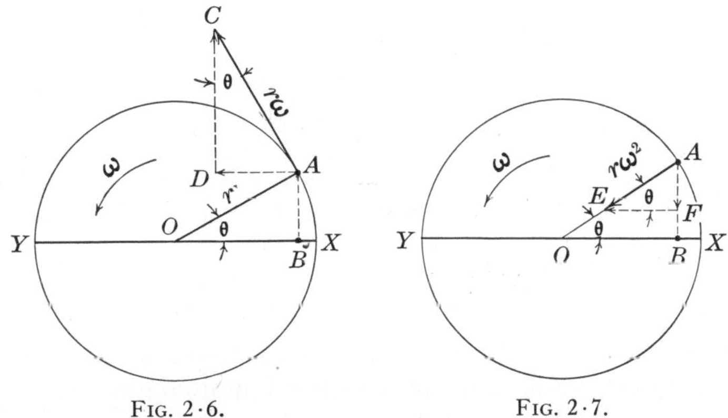

FIG. 2·6. FIG. 2·7.

The acceleration can also be shown vectorially. Since point A travels with constant angular velocity, its only acceleration is normal and acts toward the center of rotation O. It has a constant value of $r\omega^2$. In Fig. 2·7, this acceleration of point A is represented by the vector **AE**, and the component **FE** parallel to the reference diameter XY is the acceleration of point B in that direction. The acceleration of B is, from the figure, equal to $r\omega^2 \cos \omega t$.

Simple harmonic motion can be defined as a motion in which the acceleration is directly proportional to the displacement and acts in a direction toward the point of zero displacement.

Displacement-time curve for SHM To construct this curve, we take a base line representing 360° motion of the generating line (Fig. 2·8), and divide it into any number of equal spaces representing equal angles. Draw a circle whose radius is equal to that of the generating line r, with a center on the base line produced. Divide this circle into angles of the same

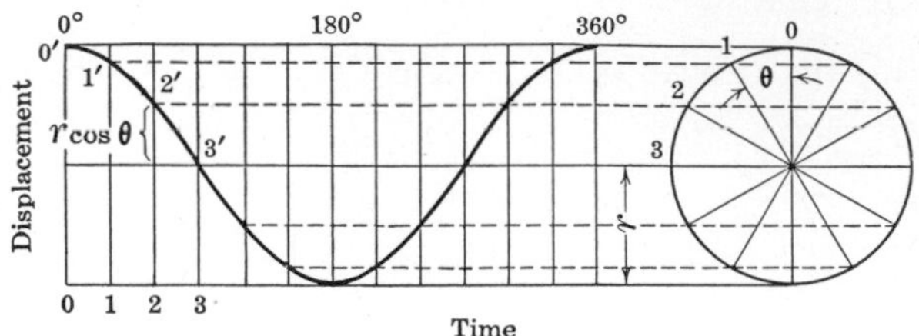

FIG. 2·8 Displacement-Time Curve for SHM.

value as the base-line intervals. The zero position is at 90° to the base line, as indicated on the diagram. Project horizontally from points 0, 1, 2, etc., to points 0′, 1′, 2′, etc. The latter are points on the curve of displacement on a base representing the crank angle, for it is evident that the ordinate for any angle θ is equal to $r \cos \theta$.

Velocity-time curve for SHM (See Fig. 2·9.) The base line, as before, is taken to represent 360° motion of the generating line and is divided into equal spaces of a convenient width. A circle is drawn with center on the base line produced, its radius representing the linear velocity $r\omega$ at the end of the generating line. This circle is divided into equal angles of the same value as the base-line divisions, starting with zero position along the

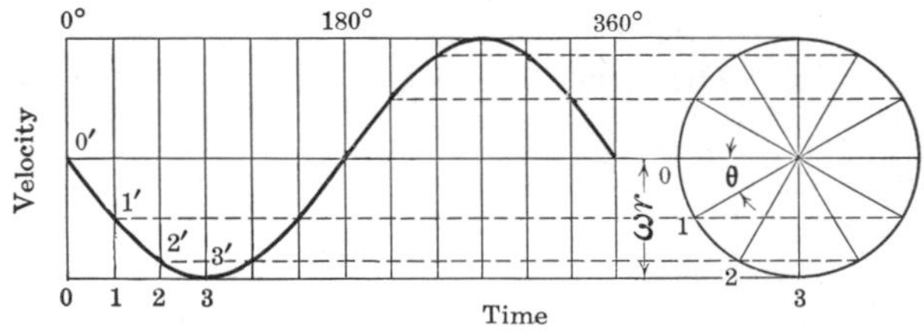

FIG. 2·9 Velocity-Time Curve for SHM.

base line as indicated. Taking points 0, 1, 2, etc., project horizontally to points 0′, 1′, 2′, etc., which are points on the required curve. For at any angle θ the ordinate is equal to $-\omega r \sin \theta$, which is the value of the velocity, by equation 2·12.

Acceleration-time curve for SHM A base line is taken to represent a complete revolution of the crank (Fig. 2·10). A circle is drawn with a center on this base line produced, and with a radius representing $\omega^2 r$. The base line and circle are divided

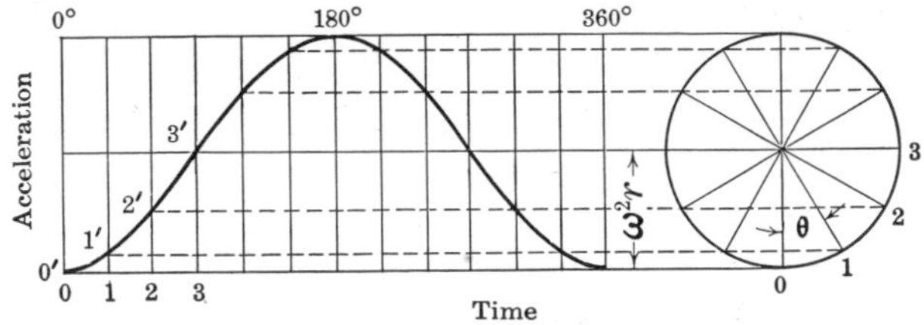

FIG. 2·10 Acceleration-Time Curve for SHM.

into equal parts, the zero position in the circle being at 90° to the base line, as for the displacement curve. Project horizontally from points 0, 1, 2, etc., to points 0′, 1′, 2′, etc., which are points on the required curve. For any angle θ the ordinate to the curve thus obtained is evidently equal to $-\omega^2 r \cos \theta$, the value of the acceleration of a point moving with SHM, by equation 2·13. It may be observed that the graphical constructions for displacement and acceleration curves are identical, except for positive and negative signs.

2·9 Polar curves for SHM

The construction for plotting a **polar displacement** curve of a point having SHM is shown in Fig. 2·11. Let XY be the path of motion. Draw a circle with center O and XY as a diameter. Draw circles with OX and OY as diameters. Then these circles are polar displacement curves on an angle base as required. This may be proved as follows: Take a radius OR in any position, making an angle θ with XY. This intercepts one of the small circles at S. Join XS. Then the angle $XSO = 90°$, since it is an angle subtended by a semicircle. Therefore,

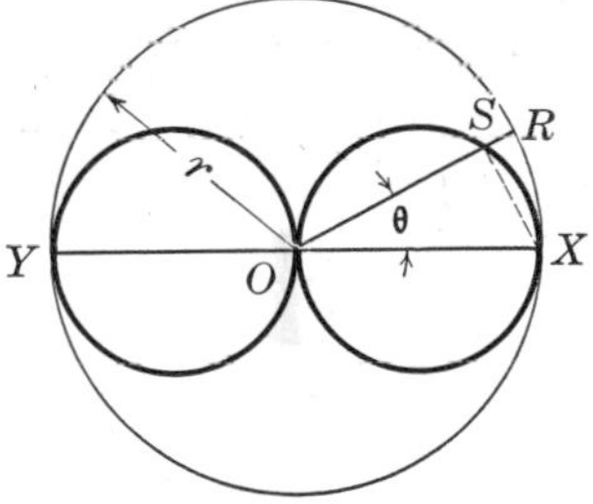

FIG. 2·11 Polar Curve for Displacement with SHM.

$$OS = OX \cos \theta = r \cos \theta$$

Consequently, the intercept OS is the displacement of the point, by equation 2·11.

The **polar velocity** curve is found as follows: Take a line OX representing the linear velocity of the outer end of the generating line (Fig. 2·12). Describe a circle with OX as radius.

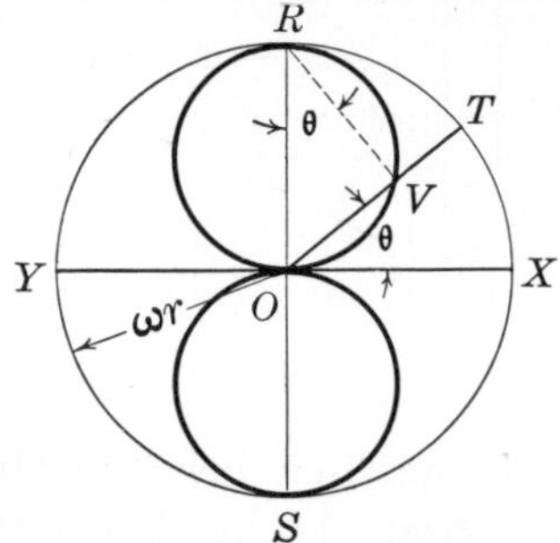

FIG. 2·12 Polar Curve for Velocity with SHM.

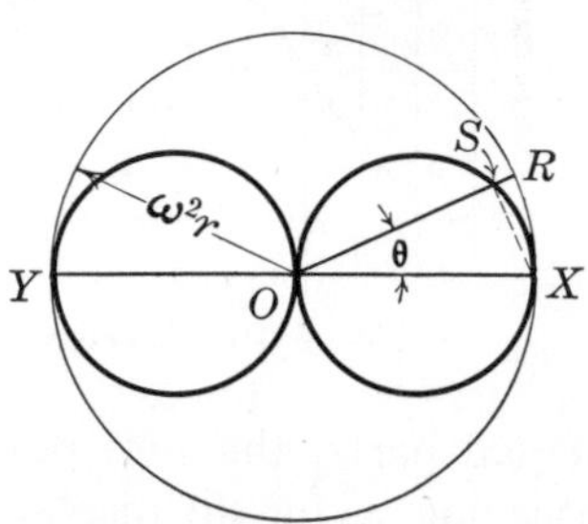

FIG. 2·13 Polar Curve for Acceleration with SHM.

Draw RS perpendicular to XY. Construct two circles with RO and OS as diameters. Then these circles are the required velocity curves.

Proof: Take any line OT making an angle θ with the line XY, intersecting the small circle at V. Join VR. Then angle $OVR = 90°$, being the angle in a semicircle. From the figure,

$$OV = OR \cos (90 - \theta) = \omega r \sin \theta$$

Therefore, the distance OV represents the velocity of the point moving with SHM by equation 2·12, which proves the construction to be correct.

The **polar acceleration** curve of Fig. 2·13 is constructed in the same manner as the displacement curve, except that the radius OX now represents $\omega^2 r$. The radiant OS at an angle θ can be shown to have the value $\omega^2 r \cos \theta$, which proves the construction.

2·10 Composition of simple harmonic motions of equal periods Machines sometimes contain two or more parts that are driven with simple harmonic motions from the same rotating member; thus they have equal periods, though they may differ in phase and amplitude. This condition is approximately attained in certain kinds of valve gears on steam engines. When designing, it is necessary to study the relative motion of such parts.

Suppose that A and B (Fig. 2·14) represent the instantaneous positions of two points moving with SHM along a line XY. The generating radii OR and OS may be unequal and have a phase difference of β. The relative displacement or distance between the points is AB at the instant considered. From O draw OT equal and parallel to RS. Then OV, the projection of OT on XY, is obviously equal to AB. It is therefore evident that OT will act as a generating radius producing SHM of the point V whose displacement from mid-position is the relative displacement of A and B.

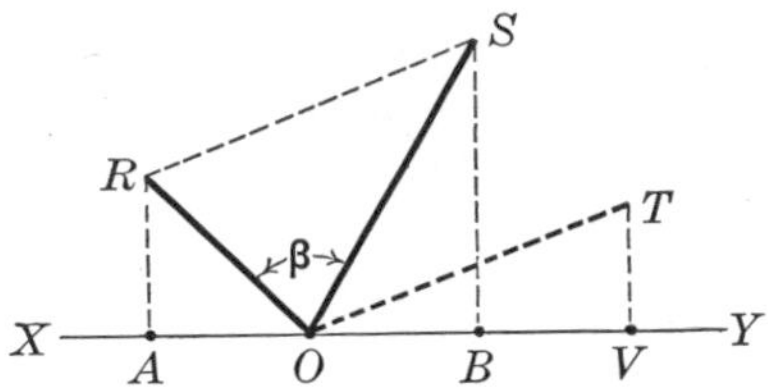

Fig. 2·14 Composition of Two Simple Harmonic Motions of Equal Periods.

Thus, two points moving with SHM of equal periods along the same straight line have a relative motion that is also simple harmonic, the phase and amplitude of this motion being determinable by the construction just outlined.

2·11 Linear velocity-time and acceleration-time curves

Frequently it is desirable to analyze the motion of a body, where data are available concerning its position at certain instants, but no data are directly obtainable concerning its velocity and acceleration. Information regarding the latter quantities can be obtained if a linear displacement-time curve is first plotted and a graphical method is then used to derive velocity-time and acceleration-time curves from the displacement-time curve.

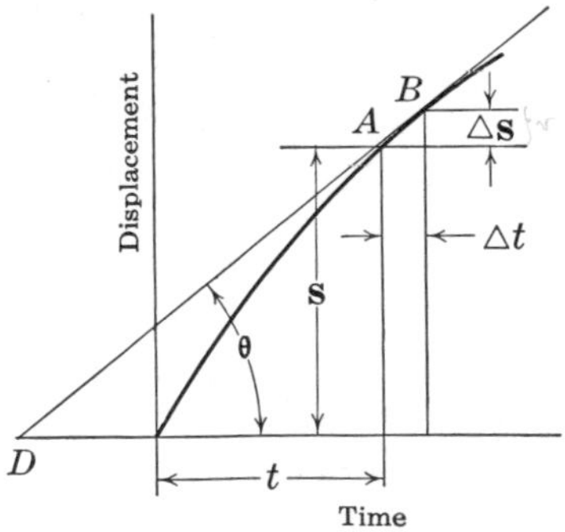

Fig. 2·15.

In Fig. 2·15 is shown a curve obtained by plotting the displacement of a moving body from a fixed reference point, on a base representing time. Thus at any point on the curve, such as A, the displacement and time are, respectively, **s** and t. At point B, after a short interval of time Δt has elapsed, the displacement is $\mathbf{s} + \Delta\mathbf{s}$ at time $t + \Delta t$. Now the average velocity during the short interval is **v** where $\mathbf{v} = \Delta\mathbf{s}/\Delta t = \tan\boldsymbol{\theta}$. $\boldsymbol{\theta}$ is the angle of slope of the line BAD. In the limit where Δt is an infinitesimal, the distance from A to B also becomes infinitesimal, and the line BAD is then a tangent to the curve. Velocity **v** becomes the instantaneous velocity, that is, the velocity existing during the infinitesimal period dt. It follows, therefore, that **the instantaneous velocity of a body is measured by the tangent of the angle of slope of the displacement-time curve at the point considered.**

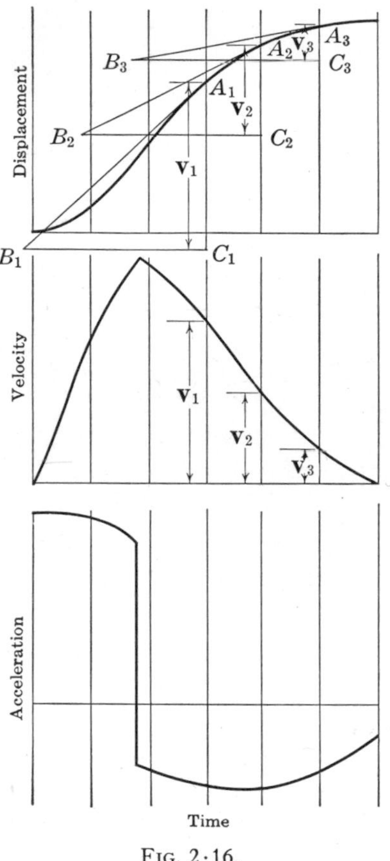

FIG. 2·16.

Since acceleration bears the same relation to velocity that velocity bears to displacement, it can be shown in the same manner that **the instantaneous acceleration of the body is equal to the tangent of the angle of slope of the velocity-time curve at the point under consideration.**

2·12 Graphical construction of velocity and acceleration curves from a known displacement curve may be carried out as follows: Select any convenient number of points on the displacement curve (Fig. 2·16), as A_1, A_2, A_3. Construct the triangles $A_1B_1C_1$, $A_2B_2C_2$, $A_3B_3C_3$ in which the AB lines are tangents to the curve and the horizontal BC lines are all of equal length.

The velocities at A_1, A_2, A_3 are proportional to the quantities

A_1C_1/B_1C_1, A_2C_2/B_2C_2, A_3C_3/B_3C_3, since these are the tangents of the slope angles. By our construction, $B_1C_1 = B_2C_2 = B_3C_3$, and therefore it is evident that the velocities are represented graphically by the lengths A_1C_1, A_2C_2, A_3C_3. These lengths are plotted as ordinates on a time base, giving the **velocity-time diagram** of Fig. 2·16.

Since acceleration bears the same relationship to velocity that velocity bears to displacement, a repetition of the construction just outlined, if applied to the velocity-time curve, will enable us to draw an **acceleration-time diagram,** as shown in Fig. 2·16.

It is somewhat difficult to draw accurate tangents to a curve of irregular form; hence the alternative construction that follows, though only an approximate one, often will produce more accurate results.

We shall assume that the following data are available in regard to the motion of a car in which distances are measured from a fixed reference point at stated time intervals:

Time, sec	Distance, ft	Time, sec	Distance, ft
0	0	25	412
5	11	30	472
10	57	35	501
15	138	40	511
20	298		

We shall plot our displacement-time diagram, using the following scales:

Distance	1 in. = 160 ft
Time	1 in. = 10 sec

For convenience in projection of points, we shall locate our curves as shown in the diagram, Fig. 2·17, the base line always representing time, and the same instant in time being represented by points on the three bases which are in the same vertical line. The construction for one point on the velocity curve corresponding to the 15–20-sec interval is as follows. Find the points a and b where the curve crosses the 15-sec and 20-sec lines, respectively. Draw ac horizontally, thus obtaining a distance bc ($= x$). Transfer x to the velocity-time diagram, plotting it opposite the middle of the 15–20-sec strip, namely, at $17\frac{1}{2}$ sec. Distance x can be stepped off 2, 3, or 4 times on this line if desirable, in order to increase the height of the velocity curve. In the diagram as drawn, it is stepped off twice.

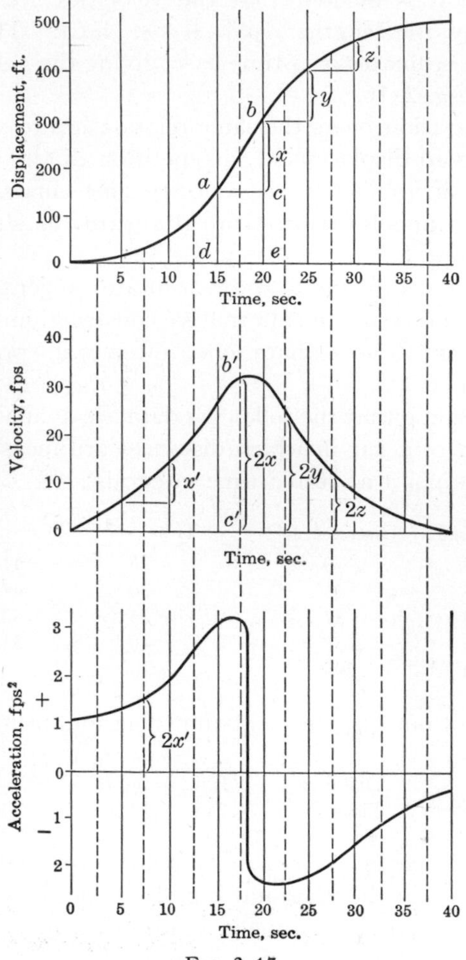

Fig. 2·17.

Then b' is one point on the velocity-time curve. The proof of this is as follows.

Since ad represents the displacement of the body at the end of 15 sec, and be the displacement at the end of 20 sec, $(be - ad)$ or x represents the displacement during the 5-sec interval.

Similar lengths, y, z, will represent in the same way the displacement during the 20–25-sec and the 25–30-sec intervals, respectively. Now the average velocities during equal time intervals are proportional to the displacements that are obtained during the corresponding time intervals. Hence x, y, z are proportional to these velocities. If we make the assumption that the average velocity for each interval is equal to the actual velocity at the middle of the interval, an assumption that is reasonably correct if the time intervals are short, we may proceed to obtain a velocity curve by plotting x, y, z (or multiples of these distances if more convenient) opposite the middle of each interval. It may be noted, however, that the error due to the approximation decreases as the time intervals are made shorter; hence, for accuracy, we must divide up our time base into narrow strips.

Since acceleration bears the same relationship to velocity that velocity does to displacement, it follows that the acceleration-time curve is obtained from the velocity-time curve in exactly the same manner as that in which the velocity time has been derived from the displacement time. This curve is shown in the figure, the ordinates being doubled as before, in order to magnify variations in the shape of the curve.

Once the velocity-time curve has been obtained, it is necessary to determine the proper ordinate scale. Let the displacement curve be plotted to a scale of 1 in. = $\mathbf{s}$ ft, and the change in height of the displacement curve during a time interval of t sec be x in. on the drawing. The actual movement of the point during the time interval t then is $x\mathbf{s}$ ft. The average velocity during this interval is $x\mathbf{s}/t$ fps. In plotting the velocity-time curve, the distance x was laid off m times. Hence the distance mx in. on the drawing represents $x\mathbf{s}/t$ fps, or $1 \text{ in.} = \dfrac{x\mathbf{s}}{t}\,\dfrac{1}{mx}$ $= \mathbf{s}/tm$ fps.

In the example, the displacement scale is 1 in. = 160 ft, and the time interval is taken as 5 sec. Assuming a value for the change in height of the displacement curve of $\frac{3}{8}$ in. (any value may be used) during this time interval means the change in displacement is $\frac{3}{8} \times 160$ or 60 ft. Since this change in displacement occurs during a 5-sec period, the average velocity is $\frac{60}{5}$ or 12 fps. In plotting this $\frac{3}{8}$ in. on the velocity diagram, the length was doubled, hence $2 \times \frac{3}{8}$ in. = 12 fps, or 1 in. = 16 fps.

In a similar manner, let the velocity scale be 1 in. = $\mathbf{v}$ fps, the time interval be t sec, and the change in height of a typical time interval be x' in. on the drawing. The change in velocity of the point during the time interval then is $x'\mathbf{v}$ fps. The average acceleration during the interval equals $x'\mathbf{v}/t$. In plotting the acceleration-time curve, the distance x' is laid off n times. Hence the distance on the drawing of nx' in. represents $x'\mathbf{v}/t$ fps^2, or

$$1 \text{ in.} = \frac{x'\mathbf{v}}{t}\frac{1}{nx'} = \frac{\mathbf{v}}{tn} \text{ fps}^2.$$

With reference to the example, the velocity scale is 1 in. = 16 fps, and the time interval is 5 sec. Assuming a value for the change in height of the velocity curve of $\frac{1}{4}$ in. (again any value may be used) during this time interval means the change in velocity is $\frac{1}{4} \times 16$, or 4 fps. Since this change in velocity occurs in a 5-sec period, the average acceleration is $\frac{4}{5}$, or 0.8 fps^2. In plotting this $\frac{1}{4}$ in. on the acceleration diagram, the length was doubled; hence, $2 \times \frac{1}{4}$ in. = 0.8 fps^2, or 1 in. = 1.6 fps^2.

In showing the scale on the drawing, it should be laid off in units that are simple to interpolate visually. Thus, for the acceleration scale, the units should be 1, 2, 3, etc. rather than 1.6, 3.2, 4.8, etc., which are difficult to interpolate.

It should be realized that, although it is quite unusual in nature for instantaneous changes of displacement or velocity to occur, the acceleration does so frequently. When the brakes are suddenly applied to a car, it instantaneously experiences a large deceleration. Similarly, when the clutch pedal is suddenly released, the car experiences a large acceleration. Numerous similar examples may be recalled. Also, it should be realized that the instant selected for time to be zero is highly arbitrary, and at that instant the body may have a displacement, velocity, or acceleration. Hence, these values need not be zero when time is considered to be zero.

2·13 Relative velocities of three points The symbol $\mathbf{v}_{A/B}$ means the relative linear velocity of point A with respect to point B. Considering three bodies, we have three relative velocities as follows: $\mathbf{v}_{1/2}$, $\mathbf{v}_{2/3}$, and $\mathbf{v}_{1/3}$. There are also the velocities $\mathbf{v}_{2/1}$, $\mathbf{v}_{3/2}$, and $\mathbf{v}_{3/1}$, but these are not independent quantities since:

$$\mathbf{v}_{1/2} = -\mathbf{v}_{2/1}; \quad \mathbf{v}_{2/3} = -\mathbf{v}_{3/2}; \quad \mathbf{v}_{1/3} = -\mathbf{v}_{3/1}$$

The truth of these statements is self-evident if we consider the following example. A passenger on an eastbound train sees any landmark receding to the west at the speed of the train. Thus two vectors, representing the velocity of the passenger relative to the earth, and of the earth relative to the passenger, are of equal length but have arrows pointing respectively east and west, or one velocity is -1 times the other.

When point A on body 3 moves relative to point B on a second body 2, which is itself moving relative to a third body 1; the motion of point A relative to body 1 may be found by vector addition. The velocity of point A relative to body 1 is given as the vectorial sum of the motion of point B relative to body 1 plus the motion of point A relative to point B. Expressed in equation form this is

$$\mathbf{v}_{A/1} = \mathbf{v}_{B/1} \not\rightarrow \mathbf{v}_{A/B}$$

The sign $\not\rightarrow$ is used to indicate a vectorial rather than an arithmetical addition. In Fig. 2·18 is shown the graphical method of summing the vectors $\mathbf{v}_{B/1}$ and $\mathbf{v}_{A/B}$, the resultant being equal to the closing line $\mathbf{v}_{A/1}$ of the triangle or parallelogram. The direction of the arrows in this figure should be carefully observed since here errors often occur. Where we have a vectorial sum the arrows point around the figure in the same sense, i.e., clockwise.

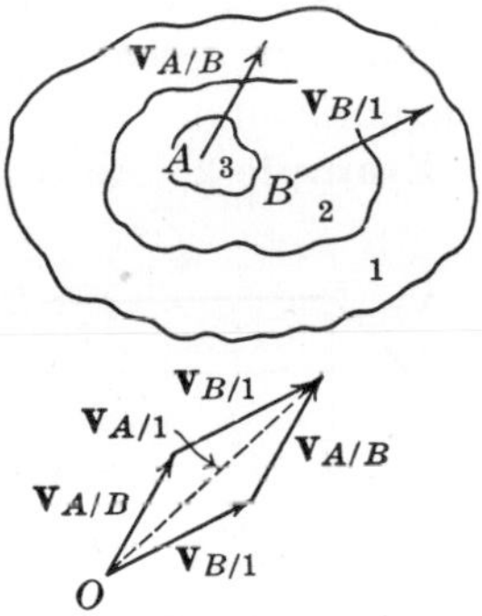

FIG. 2·18.

If we treat the subscripts $B/1$ and A/B as quantities to be multiplied, the result is $\left(\frac{B}{1}\right)\left(\frac{A}{B}\right) = \frac{A}{1}$. On the other hand, the sum of $\mathbf{v}_{B/1}$ and $\mathbf{v}_{B/A}$ would equal $\mathbf{v}_{B^2/A1}$ by the same method, and this quantity has no significance as a velocity vector. This would show that the right-hand side of the equation is incorrectly written.

Example 1 Find the velocity relative to the track of the crankpin A (Fig. 2·19) on a 60-in.-diameter locomotive driver when the locomotive is moving at the rate of 36.1 mph.

Solution The velocity of wheel center B relative to the track C is $\dfrac{36.1 \times 5280}{60 \times 60} = 53$ fps.

The angular velocity of the wheel is $\dfrac{53 \times 12}{30} = 21.2$ rad per sec. The linear velocity of A relative to B ($\mathbf{v} = \omega r$) is

$$21.2 \times 10 = 212 \text{ in. per sec}$$
$$= 17.66 \text{ fps}$$

Starting from a point O, draw vectors **OL** and **LM** representing $\mathbf{v}_{B/C}$ and $\mathbf{v}_{A/B}$ respectively. The closing line **OM** of the triangle

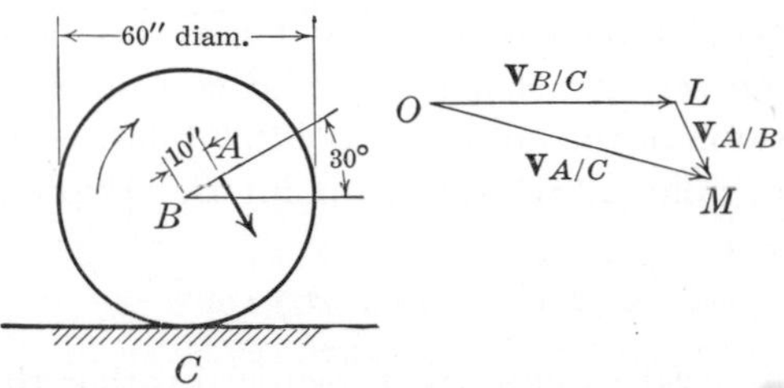

FIG. 2·19.

OLM is the required velocity $\mathbf{v}_{A/C}$. By this method **OM** is found to represent a velocity of 63.7 fps at an angle of 14° with the horizontal.

Example 2 Auto A is traveling east on a straight road with a velocity $\mathbf{v}_A$, and at the same time an auto B is traveling southwest on a straight road with a velocity $\mathbf{v}_B$. Find the relative velocities of the two autos.

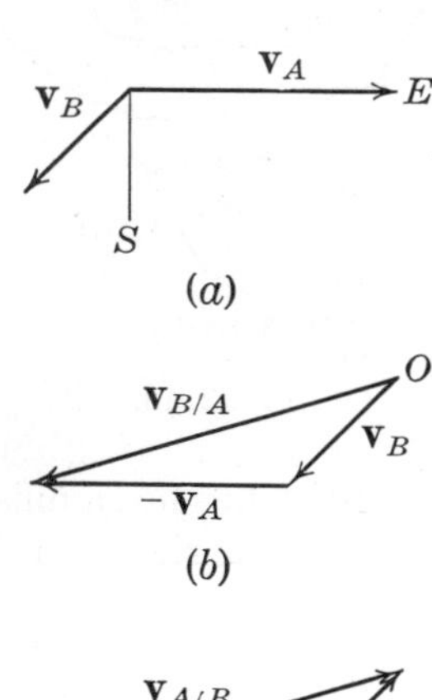

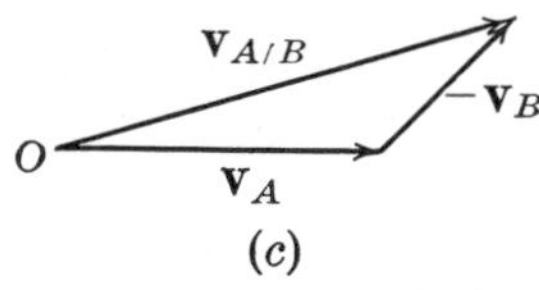

FIG. 2·20.

The known velocities of the two cars are shown in Fig. 2·20a. To find the velocity of auto B relative to that of auto A, a vector equation may be written for the motion as $\mathbf{v}_A \nrightarrow \mathbf{v}_{B/A} = \mathbf{v}_B$, or, solving for $\mathbf{v}_{B/A}$, we have $\mathbf{v}_{B/A} = \mathbf{v}_B \rightarrow \mathbf{v}_A$. To subtract $\mathbf{v}_A$ from $\mathbf{v}_B$, we reverse the direction of $\mathbf{v}_A$ and then add it to the vector $\mathbf{v}_B$ as shown in Fig. 2·20b, to obtain $\mathbf{v}_{B/A}$.

If the velocity of auto A relative to that of auto B were desired, we would first write the equation $\mathbf{v}_B \nrightarrow \mathbf{v}_{A/B} = \mathbf{v}_A$, or $\mathbf{v}_{A/B} = \mathbf{v}_A \rightarrow \mathbf{v}_B$. Reversing the direction of the vector $\mathbf{v}_B$ and adding it to that of $\mathbf{v}_A$ as shown in Fig. 2·20*c* gives $\mathbf{v}_{A/B}$. It may be observed from these figures that $\mathbf{v}_{B/A} = -\mathbf{v}_{A/B}$; that is, they have the same magnitudes but opposite directions.

QUESTIONS

2·1 Define (*a*) displacement, (*b*) velocity, (*c*) linear velocity, (*d*) angular velocity. Name a common unit for each.

2·2 Define (*a*) acceleration, (*b*) linear acceleration, (*c*) angular acceleration. Name a common unit for each.

2·3 What is meant by (*a*) tangential acceleration, (*b*) normal acceleration, of a moving point? What is the normal acceleration of a point moving in a curved path of radius r ft at a speed of $\mathbf{v}$ fps?

2·4 A train moves at the rate of 45 mph. What is its velocity in feet per second? *Ans.* 66 fps.

2·5 The wheel of an automobile is turning at the rate of 350 rpm. What is the angular velocity of the wheel in radians per second? What is the speed of the car in miles per hour? The tire diameter is 30 in.

2·6 A piece of cast iron 6 in. in diameter is to be turned in a lathe with a cutting speed of 90 fpm. At what speed must the work be rotated? *Ans.* 57.3 rpm.

2·7 In a shaper the cutting tool has a stroke of 15 in. The cutting stroke takes twice the time required for the return stroke. If it is desired to obtain an average speed during the cutting stroke of 25 fpm, what must be the rpm of the driving crank? *Ans.* 13.34 rpm.

2·8 An automobile is accelerated uniformly from 10 to 30 mph in 8 sec. Find the value of the acceleration in foot-second units. If the wheels are 28 in. in diameter, find their angular acceleration in radian-second units.

2·9 A flywheel rotates at 250 rpm, its radius being 6 ft. Find (*a*) its angular velocity in radian measure, (*b*) the linear velocity of a point 3 ft from the axis, (*c*) the normal acceleration of a point on the rim.

2·10 A flywheel 4 ft in diameter is speeded up from 120 to 380 rpm with constant angular acceleration in 2 sec. Find the total acceleration of a point on the circumference of the wheel when the speed reaches 180 rpm. *Ans.* 711 fps^2.

2·11 A point on a body moves along a curved path. At a certain instant the point has a velocity of 27 fps, a tangential acceleration of 40 fps^2, and a normal acceleration of 54 fps^2. Find (*a*) the radius of curvature of the path, (*b*) the total acceleration of the point, (*c*) the angular velocity and the angular acceleration of the body.

2·12 The speed of a flywheel rim is 50 fps, and the rpm is 200. Find (*a*) the radius of the wheel, (*b*) the normal acceleration of a point on the rim.

2·13 A reciprocating steam engine has a stroke of 24 in. and rotates at 225 rpm. Find (*a*) the linear velocity of the crankpin, (*b*) the normal acceleration of the crankpin. *Ans.* (*a*) 23.5 fps. (*b*) 554 fps^2.

2·14 A revolving body has an angular acceleration of 30 rad per $\sec^2$. A point on it is distant 12 in. from the axis of revolution. When the speed of the body reaches 200 rpm, find the normal and tangential acceleration of the point, and show how the total acceleration can be obtained graphically.

Ans. 30 fps^2; 438 fps^2.

2·15 What is meant by "simple harmonic motion"? Explain the meaning of the terms "period," "phase," and "amplitude" as applied to this form of motion.

2·16 Show how to draw a time curve of (*a*) velocity, (*b*) acceleration, for a point having SHM, given the period and amplitude.

2·17 Show how to draw a polar curve of (*a*) displacement, (*b*) velocity, for a point having SHM, given the period and amplitude. Prove your constructions.

2·18 A point has SHM of period 2 sec, amplitude 6 in. Find (*a*) its maximum velocity, (*b*) its maximum acceleration.

2·19 A point has simple harmonic motion of period 2 sec, amplitude 6 in. Find (*a*) its displacement, (*b*) its velocity, when the revolving line is at 30° with the line of motion. *Ans.* 5.2 in.; 0.785 fps.

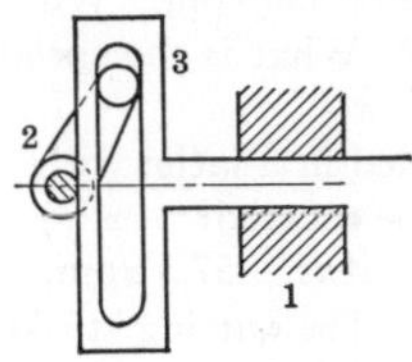

Fig. P2·20.

2·20 In the mechanism shown in Fig. P2·20, the crank 2, 12 in. long, rotates at 100 rpm. Find (*a*) the velocity of 3, and (*b*) the acceleration of 3, when the crank 2 is at 60° with the line of stroke.

2·21 The slotted link in a Scotch yoke is found to attain a maximum velocity of 6 fps, the crank length being 4 in. At what average speed does the slotted link move if the crank rotates uniformly? What is the maximum acceleration? *Ans.* 1.9 fps; 108 fps^2.

2·22 A single-cylinder steam engine has a slide valve driven by an eccentric, the eccentric radius being advanced 120° ahead of the engine crank. The total movement of the valve is 4 in., and it can be considered as simple harmonic. Find the displacement, velocity, and acceleration of the valve at the instant when the engine crank is on the dead center. The engine turns at 300 rpm.

2·23 Given a distance-time curve, show how to obtain graphically a velocity-time and acceleration-time curve.

2·24 If, in Question 2·23, the distance scale is 1 in. = **s** ft, the time base is divided into intervals representing *n* sec, and the ordinates are doubled in transferring, show that the velocity scale is

$$1 \text{ in.} = \frac{\mathbf{s}}{2n} \text{ fps}$$

2·25 If, in Question 2·23, the velocity scale is 1 in. = **v** fps, the time base is divided into intervals representing *n* sec, and ordinates are doubled in transferring to the acceleration diagram, show that the acceleration scale is

$$1 \text{ in.} = \frac{\mathbf{v}}{2n} \text{ fps}^2$$

2·26 A polar curve for the velocity of a point moving with SHM is drawn with a maximum ordinate of 2 in. (*a*) If the length of the generating radius is 6 in. and its angular velocity 150 rpm, what is the velocity scale for the polar curve? (*b*) If a polar acceleration curve for the same point has a maximum ordinate of 2 in. what is the acceleration scale?

2·27 How many different relative motions are there when three bodies are considered? when four bodies are considered? Show graphically how to find one of the relative velocities when the others are known.

2·28 A bee enters the open window of an automobile and leaves at the corresponding point on the opposite window, $4\frac{1}{2}$ ft away, just $\frac{1}{2}$ sec later. If the automobile is traveling at the rate of 12 fps, find the speed and direction of flight of the bee. *Ans.* 15.0 fps; 36° 52′ to auto axis.

2·29 A locomotive has driving wheels of 62 in. diameter. The tender wheels are 36 in. diameter. Find the angular velocity of each and the velocity ratio when the locomotive is traveling at the rate of 40 mph.

Ans. 22.7 radians per sec; 39.1 rad per sec; ratio 1:1.72.

2·30 A locomotive running at 60 mph has a stroke of 32 in. Find the velocity of the crankpin relative to the ground when the crank is in the position shown in Fig. P2·30.

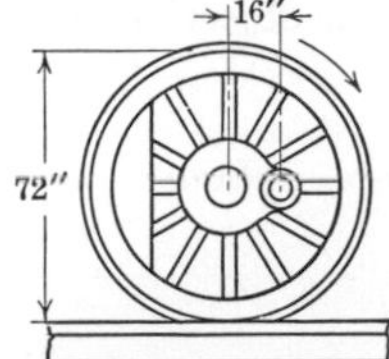

FIG. P2·30.

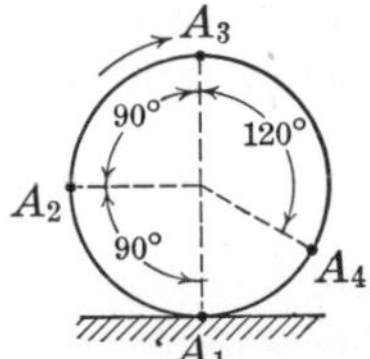

FIG. P2·31.

2·31 A locomotive is traveling at the rate of 45 mph. The driving wheels are 6 ft in diameter. Find the speed of a point on the rim of the driver when the point occupies the positions A_1, A_2, A_3, A_4 in Fig. P2·31.

2·32 A streetcar with wheels 30 in. in diameter is traveling at the rate of 35 mph. (*a*) What is the angular velocity of the wheels? (*b*) What is the linear velocity of the highest point on the tread of a wheel, relative to the track?

Ans. (*a*) 41 rad per sec. (*b*) 102.5 fps.

2·33 The pair of friction wheels 2 and 3 shown in Fig. P2·33 are, respectively, 8 and 6 in. in diameter. They roll together without slipping, 2 turning at 210 rpm. Show how to find graphically the relative velocities of point L to point M, of point L to point N, and of point M to point N.

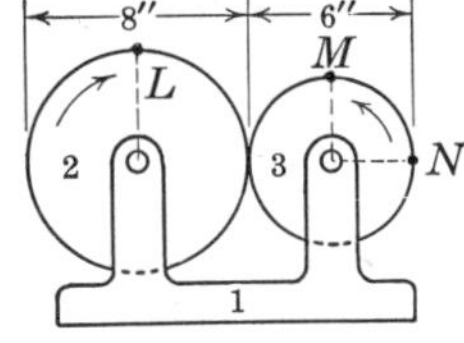

FIG. P2·33.

2·34 An airplane has a landing speed of 50 mph. Find the velocity of the end of the propeller blade relative to the ground, at the instant when the blade is in a horizontal position when landing. The propeller is 7 ft in diameter and is turning at 550 rpm.

2·35 Two points lying on a revolving disk in the same radial straight line have a relative velocity of 60 fps. If the disk turns at 420 rpm, what is the distance between the points?

2·36 The hour hand of a clock is 3 in. long, and the minute hand 5 in. long. What is the relative velocity, in inches per minute, of points at the ends of the hands at 9 o'clock?

2·37 A pilot flies a straight course from city *A* due north to city *B*, 400 miles distant. His plane has an air speed of 180 mph. A cross wind blows due east at 60 mph. In what direction must the plane be headed, and how long will the trip take? *Ans.* N 19° 30′ W; 2 hr 21 min.

2·38 A boatman heads his boat across a river 1 mile in width. He can propel the boat at the rate of 4 mph. The current in the river flows at 5 mph. How long does it take him to reach the opposite bank? What is his velocity relative to the shore in direction and magnitude? How far downstream does he land?

2·39 An airplane takes off from city *A* to fly to city *B*, due west and distant 600 miles. The wind is estimated to be blowing at 50 mph in a direction E 30° S, and the plane's course is set on this basis. If the wind actually blows at 30 mph in the direction given, how far from the starting point will the plane be at the time it should have landed at its destination? Obtain by vector diagram the distance of the plane from its objective at that time. The plane has a cruising speed of 200 mph.

3 Instant Centers

3·1 General Links of machines with plane motion may be divided into three groups: (*a*) those with angular motion about a fixed axis; (*b*) those with angular movement but not about a fixed axis; and (*c*) those with linear but not angular motion. All these motions may be studied by the use of **instant centers.**

For kinematic purposes, as pointed out in Art. 1·9, we shall disregard the thickness of the bodies perpendicular to the plane of motion, and deal with the projections of the bodies on this plane.

Let 2, Fig. 3·1, represent a body having plane motion relative to a second body 1. A point A on 2 lies in the position A_1 at a certain instant, and point B is at B_1 at the same instant. An instant later A has moved to A_2 and B to B_2. RS and TW are, respectively, the paths traced on body 1 by the two points A and B as body 2 moves. Since A and B are points on the same body, A_1B_1 and A_2B_2 are of equal length. If we bisect A_1A_2 and B_1B_2 at right angles by KL and MN, respectively, and find the intersection of these two lines at O_{21}, then it is evident that the movement of A from A_1 to A_2 and of B from B_1 to B_2 could be accomplished by rotation of the body 2 about O_{21}. If distances A_1A_2 and B_1B_2 are infinitely small, then O_{21} becomes the **instant center** for the relative motion, and is called O_{21}, meaning "the instant center for the motion of 2 with respect to 1." O_{21} can be regarded as the position of a pair of superimposed points, one on each body, the two points having for the instant no motion with respect to one another. The instant center may therefore be defined in either of the following ways:

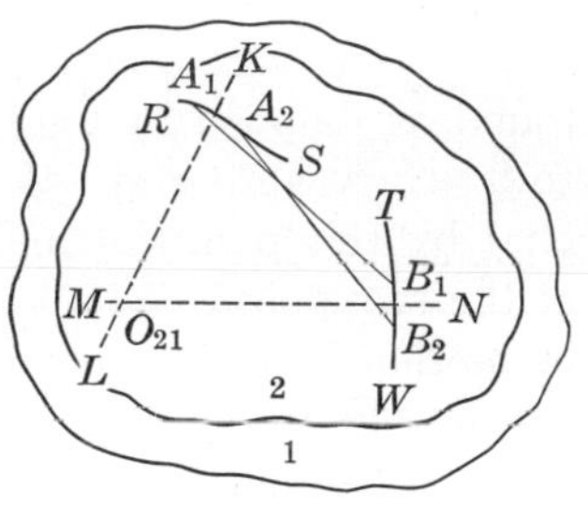

FIG. 3·1.

(*a*) When two bodies have plane relative motion, **the instant center is a point on one body about which the other rotates at the instant considered.**

(*b*) When two bodies have plane relative motion, **the instant center is the point at which the bodies are relatively at rest at the instant considered.**

3·2 Locating instant centers Instant centers are extremely useful in finding the velocities of links in mechanisms. Their use sometimes enables us to substitute for a given mechanism another which produces the same motions and is mechanically more serviceable. The methods of locating the instant centers are therefore of great importance. When a body has constrained motion, any point on it traces out a **point path** in space. When the motion is plane, the point path is a plane figure of some sort. Very frequently we can easily find the point paths corresponding to the motions of two points on a body. When this is the case the instant center is found as follows: In Fig. 3·2 body 2 has plane motion relative to 1. Curves *RS* and *TW* are, respectively, the paths traced out on 1 by two points *A* and *B* on 2. The instantaneous motions of the two points must be along tangents **v** and $\mathbf{v}_1$ to the paths of motion, and the instant center must be so placed as to give motions in these directions. To cause *A* to move in direction **v**, the body must be swung about a center somewhere on the line *KL* perpendicular to **v**. Likewise, to cause *B* to move along $\mathbf{v}_1$, the center must be somewhere along *MN*. The intersection of these lines at O_{21} is the only point that will satisfy both requirements, and this point is therefore the instant center.

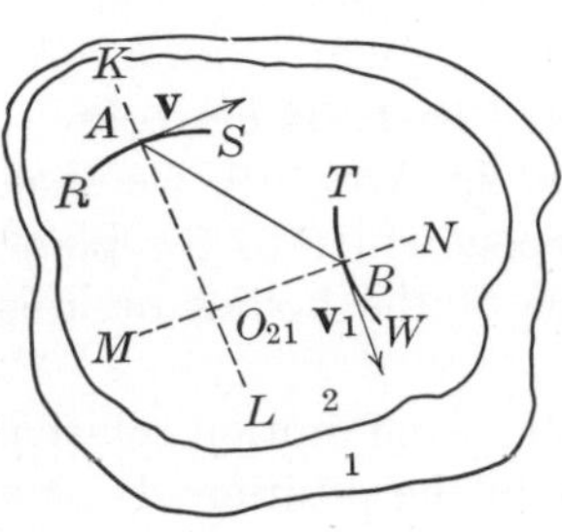

FIG. 3·2.

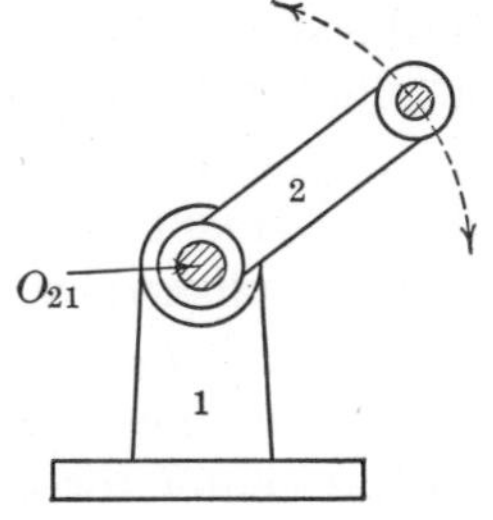

FIG. 3·3.

3·3 Special cases (*a*) When two links in a mechanism are connected by a pin joint, as for example 2 and 1, Fig. 3·3, it is evident that the pivot point is the instant center for all possible positions of the two bodies and is therefore a permanent center as well as an instant center.

(*b*) When a body has rectilinear motion with respect to a second body, as in Fig. 3·4 where block 2 slides between the flat guides 1, the instant center is at infinity. This must be the case, since, if we take any two points, such as A and B, on 2 and draw KL and MN perpendicular to the directions of motion, these lines are parallel and meet at infinity.

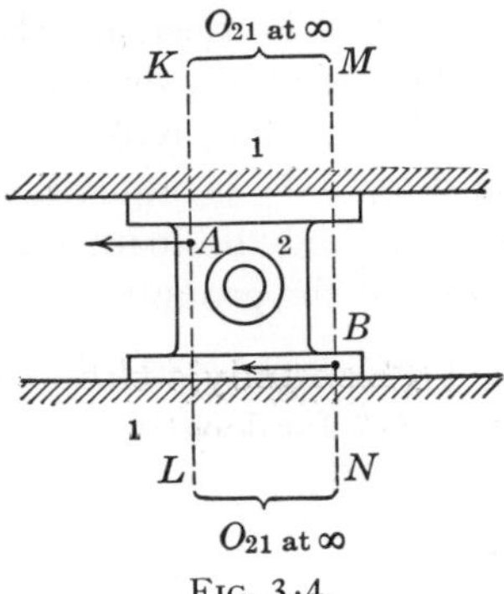

FIG. 3·4.

(*c*) Where two bodies slide on one another, maintaining contact at all times, as 2 and 3, Fig. 3·5, the instant center must lie along the perpendicular to the common tangent. This follows, since the relative motion of contact point Q_2 on 2 to contact point Q_3 on 3 is along the common tangent XY; otherwise the two surfaces would either separate or cut into one another. Relative motion along the common tangent can be effected only by swinging about a center somewhere along the perpendicular KL; hence the instant center is on this line.

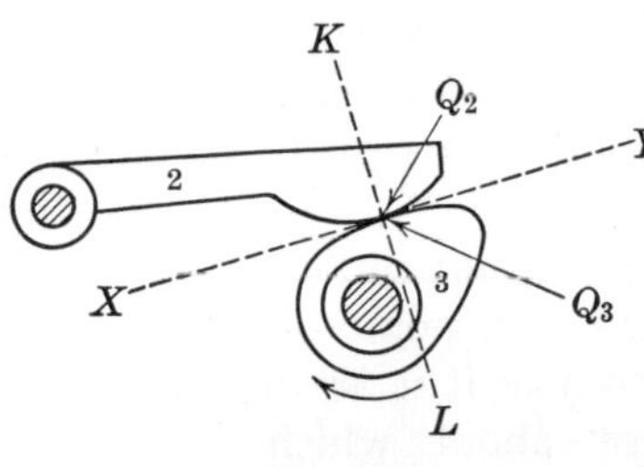

FIG. 3·5.

(*d*) When one body rolls on the surface of a second, the instant center is then the point of contact, since at this point the bodies have no relative motion. This may be illustrated by Fig. 3·6, which represents a wheel 2 having radial spokes but no rim. As

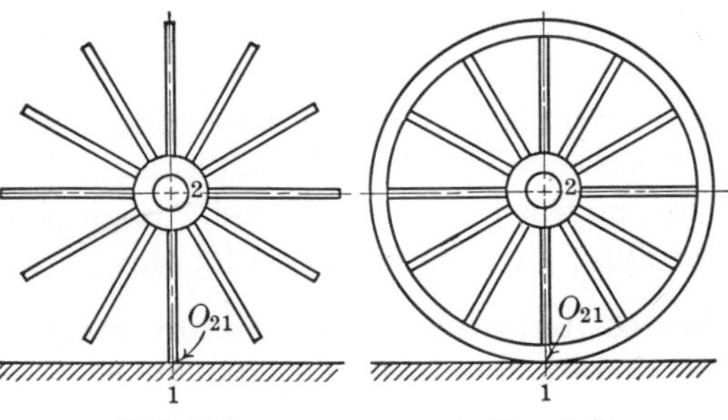

FIG. 3·6. FIG. 3·7.

the wheel is rolled on the ground 1, the successive positions of the pivot point, or instant center, are at the end of the spoke making contact with the ground. Replacing the rim, as shown in Fig. 3·7, is equivalent to inserting an infinite number of spokes, and the instant center O_{21} is the point of contact of the rim and the ground.

3·4 Kennedy's theorem The methods described in Arts. 3·1 and 3·2 for locating the instant centers are generally unwieldy to use. The centers may be easier located by means of Kennedy's theorem. This theorem states that **the instant centers for any three bodies having plane motion lie along the same straight line.** It is proved as follows:

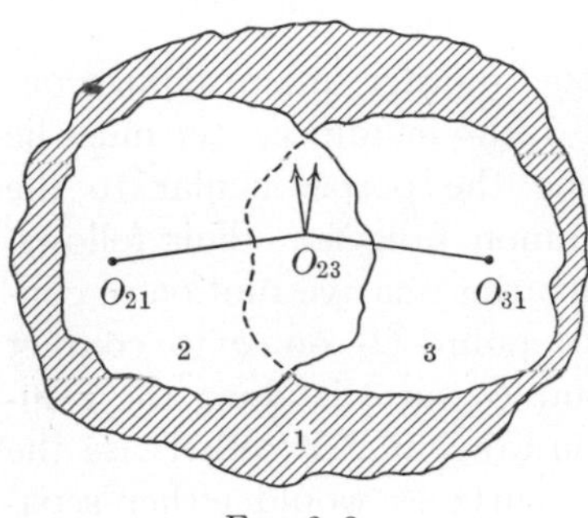

Fig. 3·8.

Let 1, 2, 3 (see Fig. 3·8) be any three bodies having plane motion with respect to one another. Let O_{21}, O_{31}, O_{23} be the three instant centers.

O_{23} is a point on either 2 or 3, because it is an instantaneous pivot about which one body swings with reference to the other. First consider O_{23} as a point on 2. Then it is moving relative to 1 about the instant center O_{21}, and its direction of motion is perpendicular to the line $O_{21}O_{23}$. Next consider O_{23} as a point on 3. It is now moving relative to 1 about the instant center O_{31}, and its direction of motion is perpendicular to the line $O_{31}O_{23}$. But the point O_{23} cannot have two different motions relative to 1 at the same time. Therefore, the perpendiculars to the lines $O_{21}O_{23}$ and $O_{31}O_{23}$ must coincide. This can occur only when $O_{21}O_{23}O_{31}$ is a straight line.

Kennedy's theorem is very useful in locating instant centers in mechanisms in cases where two instant centers for three links are known and the third has to be found. Examples given later in the chapter illustrate its application for this purpose.

3·5 Number of instant centers In any mechanism having plane motion, there is one instant center for each pair of links. The number of instant centers is therefore equal to the number of pairs of links. With n links, the number of instant centers is equal to the number of combinations of n objects taken two at a time, namely, $\frac{n(n-1)}{2}$.

3·6 Four-bar linkage (Fig. 3·9.) This consists of four links connected by turning pairs at K, L, M, N. The number of instant centers is, by Art. 3·5, $\frac{4 \times 3}{2} = 6$. Four of these centers are found by inspection (Art. 3·3a) to be at the pivot points.

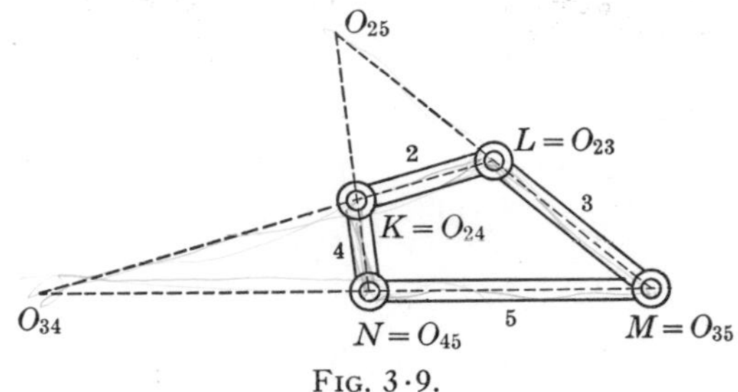

Fig. 3·9.

These are O_{23}, O_{24}, O_{35}, and O_{45}. The remaining two, namely, O_{25} and O_{34}, may be located by (a) the point-path method of Art. 3·2, or (b) the use of Kennedy's theorem of Art. 3·4. Both methods will now be described.

(a) In applying the point-path method to find the instant center of two bodies, it is convenient to consider one of the bodies as being fixed and then to note the direction of motion of two points on the other. Thus, to find O_{25}, we regard 5 as a fixed link and observe the direction of movement of points K and L. Point K is moving about a center at N in a direction normal to KN. Likewise, L is moving about M in a direction normal to LM. The intersection of KN and LM is, therefore, O_{25}, by Art. 3·2.

In a similar way, by regarding 3 as fixed, we can find O_{34} at the intersection of KL and MN.

(b) In using Kennedy's theorem to find O_{25}, we select two groups of bodies, each group consisting of the two bodies 2, 5, plus a third. The instant centers for each group must lie in one straight line, by the theorem. If we take 2, 5, 3 as one group, O_{25} must lie on a straight line with $O_{23}O_{35}$. If we take 2, 5, 4 as the other group, O_{25} must lie along $O_{24}O_{45}$. Therefore, O_{25} is at the intersection of the lines $O_{23}O_{35}$ and $O_{24}O_{45}$. The instant center O_{34} is found in a similar manner.

3·7 Instant centers for the slider-crank mechanism It is important that the student be able to recognize the slider-crank mechanism in any of its many forms since it is applied to a large variety of practical uses. It may be described as a four-link chain in which one pair of links have rectilinear motion with respect to each other, while the relative motion of any other pair of adjacent links is that of rotation. The mechanism, therefore, contains three turning pairs and one sliding pair.

Figures 3·10, 3·11, and 3·12 illustrate three forms of the slider-crank mechanism, corresponding links bearing the same

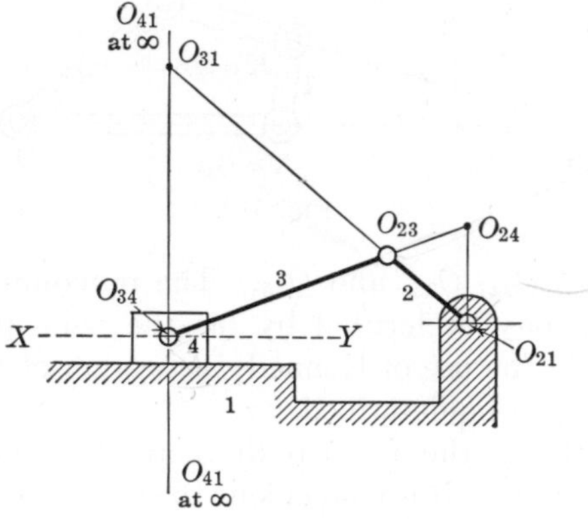

FIG. 3·10.

letter. There are six instant centers, three of them, O_{21}, O_{23}, O_{34}, being located at the pivot points. One, O_{41}, is at infinity, as the relative motion of 1 and 4 is rectilinear.

The two remaining centers, O_{24} and O_{31}, may be found as follows:

(*a*) By the method of Art. 3·2, to locate O_{31}, 1 is considered to be fixed; then the point O_{34} moves along XY, and the point O_{23} moves perpendicularly to link 2. As these are two points on link 3, the instant center O_{31} is at the intersection of the perpendiculars to the directions of motion of these points (see figures). Similarly, for O_{24}, if 4 is fixed, O_{21} is constrained to move parallel to XY, and point O_{23} perpendicular to the centerline of 3. The normals to these directions of motion meet at O_{24}.

(*b*) The same results may be obtained using Kennedy's theorem. As before, the location of the instant centers O_{21}, O_{23}, O_{34}, and O_{41} are known. The instant center O_{24} will be located at the intersection of lines drawn through $O_{21}O_{41}$ and

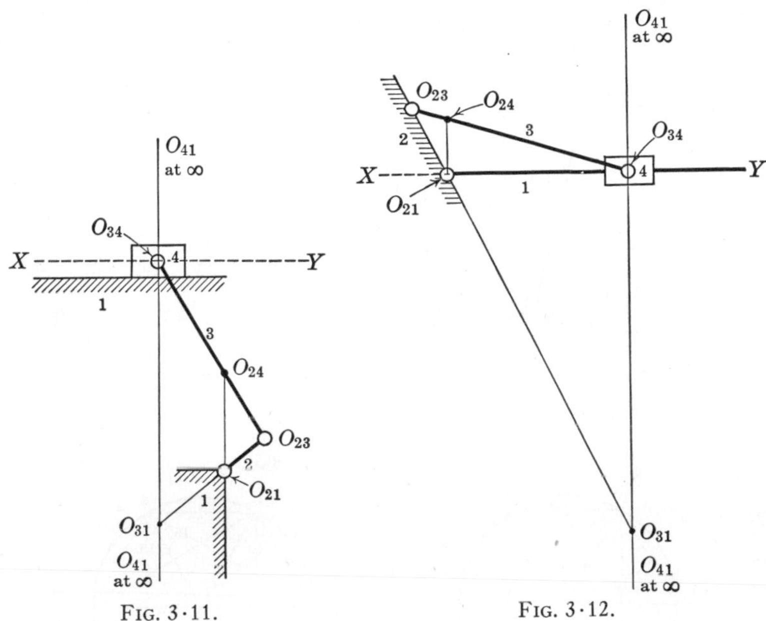

FIG. 3·11.

FIG. 3·12.

$O_{23}O_{34}$. The instant center O_{31} is at the intersection of lines drawn through $O_{21}O_{23}$ and $O_{34}O_{41}$. Since the instant center O_{41} is located at infinity, and parallel lines meet at infinity where O_{41} is located, it is possible to draw lines through this point by moving the line parallel to itself.

3·8 Tabulation of centers When a mechanism has six links, the number of instant centers to be located is fifteen. It is then desirable to have a systematic method of recording progress and assisting in the determination. This may be done by means of a circle diagram, or by the use of tables. Both methods will be given and illustrated by an example.

(a) Circle diagram A diagram of the form shown in Fig. 3·13*b* is useful when finding instant centers since it gives a visual indication of the order in which the centers can be located by means of Kennedy's theorem and also, at any stage in the process, it shows what centers remain to be found. The circle diagram will be used for finding the centers in the six-link mechanism of Fig. 3·13*a*. The following procedure is used to locate them.

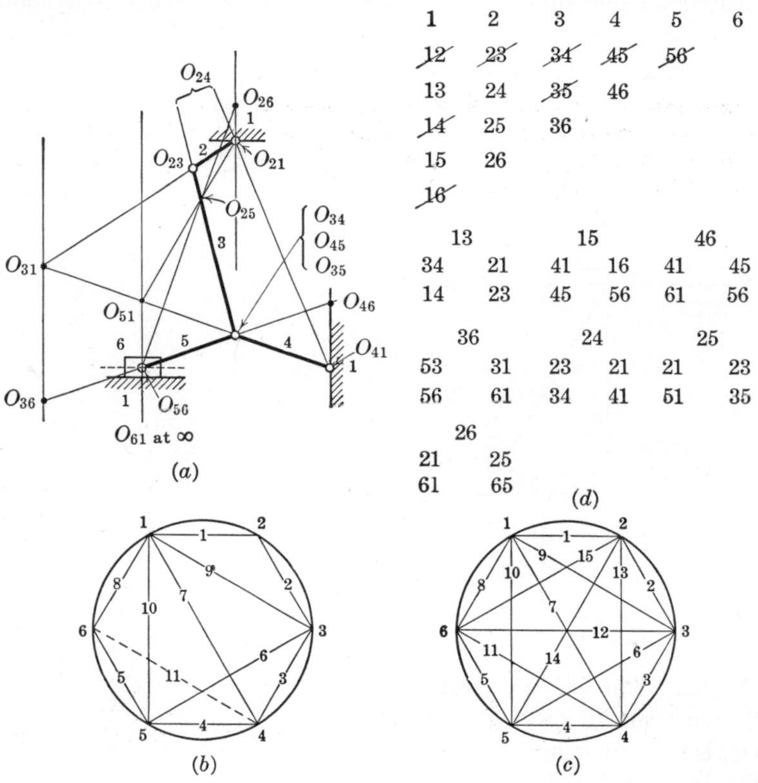

FIG. 3·13 Crusher Mechanism.

Draw a circle, as in Fig. 3·13*b*, and mark points, 1, 2, 3, 4, 5, 6, around the circumference, representing the six links in the mechanism. As the instant centers are located, draw lines connecting the points with corresponding numbers on this diagram. Thus line 12 is drawn when the instant center O_{12} is found. The figure will have lines connecting all pairs of points when all the instant centers have been determined. Numbers on the lines, indicating the sequence in which they are drawn, facilitate checking. At one stage in the process (after 10 of the centers have been found) the diagram will appear as shown in Fig. 3·13*b*. From inspection of the diagram we note that by joining 46 we complete two triangles 465 and 461. Since this is the case, we locate the instant center O_{46} at the intersection of $O_{41}O_{61}$ and $O_{45}O_{56}$. Had we drawn 62 instead, only one triangle, namely 621, would have been formed; hence, the center O_{62} could not be found at this stage, though it can be after O_{25} (line 14) is placed. The line 62 is therefore taken as number 15. The procedure is the same for the remaining points.

If each line is first drawn dashed while the center is being located and made solid as soon as the center is found, errors are less likely to occur. Figure 3·13*a* shows the location of all the instant centers, and Fig. 3·13*c* the completed circle diagram.

(b) Tabular method An alternative method of locating instant centers in common use is the tabular method. In this procedure a main table is set up and used with supplementary tables as illustrated in Fig. 3·13*d*.

Across the top of the main table are listed the numbers of the links in the mechanism. In the first column are listed the number at the top of the column combined with those numbers to the right of it. In the second column the number at the top of that column combined with those to the right. Continuing this procedure to the end of the table gives a complete list of all the centers to be found. As the centers are located on the drawing, they are crossed off on the table as shown. Usually about half the centers may be found by inspection and crossed off immediately. Thus, in the example of Fig. 3·13, eight of the centers O_{12}, O_{23}, O_{34}, O_{45}, O_{56}, O_{14}, O_{16}, and O_{35} may be found by inspection. The remainder will have to be found by the use of Kennedy's theorem and with the aid of supplementary tables. Suppose now it is desired to locate the center O_{31}. A supplementary table is set up in which links 1 and 3 are considered with a third link, say 4. Then the centers O_{34}, O_{14}, and O_{13} must lie on a straight line, by Kennedy's theorem. The third link might also be 2, when the centers O_{21}, O_{23}, and O_{13} will lie on a straight line. These centers are listed in a supplementary table under the heading 13. Reference to the main table shows that the centers O_{34}, O_{14}, O_{21}, and O_{23} have been crossed off, hence have been located, and are available. Drawing lines through them locates O_{31}. In a similar manner, by using the tables, all of the centers may be located. The supplementary tables in Fig. 3·13*d* show the procedure.

Frequently it may be found that the third link chosen may require centers which have not been located. In such cases another third link would have to be tried. In the early stages it may be found that no third link will be satisfactory. In that case the search for that particular center will have to be temporarily abandoned until more centers are found.

3·9 Centrodes The path of the instant center of a moving body is known as a centrode. With reference to Fig. 3·14, *A*

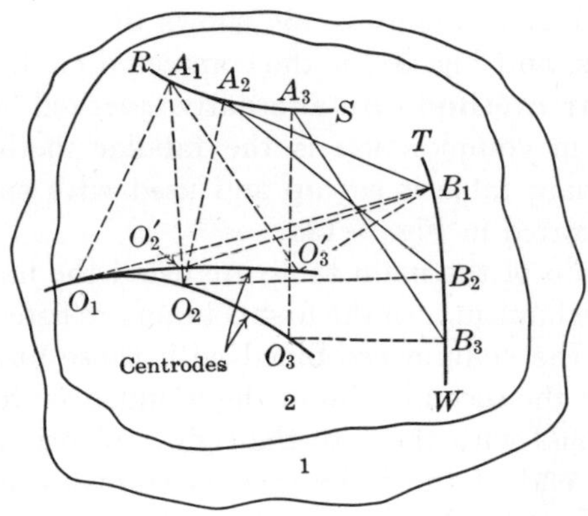

FIG. 3·14.

and *B*, two points on a moving body 2, trace out point paths *RS* and *TW* on a fixed body 1. A_1, A_2, A_3 are instantaneous positions of point *A*, and B_1, B_2, B_3 are corresponding positions of point *B* at the same instants of time. Erecting perpendiculars to the point paths at A_1 and B_1, we find the instant center O_1 at the intersection. O_2 and O_3 are found in similar fashion by intersections of perpendiculars at A_2, B_2, and A_3, B_3, respectively. O_1, O_2, O_3 are points on the centrode for the relative motion as drawn on the fixed body 1.

Since the instant center is a point on either body, we can find a second centrode traced out by the instant centers on the surface of 2. That is, we now consider *O* as a point attached to and moving with 2. To construct this centrode we must choose a "reference" position of the points *A* and *B*, say, at A_1B_1, and refer the instant centers O_2 and O_3 back to it. O_1 then becomes a common point on both centrodes, and the points O'_2 and O'_3 are found by sliding back the triangles $A_2B_2O_2$ and $A_3B_3O_3$ so that the "AB" sides coincide with A_1B_1. Thus, triangle $A_1B_1O'_2$ is made equal to $A_2B_2O_2$, and triangle $A_1B_1O'_3$ equals $A_3B_3O_3$. A curve drawn through $O_1O'_2O'_3$ is the centrode attached to 2.

An alternative method of drawing the second centrode attached to the moving link is to invert the mechanism, making this link the fixed one. By this method, 2 in the figure would become the fixed link and 1 would be allowed to move. This construction becomes difficult when the point paths have an irregular shape. A case suitable for this method is considered in the next article.

3·10 Properties of centrodes When one body has constrained motion relative to another, it may be observed that, for any relative position of the two bodies, the two centrodes are in contact at a point, this point being the instant center for that position. As relative motion continues, it follows that the two centrodes will roll on one another. Consequently, it is possible to substitute for a given mechanism an equivalent mechanism containing two rolling surfaces which will produce the same motion of a selected link as it had in the original. An example of this will now be shown.

In Fig. 3·15 is illustrated one form of the **double slider-crank mechanism,** consisting of a bar link 3 pivoted to blocks 2 and 4, the latter sliding in guides on a frame 1. Points A and B on 2 and 4 have straight-line motion along XY and XZ, respectively. In the position A_1, B_1 (Fig. 3·16), the instant center is at O_1, the intersection of perpendiculars to XY and XZ at A_1 and B_1, respectively. The centrode attached to the frame 1 is drawn through points O_1, O_2, etc., the latter being found in the same way as O_1. This is the curve MO_1O_2N.

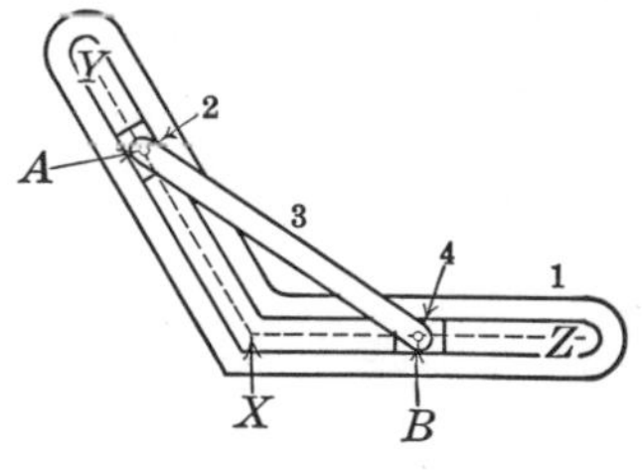

FIG. 3·15.

Two methods may be used to find the centrode attached to 3.

(*a*) In Fig. 3·16 is shown the same construction as was used in Art. 3·9. For the reference position, AB is taken as coincident with XY. Triangle XYO'_1 is made equal to $A_1B_1O_1$; XYO'_2

equals $A_2B_2O_2$, etc. The curve $MO'_1O'_2P$ is the centrode attached to 3.

(b) In Fig. 3·17 link 3 is held fixed, and 1 is moved around it. As the frame, represented by the lines XY and XZ, is moved around the body 3, represented by the line AB, XY must always

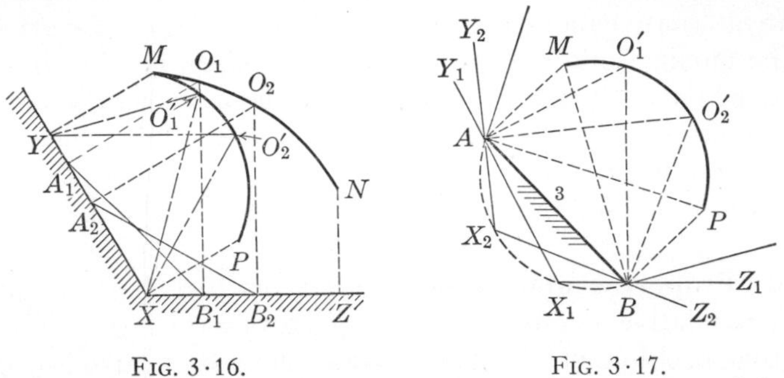

Fig. 3·16. Fig. 3·17.

pass through A, and XZ must pass through B. The angle YXZ being constant, the apex X will trace out a circular arc AX_2X_1B. When X is in position X_1, the instant center is at O'_1, a point found by the intersection of perpendiculars to X_1Y_1 and X_1Z_1 through A and B, respectively. Similarly, O'_2 corresponds to position X_2. The centrode attached to 3 is the curve $MO'_1O'_2P$.

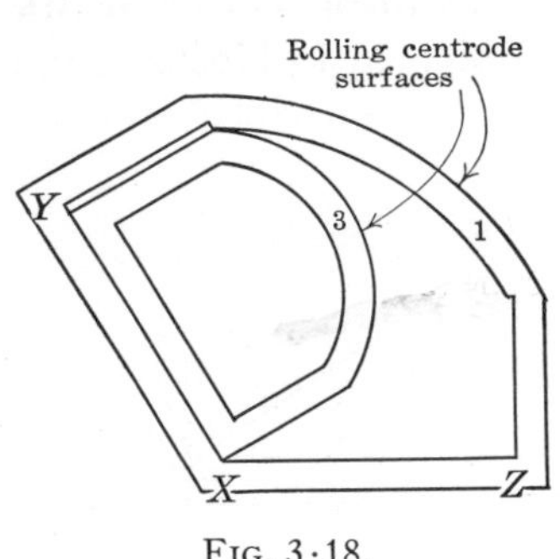

Fig. 3·18.

We can now construct a mechanism as shown in Fig. 3·18 in which we have replaced the sliding blocks 2, 4 and their guides (Fig. 3·15) by two surfaces whose profiles are the two centrodes, one surface being attached to 3 and the other to 1. The motion of 3 relative to 1 in Fig. 3·18, obtained by rolling together the centrode surfaces, is the same as for the corresponding links of Fig. 3·15.

Figure 3·18 is an example of the substitution of higher pairing with rolling contact for lower pairing with sliding contact. This principle has been employed in the valve gears of certain gas engines of German manufacture.

QUESTIONS

3·1 Define "instant axis." What convention do we use, for simplicity, when referring to the instant axis of a body having plane motion?

3·2 Show how to find the instant center for the motion of a body when the directions of motion of two points on it are known.

3·3 Show how to find one position of the instant center of a moving body when the paths of two points on it are known.

3·4 Prove that when three bodies have plane relative motion the instant centers must lie in one straight line.

3·5 Prove that the number of instant centers for n bodies equals

$$\frac{n(n-1)}{2}$$

3·6 Locate all the instant centers in the mechanisms shown in Figs. P3·6*a* to *h*. In each case explain the methods employed.

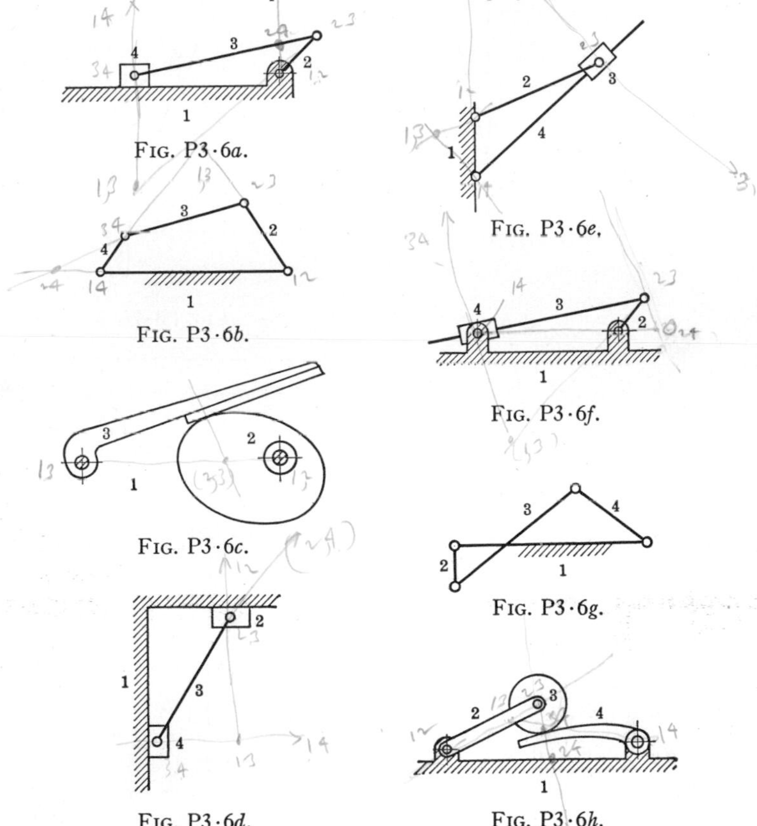

FIG. P3·6*a*.

FIG. P3·6*b*.

FIG. P3·6*c*.

FIG. P3·6*d*.

FIG. P3·6*e*.

FIG. P3·6*f*.

FIG. P3·6*g*.

FIG. P3·6*h*.

3·7 In the compound mechanisms shown in Figs. P3·7*a* to *g* determine the number of instant centers; locate all the instant centers.

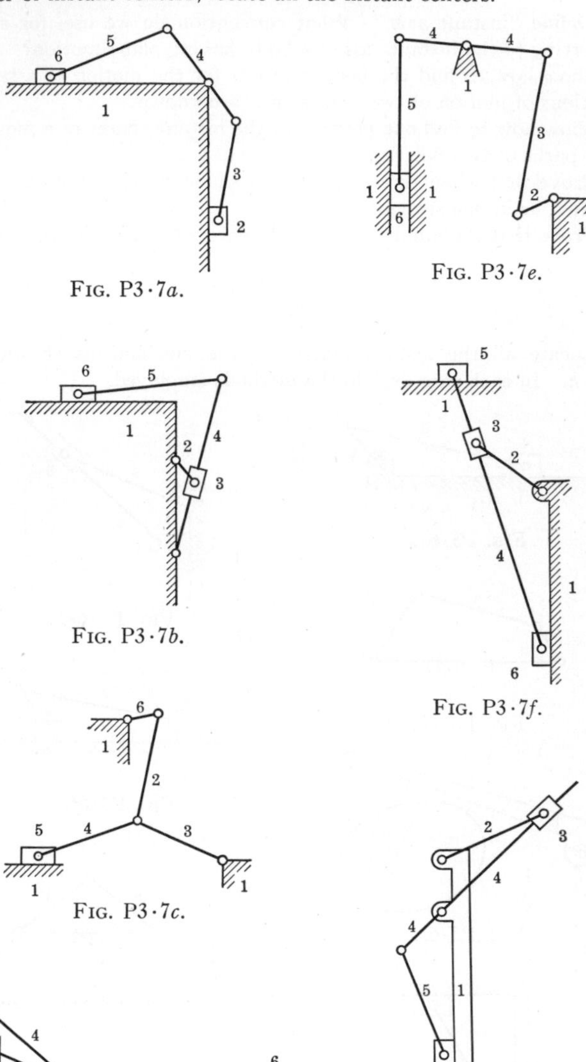

FIG. P3·7*a*.

FIG. P3·7*e*.

FIG. P3·7*b*.

FIG. P3·7*f*.

FIG. P3·7*c*.

FIG. P3·7*d*.

FIG. P3·7*g*.

3·8 Show how to plot the centrodes for the motion of link 3 relative to 1 in the mechanisms shown in Figs. P3·8*a* to *d*. (Find at least two points on each centrode.)

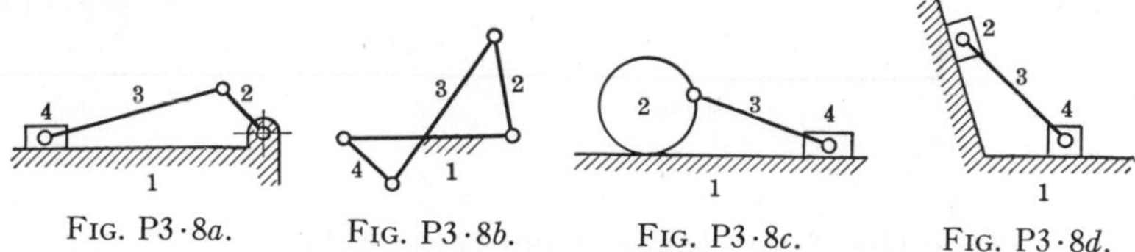

FIG. P3·8*a*. FIG. P3·8*b*. FIG. P3·8*c*. FIG. P3·8*d*.

3·9 What is the valuable property of centrodes in relation to their application to the design of mechanisms?

3·10 Illustrate the manner in which a mechanism can be altered so as to use rolling centrodes instead of turning and sliding pairs.

3·11 Locate all the instant centers in the mechanisms shown in Figs. P3·11*a* to *e*. In each case explain the methods employed.

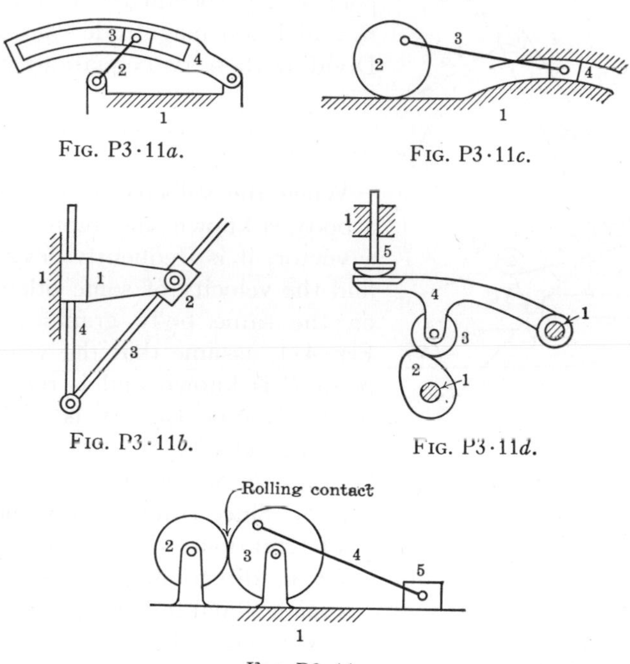

FIG. P3·11*a*. FIG. P3·11*c*.

FIG. P3·11*b*. FIG. P3·11*d*.

FIG. P3·11*e*.

3·12 Locate all the instant centers of the mechanisms shown for problems 9, 10, and 11 at the end of Chapter 4.

3·13 Two bodies having rolling contact consist of a cylinder and a straightedge. What is the centrode if (*a*) the cylinder is held fixed, (*b*) the straightedge is held fixed?

4 Velocity and Acceleration in Plane Motion

4·1 Velocities from instant centers When a body rotates about a center, the velocity of any point on it will be in a direction perpendicular to the radius and its magnitude is proportional to the radius. Thus in Fig. 4·1, where body 2 is pin-connected to body 1, the velocity of point P is perpendicular to the radius r_P and has a magnitude $\mathbf{v}_P = \omega_{2/1} r_P$. Similarly, the velocity of point Q is perpendicular to the radius r_Q and has a magnitude $\mathbf{v}_Q = \omega_{2/1} r_Q$. Dividing these two equations yields

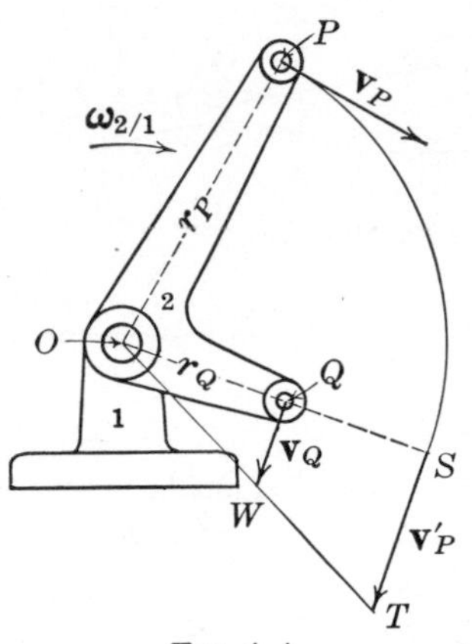

FIG. 4·1.

$$\frac{\mathbf{v}_Q}{\mathbf{v}_P} = \frac{r_Q}{r_P} \quad \text{or} \quad \mathbf{v}_Q = \mathbf{v}_P \frac{r_Q}{r_P} \qquad (4\cdot 1)$$

When the velocity of one point on a body is known and represented by a vector, it is frequently desirable to find the velocity of some other point on the same body graphically. In Fig. 4·1, assume that the velocity of point P is known and is represented by the vector $\mathbf{v}_P$. It is desired to find the velocity of point Q. With O as a center and a radius OP, or r_P, an arc is drawn intersecting OQ, produced if necessary, at S. Since S and P are the same distance from the center of rotation, their velocities are equal in magnitude but differ in direction. The vector $\mathbf{ST}$, drawn perpendicular to OS, is made equal in length to vector $\mathbf{v}_P$. This is labeled $\mathbf{v}'_P$, since it represents the magnitude of the velocity of P but not the correct direction. Drawing the line OT and the vector $\mathbf{QW}$ perpendicular to OQ, or r_Q, gives the similar triangles OQW and OST. Hence:

$$\frac{\mathbf{QW}}{\mathbf{ST}} = \frac{OQ}{OS} \quad \text{or} \quad \frac{\mathbf{v}_Q}{\mathbf{v}_P} = \frac{r_Q}{r_P}$$

which checks equation 4·1, and **QW** represents the velocity of point Q in magnitude and direction to the same scale that $\mathbf{v}_P$ represents the velocity of point P.

The same result could be obtained by swinging point Q about the center O to point X on line OP (see Fig. 4·2). Drawing the line OY, and the vector **XZ** perpendicular to OP, or r_P, gives again two similar triangles. Consequently, **XZ** represents the magnitude of the velocity of point Q to the same scale that **PY** represents the velocity of point P. Vector **XZ** is labeled $\mathbf{v}'_Q$ since it is the magnitude of $\mathbf{v}_Q$ but not the correct direction. Swinging this vector about O to point Q gives the velocity $\mathbf{v}_Q$.

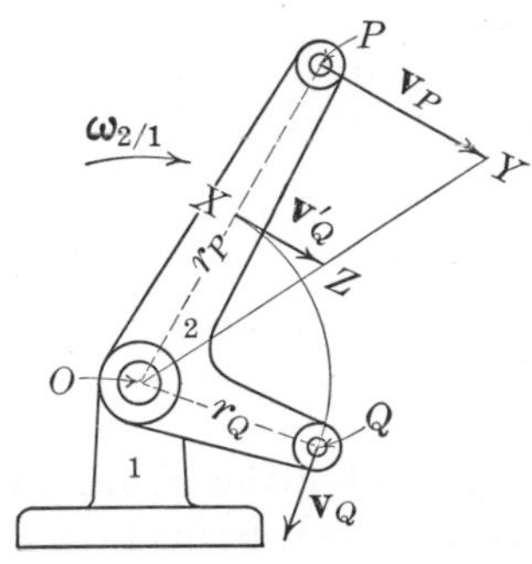

Fig. 4·2.

As instantaneous conditions only have been considered, this graphical construction applies whether the point about which the body rotates is an instant center or a permanent center.

Sometimes the instant center is inaccessible and the above graphical construction becomes impossible. In this case the following alternative is useful:

Let P and Q (Fig. 4·3) represent two points on a body 2, in motion with reference to a second body 1. The known velocity of P is represented in magnitude and direction by the vector $\mathbf{v}_P$. The instant center is at some inaccessible point O_{21} which is located at the intersection of perpendiculars to $\mathbf{v}_P$ and $\mathbf{v}_Q$.

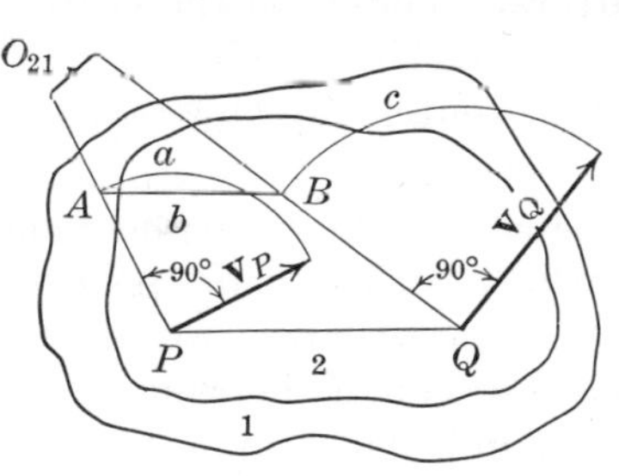

Fig. 4·3.

With P as center, arc a is swung through 90°, locating the point A on the line PO_{21}, the normal to the direction of motion of P. From A the line b is drawn parallel to PQ, meeting QO_{21} at B. With center Q and radius QB, arc c is described, subtending 90° at Q. Then it can be shown that vector $\mathbf{v}_Q$ represents the velocity of Q. The proof follows.

Since AB is parallel to PQ, triangles $O_{21}AB$ and $O_{21}PQ$ are similar. As a result,

$$\frac{O_{21}Q}{O_{21}P} = \frac{BQ}{AP}$$

But, by equation 4·1,

$$\frac{\mathbf{v}_Q}{\mathbf{v}_P} = \frac{O_{21}Q}{O_{21}P}$$

Hence,

$$\frac{\mathbf{v}_Q}{\mathbf{v}_P} = \frac{BQ}{AP}$$

If $\mathbf{v}_P$ is represented in magnitude by AP, then BQ represents $\mathbf{v}_Q$ to the same velocity scale.

4·2 Velocities from instant centers. Points on different links Very frequently it is necessary to find the velocity of a point on a certain link of a mechanism from the known velocity of another point located on a different link. Several methods are usually available, each having advantages for particular cases. It is highly desirable that the student grasp the principles of each of these methods so that he may use the one best suited to a particular problem or use one method to check the other. Some problems may best be solved by a combination of these methods.

Before outlining the methods, it is desirable to classify some of the instant centers as **pivot centers.** These are the centers related to the fixed link 1 and hence have its number in their subscript. Thus, in Fig. 4·4, the pivot centers are O_{21}, O_{31}, and O_{41}.

(a) Connecting-link method This is a step-by-step method whereby we start with the link on which is located the point of known velocity, and work through its instant center with respect to a connecting link and then along the connecting link to its instant center with respect to the next link. Continuing in this manner, we finally reach the link containing the point whose velocity is required. In general it is necessary to begin by locating all the pivot centers and the instant centers of each link with respect to its adjacent link.

To illustrate the method, consider the four-bar linkage of Fig. 4·4, in which link 1 is fixed. We shall assume that the velocity of a point P on link 2 is known, and the velocity of point Q on link 4 is required. In this example links 2 and 4 are connected by link 3, and we work through the latter from 2 to 4.

We first locate the instant centers O_{21}, O_{23}, O_{31}, O_{34}, and O_{41} as shown on the figure. The velocity of point P is given and represented by the vector $\mathbf{v}_P$, perpendicular to a line from P to the pivot center O_{21}. Considering the two points P and O_{23}

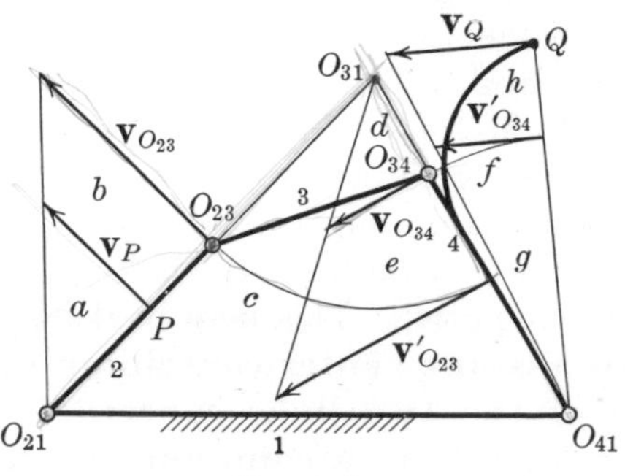

FIG. 4·4.

as points on link 2, we make the construction (by Art. 4·1) shown by the similar triangles a and b to find the velocity vector $\mathbf{v}_{O_{23}}$ for the point O_{23}.

By the definition of an instant center, O_{23} is a point on link 3 as well as on link 2. As a point on link 3 it rotates about the pivot center O_{31}; just as a point on link 2 it rotates about the pivot center O_{21}. Hence, the velocity vector $\mathbf{v}_{O_{23}}$ is swung (arc c) about the pivot center O_{31} to a line through O_{31} and O_{34}. Considering the revolved position of O_{23} and the center O_{34} as points on link 3, we make the construction (by Art. 4·1) shown by the triangles d and e; using O_{31} as the pivot center to find the velocity vector $\mathbf{v}_{O_{34}}$ for the point O_{34}. Now, O_{34} and Q are both points on link 4, which rotates about the pivot center O_{41}. Hence, $\mathbf{v}_{O_{34}}$ may be swung about this pivot center to the line $O_{41}Q$ (arc f). Drawing the similar triangles g and h, we find the velocity vector $\mathbf{v}_Q$ representing the required velocity of point Q. It is perpendicular to a line from Q to the pivot center O_{41}.

From this description it should be evident that: **the rotation of any link relative to the fixed link occurs about the pivot center containing the number of that link and the fixed**

link. The absolute velocity of any point on a link is in a direction perpendicular to a line from the point to the pivot center of that link, and the vertex of the similar triangle construction given in Art. 4·1 is always at the pivot center of the link considered.

In this example pin joints connect the three links 2, 3, and 4. The connection between these links may, however, take any form, and the method can be applied to any mechanism, provided that the needed instant centers are accessible.

(b) Direct method When a mechanism has many links, the connecting-link method may become rather tedious. The direct method may frequently be used to shorten the labor involved in such cases. As the name implies, we go directly from the link containing the known velocity to the link containing the point whose velocity is required. This may be done by **finding the velocity of the instant center containing in its subscript the numbers of the two links concerned, since at this point the two links have a common velocity.** Hence it is necessary to locate only three instant centers. If the fixed link is 1, and the two links concerned are m and n, the centers to be located are O_{mn}, O_{m1} and O_{n1}. The latter two centers are the pivot centers, and the principles of the connecting-link method regarding the construction apply equally well here.

Thus in Fig. 4·5, which is the same four-bar linkage used in the previous example, the velocity of point P on link 2 is given, and it is required to find the velocity of point Q on link 4. Hence we locate the common center O_{24} and the two pivot centers O_{21} and O_{41}.

The points P and O_{24} are both points on link 2 and hence rotate about the pivot center O_{21}. As the velocity of P is known, the velocity of O_{24} may be found graphically by the method of Art. 4·1 and is labeled $\mathbf{v}_{O_{24}}$. As link 2 pivots about O_{21}, the triangle a is drawn, one side representing $\mathbf{v}_P$. Triangle b, similar to a, will have a corresponding side representing the velocity of O_{24} as indicated. As a point on link 4, O_{24} has the same velocity $\mathbf{v}_{O_{24}}$; hence we now know the velocity of one point on 4 and can find the velocity of any other point, such as Q. Since link 4 pivots about O_{41}, we construct the triangle c, and then the similar triangle d. The latter has a side representing $\mathbf{v}_Q$, which is labeled $\mathbf{v}'_Q$. This vector is swung about O_{41} up to point

Q, where it is perpendicular to a line from Q to the pivot center O_{41}. It represents the velocity of Q in both magnitude and direction.

The construction can be applied to any form of mechanism provided that the instant center for the two links on which the points are located is available. When it is not accessible, some

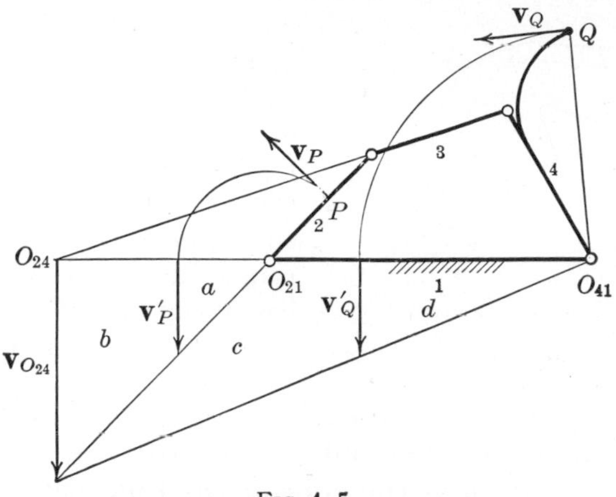

FIG. 4·5.

other method must be used. In some cases the location of this center may require much labor, and it may be simpler to use another method.

It should be realized that, if one of the pivot centers is at infinity, all points on that link will have the same velocity in both magnitude and direction. Hence, if the velocity of the common center is found, and the pivot center of the link on which the velocity is desired is at infinity, it is not possible, or necessary, to swing arcs as the velocity of the point is the same as that of the common center in both magnitude and direction (see Art. 4·9*b*).

4·3 Linear velocities by resolution If the magnitude and direction of motion of one point on a moving body and the direction of motion of a second point on the same body are known, the magnitude of the velocity of the latter point can be found by resolution. This method depends on the fact that the distance between the two points is constant if the body is rigid.

Let P and Q (Fig. 4·6) be two points on a body 2 in motion with respect to body 1. The velocity of P is indicated in magnitude and direction by the vector $\mathbf{v}_P$ at the instant considered. The point Q has motion in the direction QA at the same instant. The distance PQ is constant, and so the components of the velocities in a direction parallel to PQ must be the same; otherwise the distance between them would increase or decrease. By drawing triangle a we find the vector $\mathbf{v}_1$, the component parallel to PQ. Triangle b can now be drawn, since the vector $\mathbf{v}'_1$, representing the component of Q's velocity parallel to PQ, is equal to $\mathbf{v}_1$; also one side is perpendicular to PQ and the third lies along QA. The side last mentioned is $\mathbf{v}_Q$ and represents the velocity of Q.

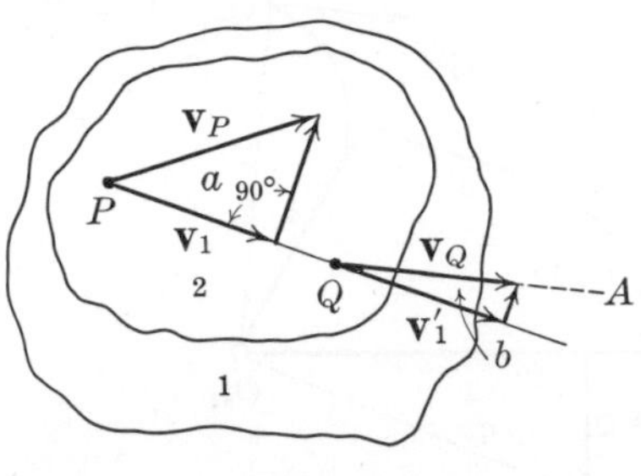

FIG. 4·6.

In drawing the components of a resultant, they should always be made parallel and perpendicular to the link, or a line drawn through the ends of the link, but **never** perpendicular to the resultant. If they are not drawn perpendicular to the link, these components will have another component of themselves along the link, which will destroy the principle on which the method is based.

The resolution method cannot be applied to two points lying on a radial line of a link having pure rotation. In such cases there is no component of motion along this line. In such situations we must resort to the procedure outlined in Art. 4·1.

By working from point to point through connecting links the method of resolution can be used in many cases to find the velocity of any point on a mechanism when the velocity of one point, not necessarily on the same link, is known.

The application of this method may be described using the same mechanism employed previously, as shown in Fig. 4·7. The velocity of point P is given and the velocity of point Q required. Since point P and the instant center O_{23} lie on a radial line, the resolution method cannot be used to find $\mathbf{v}_{O_{23}}$, and the similar triangle construction of Art. 4·1 must be employed. The velocity of O_{23} is now completely established, but only the direction of the resultant velocity of O_{34} (perpendicular to link 4, or $O_{34}O_{41}$) is known. The velocity of point O_{23} may be broken into two components: one perpendicular to link 3, and the other along it. The latter is labeled $\mathbf{v}_1$. This component must be the same at the right end, or link 3 would be elongated or compressed. Hence $\mathbf{v}'_1$, equal in length to $\mathbf{v}_1$, is laid off at O_{34} and a perpendicular to link 3 drawn at the end of this vector. Where this perpendicular intersects a vector perpendicular to link 4, or $O_{34}O_{41}$, determines the end of the vector $\mathbf{v}_{O_{34}}$.

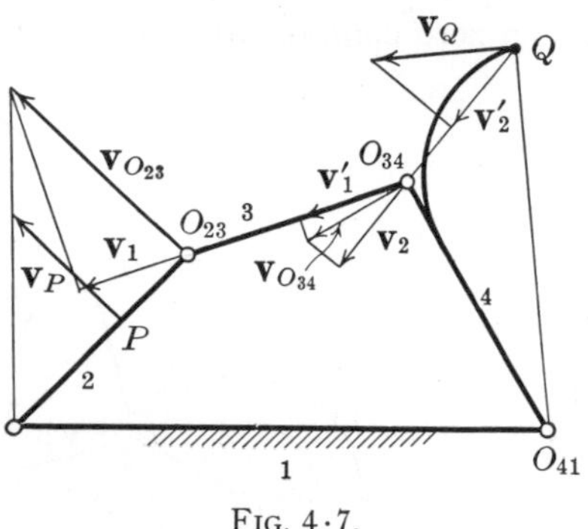

FIG. 4·7.

As O_{34} and point Q do not lie on a radial line from the point of rotation of link 4, resolution may again be used to find the velocity of Q. A line from O_{34} to Q is always the same length, as link 4 is assumed to be rigid. Hence, $\mathbf{v}_{O_{34}}$ may be broken into two components: one perpendicular to the line $O_{34}Q$, and the other along it. The component along this line is labeled $\mathbf{v}_2$ and must have the same length at point Q as at O_{34}. The resultant velocity of point Q is perpendicular to a line from Q to the pivot center O_{41}. Hence the tip of the $\mathbf{v}_Q$ vector will lie at the intersection of a line perpendicular to $O_{34}Q$ at the tip of the $\mathbf{v}'_2$ component, and it is perpendicular to QO_{41}.

A second example of the use of the resolution method is given in Fig. 4·8. This illustrates a compound mechanism often used in shapers as a means of driving the ram which carries the cutting tool. The slope of link 5 has been exaggerated to illustrate the construction more clearly.

We shall suppose that the velocity of the point P on the driving crank 2 is known and that the velocity of the point Q on the ram 6 is required.

Point P on link 2 and a coincident point P' on link 4 must have the same velocity normal to the line of slide of 3 on 4. If this were not the case, P would move off the line RO_{41}; this is an impossibility, owing to the constraining effect of the sliding pair. If $\mathbf{v}_P$ is resolved into two components parallel and normal to RO_{41} by drawing triangle a, then the normal component represents $\mathbf{v}'_P$, the velocity of point P' on 4, and the other component the rate at which link 3 slides on link 4.

P' and R are two points on link 4 pivoting about O_{41}. By use of the graphical construction given in Art. 4·1 and shown by triangles b and c, we find vector $\mathbf{v}_R$ representing the velocity of R. The resolution method cannot be used here, because $\mathbf{v}'_P$ has a zero component along RO_{41}.

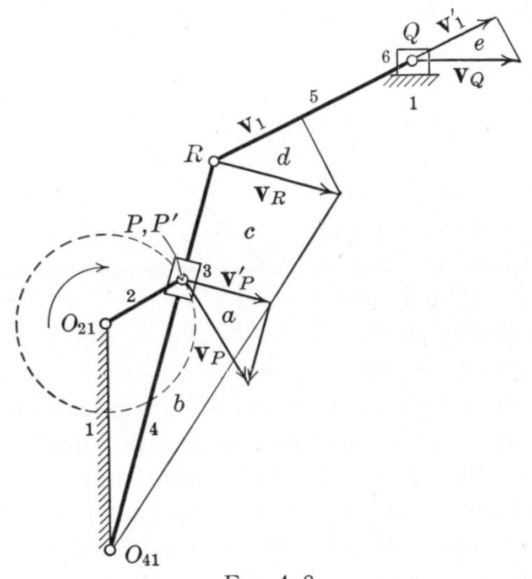

FIG. 4·8.

Finally, R and Q are points on link 5 and therefore have equal velocity components along 5. The resolution method, requiring the construction of triangles d and e, fixes the length of the vector $\mathbf{v}_Q$ which represents the velocity of Q.

4·4 Angular velocities When two bodies are in motion, it can be shown that their instantaneous angular velocities with respect to a third body are inversely as the distances from their common instant center to the instant centers about which they are pivoting on the third body. Thus, in Fig. 4·9, 2 and 3 are two bodies in motion with respect to 1. The three instant centers O_{21}, O_{23}, and O_{31} are assumed to be located as shown in the figure, and they lie on one straight line in accordance with Kennedy's theorem.

O_{23} is a point common to 2 and 3. As a point in 2, its instantaneous linear velocity is $\omega_{2/1}(O_{23}O_{21})$. As a point in 3, O_{23} is moving with a linear velocity $\omega_{3/1}$ $(O_{23}O_{31})$. Therefore,

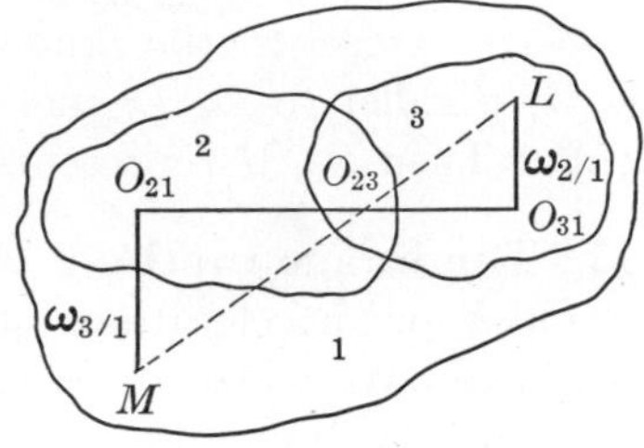

Fig. 4·9.

$$\omega_{2/1}(O_{23}O_{21}) = \omega_{3/1}(O_{23}O_{31})$$

or

$$\frac{\omega_{2/1}}{\omega_{3/1}} = \frac{O_{23}O_{31}}{O_{23}O_{21}}$$

When one of these angular velocities is known, the other can be determined graphically. The construction is indicated in Fig. 4·9. Suppose $\omega_{2/1}$ is known and $\omega_{3/1}$ is to be determined. Draw $O_{31}L$ perpendicular (or at any convenient angle) to $O_{31}O_{21}$ of a length representing $\omega_{2/1}$. Join LO_{23} and produce this line to meet $O_{21}M$, parallel to $O_{31}L$. From similar triangles,

$$\frac{O_{21}M}{O_{31}L} = \frac{O_{23}O_{21}}{O_{23}O_{31}} = \frac{\omega_{3/1}}{\omega_{2/1}}$$

Hence, $O_{21}M$ represents $\omega_{3/1}$ to the same scale as $O_{31}L$ represents $\omega_{2/1}$.

When O_{23} falls between O_{21} and O_{31}, the bodies 2 and 3 turn in **opposite** senses; but, when it falls on $O_{21}O_{31}$ produced, the bodies 2 and 3 turn in the **same** sense.

Example Figures 4·10 and 4·11 show the same slider-crank mechanism in two positions. In each case, assuming that the

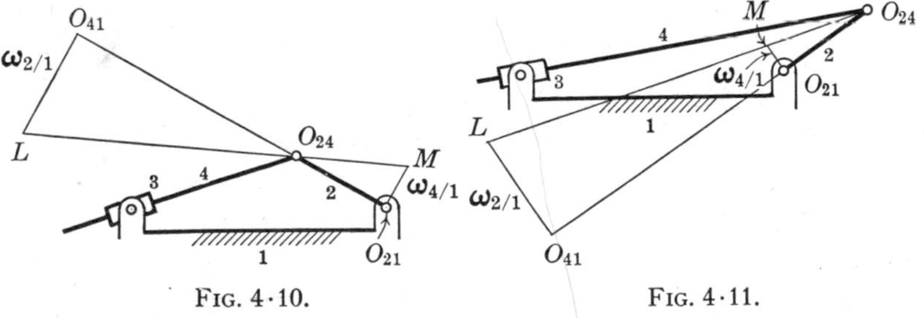

Fig. 4·10. Fig. 4·11.

angular velocity of the crank 2 ($\omega_{2/1}$) is known, find graphically the angular velocity of link 4 ($\omega_{4/1}$).

Construction. Find the three instant centers for links 1, 2, and 4. These centers lie on a straight line by Kennedy's theorem. Draw the triangle $LO_{41}O_{24}$ in which $O_{41}L$, perpendicular to $O_{41}O_{24}$, represents the known angular velocity $\boldsymbol{\omega}_{2/1}$. Draw $O_{21}M$, parallel to $O_{41}L$, meeting LO_{24}, produced, if necessary, at M. Then $O_{21}M$ represents the desired angular velocity $\boldsymbol{\omega}_{4/1}$.

4·5 The image method A graphical method of determining velocities and accelerations of points in mechanisms, which has proved to have wide application and very considerable practical importance, will now be considered. This is generally known as the "image method." It is given by Professor Burmester in his *Kinematik*. The construction of the acceleration diagram often requires the prior determination of certain velocities; hence the latter problem will be taken up first.

4·6 The velocity image If there are two points *A* and *B* on a body in plane motion, then the absolute velocity of *B* is equal to the vectorial sum of the absolute velocity of *A* and the relative velocity of *B* with respect to *A*. The velocity image method is based on this statement.

Assume a link as shown in Fig. 4·12*a*, pivoted at point *O* and containing three points *A*, *B*, and *C*. It is rotating clockwise

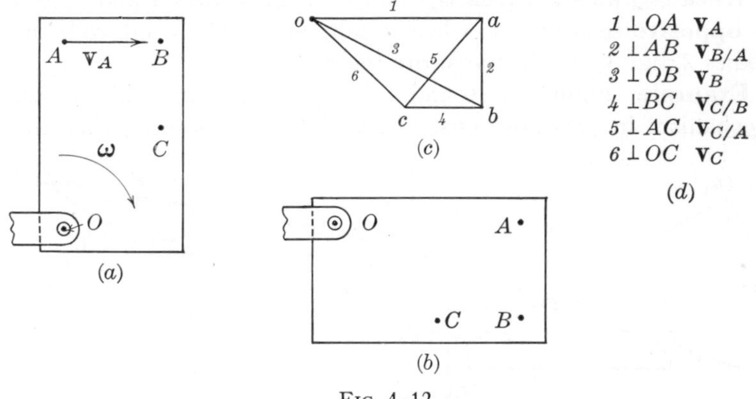

FIG. 4·12.

with an angular velocity $\boldsymbol{\omega}$. The velocity of point A is known and given by the vector $\mathbf{v}_A$. It is desired to find the velocity of points B and C. This, of course, could be done by the method of Art. 4·1, but this discussion is based on the principle outlined in the preceding paragraph. As the link rotates, point B will rotate about point A with the same angular velocity (both magnitude and direction) as A rotates about the pivot O. This is shown in Fig. 4·12b, where the link is revolved through 90° from that given in Fig. 4·12a. It may be noted that B is now below A rather than to its right, i.e., has rotated about A through the same angle that A has rotated about O. This may be made clearer by marking the letters on a piece of paper, representing the link, and pivoting it between the fingers at point O. For the position shown in Fig. 4·12a, the velocity of point B relative to point A is in a vertical direction.

By using these facts and the basic principle stated above, the velocity image diagram, shown in Fig. 4·12c, may be drawn. The lines on this diagram are numbered in the order in which they are drawn. A table of explanation giving the direction of the lines and what they represent is given in Fig. 4·12d. From an assumed point or "pole" o, the line **oa** is drawn perpendicular to OA, representing $\mathbf{v}_A$ (equal to $\boldsymbol{\omega} OA$) to any convenient velocity scale. The relative velocity of B to A, ($\mathbf{v}_{B/A}$), acts in a direction perpendicular to AB. The absolute velocity of point B is in a direction perpendicular to a line from B to O. Hence, from the pole o, draw line *3* perpendicular to OB of Fig. 4·12a. It meets line *2* at point b, and **ob** represents the absolute velocity of point B to the same scale that **oa** represents the velocity of point A. Also, **ab**, or line *2*, on Fig. 4·12c represents to the same scale the velocity of point B relative to A. Note that **ba** is the velocity of point A relative to point B; i.e., it has the same magnitude but the opposite direction.

If the process is continued by drawing lines *4*, *5*, and *6* as outlined in the table (Fig. 4·12d), all the absolute and relative velocities are found. It will be observed that it is only necessary to calculate, or be given, one velocity, and the remainder are determined by the direction of the various lines. This is true since the angular velocity of the link is the same for all the points about each other, as shown above. Also it may be noted that the diagram is geometrically similar to the original link, but rotated in the direction of rotation by 90°. Hence, if the original link is rotated 90°, and the proper velocity scale is chosen, we automatically have the velocity diagram.

It should be noted that any line originating at the pole *o* is an absolute velocity (i.e., relative to the fixed link), whereas the lines between the other points represent the velocity of one of these points relative to the other.

Example In the four-bar linkage of Fig. 4·13*a*, link *AB* rotates with a constant angular velocity $\boldsymbol{\omega}_{2/1}$. It is required to find the absolute velocities of points *B*, *C*, and *E* on the adjacent link.

The velocity of point *B* can be calculated as it is equal to $\boldsymbol{\omega}_{2/1}AB$. It acts in a direction perpendicular to *AB*. This is

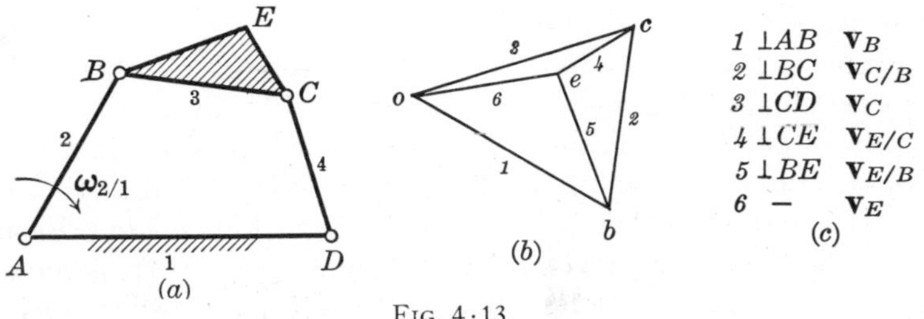

FIG. 4·13.

laid off to some convenient velocity scale as line *1* from the pole *o* in Fig. 4·13*b*. The motion of point *C* relative to *B* is in a direction perpendicular to *BC*; hence from *b*, line *2* is drawn in that direction. The absolute velocity of point *C* is normal to link *CD*; so line *3* is drawn from the pole *o* perpendicular to *CD* to intersect line *2* at *c*. Then line *3*, or **oc**, is the absolute velocity of point *C*, whereas line *2*, or **bc**, is the velocity of point *C* relative to point *B*.

The velocity of point *E* relative to *C* is perpendicular to line *CE* and is drawn from point *c* (line *4*), while the velocity of point *E* relative to *B* is perpendicular to line *BE* and is drawn from point *b* (line *5*). The intersection of lines *4* and *5* locates point *e*. A line from *o* to *e* gives the absolute velocity of point *E* (line *6*). The direction of the velocity of point *E* could be checked by locating the instant center O_{31}. Line *6* should be perpendicular to a line from this center to point *E*. The numbers on the lines of the image indicate the order in which they are drawn, and the table gives their direction and meaning.

4·7 The acceleration image This is based on the same general principle concerning accelerations as that underlying the velocity-image construction, which may be stated as follows: **For two points A and B on a body in plane motion, the absolute acceleration of B is equal to the vectorial sum of the absolute acceleration of A and the acceleration of B relative to A.**

As pointed out in Art. 2·4, a point P (Fig. 4·14) on a body moving about an instant center O is subject to a tangential acceleration $\mathbf{a}^t$ acting tangentially to the motion, and a normal acceleration $\mathbf{a}^n$ acting toward the center of curvature, where

$$\mathbf{a}^t = \alpha OP$$

$$\mathbf{a}^n = \omega^2 OP = \mathbf{v}^2{}_P/OP$$

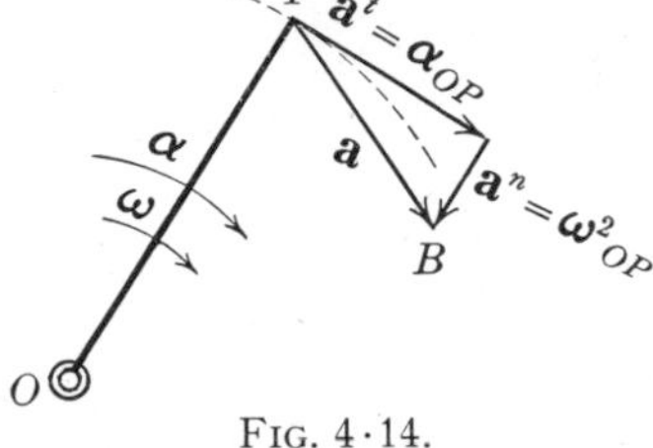

FIG. 4·14.

ω and α being, respectively, the angular velocity and angular acceleration of the point P. Distance **PB** represents the total acceleration $\mathbf{a}$ and equals the vectorial sum of $\mathbf{a}^t$ and $\mathbf{a}^n$.

If the point O is a fixed point, then **PB** is the absolute acceleration of point P. If, however, both P and O are in motion, then **PB** is the relative acceleration of P with respect to O.

In Fig. 4·15*a*, which is similar to Fig. 4·12*a* except that point C is omitted, A and B are two points on a body that has a known angular velocity ω and angular acceleration α and is pivoted at a fixed point O. It is desired to find the absolute acceleration of points A and B.

Calculate the value of $\omega^2 OA$, the normal acceleration of point A, and from an assumed pole o' draw line *1'*, or $\mathbf{o'a'}_1$, parallel to OA to represent this acceleration to some convenient acceleration scale (see Fig. 4·15*b*). Then calculate the value of αAO, the tangential acceleration of A; and from a'_1 draw a line $\mathbf{a'}_1\mathbf{a'}$, or line *2'*, perpendicular to AO representing this acceleration. Join o' and a' to get line *3'*. Then $\mathbf{o'a'}$ represents the total and absolute acceleration of point A.

The relative acceleration of point B to point A must next be found. This requires the calculation of the normal ($\omega^2 AB$) and the tangential (αAB) accelerations. Starting from a' lines *4'* and *5'*, or $\mathbf{a'b'}_1$ and $\mathbf{b'}_1\mathbf{b'}$, are drawn, respectively, parallel and perpendicular to BA. If point b' is joined to the pole o', the line $\mathbf{o'b'}$, or line $7'$, represents the absolute acceleration of point B. Line $6'$ drawn from a' to b' represents the total relative acceleration of point B relative to point A. A table, similar to that used for the velocity image, is given in Fig. 4·15*c* to help clarify the procedure.

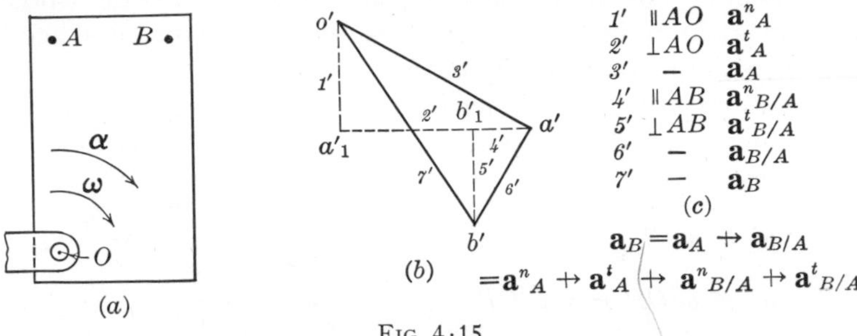

Fig. 4·15.

If only the solid lines $3'$, $6'$, and $7'$ are considered, two facts become apparent. The first is that the acceleration image is similar to the velocity image, as these lines correspond to lines *1*, *2*, and *3* of Fig. 4·12*c* and clarify the statement at the beginning of this article. The second is that the triangle formed by these lines is similar to that formed by points OAB in Fig. 4·15*a*. It is rotated forward in the direction of the angular velocity through an angle of $[90 + \tan^{-1} \omega^2/\alpha]$. The fact that the two figures are similar is the basis for the term "image" in the name of the construction, and may be used in checking.

In constructing the acceleration diagram, care should be exercised to insure that the normal acceleration vector for each point is drawn in a direction **toward** and not away from the other point to which the acceleration is referred. The tangential acceleration line must be drawn in the direction opposite to that of the velocity of the point if the angular acceleration is negative in character, that is, when the angular velocity is decreasing. Thus, in Fig. 4·15, if α were negative or opposite in sense to ω, then $\mathbf{a'}_1\mathbf{a'}$ must be drawn in the reverse direction to that shown in the figure.

4·8 Graphical construction of the normal acceleration When the velocity of a point relative to a second point on the same body is known, and also its distance from the other point, then the relative normal acceleration may be found graphically. In Fig. 4·16, let AO represent the distance (S) between points A and O to a scale of $1'' = k$ ft. Also let AB at 90° to AO

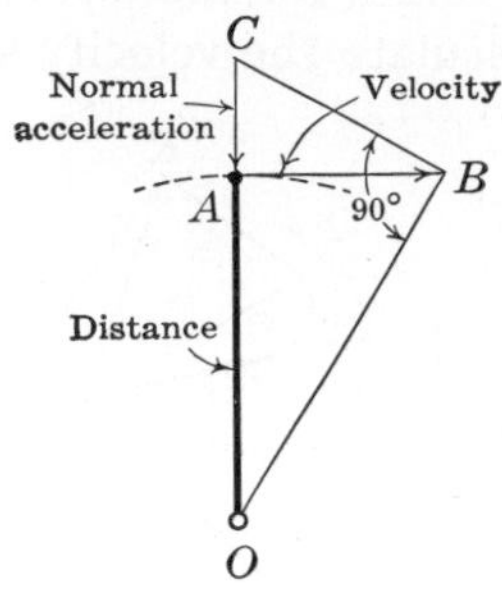

FIG. 4·16.

represent the velocity ($\mathbf{v}_{A/O}$), to a scale of $1'' = m$ fps. Thus $S = k\,AO$ ft and $\mathbf{v}_{A/O} = m\,AB$ fps, where AO and AB are in inch units.

Now the relative normal acceleration of A to O is

$$\frac{(\mathbf{v}_{A/O})^2}{S} = \frac{(m\,AB)^2}{k\,AO} = \frac{m^2}{k}\frac{(AB)^2}{AO}$$

In Fig. 4·16 draw BC perpendicular to BO, meeting OA produced at C. From the similarity of triangles CAB and BAO,

$$\frac{CA}{AB} = \frac{AB}{AO} \quad \text{or} \quad CA = \frac{(AB)^2}{AO}$$

The normal acceleration of A is therefore equal to $\dfrac{m^2}{k}\,CA$. In other words, CA represents the acceleration to a scale of $1'' = n$ fps^2 where $n = m^2/k$ or $m = \sqrt{kn}$.

The example that follows will indicate the method of using this graphical construction in drawing an acceleration diagram.

Example 1 In the slider-crank mechanism of Fig. 4·17a, the angular velocity of the crank AB is constant and equal to $\boldsymbol{\omega}$. Find the accelerations of three points B, C, and D on the connecting rod.

The velocity diagram is considered first, since it is needed in constructing the acceleration diagram.

To make it possible to find the normal accelerations by the graphical method just outlined, the scale for the velocity diagram should be $1'' = \sqrt{kn}$ velocity units. Generally it is more convenient to fix suitable values for the displacement and acceleration scales and then calculate the velocity scale.

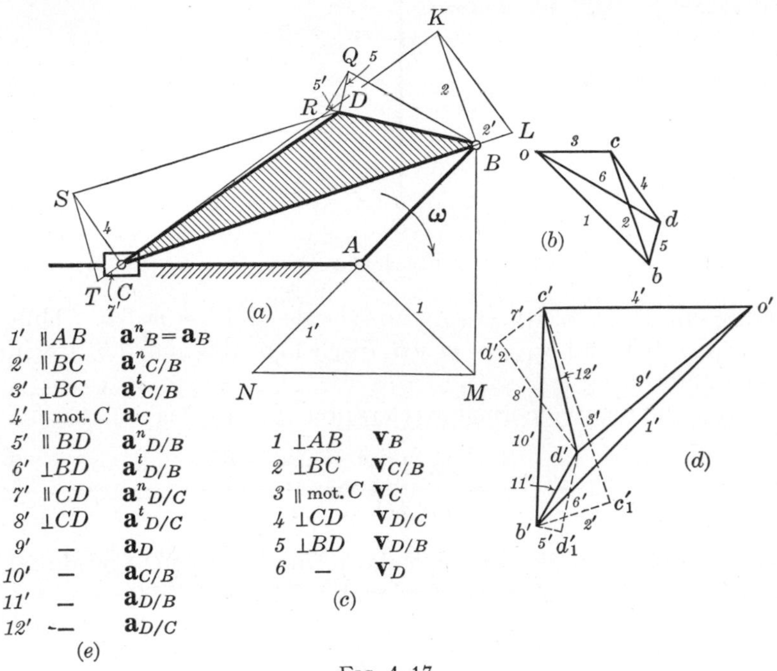

FIG. 4·17.

Point B is moving perpendicular to AB with a velocity $\boldsymbol{\omega}\,AB$, which must be calculated. Point C has an absolute velocity along CA, and its velocity relative to B is in a direction normal to BC. With this information we can draw the triangle *obc* in Fig. 4·17*b*, as lines *1*, *2*, and *3*. The velocity of point D relative to point C is perpendicular to the line CD, while that of point D relative to point B is normal to line BD. These lines are drawn on part *b* of the figure as lines *4* and *5*. Their intersection locates point *d*. Line *6* from the pole *o* to point *d* gives the absolute velocity of point D. A table explaining the meaning of the lines is given in Fig. 4·17*c*. Having determined the various velocities we are now ready to undertake the acceleration-image diagram.

Pole o' is the starting point for the acceleration diagram, which will be drawn double-size for clarity. Point B has no tangential acceleration as the crank AB is assumed to be moving with constant angular velocity. Hence, its total acceleration is a normal one, equal to $\boldsymbol{\omega}^2 AB$ acting toward A. The value of this quantity is found graphically by drawing AM normal to AB and equal in length to **ob**, or line *1* of the velocity-image diagram. Completing the right-angled triangle construction, we obtain the length AN, equal to $\mathbf{v}^2_B/AB$ or $\boldsymbol{\omega}^2 AB$. On the acceleration diagram line *1'*, or **o'b'** is drawn twice the length of AN in a direction parallel to BA.

Point C will have both a normal and tangential acceleration relative to point B. The normal acceleration of C relative to B is given by the right-angled triangle CKL in which BK equals the length of line *2*, or $\mathbf{v}_{C/B}$; and BL is the relative normal acceleration. It is laid off double-size from point b' as line *2'*, parallel to BC. The tangential acceleration of C relative to B will act normal to BC and is drawn of indefinite length as line *3'*.

The absolute acceleration of point C must be horizontal as its motion is limited to that direction. Hence line *4'* is drawn from the pole o' to meet line *3'* at c'. The acceleration of point C is then line *4'*, or **o'c'**.

By a similar construction, the acceleration of point D relative to B may be found. The right-angled triangle BQR, using line *5*, or **bd**, of the velocity image gives RD, the normal acceleration of point D relative to B. It is laid off double-size from b' as line *5'*. The tangential acceleration of D relative to B is perpendicular to this and drawn as line *6'*.

Again, the normal acceleration of point D relative to C is found from the triangle DST using line *4*, or **cd**, of the velocity image, as CT. This length is laid off double size from c' as line *7'*. The tangential acceleration of D relative to C is perpendicular to this and drawn as line *8'*.

The intersection of lines *6'* and *8'* locates point d', and **o'd'**, or line *9'*, is the absolute acceleration of point D. The total relative acceleration of C to B is line *10'*, drawn from c' to b'; of D to B is line *11'*, drawn from d' to b'; of D to C is line *12'*, drawn from d' to c'.

It may be observed that the triangle $b'c'd'$ is similar to triangle BCD. Considering only the solid lines of Fig. 4·17*d*, it may be seen that the basic principle of the acceleration-image diagram applies; i.e., the acceleration of point D (line $9'$) equals the vectorial sum of the absolute acceleration of point B (line $1'$) and the acceleration of point D relative to point B (line $11'$). A similar statement may be made regarding points D and C.

A table giving the direction and meaning of the various lines of the acceleration-image diagram is given in Fig. 4·17*e*.

Example 2 Figure 4·18 shows a cam mechanism with a pivoted roller follower. The cam profile is in the form of a circular

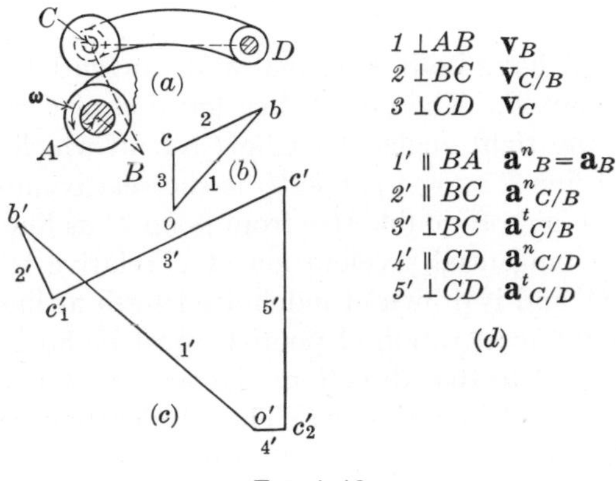

FIG. 4·18.

arc with center at B. It is required to find the angular velocity and angular acceleration of the follower, assuming a constant angular velocity of the cam.

The distance BC from center of curvature of the cam profile to center of the roller is constant. Hence the equivalent mechanism is a four-bar linkage with links AB, BC, CD and DA (fixed).

The velocity triangle *obc* has sides respectively perpendicular to AB, BC, and CD. Length $\mathbf{ob}$ is equal to $\boldsymbol{\omega}\, AB$ where $\boldsymbol{\omega}$ is the angular velocity of the cam. Length $\mathbf{oc}$ represents the velocity of C. The angular velocity of the follower is equal to $\mathbf{oc}/CD$ when $\mathbf{oc}$ is expressed in velocity units and CD is the real length of the arm.

For the acceleration diagram, the lines are drawn in the order shown by figures on the diagram starting from the pole o'. The two tables on the figure give the direction and meaning of each line drawn.

The three normal accelerations $\mathbf{o'b'}$, $\mathbf{b'c'_1}$, and $\mathbf{o'c'_2}$, corresponding to lines *1'*, *2'*, and *4'*, respectively, may be either calculated or found graphically. In the latter case the scales of displacement, velocity, and acceleration must bear the relationship stated in Art. 4·8.

The lines of the acceleration image are drawn in the numbered order indicated. The location of point c' is at the intersection of lines *3'* and *5'*. The required angular acceleration of the follower is equal to the tangential acceleration of C, namely $\mathbf{c'_2c'}$, or line *5'*, divided by the actual length of CD.

4·9 Summary example To illustrate the various methods of finding velocities and accelerations described in this chapter, consider the six-link mechanism shown in Fig. 4·19*a*, on which most of the instant centers are located. The velocity of point R is given by the vector $\mathbf{v}_R$, and it is desired to find the velocity of point T by (*a*) the connecting-link method, (*b*) the direct method (considering R as a point on link 2, and T as a point on link 6), (*c*) the resolution method, and (*d*) the velocity-image method. (*e*) If the angular velocity of link 2 ($\boldsymbol{\omega}_{2/1}$) is represented by a line $\frac{1}{2}$ in. long, find the corresponding angular velocities of links 3 and 4. (*f*) Assuming that the velocity of point R is constant in magnitude (that is, $\boldsymbol{\omega}_{2/1}$ is constant), find the acceleration of point T by the acceleration image.

(a) Connecting-link method Points R and S are both on link 3 and hence rotate about the pivot center O_{31}. On Fig. 4·19*a*, point R is swung about O_{31} to link 4, and the triangle $O_{31}GS$ drawn to find the velocity of S. Both S and T are points on link 5 and hence rotate about the pivot center O_{51}. Point T is swung about O_{51} to link 4 extended, and the triangle $O_{51}HT'$ is drawn to find the velocity $\mathbf{v'}_T$. This vector is then swung back about O_{51} to point T to give the velocity of T.

(b) Direct method Considering R as a point on link 2 and T as a point on link 6, the three instant centers to be used are O_{21}, O_{26}, and O_{61}. These are located on Fig. 4·19*a*. Points R and the instant center O_{26} are both points on link 2 and hence rotate about the pivot center O_{21}. The vector $\mathbf{v}_R$ is then swung about O_{21} to a line through $O_{21}O_{26}$, and the triangle $O_{21}O_{26}J$ is drawn to find the velocity of O_{26}. This should then be related in a similar manner to point T. However, the pivot center O_{61}

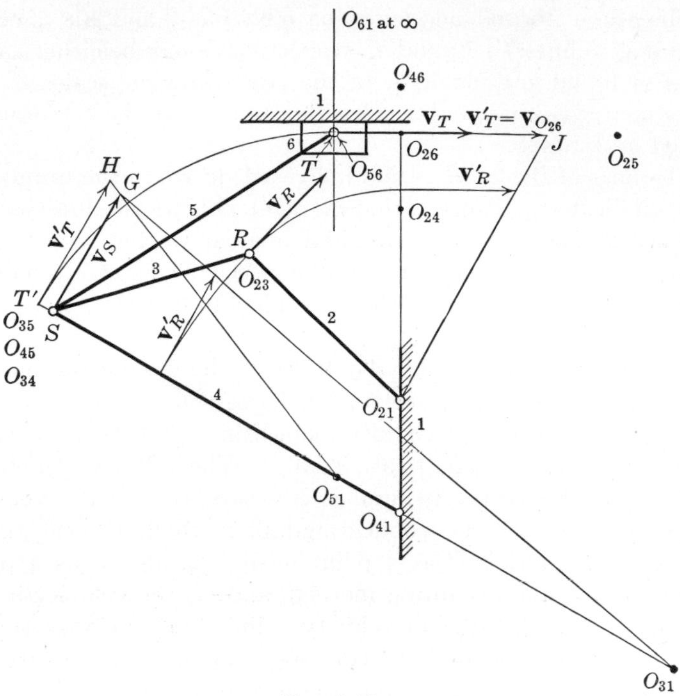

Fig. 4·19*a*.

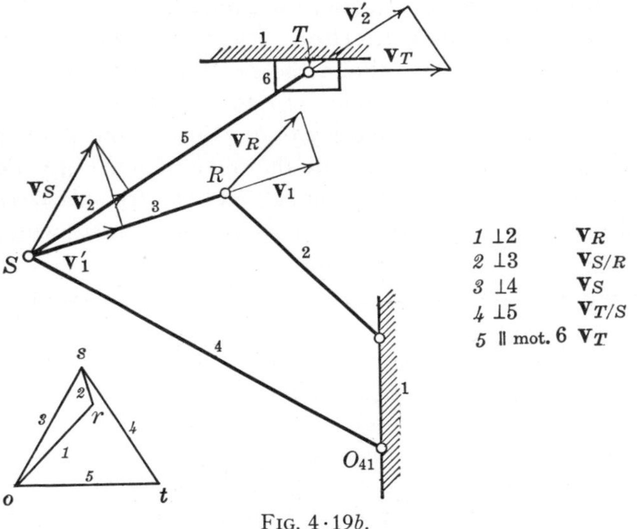

Fig. 4·19*b*.

is at infinity, which means that any point on link 6 has the same magnitude and direction of velocity. Hence the velocity of O_{26}, a point on link 6, is the same as the velocity of T, and the vector is merely transferred to point T.

(c) Resolution method The velocity $\mathbf{v}_R$ of point R may be broken into two components; one along link 3, which is labeled $\mathbf{v}_1$, and one perpendicular to this link as shown on Fig. 4·19*b*. The component along the link must be the same at either end and hence is shown as $\mathbf{v}'_1$ at point S. From the end of the $\mathbf{v}'_1$ component at S, a normal line is drawn to link 3 representing the other component. Where it intersects the resultant velocity vector of S, which is perpendicular to link 4, determines the velocity of S. Again this resultant velocity of S may be broken into two components, one along link 5, which is labeled $\mathbf{v}_2$, and the other perpendicular to link 5. The component along the link must be the same at either end and hence is also shown at point T as $\mathbf{v}'_2$. The absolute velocity of point T must be horizontal, as that is the only direction in which it can move. Drawing a normal at the end of the $\mathbf{v}'_2$ vector at its tip determines the magnitude of the velocity of point T, or $\mathbf{v}_T$.

(d) Velocity-image method Starting from a pole o (Fig. 4·19*b*), the given velocity of point R is laid off perpendicular to link 2. The velocity of point S relative to R is in a direction perpendicular to line RS, or link 3. Hence, from r on the diagram draw line *2* perpendicular to link 3. The velocity of point S is in a direction perpendicular to link 4. As the velocity of S is an absolute one, or relative to the fixed link, line *3* is drawn from the pole o perpendicular to link 4. The intersection of lines *2* and *3* locates points s; and **os**, or line *3*, is the velocity of point S.

The velocity of point T relative to S is in a direction perpendicular to link 5; hence line *4* is drawn from s normal to link 5. The velocity of point T must be horizontal. Since it is relative to the fixed link, it is drawn from the pole o. The intersection of lines *4* and *5* determines point t; and **ot**, or line *5*, represents the velocity of point T.

(e) Angular velocities To find the angular velocity of link 4, knowing the angular velocity of link 2, three centers are used, namely O_{21}, O_{24}, and O_{41}. The line representing the angular velocity of link 2 is laid off at O_{41} (Fig. 4·19*c*), and the triangle $O_{24}O_{41}K$ is drawn. At O_{21} a line parallel to the line representing

$\omega_{2/1}$ is drawn to meet the hypotenuse of this triangle. The length of this line represents $\omega_{4/1}$ to the same scale that the first line, $O_{41}K$, represents $\omega_{2/1}$.

To find the angular velocity of link 3, if we know the angular velocity of link 2, the three centers to be used are O_{31}, O_{23}, and

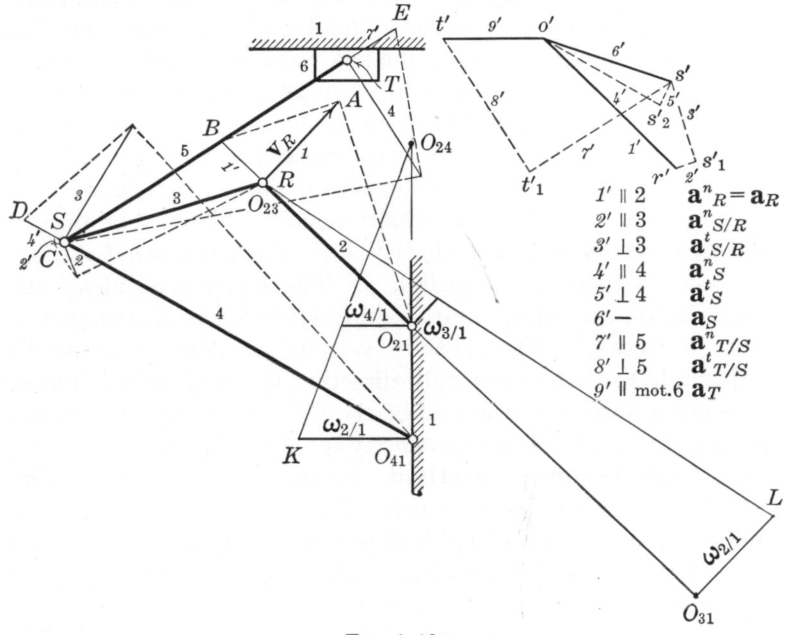

FIG. 4·19*c*.

O_{21}. The line $O_{31}L$, representing the angular velocity of link 2, is drawn at O_{31}, and then the triangle $O_{23}O_{31}L$ is constructed. From O_{21} a line is drawn parallel to $O_{31}L$ representing $\omega_{3/1}$.

(f) Acceleration image The absolute and relative velocities needed in drawing this diagram are taken from the velocity-image diagram of Fig. 4·19*b*. As the velocity of point R is assumed to be constant, it has only a normal acceleration. Its magnitude is found by the right-angled triangle ABO_{21} to be BR (see Fig. 4·19*c*). The acceleration image is drawn triple size for clarity; hence this distance is laid off from the pole o' parallel to link 2 triple size to give line *1'*, or **o'r'**.

Point S will have both a normal and tangential acceleration relative to point R. The normal acceleration is found by laying off line *2* of the velocity image at S; and the distance CS, found by the right-triangle construction, is laid off triple size from r' parallel to link 3 to give line *2′*. The tangential acceleration of S relative to R is perpendicular to this line and is labeled *3′*. The absolute acceleration of point S relative to the ground is the vector sum of the normal and tangential accelerations. If we use line *3* of the velocity image at point S, the length SD is the normal acceleration of S relative to the fixed link 1. Since this is an absolute value, it is laid off triple size from the pole o' parallel to link 4 as line *4′*. The tangential acceleration of S relative to the ground is normal to link 4 and is drawn as line *5′*. The intersection of lines *3′* and *5′* locates s'. Line *6′* from the pole o' to s' represents the absolute acceleration of point S.

Point T has both a normal and tangential acceleration relative to point S. Placing line *4* of the velocity image at point T and drawing the right-angled triangle gives TE as the normal acceleration of T relative to S. This is laid off triple size as line *7′* from s' parallel to link 5. The tangential acceleration is perpendicular to this and is shown as line *8′*. Any absolute acceleration of the slider 6, or point T, must be horizontal. Hence line *9′* is drawn from the pole o' to intersect line *8′* at t'. Line *9′*, or $\mathbf{o't'}$ is then the absolute acceleration of point T. The tabulation given in Fig. 4·19*c* summarizes the steps just outlined.

4·10 Coriolis' acceleration The image method of determining accelerations is applicable only to points located on a rigid body. Referring to the mechanism of Fig. 4·20*a*, we may write the vector equation:

$$\mathbf{a}_{Q/1} = \mathbf{a}_{P/1} +\!\!\!\!\!\rightarrow \mathbf{a}_{Q/P} = \mathbf{a}^n{}_{P/1} +\!\!\!\!\!\rightarrow \mathbf{a}^t{}_{P/1} +\!\!\!\!\!\rightarrow \mathbf{a}^n{}_{Q/P} +\!\!\!\!\!\rightarrow \mathbf{a}^t{}_{Q/P}$$

In writing this equation, which is the basis of the acceleration image, we are dealing entirely with points located on the rigid link 3.

Occasionally problems arise in which it is necessary to find the acceleration of points not on the same rigid body.* For such problems it is necessary to use Coriolis' law. To illustrate, sup-

* "How Acceleration Analysis Can Be Improved," by A. S. Hall and E. S. Ault, *Machine Design*, February, 1943, p. 100; March, 1943, p. 90. "Teaching Coriolis' Law," by A. S. Hall, *Journal of Engineering Education*, June, 1948, p. 757.

pose that a point Q on body 3 is traveling along a curved path CD on body 2, as body 2 rotates about point O (see Fig. 4·20b). Point P on body 2 at the instant considered lies directly beneath point Q, i.e., is coincident with it. The radius of curvature of the path CD is R. The acceleration of point Q relative to point P is given by the vector equation:

$$\mathbf{a}_{Q/P} = \mathbf{a}^n{}_{Q/P} \nrightarrow \mathbf{a}^t{}_{Q/P} \nrightarrow 2\mathbf{v}_{Q/P}\boldsymbol{\omega}_{2/1}$$

The normal acceleration of Q relative to P, which changes the direction of the relative velocity $\mathbf{v}_{Q/P}$, is $\mathbf{a}^n{}_{Q/P} = \mathbf{v}^2{}_{Q/P}/R$

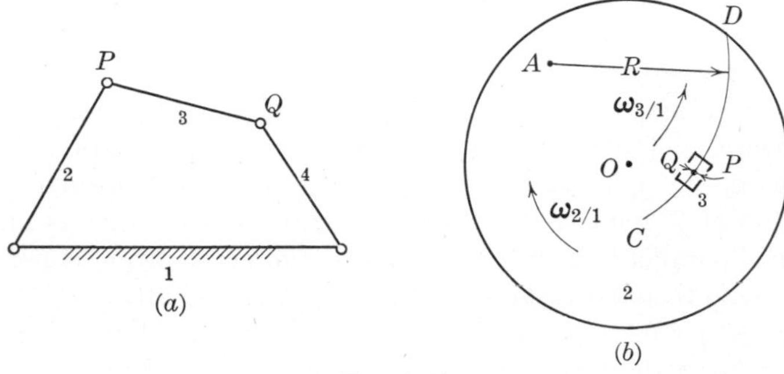

FIG. 4·20.

$= R\omega^2{}_{3/2}$, and it acts toward the center of curvature A of the path CD which Q traces on body 2. If there is no change in the direction of $\mathbf{v}_{Q/P}$, the radius R is infinite, and the relative normal acceleration equals zero. The direction of the tangential acceleration of Q relative to P, which changes the magnitude of the relative velocity $\mathbf{v}_{Q/P}$, is parallel to the $\mathbf{v}_{Q/P}$ vector, and it acts in the direction of $\boldsymbol{\alpha}_{3/2}$. The direction of action of the Coriolis vector, $2\mathbf{v}_{Q/P}\boldsymbol{\omega}_{2/1}$ is found by rotating the $\mathbf{v}_{Q/P}$ vector 90° in the same sense as $\boldsymbol{\omega}_{2/1}$. If the acceleration of point P on body 2 is known or can be found, the acceleration of point Q is then given by the vector equation: *

$$\mathbf{a}_{Q/1} = \mathbf{a}_{P/1} \nrightarrow \mathbf{a}_{Q/P} = \mathbf{a}^n{}_{P/1} \nrightarrow \mathbf{a}^t{}_{P/1} \nrightarrow \mathbf{a}^n{}_{Q/P} \nrightarrow \mathbf{a}^t{}_{Q/P} \nrightarrow 2\mathbf{v}_{Q/P}\boldsymbol{\omega}_{2/1}$$

In some cases no points on the bodies overlap. Then it is necessary, for purposes of analysis, to assume that one of the

* A derivation of this equation with a physical picture of the various accelerations is given in Chapter 14 of *Analytical Mechanics for Engineers*, by Seely and Ensign, 3d Ed., John Wiley & Sons.

bodies is extended to secure a coincident point. The principles just outlined, and a physical concept of the action taking place, may be understood more clearly with the aid of a few examples.

Example 1 For the first example consider a case which may be solved by both the acceleration image and Coriolis' law methods. This is to determine the acceleration of the weight B of an inertia governor. The weight swings at the end of an arm 3 attached to a flywheel 2 at point A, as shown diagrammatically in Fig. 4·21a. Let it be assumed that at the instant considered

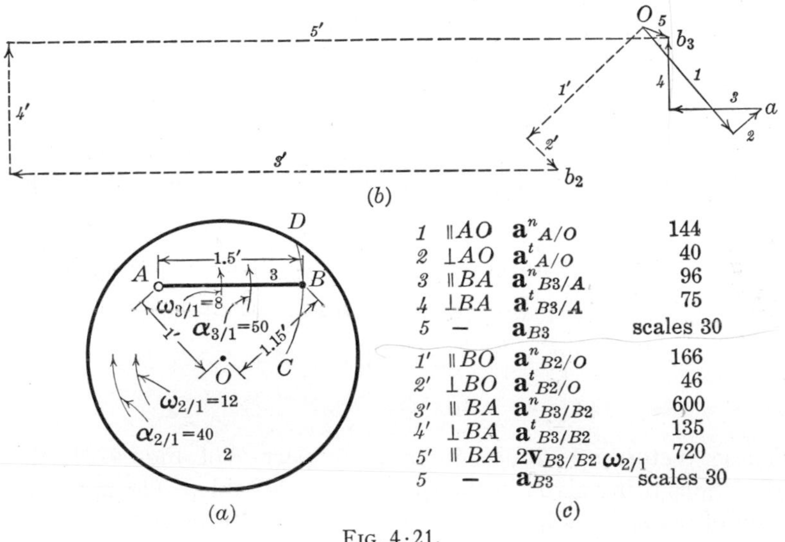

FIG. 4·21.

point B on link 3 ($B3$) has an angular velocity $\omega_{3/1}$ of 8 rad per sec counterclockwise about point A, and a counterclockwise angular acceleration $\alpha_{3/1}$ of 50 rad per sec^2 about point A. The flywheel 2 at this instant has an angular velocity $\omega_{2/1}$ of 12 rad per sec clockwise and a clockwise angular acceleration of $\alpha_{2/1} = 40$ rad per sec^2. The coincident point B on the flywheel, or link 2, will be designated as $B2$.

Before determining the acceleration of point $B3$ it is desirable to understand the action clearly. It should be realized that the linear velocity and acceleration of point $B3$ relative to point $B2$ is not the same as that of $B3$ relative to point A. The velocity of $B3$ relative to $A = AB\omega_{3/1}$. As the arm and all points on the flywheel are rotating about O with an angular velocity $\omega_{2/1}$, the velocity of $B3$ relative to $B2$ is $\mathbf{v}_{B3/B2} = AB(\omega_{3/1} \pm \omega_{2/1}) = AB\omega_{3/2}$. If $\omega_{3/1}$ and $\omega_{2/1}$ are in the same sense, the net angular velocity $\omega_{3/2}$ is the difference between $\omega_{3/1}$ and $\omega_{2/1}$; if they are in opposite senses, the net angular velocity is the sum, and a plus sign is used. Similarly for the accelerations: $\mathbf{a}^t_{B3/A} = AB\alpha_{3/1}$, while $\mathbf{a}^t_{B3/B2} = AB(\alpha_{3/1} \pm \alpha_{2/1}) = AB\alpha_{3/2}$. If the flywheel 2 is not rotating, i.e., is either stationary or moving with translation, $\omega_{2/1}$ and $\alpha_{2/1}$ equal zero, so that both $\mathbf{v}_{B3/A}$ and $\mathbf{v}_{B3/B2} = AB\omega_{3/1}$ and both $\mathbf{a}^t_{B3/A}$ and $\mathbf{a}^t_{B3/B2} = AB\alpha_{3/1}$.

In this example $\omega_{2/1} = 12$ and $\omega_{3/1} = 8$, and they act in opposite senses; hence $\mathbf{v}_{B3/A} = AB\omega_{3/1} = 1.5 \times 8 = 12$ fps, and $\mathbf{v}_{B3/B2} = AB(\omega_{3/1} + \omega_{2/1}) = 1.5(8 + 12) = 30$ fps. Similarly for the accelerations: $\mathbf{a}^t_{B3/A} = AB\alpha_{3/1} = 1.5 \times 50 = 75$ fps^2, and $\mathbf{a}^t_{B3/B2} = AB(\alpha_{3/1} + \alpha_{2/1}) = 1.5(50 + 40) = 135$ fps^2.

Using first the familiar acceleration image, we may write the equation:

$$
\begin{aligned}
\mathbf{a}_{B3/1} &= \mathbf{a}_{A/1} +\!\!\!\!\rightarrow \mathbf{a}_{B3/A} = \mathbf{a}^n_{A/1} +\!\!\!\!\rightarrow \mathbf{a}^t_{A/1} +\!\!\!\!\rightarrow \mathbf{a}^n_{B3/A} +\!\!\!\!\rightarrow \mathbf{a}^t_{B3/A} \\
&= OA\omega^2_{2/1} +\!\!\!\!\rightarrow OA\alpha_{2/1} +\!\!\!\!\rightarrow AB\omega^2_{3/1} +\!\!\!\!\rightarrow AB\alpha_{3/1} \\
&= 1 \times 12^2 +\!\!\!\!\rightarrow 1 \times 40 +\!\!\!\!\rightarrow 1.5 \times 8^2 +\!\!\!\!\rightarrow 1.5 \times 50 \\
&= 144 +\!\!\!\!\rightarrow 40 +\!\!\!\!\rightarrow 96 +\!\!\!\!\rightarrow 75
\end{aligned}
$$

These vectors are drawn in order in part b of Fig. 4·21, the directions being given in the supplementary table. The acceleration of point $B3$ is line 5, which is scaled as 30 fps^2.

If we use Coriolis' law, the equation is:

$$
\begin{aligned}
\mathbf{a}_{B3/1} &= \mathbf{a}_{B2/1} +\!\!\!\!\rightarrow \mathbf{a}_{B3/B2} = \mathbf{a}^n_{B2/1} +\!\!\!\!\rightarrow \mathbf{a}^t_{B2/1} +\!\!\!\!\rightarrow \mathbf{a}^n_{B3/B2} +\!\!\!\!\rightarrow \mathbf{a}^t_{B3/B2} +\!\!\!\!\rightarrow 2\mathbf{v}_{B3/B2}\omega_{2/1} \\
&= OB\omega^2_{2/1} +\!\!\!\!\rightarrow OB\alpha_{2/1} +\!\!\!\!\rightarrow AB(\omega_{3/1} + \omega_{2/1})^2 +\!\!\!\!\rightarrow AB(\alpha_{3/1} + \alpha_{2/1}) +\!\!\!\!\rightarrow 2\mathbf{v}_{B3/B2}\omega_{2/1} \\
&= 1.15(12)^2 +\!\!\!\!\rightarrow 1.15 \times 40 +\!\!\!\!\rightarrow 1.5(8 + 12)^2 +\!\!\!\!\rightarrow 1.5(50 + 40) +\!\!\!\!\rightarrow 2 \times 30 \times 12 \\
&= 166 +\!\!\!\!\rightarrow 46 +\!\!\!\!\rightarrow 600 +\!\!\!\!\rightarrow 135 +\!\!\!\!\rightarrow 720
\end{aligned}
$$

These vectors are drawn with primed numbers in part b of Fig. 4·21 with dashed lines, the directions being given in the supplementary table. The acceleration of point $B3$ checks the value of 30 fps^2 found previously. It may be observed that the Coriolis component of $2\mathbf{v}_{B3/B2}\omega_{2/1}$ is drawn horizontally to the right in accordance with the rule that its direction is found by rotating the $\mathbf{v}_{B3/B2}$ vector 90° in the direction of $\omega_{2/1}$.

Using this example as a basis, let us now inquire into the physical significance of the Coriolis expression, $\mathbf{a}_{B3/B2} = \mathbf{a}^n{}_{B3/B2} \nrightarrow \mathbf{a}^t{}_{B3/B2} \nrightarrow 2\mathbf{v}_{B3/B2}\boldsymbol{\omega}_{2/1}$. If we momentarily consider link 2, or the curve *CD*, fixed, it is apparent that the term $\mathbf{a}^n{}_{B3/B2}$ cares for the change in direction of the velocity $\mathbf{v}_{B3/B2}$ traveling along the curve, whereas the term $\mathbf{a}^t{}_{B3/B2}$ cares for the change in magnitude of this velocity vector. The Coriolis component, $2\mathbf{v}_{B3/B2}\boldsymbol{\omega}_{2/1}$, is based on two effects occurring during the rotation of the path. The first is that the velocity vector $\mathbf{v}_{B3/B2}$ is rotating with the angular velocity $\boldsymbol{\omega}_{2/1}$; hence its direction is continually changing. The resulting acceleration then is $\mathbf{v}_{B3/B2}\boldsymbol{\omega}_{2/1}$. The second effect is caused by the fact that as the point *B*3 travels outward along the curve *CD*, it is continually approaching a point having a velocity different in magnitude or direction from the one just left, giving a second acceleration of $\mathbf{v}_{B3/B2}\boldsymbol{\omega}_{2/1}$.

Example 2 For the second example, let us consider a case which may be solved only by the use of Coriolis' law. This is illustrated in Fig. 4·22*a*, where we have a cam rotating at a constant angular velocity of 20 rad per sec counterclockwise. A flat face on the cam is in contact with a roller follower, and it is desired to determine the acceleration of the follower for the position shown.

To obtain the coincident points needed in the analysis, we can imagine the cam (link 2) is extended to include the center of the roller *B* of the follower (link 3). Hence again we have coincident points *B*2 and *B*3 on links 2 and 3, respectively. The path of point *B*3 on link 2 will be a straight line parallel to the flat face of the cam; i.e., considering the cam fixed and the follower rolling along the flat face, its center *B*3 will trace a straight line parallel to the cam face as shown by the dashed line.

The velocity triangle may now be drawn as shown in Fig. 4·22*b*. The velocity of point *B*2 equals $OB\boldsymbol{\omega}_{2/1} = 6 \times 20 = 120$ in. per sec; the direction of the velocity of *B*3 is known to be vertically upward, whereas that of $\mathbf{v}_{B3/B2}$ is parallel to the cam face. Lines *2*, or $\mathbf{v}_{B3/B2}$, and *3*, or $\mathbf{v}_{B3}$, are scaled as 137 and 97 in. per sec, respectively.

Using the Coriolis expression, we may write:

$$\mathbf{a}_{B3/1} = \mathbf{a}_{B2/1} \nrightarrow \mathbf{a}_{B3/B2}$$

$$= \mathbf{a}^n{}_{B2/1} \nrightarrow \mathbf{a}^t{}_{B2/1} \nrightarrow \mathbf{a}^n{}_{B3/B2} \nrightarrow \mathbf{a}^t{}_{B3/B2} \nrightarrow 2\mathbf{v}_{B3/B2}\boldsymbol{\omega}_{2/1}$$

We will discuss these terms in turn. $\mathbf{a}^n{}_{B2/1} = OB\boldsymbol{\omega}^2{}_{2/1} = 6(20)^2 = 2400$ in. per sec^2, and it acts downward in a direction parallel to OB. $\mathbf{a}^t{}_{B2/1} = 0$, since $\boldsymbol{\omega}_{2/1}$ is constant. $\mathbf{a}^n{}_{B3/B2} = 0$, as the direction of $\mathbf{v}_{B3/B2}$ is along a straight line, or the radius of this rotation is infinite. If the cam surface were curved at the point of contact with the follower, we would have to determine its radius of curvature R and use the equation $\mathbf{a}^n{}_{B3/B2} = \mathbf{v}^2{}_{B3/B2}/R$. The magnitude of $\mathbf{a}^t{}_{B3/B2}$ is unknown, but its direction is parallel to the cam face, or path of motion of $B3$ relative to link 2. The Coriolis component $2\mathbf{v}_{B3/B2}\boldsymbol{\omega}_{2/1} = 2 \times 137 \times 20 = 5480$ in. per sec^2, its direction being perpendicular to the cam surface and acting upward to the left, i.e., in the direction of the $\mathbf{v}_{B3/B2}$ vector rotated 90° in the direction of $\vec{\boldsymbol{\omega}}_{2/1}$. The acceleration of point $B3$ must be vertically upward; hence the diagram may be drawn as shown in Fig. 4·22*c*. Point b'_3 lies at the intersection of lines *3′* and *4′*. The supplementary table outlines the procedure. The distance $\mathbf{o'b'}_3$ represents the acceleration of point $B3$, and hence the follower. This distance scales as 4300 in. per sec^2.

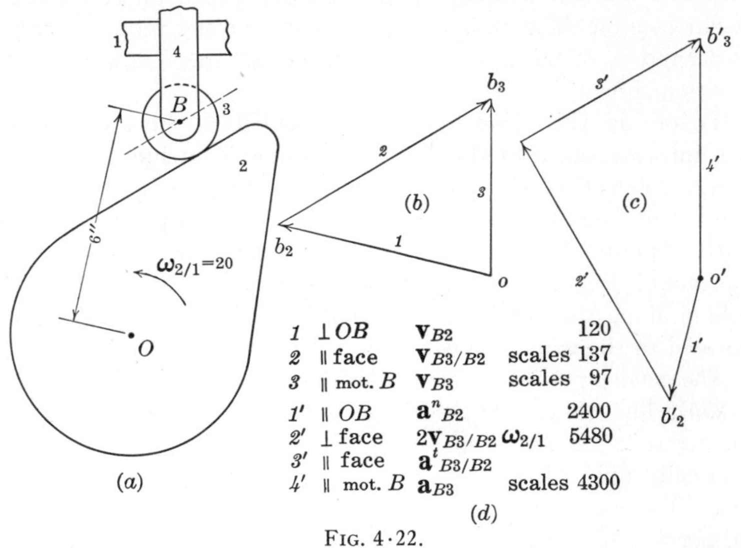

FIG. 4·22.

Example 3 For the final example let us consider the mechanism shown in Fig. 4·23*a*, in which link 2 rotates with a constant

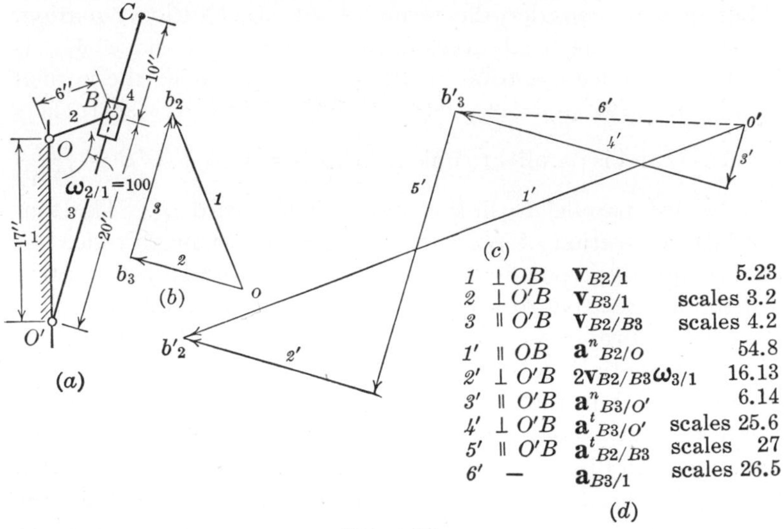

1	$\perp OB$	$\mathbf{v}_{B2/1}$	5.23
2	$\perp O'B$	$\mathbf{v}_{B3/1}$	scales 3.2
3	$\parallel O'B$	$\mathbf{v}_{B2/B3}$	scales 4.2
1′	$\parallel OB$	$\mathbf{a}^n_{B2/O}$	54.8
2′	$\perp O'B$	$2\mathbf{v}_{B2/B3}\omega_{3/1}$	16.13
3′	$\parallel O'B$	$\mathbf{a}^n_{B3/O'}$	6.14
4′	$\perp O'B$	$\mathbf{a}^t_{B3/O'}$	scales 25.6
5′	$\parallel O'B$	$\mathbf{a}^t_{B2/B3}$	scales 27
6′	—	$\mathbf{a}_{B3/1}$	scales 26.5

(d)

FIG. 4·23.

angular velocity of 100 rpm counterclockwise. It is desired to find the acceleration of point C on link 3. Using Coriolis' law and considering the coincident points $B2$ and $B3$, we could write the equation:

$$\mathbf{a}_{B3/1} = \mathbf{a}_{B2/1} \mathrel{+\!\!\!\!\rightarrow} \mathbf{a}^n_{B3/B2} \mathrel{+\!\!\!\!\rightarrow} \mathbf{a}^t_{B3/B2} \mathrel{+\!\!\!\!\rightarrow} 2\mathbf{v}_{B3/B2}\boldsymbol{\omega}_{2/1}$$

but it would be necessary to know the path of point $B3$ on link 2, which is not obvious. However, we do know that the path of point $B2$ on link 3 is a straight line, or link 3 itself. Hence we may write the equation:

$$\mathbf{a}_{B2/1} = \mathbf{a}_{B3/1} \mathrel{+\!\!\!\!\rightarrow} \mathbf{a}^n_{B2/B3} \mathrel{+\!\!\!\!\rightarrow} \mathbf{a}^t_{B2/B3} \mathrel{+\!\!\!\!\rightarrow} 2\mathbf{v}_{B2/B3}\boldsymbol{\omega}_{3/1}$$

Since we know the velocity of point $B2$ to be $OB\boldsymbol{\omega}_{2/1} = \frac{6}{12}(100 \times 2\pi/60) = 5.23$ fps, the velocity polygon is drawn in Fig. 4·23b by resolving this velocity into components parallel and perpendicular to link 3. Scaling these values from the polygon gives $\mathbf{v}_{B2/B3}$ as 4.2 fps and $\mathbf{v}_{B3/O'}$ as 3.2 fps. The angular velocity of link 3 is $\boldsymbol{\omega}_{3/1} = \mathbf{v}_{B3/O'}/O'B = \dfrac{3.2}{20/12} = 1.92$ rad per sec.

Let us now consider the terms of the acceleration equation. There is no tangential acceleration of point $B2$ since $\boldsymbol{\omega}_{2/1}$ is constant. Hence the total acceleration $\mathbf{a}_{B2/0}$ equals the normal $\mathbf{a}^n{}_{B2/0}$, or $OB\omega^2{}_{2/1} = \frac{6}{12}(100 \times 2\pi/60)^2 = 54.8$ fps^2. It acts towards O and is parallel to link 2. $\mathbf{a}^n{}_{B3/0'} = \mathbf{v}^2{}_{B3/0'}/O'B = \dfrac{3.2^2}{20/12}$ $= 6.14$ fps^2 parallel to link 3 and acting toward O'. The tangential acceleration of point $B3$ is unknown in magnitude, but its direction is perpendicular to link 3. The normal acceleration of point $B2$ relative to point $B3$ equals zero since the motion is straight line or the radius of curvature is infinite. The magnitude of the tangential acceleration of point $B2$ relative to point $B3$ is unknown, but the direction is along link 3. The Coriolis component $2\mathbf{v}_{B2/B3}\boldsymbol{\omega}_{3/1} = 2 \times 4.2 \times 1.92 = 16.13$ fps^2, and its direction found by rotating the $\mathbf{v}_{B2/B3}$ vector 90° in the direction of $\boldsymbol{\omega}_{3/1}$, or to the left. This polygon is shown in Fig. 4·23*c*; the table in part *d* of this figure explains the procedure. The terms on the right side of the equation are added vectorially to equal the term (line *1′*) on the left side. The acceleration of point $B3$ is scaled from line 6′ of the figure to be 26.5 fps^2. The acceleration of point C may then be found by proportion, as the acceleration is directly proportional to the radius; or $\mathbf{a}_{C/1} = \mathbf{a}_{B3/1}(O'C/O'B)$ $= 26.5(30/20) = 39.7$ fps^2.

Conclusion It was not possible to use the acceleration-image method in the last two examples since the points concerned could not be considered to lie on a rigid link. It was necessary to select a pair of coincident points lying on different links. These points have relative motion, and the acceleration of this relative motion had to be found.

To outline the general procedure to be followed in solving a problem by Coriolis' law, assume that we know the acceleration of all points on body 2 and that the acceleration of a point on body 3 is required. The first step is to select a pair of coincident points P_2 and P_3 on the two bodies, or the bodies extended, whose motion is known or easily determined. We consider body 2 as fixed and find the path of point P_3 on it, and then consider body 3 as fixed and find the path of point P_2 on it. If the coincident points were properly selected, one of these paths should be either a straight line or a circle arc whose radius of curvature is known. This is the motion to be used, and the Coriolis equation may be written. If P_3 traces a circular arc or straight line on body 2, we would write the equation as

$$\mathbf{a}^n_{P3/1} \nrightarrow \mathbf{a}^t_{P3/1} = \mathbf{a}^n_{P2/1} \nrightarrow \mathbf{a}^t_{P2/1} \nrightarrow \mathbf{a}^n_{P3/P2} \nrightarrow \mathbf{a}^t_{P3/P2} \nrightarrow 2\mathbf{v}_{P3/P2}\boldsymbol{\omega}_{2/1}$$

If P_2 traces a circular arc or straight line on body 3, we would write the equation as

$$\mathbf{a}^n_{P2/1} \nrightarrow \mathbf{a}^t_{P2/1} = \mathbf{a}^n_{P3/1} \nrightarrow \mathbf{a}^t_{P3/1} \nrightarrow \mathbf{a}^n_{P2/P3} \nrightarrow \mathbf{a}^t_{P2/P3} \nrightarrow 2\mathbf{v}_{P2/P3}\boldsymbol{\omega}_{3/1}$$

Note that the "denominator" of the subscript terms in the relative acceleration expressions is referred to the body temporarily considered to be fixed; and that the subscript of the $\boldsymbol{\omega}$ term is also that of the body considered to be temporarily fixed relative to the link which is actually fixed. The magnitudes and/or directions of each term are then determined (some magnitudes may equal zero), and the vector diagram is drawn. The sequence of drawing the lines need not follow the order given in the equation; generally those lines whose magnitude is unknown are drawn last. In either equation, $\mathbf{a}^n_{P3/1} \nrightarrow \mathbf{a}^t_{P3/1}$ represents the total acceleration of a point on body 3 and so should be drawn in succession.

QUESTIONS

4·1 State the relationship between the linear velocities of two points on a moving link whose instant center is known.

4·2 Two points are located on different links of the same mechanism, the instant center of the links being known. When we know the velocity of one point, what property of the instant center is used in finding the velocity of the second point?

4·3 Show how to find by the resolution method the velocity of a point B which moves in a known direction, it being assumed that the velocity of a second point A on the same body is known both in magnitude and direction.

4·4 When two bodies are so connected as to have relative rectilinear motion, what components of their linear velocities with respect to a third body have equal value?

4·5 In Figs. P4·5*a* to *g* assume a known velocity for the point *A*, and show how to find graphically the velocities of points *B*, *C*. Mark the positions of all instant centers used in the constructions you employ.

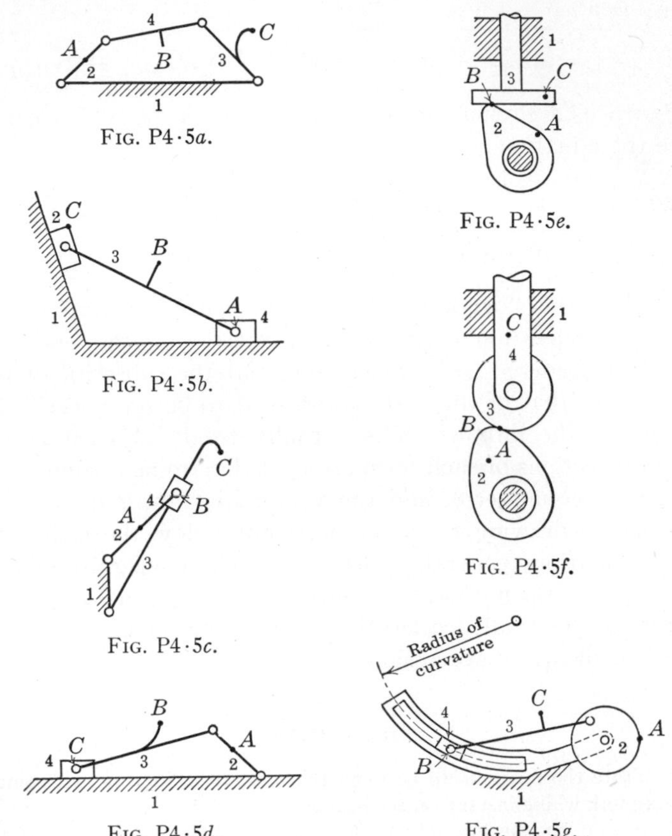

FIG. P4·5*a*.

FIG. P4·5*b*.

FIG. P4·5*c*.

FIG. P4·5*d*.

FIG. P4·5*e*.

FIG. P4·5*f*.

FIG. P4·5*g*.

4·6 In Figs. P4·5*a*, *c*, *d*, *f*, and *g* assume a known angular velocity for link 2 and find the angular velocity of link 3.

4·7 In Fig. P4·5*a* assume that link 2 rotates at a known constant angular velocity in a clockwise sense. By use of the image method, show how to find graphically (1) the linear velocity and (2) the linear acceleration of the point *B*.

4·8 Using Fig. P4·5*d*, find by the image method the linear velocity and linear acceleration of the point *B*, assuming that the link 2 has a known constant angular velocity in a counterclockwise sense.

4·9 (*a*) In Figs. P4·9*a* to *d* assume a known linear velocity for point *P*, and show how to find graphically the velocities of points *Q* and *R*.

(*b*) In Figs. P.4·9*a* to *d* assume a known angular velocity for link 2, and show how to obtain graphically the angular velocities of links 3 and 4.

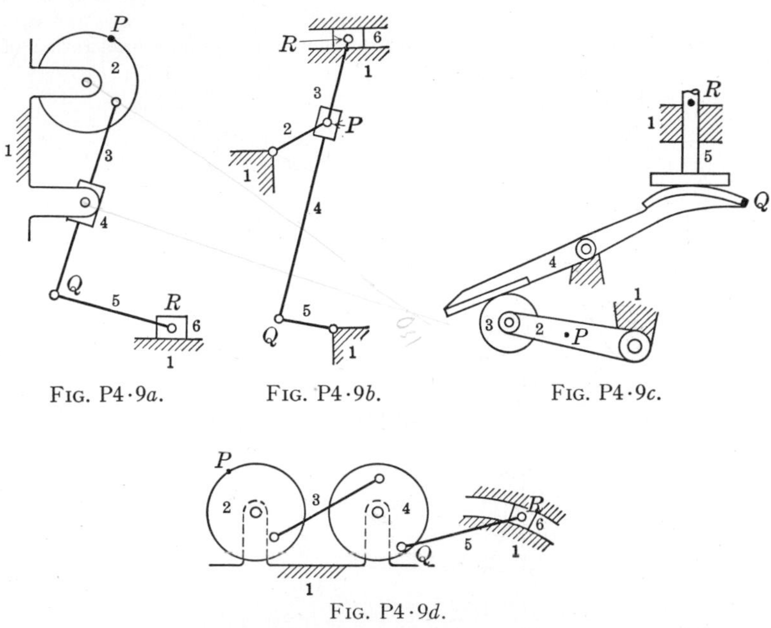

FIG. P4·9*a*. FIG. P4·9*b*. FIG. P4·9*c*.

FIG. P4·9*d*.

4·10 In Fig. P4·10 link 5 rotates and rubs against link 4 in a camlike action. The velocity of point P on link 5 is shown by the vector $\mathbf{v}_P$. Find the velocity of points R, S, and T by (*a*) the connecting-link method, (*b*) the

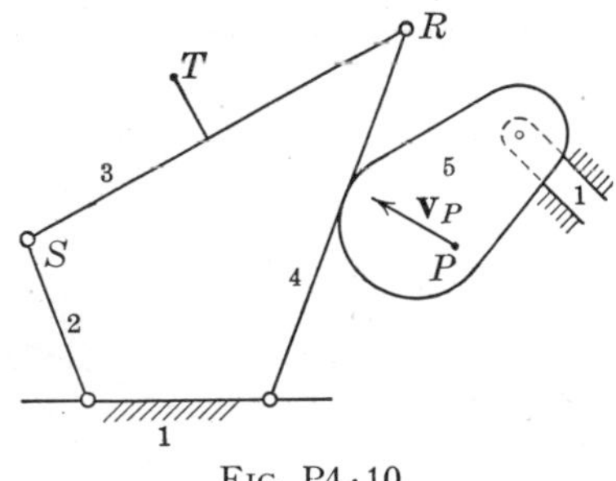

FIG. P4·10.

direct method, considering P as a point on link 5 and the other points as being on link 3, and (*c*) the resolution method (find the magnitude and the direction of the velocity of point T from the velocities of points R and S alone).

4·11 In Figs P4·11*a*, *b*, and *c* the velocity of point R is shown by the vector $\mathbf{v}_R$. Find the velocity of point T by (*a*) the connecting-link method, (*b*) the direct method, (*c*) the resolution method, and (*d*) the image method. (*e*) If $\omega_{2/1}$ is represented by a line 1 in. long, find graphically $\omega_{3/1}$ and $\omega_{4/1}$. (*f*) If the velocity of point R is constant, find the absolute acceleration of point T by the image method.

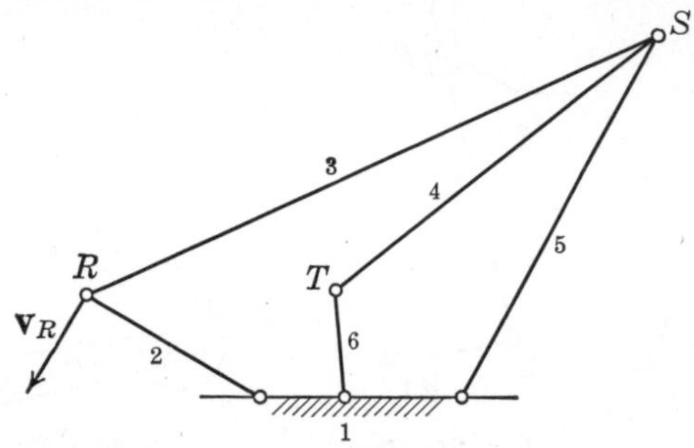

FIG. P4·11*a*.

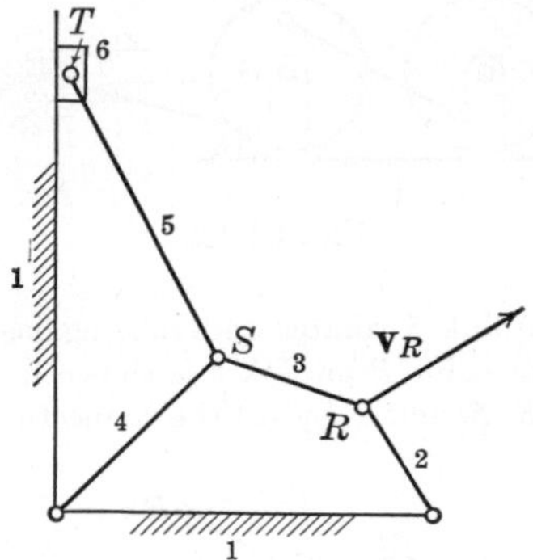

FIG. P4·11*b*.

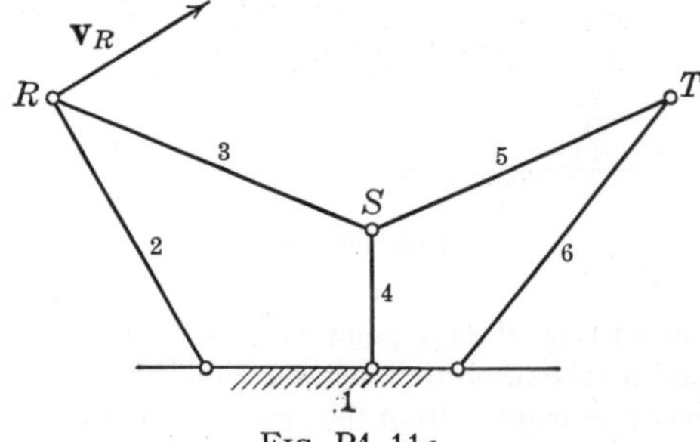

FIG. P4·11*c*.

4·12 Assume that the crank OA of the slider-crank mechanism shown in Fig. P4·12 is extended to include the wrist pin B, and find the acceleration of the slider 4 by the use of Coriolis' law. The crank 2 rotates at a constant speed. Check your result by using the acceleration image.

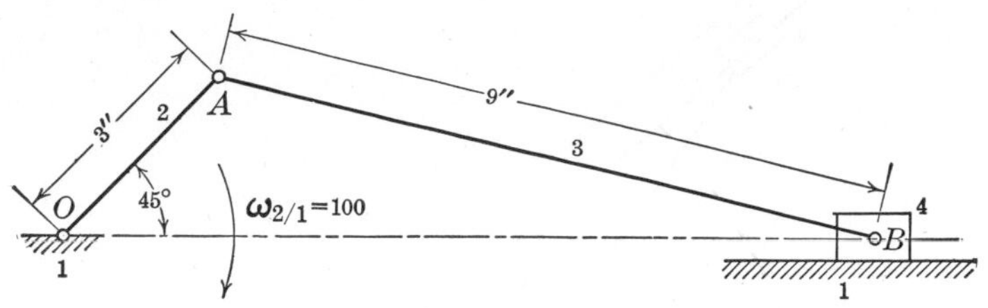

FIG. P4·12.

4·13 Using Coriolis' law find the angular acceleration of the pivoted flat-faced follower for the position of the mechanism shown in Fig. P4·13. The cam rotates counterclockwise with a constant angular velocity of 15 rad per sec. *Ans.* 41.8 rad per sec^2.

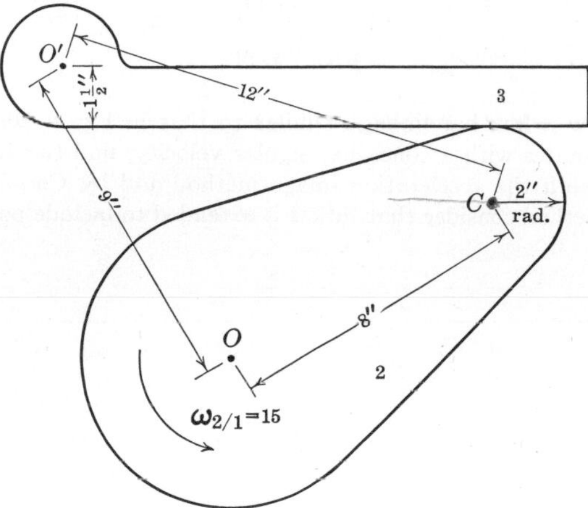

FIG. P4·13.

4·14 Find the angular acceleration of link 3 in the mechanism shown in Fig. P4·14 by Coriolis' law, assuming that link 2 rotates with a constant angular velocity of 100 rpm counterclockwise. *Ans.* 11.23 rad per sec^2.

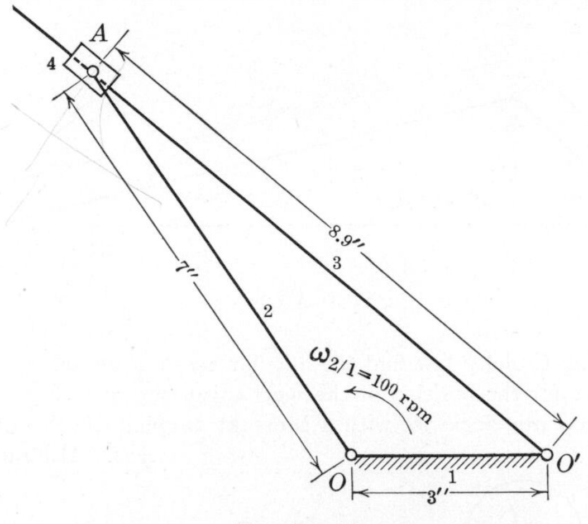

FIG. P4·14.

4·15 Draw a four-bar linkage similar to that in Fig. 4·20*a*. Assuming that link 2 rotates with a constant angular velocity, find the acceleration of point Q by both the acceleration-image method and by Coriolis' law. For the second method consider that link 2 is extended to include point Q.

5 Slider-Crank Mechanisms

5·1 General The uses of the **slider-crank mechanism** in its various forms are so many and important that it merits careful consideration. It can be described as a simple four-link mechanism with plane relative motion among its parts, three pairs of constraining surfaces being pin joints and the fourth a slider and guide allowing relative rectilinear movement of a pair of adjacent links.

Figures 5·1, 5·2, and 5·3 show a process of development of the slider-crank mechanism from a four-bar linkage. Figure 5·1 illustrates a four-bar linkage; Fig. 5·2 shows a device derived from it by altering the form of the constraining surfaces.

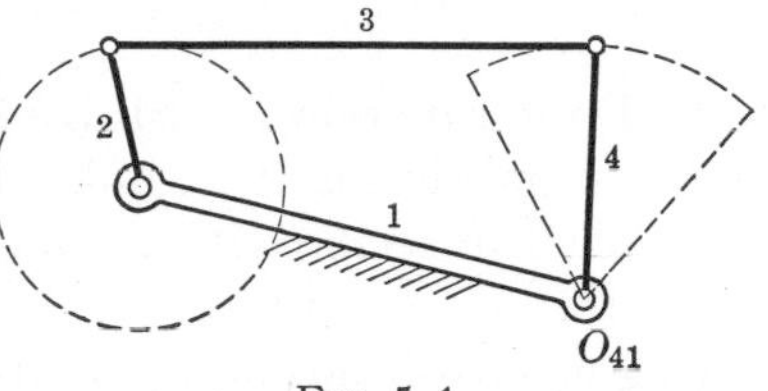

FIG. 5·1.

The pin joint between links 4 and 1 in Fig. 5·1 has been altered to a block and circular slotted guide in Fig. 5·2. If, however, the mean radius of the slot in 1 is made equal to the length of 4

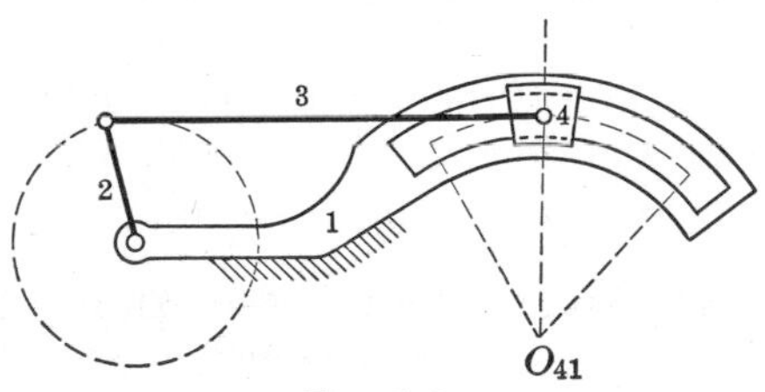

FIG. 5·2.

in the former mechanism, the movements of corresponding links in both are identical. The material pin at O_{41}, about which 4 moves with respect to 1 in the four-bar mechanism, is replaced by an imaginary pivot O_{41} in the latter.

If the linkage is further altered by giving the slot in 1 an infinite radius, so that O_{41} moves out to infinity, it becomes a common form of the slider-crank mechanism as illustrated in Fig. 5·3.

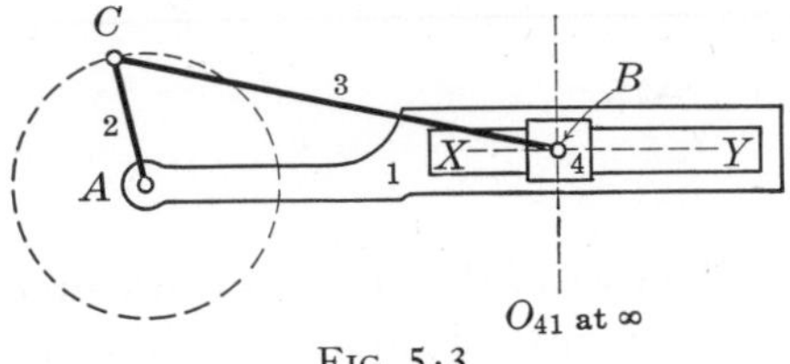

FIG. 5·3.

The slider crank having four links, any one of which may be fixed, four inversions are possible. These inversions are taken up in detail in the paragraphs that follow.

5·2 First inversion. Sliding block linkage In this mechanism, shown in Fig. 5·3, link 1 becomes the stationary member. As applied to reciprocating engines, 1 is the frame, 2 the crank, and 3 the connecting rod. Link 4 is the piston in some engines having no crosshead; in others it consists of the crosshead, piston rod, and piston, since these parts move as a single rigid piece of material.

The mechanism is said to be "offset" when (as in Fig. 5·3) the straight line XY, which is the path of motion of the point B, does not pass through point A.

The crank, in practical engines employing this mechanism, generally rotates with an angular velocity which is approximately constant. For purposes of design it is necessary to analyze the velocity and acceleration of the piston. The analysis is commonly made with the assumption that the crank velocity is exactly constant, the error involved being of small proportions.

5·3 Piston velocity. Graphical method The direct instant center method, as described in Art. 4·2*b*, may be used to find the piston velocity when the crankpin velocity is known. However, the alternative method shown in Fig. 5·4 is shorter and generally more convenient. The construction in this figure is as follows:

The centerline of the connecting rod 3 is produced to meet at D a line AD drawn in a direction perpendicular to the line of

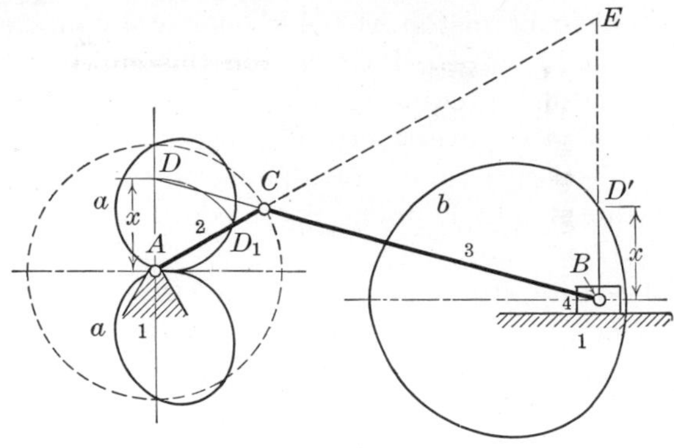

FIG. 5·4.

stroke. It can be shown that the distance AD represents the piston velocity to the same scale as the crank length AC represents the crankpin velocity. This statement is proved as follows:

Produce AC to meet at E a line BE drawn perpendicular to the path of B. Then E is O_{31}, and hence

$$\frac{\text{Linear velocity of } B}{\text{Linear velocity of } C} = \frac{EB}{EC}$$

Also $\dfrac{EB}{EC} = \dfrac{AD}{AC}$ (from similarity of triangles BEC and CDA).

Therefore,

$$\frac{\mathbf{v}_B}{\mathbf{v}_C} = \frac{AD}{AC} \quad \text{or} \quad \mathbf{v}_B = \frac{\mathbf{v}_C}{AC} \times AD \tag{5·1}$$

Now $\mathbf{v}_C$ is the crankpin velocity, which is constant when the crank rotates at a uniform speed. AC, also, is a fixed length.

Consequently, we may write

$$\text{Piston velocity} = \mathbf{v}_B = \text{a constant} \times AD$$

When AD has a length of 1 in., $\mathbf{v}_B = \dfrac{\mathbf{v}_C}{AC} \times 1$; that is, 1 in. represents $\mathbf{v}_C/AC$ units of velocity. As an easy way of remembering the scale, we may note that **the piston velocity is represented by the length *AD* to the same scale as the crank length *AC* on our drawing represents the crankpin velocity.**

A **polar curve** of piston velocity on a crank-angle base is shown at (*a*) in Fig. 5·4. Point D_1 on this curve is found by making the length AD_1 equal to AD.

A **velocity-displacement curve** is also drawn at (*b*) in Fig. 5·4. Point D' on this curve corresponds to the position of the mechanism shown and is found by erecting an ordinate BD' equal to AD.

A **velocity-time curve** (Fig. 5·5) is constructed by plotting the same velocity ordinates on a base on which equal crank angles are represented by equal spaces; time and angular

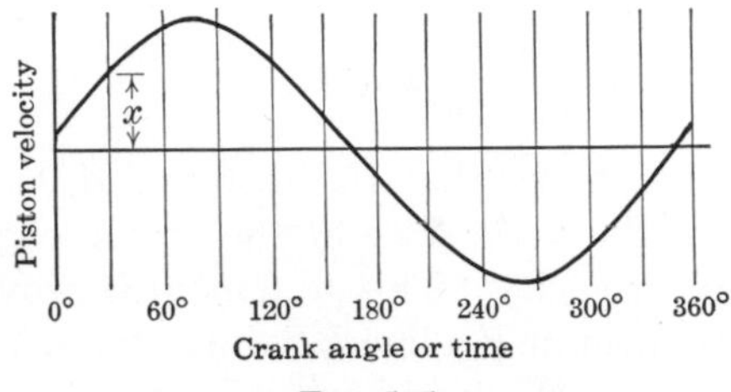

FIG. 5·5.

crank displacement are proportional to each other, and, the crank velocity being constant, the same base will serve for both. Thus, distance x in Fig. 5·5 is made equal to the length similarly marked in Fig. 5·4.

5·4 Characteristics of piston motion Figure 5·6 shows the **velocity-displacement curve** for the piston motion in an

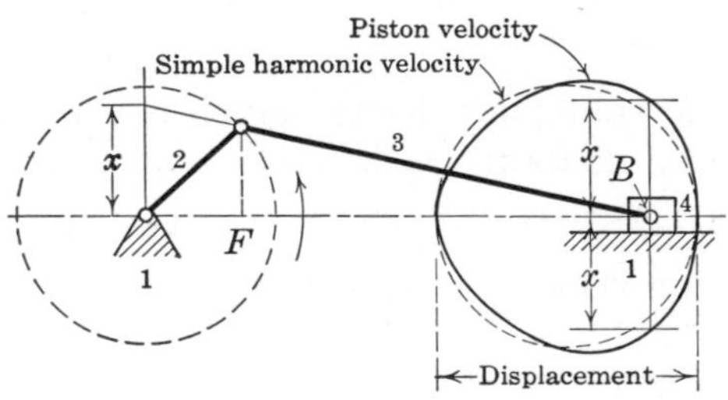

FIG. 5·6.

engine with no offset. It may be observed that the maximum velocity is attained somewhat before midstroke, when the piston is moving away from the out dead center, the curve being unsymmetrical about a vertical line at half stroke but symmetrical about the horizontal axis. When offset exists, as in Fig. 5·4, it is unsymmetrical in both ways. Point *F* (Fig. 5·6), the projection of the crankpin center on the line of stroke, has simple harmonic motion when the crank rotates with uniform velocity. The curve (a circle) drawn in dashed lines represents the velocity of *F*. This curve differs somewhat from the piston-velocity curve. If the connecting rod always made a constant angle with the line of stroke, its projection *BF* on that line would have a constant length. That is, points *B* and *F* would have equal velocity at all times; the piston would move with simple harmonic motion. Since this is not the case, *B* cannot move with simple harmonic motion. The larger the angular movement of the connecting rod, the greater the variation from simple harmonic motion becomes. By increasing the length of the connecting rod in proportion to the crank length we decrease the angular displacement of the former, and the piston motion tends to approach simple harmonic. If the connecting rod were of infinite length, this condition would be exactly attained.

This distortion of the piston motion from simple harmonic has been aptly termed the **connecting-rod effect.** The design of valve gears and the balancing of engines would be much simplified if it did not exist. By reference to Fig. 5·6 it may be seen that it tends to increase the piston velocity during periods before and after the crank passes the out dead center and has the opposite effect during the other portions of the stroke. Maximum piston velocity is attained somewhat before half stroke.

5·5 Piston acceleration. Klein's graphical construction A line whose length represents the piston acceleration may be obtained by the use of Klein's construction, as shown in Fig. 5·7, which applies whether the line of the slider motion passes through the crank center *A* or is offset.

In Fig. 5·7*a*, point *D* is found by extending the connecting rod *BC* to meet a vertical line *AD* passing through the crank center *A*. A semicircle *CLB* is then drawn, with *BC* as a diameter. This is intersected at *E* by an arc drawn with *C* as a center and *CD* as a radius. From *E* a line *EGH*, perpendicular to *BC* is drawn, meeting at *H* a line *AH* parallel to the line of the piston motion. The length of the line *AH* is then equal to the piston acceleration to a given scale.

This may be proved and the scale determined from the acceleration-image diagram. Applying the principles of Art. 4·6 to the slider crank of Fig. 5·7*a*, we first draw the velocity image as shown in part *b*, the explanation of the lines being given in the table. The length of line *1*, representing the velocity of the

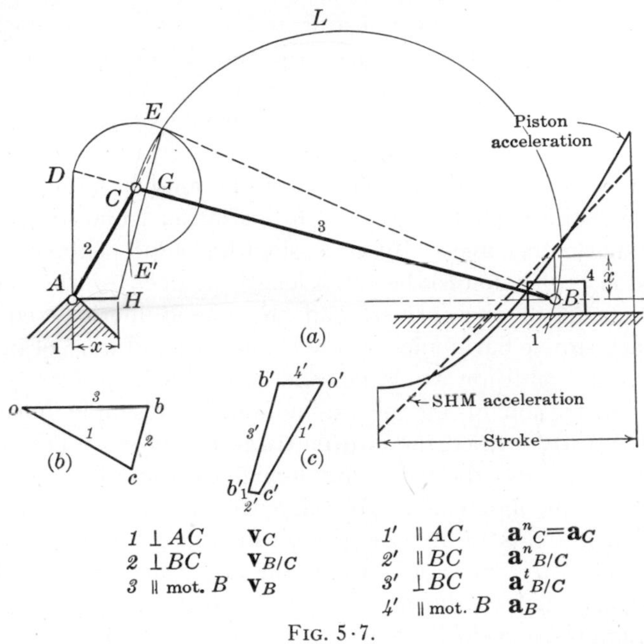

FIG. 5·7.

crankpin *C*, is made equal to the length of the crank *AC*. Incidentally, it may be noted that the triangle *obc* of the velocity image is identical with the triangle *ACD* of part *a*, but rotated forward 90°. This represents an additional proof to that given in Art. 5·3 that the length *AD* represents the velocity of the slider *B* to the same scale that the length of the crank represents the velocity of the crankpin *C*.

Line *1′* of the acceleration image in Fig. 5·7*c* represents the normal and, as the crank is rotating at a constant angular velocity, the absolute acceleration of *C*. Let its length be made equal to that of the crank *AC*. The remainder of the diagram is drawn in the conventional manner, which is explained in the table.

A comparison of Fig. 5·7*a* with the acceleration image of part *c* shows that the figures *ACGH* and $o'c'b'_1b'$ are similar since their respective sides are parallel to each other. They may be proved to be identical if it can be shown that two of these sides have the same length. Line *1′* was drawn equal in length to *AC*. To show that line *2′* is equal to the length *CG*, we must consider the two triangles *CEB* and *CEG* of Fig. 5·7*a*. These triangles are similar as they both have right angles and also a common angle *GCE*. By proportion we can state that

$$\frac{CG}{CE} = \frac{CE}{BC} \quad \text{or} \quad CG = \frac{CE^2}{BC}$$

By construction, *CE* equals *CD*, which from the velocity image equals the velocity of point *B* relative to *C*, or $\mathbf{v}_{B/C}$; and *BC* is the radius with which point *B* is rotating relative to point *C*. Hence: $\dfrac{\mathbf{v}^2_{B/C}}{r_{B/C}} = \dfrac{CE^2}{BC} = CG$, which is the normal acceleration of point *B* relative to point *C*. As this is the same as line *2′* of the acceleration image, their lengths must be equal, and the two figures, *ACGH* and $o'c'b'_1b'$, are identical. Hence *AH* by Klein's construction, which is parallel to **o′b′**, represents the acceleration of the slider *B* for any position of the mechanism. The scale of the acceleration is found by dividing the normal acceleration of the crankpin *C* by the length of the crank *AC* as it appears on the drawing.

An acceleration-displacement diagram is drawn by laying off the acceleration (*AH*, or *x*) at the corresponding position of point *B* as shown in Fig. 5·7*a*. If the slider is not offset, the curve retraces itself during each half-cycle.

5·6 Piston velocity and acceleration. Analytical method

Although the graphical method of analysis is usually to be preferred, there are cases where an analytical method is necessary. The case of a mechanism with no offset will be considered. In Fig. 5·8, let *r* be the crank length and *nr* be the connecting-rod length, *n* being the ratio of connecting-rod length to crank length. Suppose the crank to be at any angle θ with the line of stroke, and ϕ the corresponding inclination of the connecting rod. *x* is the distance from the center of the crosshead pin to the center of the crankshaft. At midstroke, evidently, $x = nr$. At any crank angle θ the piston displacement $\mathbf{s}$ from mid-position $= x - nr$.

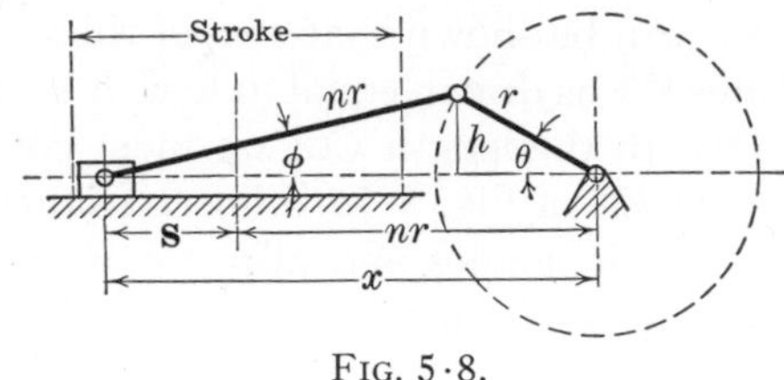

FIG. 5·8.

From Fig. 5·8, $x = r\cos\theta + nr\cos\phi$, and the

$$\begin{aligned}\text{Piston displacement } \mathbf{s} &= x - nr \\ &= r\cos\theta + nr\cos\phi - nr \\ &= r(\cos\theta + n\cos\phi - n) \qquad (5\cdot 2)\end{aligned}$$

Also,

$$\sin\theta = \frac{h}{r} \quad \text{and} \quad \sin\phi = \frac{h}{nr}$$

By division,

$$\sin\phi = \frac{\sin\theta}{n}$$

Now,

$$\cos\phi = \sqrt{1 - \sin^2\phi} = \sqrt{1 - \frac{\sin^2\theta}{n^2}} = \frac{1}{n}\sqrt{n^2 - \sin^2\theta}$$

Substituting this value of $\cos\phi$ in equation 5·2 yields

$$\text{Piston displacement} = \mathbf{s} = r(\cos\theta + \sqrt{n^2 - \sin^2\theta} - n) \qquad (5\cdot 3)$$

Thus we have the piston displacement in terms of the crank angle.

If the piston moved with simple harmonic motion, its displacement at crank angle θ would be $r\cos\theta$. The "connecting-rod effect," due to the obliquity of this member with the line of stroke, is represented by the term $r(\sqrt{n^2 - \sin^2\theta} - n)$.

The **piston velocity** is equal to $d\mathbf{s}/dt$ where $\mathbf{s}$ is the piston displacement. Substituting the value of $\mathbf{s}$ from equation 5·3 gives

$$\text{Piston velocity} = \frac{d}{dt}[r(\cos\theta + \sqrt{n^2 - \sin^2\theta} - n)]$$

$$= r\left[-\sin\theta\frac{d\theta}{dt} + \frac{1}{2}(n^2 - \sin^2\theta)^{-1/2} \times \frac{d(n^2 - \sin^2\theta)}{dt}\right]$$

$$= -r\frac{d\theta}{dt}\left[\sin\theta + \frac{2\sin\theta\cos\theta}{2\sqrt{n^2 - \sin^2\theta}}\right]$$

$$= -r\omega\left[\sin\theta + \frac{\sin 2\theta}{2\sqrt{n^2 - \sin^2\theta}}\right] \qquad (5\cdot4)$$

since $d\theta/dt = \omega$ = angular velocity of the crank

An approximate form of this equation is obtained by neglecting $\sin^2\theta$ in the denominator. The error involved is not very large, the value of n in engine design being seldom less than 4, and $\sin^2\theta$ being equal to 1 as a maximum. Equation 5·4 then reduces to the following form:

$$\text{Piston velocity} = -r\omega\left(\sin\theta + \frac{\sin 2\theta}{2n}\right) \qquad (5\cdot5)$$

The **piston acceleration** is equal to $d\mathbf{v}/dt$. By taking the exact velocity equation 5·4, differentiating, and dividing by dt, it can be shown that

Piston acceleration

$$= r\omega^2\left[\cos\theta + \frac{\cos^4\theta + \cos 2\theta(n^2 - 1)}{(n^2 - \sin^2\theta)^{3/2}}\right] \qquad (5\cdot6)$$

Treating the approximate equation 5·5 in the same manner, we have

$$\text{Piston acceleration} = \frac{d}{dt}\left[r\omega\left(\sin\theta + \frac{\sin 2\theta}{2n}\right)\right]$$

$$= r\omega^2\left(\cos\theta + \frac{\cos 2\theta}{n}\right) \qquad (5\cdot7)$$

Equation 5·7 is so much simpler than equation 5·6 that it is generally used where extreme accuracy is not required.* When

* Tables and curves for displacement, velocity and acceleration, derived by use of the exact formulas, will be found in an article by J. L. Bogert in *Marine Engineering*, December, 1920.

n is equal to 4 the approximate equation shows a maximum error of about 0.6 per cent of the greatest acceleration.

5·7 Discussion of slider-crank equations Several interesting relationships may be found from the equations derived in the previous article.

The angle of the crank when the piston is at midstroke may be found by letting the displacement **s** equal zero in equation 5·3.

$$O = r(\cos\theta + \sqrt{n^2 - \sin^2\theta} - n)$$

or

$$n - \cos\theta = \sqrt{n^2 - \sin^2\theta}$$

Squaring both sides gives

$$n^2 - 2n\cos\theta + \cos^2\theta = n^2 - \sin^2\theta$$

or

$$2n\cos\theta = \cos^2\theta + \sin^2\theta = 1$$

Hence:

$$\cos\theta = \frac{1}{2n}$$

The values of the crank angle θ at which the piston is in its mid-position for values of n of 3, 4, 5, and 6 are then approximately 80.4°, 82.8°, 84.2°, and 85.2°, respectively. If n is infinite, simple harmonic motion of the piston is obtained, and the angle is then 90°.

The position of the crank when the piston velocity is a maximum occurs when the acceleration is zero. Setting the approximate equation for the acceleration (equation 5·7) equal to zero gives

$$O = r\omega^2\left(\cos\theta + \frac{\cos 2\theta}{n}\right)$$

or

$$O = n\cos\theta + \cos 2\theta = n\cos\theta + \cos^2\theta - \sin^2\theta$$

$$= n\cos\theta + \cos^2\theta - 1 + \cos^2\theta$$

$$= 2\cos^2\theta + n\cos\theta - 1$$

and

$$\cos\theta = \tfrac{1}{4}(-n \pm \sqrt{n^2 + 8})$$

It will be found that the plus sign for the second term in the equation should be used rather than the minus sign. The values of crank angle θ at which the piston velocity will be a maximum, or its acceleration zero, for values of n of 4, 5, and 6 are then approximately 77.0°, 79.3°, and 80.9°, respectively. If the exact equation is used, as calculated by Bogert, the values are 76.72°, 79.10°, and 80.78°.

5·8 Quick-return motion The slider-crank mechanism can be used as a quick-return motion when offset as shown in Fig. 5·9. That is, the piston link 4 executes its strokes to right and left in unequal periods of time. The mechanism is shown by dashed lines in the two positions where the piston link has reached the end of its travel to right and left, respectively. At these positions the crank and connecting-rod links lie along the same straight line. With the crank turning clockwise, the piston stroke to the left takes place while the crank rotates through the angle θ_a and the return stroke requires a crank movement of θ_r. If a constant crank velocity is assumed, the time ratio of the two strokes is equal to θ_a/θ_r. This ratio is unity when the offset is zero and increases with the offset.

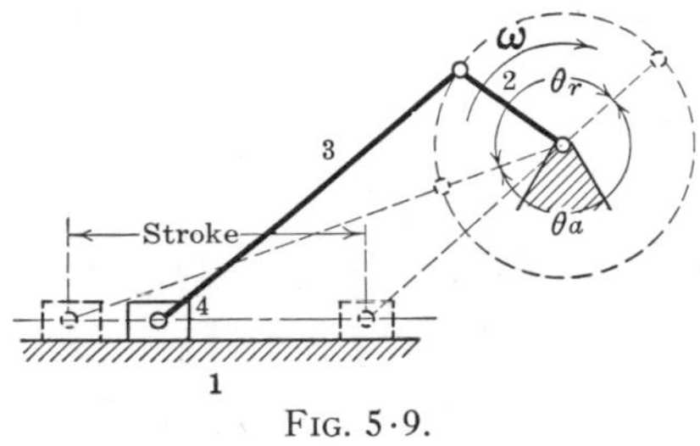

FIG. 5·9.

5·9 Second inversion In this mechanism, shown in Fig. 5·10, the link 1, corresponding to the connecting rod 3 in the direct-acting engine mechanism, is the fixed link. Figure 5·11 illustrates the application to an oscillating steam engine, link 4 taking the form of a cylinder pivoted so as to oscillate about trunnions at B. Link 3 becomes the piston and piston rod. Before the design of steam engines became standardized, this type was occasionally used.

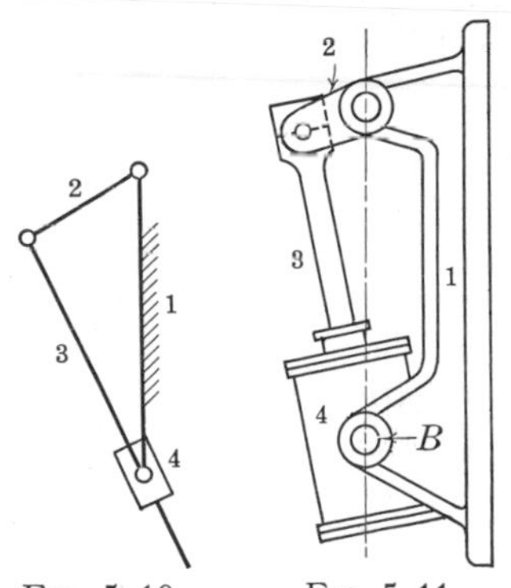

FIG. 5·10. FIG. 5·11.

It is still employed on some toy steam engines where the engine is mounted on the boiler.

5·10 Third inversion. Shaper mechanisms Examples of this mechanism are shown in Figs. 5·13 and 5·15. The link 1,

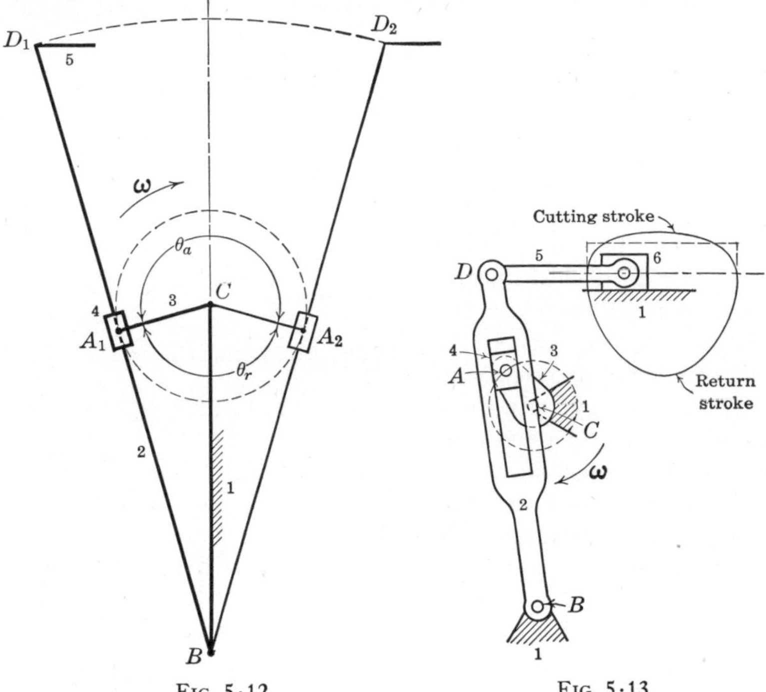

FIG. 5·12.

FIG. 5·13.

corresponding to the crank 2 in the first inversion, is the fixed link. These units are used to obtain quick-return motions in machine tools.

Figure 5·13 shows the **crank-shaper quick-return mechanism.** Link 3 is the driving crank, attached to which is the block 4. The latter slides between guides formed on lever 2. The lever 2 drives ram 6 through the rod 5. As applied to a shaper, ram 6 carries the cutting tool. This has a reciprocating motion, the return stroke being performed in a shorter time than the cutting stroke.

If we assume that the crank 3 turns clockwise, the lever 2 will reach its extreme position to the left when the crank 3 is at

A_1C (Fig. 5·12) perpendicular to BA_1D_1. Likewise 2 will reach the other extreme position when the crank is in position A_2C. The crank meanwhile turns through an angle θ_a. The return stroke takes place during a crank movement θ_r. Consequently, assuming constant crank 3 angular velocity, the ratio of the

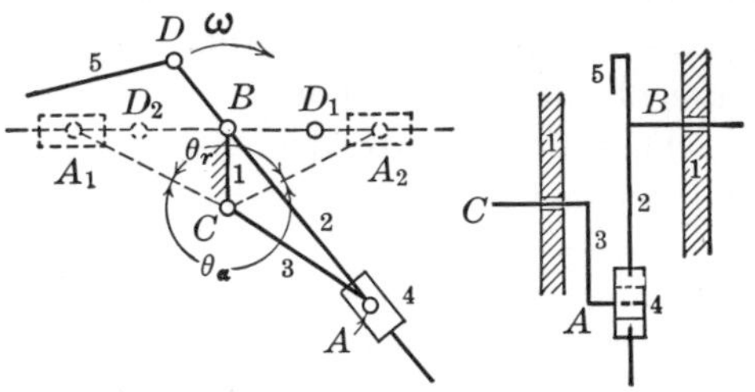

FIG. 5·14.

times of advance to return strokes is equal to θ_a/θ_r. This ratio can be given any required value from one to infinity by the proper choice of the ratio of link lengths AC/BC or 3/1.

Another example of the third inversion, illustrated in Figs. 5·14 and 5·15, is the **Whitworth quick-return mechanism,**

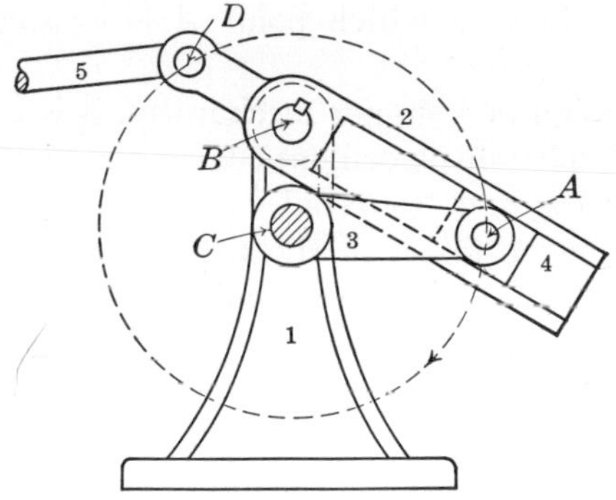

FIG. 5·15.

another application employed in machine tools and other cases where it is desired to produce a reciprocating motion with a rapid return stroke.

The driving crank is 3, rotating with constant angular velocity and driving the slotted link 2 by means of the block 4. Link 2 rotates through a complete circle with variable velocity, and a connecting link 5 may be attached to drive a reciprocating member.

Referring to Fig. 5·14, link 2 turns clockwise from a horizontal position A_1B through 180° to position A_2B, while the driving crank 3 is turning through the angle θ_r. It executes the next half revolution while the driving crank moves through the angle θ_a. The time ratio of advance to return strokes is therefore θ_a/θ_r. Reduction of the length of link 1 without altering that of 3 will cause the ratio θ_a/θ_r to decrease, its value becoming unity in the limit when 1 has zero length.

A comparison of Figs. 5·12 and 5·14 shows that the difference between the two mechanisms is that in Fig. 5·12, the crank-shaper mechanism, the length of link 1 is greater than the length of 3; whereas in Fig. 5·14, the Whitworth mechanism, the length of link 1 is less than the length of link 3. As the ratio of the lengths 1/3 approaches unity—that is, the length of link 1 approaches that of link 3—the time ratio of advance to return strokes θ_a/θ_r approaches infinity. In actual machines the length of link 1 may be varied by raising or lowering the pivot B or C by mounting it on the nut of a power screw. In a similar manner the driving link 3 may contain a power screw which, when rotated, moves a slider on which point A is located to vary the length AC.

During the design of a shaper mechanism, it is generally desirable to plot a velocity-displacement curve of the cutter or reciprocating tool. This is done to avoid varying cutting speeds which may cause an uneven finish in the work produced by the unit. The velocity of point A on the driving link 3 is known, and, by the methods described in Chapter 4, the velocity of the cutter may be found. A typical curve is shown on Fig. 5·13 along the path of the slider 6. The upper portion represents the velocities during the cutting stroke, while the lower portion is the velocities during the return stroke. The ideal cutting-curve shape from a production standpoint is a rectangle, as shown by the dashed lines in the figure. Then the cutter would hold a constant velocity during the entire stroke. This is not attainable or desirable because of the heavy shock loads resulting at the ends of the stroke. As in most engineering problems, two conflicting factors must be balanced to obtain the most satisfactory compromise.

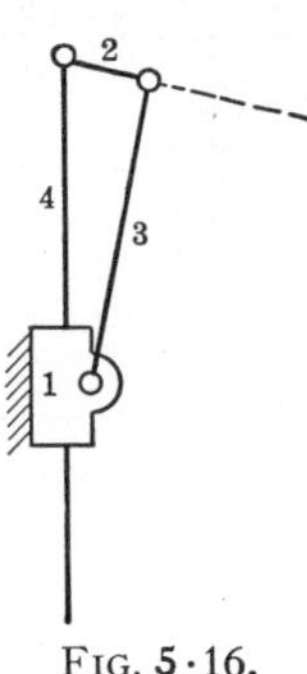

FIG. 5·16.

5·11 Fourth inversion. Fixed-block linkage The remaining inversion of the slider-crank chain is obtained by fixing the block 1 (Fig. 5·16). The most common application of this linkage is found in hand-operated water pumps. It is also used in certain direct-driven reciprocating steam pumps. In the hand-pump application, 1 becomes the pump barrel and 4 the pump rod, to the lower end of which the plunger is attached. The dotted extension of 2 forms the pump handle.

QUESTIONS

5·1 Draw skeleton diagrams of the four inversions of the slider-crank mechanism. Name a practical application of each.

5·2 Show how to draw a polar curve of piston velocity on a crank-angle base for the slider-crank mechanism.

5·3 Show how to find graphically the velocity of the piston in the direct-acting steam-engine mechanism. Prove your construction to be correct.

5·4 Show how to draw velocity and acceleration curves for the crosshead of a direct-acting engine on a base representing the crosshead position. How is the scale for the diagram obtained?

5·5 Sketch and explain Klein's construction for finding the acceleration of the piston in the direct-acting steam-engine mechanism. If the diagram is drawn to a scale of 1 in. = n in., what is the acceleration scale when the ordinates are measured in inches and ω is in radians per second?

5·6 Prove that the velocity of the piston in the direct-acting steam engine is not simple harmonic. How can the motion be made to approach simple harmonic?

5·7 A steam engine has a stroke of 12 in., and the connecting rod is 24 in. long. Show how to find graphically the piston velocity and acceleration when the crank makes an angle of (*a*) 45° and (*b*) 90° and (*c*) 120° with the line of stroke. Also determine the velocity and acceleration scales in foot-second units if the drawing of the mechanism is one-fourth full size and the engine rotates at 240 rpm. *Ans.* 1 in. = 8.38 fps; 1 in. = 210.5 fps^2.

5·8 A steam engine, 8-in. bore and 10-in. stroke, runs at 300 rpm. Assuming a constant angular velocity of the crank, calculate the piston velocity and acceleration corresponding to the following crank angles: 0°, 45°, 90°, 135°, 180°. The connecting rod is 25 in. long.

Ans. At 45°, vel. = 10.56 fps; Acc. = 290.5 fps^2.

5·9 If the average piston speed of an internal-combustion engine, $3\frac{1}{2}$-in. bore and 5-in. stroke, with a connecting rod 11 in. long, is 3000 fpm, at what speed does the engine run? Find, also, the maximum piston velocity and maximum piston acceleration. At what angles are these maximum values obtained?

5·10 In a four-cylinder gasoline engine with a stroke of $4\frac{1}{2}$ in. and a connecting rod 9 in. long, two cranks are on the top dead center when the other two are on the bottom dead center. Compare the piston accelerations for this position of the cranks if the rpm is 3600. What is the average piston velocity?

5·11 Compare the calculated piston accelerations of Problem 5·10 with those obtained under the assumption that the pistons have SHM. Express the differences as a percentage.

5·12 Sketch the crank-shaper quick-return motion. How is the time ratio of advance to return obtained graphically? How is the stroke of the shaper altered? Does this affect the time ratio of the strokes?

5·13 Sketch the Whitworth quick-return motion. Show how to find graphically the time ratio of advance and return strokes. What alteration would be required to increase this ratio?

5·14 Sketch an inversion of the slider-crank mechanism used in hand pumps, and name and indicate the essential parts in this application.

5·15 A crank-shaper quick-return motion has a driving crank 4 in. long. Find the distance between the pivot points of driving crank and swinging link if the time ratio of advance to return stroke is 3:1. What is the new time ratio obtained when the crank length is reduced to 2 in.?

5·16 Find graphically the time ratio of advance to return for the driven block 4 in the mechanisms shown in Figs. P5·16*a* to *c*, assuming that the driving crank 2 rotates with constant angular velocity. Which figure is a Whitworth and which a crank-shaper mechanism? Explain fully the reasons for your selections.

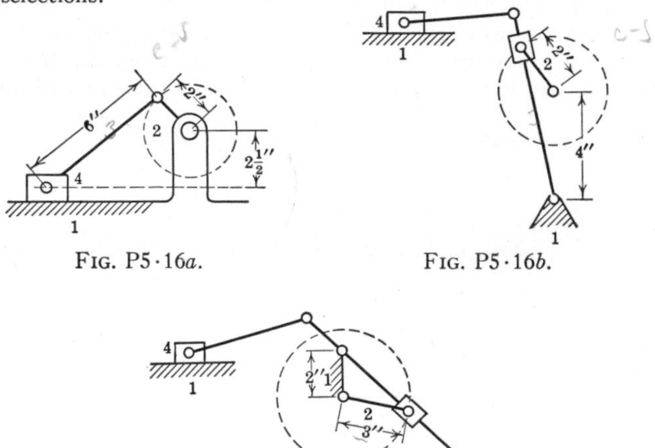

FIG. P5·16*a*.

FIG. P5·16*b*.

FIG. P5·16*c*.

5·17 Show how the first inversion of the slider-crank mechanism may be used to give a quick-return motion. Show how to find this ratio graphically. State two ways of increasing this ratio. How will they affect the length of the stroke?

6 Cams

6·1 Cam mechanisms are extensively used in machinery because of the ease with which the design can be carried out to produce any desired motion. The motions needed in machine parts are often of such a nature that it would be difficult to obtain them by any other mechanism of equal simplicity and practicability. Thus cam mechanisms are commonly used for operating valves in internal-combustion engines, in printing machinery, shoemaking machinery, automatic screw machines, stamp mills, clocks, locks, etc. It is difficult to find a machine of the type we term "automatic" that does not employ one or more cam mechanisms.

All cam mechanisms are composed of at least three links: (*a*) the **cam,** which has a contact surface either curved or straight; (*b*) the **follower,** whose motion is produced by contact with the cam surface; and (*c*) the **frame,** which supports and guides the follower and cam.

6·2 Types of cams There are many types of cams; a few of the more common are described here. In a **translation cam,** the profile is cut on one side of a block or sheet of metal or other material, and the cam has a reciprocating motion along a surface as shown in Fig. 6·1. It is the basic form, as all cams may

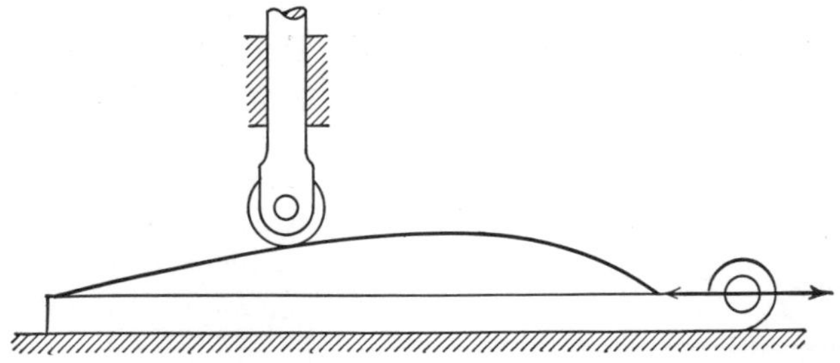

FIG. 6·1 Translation Cam.

be regarded as wedges having surfaces of uniform or, more frequently, variable slope. The disadvantage of this type is that the same motion must be taken in the reverse order during the return stroke. This may be avoided by wrapping the wedge around the circumference of a disk (Fig. 6·2) to form a **disk cam.** When the wedge is formed on the surface or end of a cylinder, as shown in Figs. 6·3 and 6·4, a **cylinder cam** results.

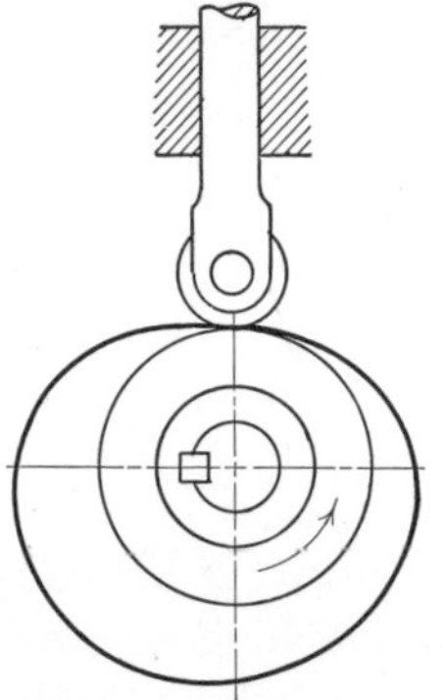

FIG. 6·2 Disk Cam.

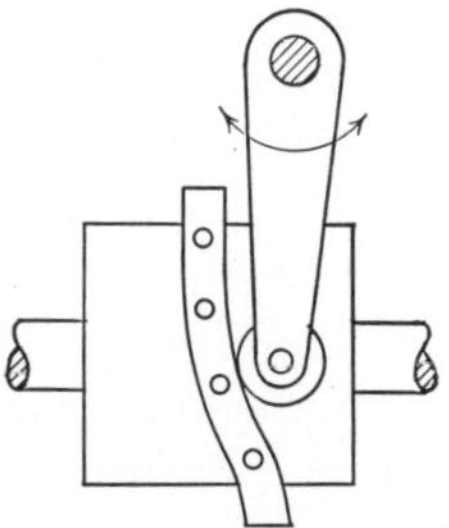

FIG. 6·3 Cylinder Cam.

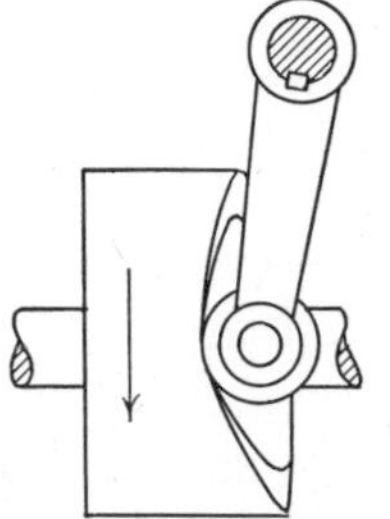

FIG. 6·4 Cylinder Cam.

It should be realized that the follower may be made to move in a straight line or be pivoted to give an oscillatory motion for any of the cam types mentioned.

6·3 Constraint of follower In the mechanisms shown, it may be noted that the form of the cam is such that it does not completely constrain the motion of the follower, as no means of maintaining contact between cam and follower is indicated. Continuous contact is usually effected by utilizing either the forces of gravity or spring pressure (see Fig. 6·47).

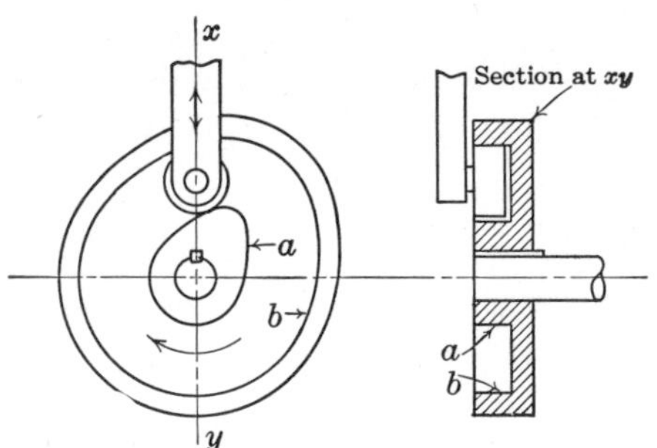

FIG. 6·5 Positive-Motion Cam.

A **positive-motion cam mechanism** (Fig. 6·5) is one in which the follower is compelled to move in a definite path by constraining surfaces and without the application of external forces. Failure to do so can be due only to breakage of some part.

Methods of accomplishing this result are taken up in detail in a later article.

DISPLACEMENT DIAGRAMS

6·4 Profile design The shape of a cam profile is governed by the requirements in regard to the motion of the follower. These requirements depend on the function the mechanism performs in the machine to which it is applied. The cycle of events for the follower, determined by such considerations, may call for certain "rest" periods, during which no follower motion occurs, and certain periods of motion of a specified nature. It is generally found convenient to start on the cam-design problem by first making a graphical representation of the follower movement, which we call a **displacement diagram.** This is a linear curve in which abscissas represent cam displacements and ordinates represent follower displacements. Since both members may have either linear or angular motion, these displacements may be either linear or angular, depending on the particular form of mechanism under consideration. Linear follower displacement is often referred to as the "lift," even though the movement may not be in a vertical direction.

Followers in practical applications frequently move exactly or approximately in accord with one of the following conditions:

(*a*) Motion at **constant velocity.**
(*b*) Motion with **constant acceleration** or **deceleration.**
(*c*) **Simple harmonic motion.**
(*d*) **Cycloidal.**

The displacement diagrams corresponding to these four cases, together with certain modifications, are next considered.

The cam shaft, where the cam has angular motion, is assumed to rotate at a constant speed. The discussion that follows is based on this assumption. Hence the displacement curve is one in which the base represents **time** as well as **cam displacement,** the two quantities being proportional to each other.

6·5 Constant velocity In Fig. 6·6 is shown a displacement diagram for a cam mechanism in which the follower rises with constant velocity during 90° motion of the cam, rests for 90°, falls with constant velocity during 90°, and rests for the remainder of the cycle.

When a body moves with constant velocity, its displacement is directly proportional to the elapsed time. If a constant cam velocity is assumed, the follower displacement is consequently proportional to the cam displacement. The curve *AB* for the first 90° must therefore be a straight line. During the second 90° period a horizontal straight line *BC* represents the rest period. The drop period during the next 90° of cam motion is indicated by another straight line *CD*, since here again we have constant velocity. *DE* is drawn horizontally for the final period.

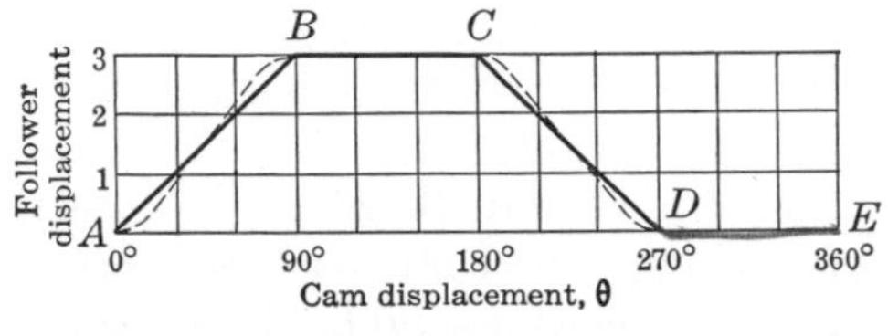

FIG. 6·6.

For a practical application the diagram would probably be modified to the form shown by the dashed lines, unless the cam turns very slowly. This is done to avoid sudden changes of motion when the lift begins and ends, and it substitutes a gradual change of velocity which eliminates shock and noise. Further reference to this matter is made in Art. 6·8.

6·6 Constant acceleration For any body moving with constant acceleration, $\mathbf{s} = \frac{1}{2}\mathbf{a}t^2$ by equation 2·6, where **s** is the displacement, **a** the acceleration, and t the time interval. The distance moved is therefore proportional to the square of the time. If we take cam displacement intervals of 1, 2, 3, 4, etc., time units, the displacements of the follower at the ends of these intervals will be proportional to the quantities 1^2, 2^2, 3^2, etc., or 1, 4, 9, etc. This principle is applied in the displacement diagram shown in Fig. 6·7.

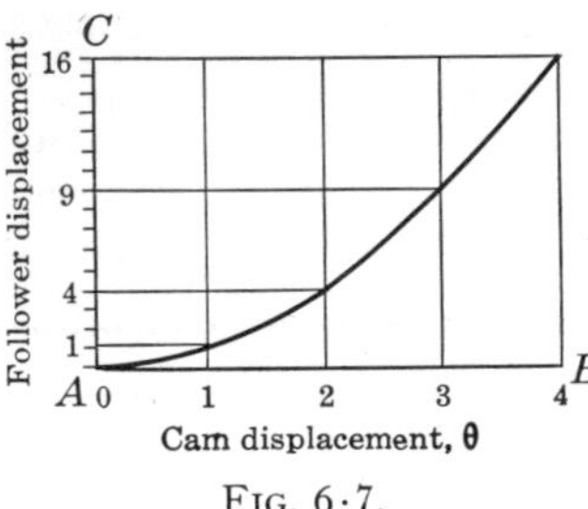

FIG. 6·7.

Here the requirement is that the follower shall move a distance *AC* during a cam displacement *AB*. The construction is as follows:

AB is divided into any convenient number of equal spaces; in the figure these are four in number. Each of these spaces represents an equal time interval under the assumption that the cam has uniform velocity. The follower displacements up to the ends of these intervals are proportional to the numbers 1, 4, 9, 16. But AC is the displacement at the end of the fourth interval. Therefore, we divide AC into sixteen equal parts and project from the first, fourth, ninth, and sixteenth division, as shown in the figure, thus locating points on the required curve.

6·7 Constantly accelerated and decelerated motion Acceleration lasting to the end of the follower travel would result in maximum velocity being attained just before the follower comes to rest, and this would cause a shock unless the cam speed were very slow. Consequently, the acceleration period should last only part of the lift interval and be succeeded by a "deceleration," which will bring the follower to rest gradually. Giving these quantities constant values will often result in smooth cam action. The constant acceleration may or may not be equal to the constant deceleration; a cam profile can be designed to give any desired ratio of acceleration to deceleration. The displacement diagram for such a case is considered next.

Let $\mathbf{a}_1$ be the constant acceleration during the first part of the follower motion, $\mathbf{s}_1$ and t_1 being the corresponding displacement and time. Let $\mathbf{a}_2$ be the deceleration during the latter part of the motion, $\mathbf{s}_2$ and t_2 being the displacement and time for the same interval. The ratio $\mathbf{a}_1/\mathbf{a}_2$ is the given acceleration-deceleration ratio. Now $S = \mathbf{s}_1 + \mathbf{s}_2$, where S is the total follower movement.

If $\mathbf{v}$ = the velocity at the end of the acceleration period, by equation 2·8,

$$\mathbf{v}^2 = 2\mathbf{a}_1\mathbf{s}_1 = 2\mathbf{a}_2\mathbf{s}_2 \quad \text{or} \quad \frac{\mathbf{a}_1}{\mathbf{a}_2} = \frac{\mathbf{s}_2}{\mathbf{s}_1}$$

Also, by equation 2·7,

$$\mathbf{v} = \mathbf{a}_1 t_1 = \mathbf{a}_2 t_2 \quad \text{or} \quad \frac{\mathbf{a}_1}{\mathbf{a}_2} = \frac{t_2}{t_1}$$

That is, the displacements and time intervals are to each other inversely as the acceleration-deceleration ratio.

Example Draw the displacement diagram for a cam mechanism in which the follower moves 2 in. during 180° of cam displacement, acceleration and deceleration being constant and having the ratio of 3 to 1.

From the foregoing discussion it is evident that the displacements and times corresponding to the two intervals are in the ratio of 1 to 3. For the acceleration period the displacement is therefore one fourth of the total displacement and the period lasts for one fourth of the total time, ending at 45° cam displacement (Fig. 6·8). This fixes the position of the point B on the

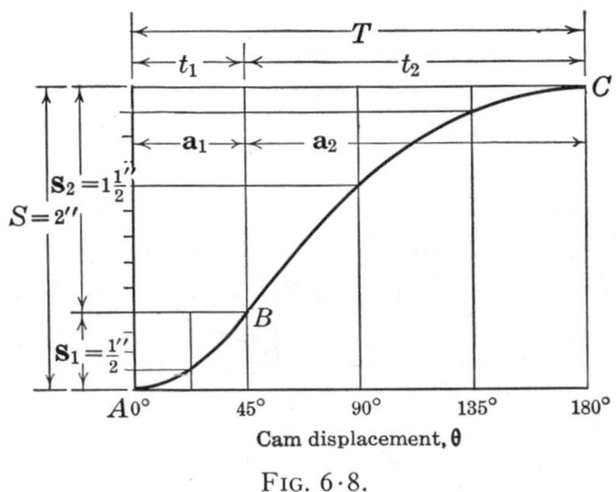

FIG. 6·8.

45° line, the ordinate being $\frac{1}{2}$ in. The construction for other points on the acceleration curve is the same as that used in Fig. 6·7. Points on the deceleration curve BC are found in the same way by working from C toward the left.

6·8 Practical modification of the constant-velocity diagram As noted in Art. 6·5, the displacement diagram for the constant-velocity cam is modified somewhat from the theoretical form in practical applications, for the purpose of avoiding sudden changes of velocity at the beginning and end of the lift period.

This modification can best be made by using a short period of constant acceleration at the beginning of lift, lasting until a suitable velocity has been attained. The follower then moves with constant velocity until near the end of the lift period, when a constant deceleration is applied, and the follower is brought to rest without shock.

The construction of the lift diagram for such a case is now considered.

Suppose it is specified that the follower is to lift during 150° of cam motion, the displacements being those due to constant acceleration for 30°, constant velocity for 90°, and constant deceleration for the remaining 30°.

When a body is accelerated uniformly from rest to a velocity **v** in t units of time, it is evident that the average velocity for the period is $\mathbf{v}/2$ and the distance moved is $\mathbf{v}t/2$. If, instead, the body has a constant velocity **v**, it will move the same distance $\mathbf{v}t/2$ in time $t/2$. Consequently, the follower in question will move the same distance during the first 30°, where it has constant acceleration, that it does in subsequent 15° intervals with constant velocity. The total lift can therefore be regarded as composed of eight equal increments, the first being executed in the first 30° period, the next six in the succeeding six 15° intervals, and the last in the final 30° period. We therefore divide the total lift (Fig. 6·9) into eight equal parts, obtaining the points 1, 2, 3, etc., and project from 1 to 1′, 2 to 2′, etc. Connecting 0, 1′, 2′, 3′ by a smooth curve completes the diagram. Intermediate points on the acceleration and deceleration curves may be found as in Fig. 6·7.

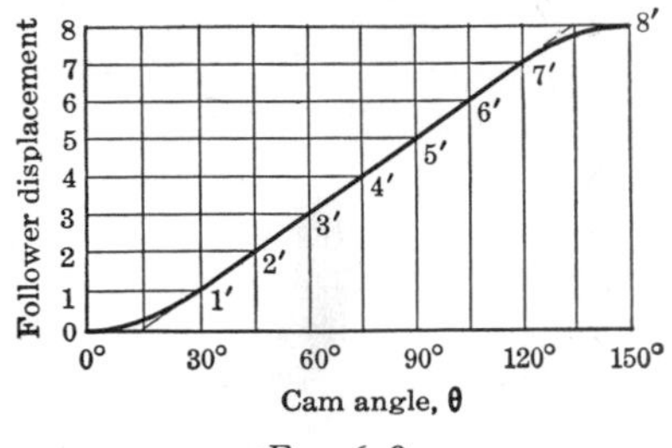

Fig. 6·9.

6·9 Simple harmonic motion The construction of the displacement diagram for harmonic motion of the follower is the same as that described in Art. 2·8, for drawing a time-displacement curve of a point moving with harmonic motion. Figure 6·10 illustrates a case in which the follower lifts during 180° of cam motion, then rests for 90°, and falls to initial position in 90°.

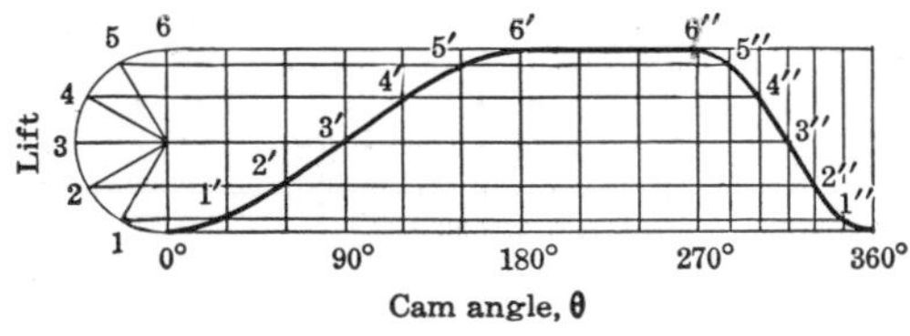

Fig. 6·10.

A semicircle is drawn as shown, the lift being used as a diameter. The cam angle for the lift period, 180°, is divided into any convenient number of equal parts; in the figure each of these represents 30°. The semicircle is divided into the same number of equal arcs, and thus points 1, 2, 3, 4, etc., are found. Horizontal projection then locates points 1′, 2′, 3′, etc., on the required curve. For the "drop" period, projection from the same points, 1, 2, 3, may be made if the cam angle corresponding to this period is divided into the same number of parts as the semicircle.

6·10 Cycloidal cam Recently a cycloidal cam has been found to have many practical advantages in securing smooth action considering vibration effects.*

The equation of this motion is $\mathbf{s} = S\frac{\boldsymbol{\theta}}{\theta_0} - \frac{S}{2\pi}\sin 2\pi\frac{\boldsymbol{\theta}}{\theta_0}$, where S is the total displacement taking place during a total cam angle θ_0, and $\mathbf{s}$ is the displacement occurring at any intermediate cam angle $\boldsymbol{\theta}$.

The graphical method of constructing this curve is shown in Fig. 6·11 for a lift S taking place during a cam angle θ_0. The

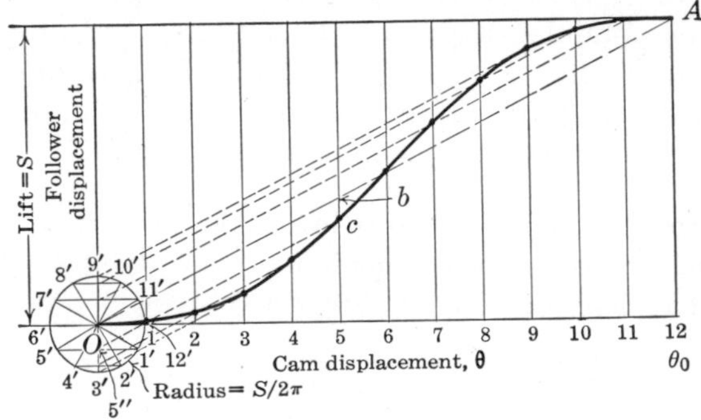

FIG. 6·11.

total time or cam angle is divided into a convenient number of equal parts, in this case twelve. A diagonal dashed line, labeled OA, is then drawn across the diagram to represent the first term

* J. A. Hrones, "An Analysis of the Dynamic Forces in a Cam-Driven System," Paper 47-A-46, *ASME Transactions*, 1948; and D. B. Mitchell, "Tests on Dynamic Response of Cam-Follower Systems," Paper 50-S-14, *Mechanical Engineering*, June 1950, pp. 467–71.

of the equation. In the lower left corner of the diagram a circle is drawn having a radius of $S/2\pi$, and its circumference divided into the same number of divisions as the abscissa of the diagram. These points are labeled clockwise as shown in the figure. They are then projected horizontally to the vertical centerline of the circle, and then parallel to the diagonal line OA to the corresponding time or cam-angle division. This latter construction fulfills the second term of the equation, which is subtracted from the first term or straight line OA. To illustrate, consider one point, 5. The distance $O5''$ on the vertical centerline of the circle equals $S/2\pi \sin 2\pi\theta/\theta_0$ since the radius is $S/2\pi$ and the angle on the circle $12'O5'$ equals $2\pi\,\theta/\theta_0$. Drawing the parallelogram $O5''cb$ transfers this distance $O5''$ from the circle to the required point on the displacement diagram to locate point c on the desired curve.

6·11 Selection of motion In many cases of cam design, the type of motion is based on the requirements of the machine. In the design of automatic machinery, however, the problem is frequently to secure a movement through a given distance in a given time; the only restriction on the type of motion is that it be smooth and have minimum shock, or unbalanced forces. In such cases an unmodified constant-velocity curve would be undesirable because of the tremendous acceleration and deceleration at the ends of the motion. The choice then lies among simple harmonic motion, a cycloidal cam, or constant acceleration and deceleration in equal amounts of time. Figure 6·12 is a comparison of these four motions when they connect two rest periods. The top portion shows the displacement curves for the follower moving a unit distance in unit time for constant velocity V; simple harmonic motion SHM; constant acceleration and deceleration in equal amounts, or gravity G; and a cycloidal cam C. By the principles of Art. 2·12, the velocity and acceleration curves are found and plotted beneath those of the displacement. Of these curves the acceleration-time curve is of greatest interest, since the magnitude of the shock forces is a function of the follower mass and its acceleration.

It may be observed that the maximum value of the acceleration during any of these motions is the least for a "gravity" cam, which would indicate that it is the most desirable motion to use.

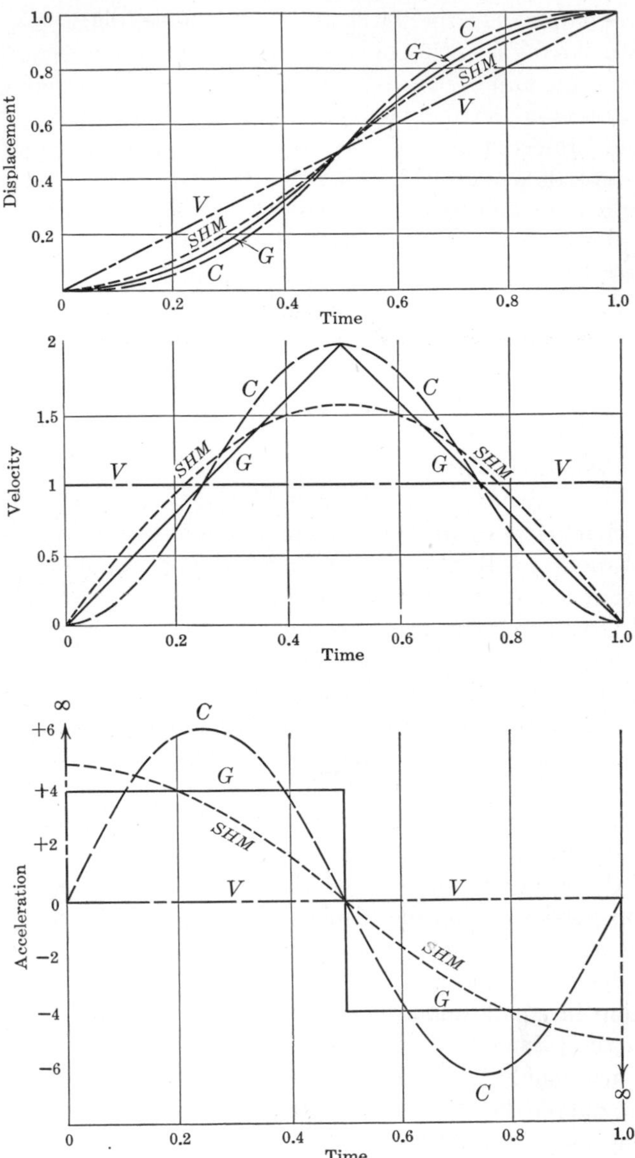

FIG. 6·12 Comparison of Displacement, Velocity, and Acceleration for Various Follower Motions.

However, for both the gravity and simple harmonic motions the maximum acceleration, and hence the maximum inertia force, is applied suddenly at the beginning of the travel. This causes severe vibratory disturbances (see reference in footnote on page 110) which may be reduced by using a cycloidal cam where the acceleration is applied gradually.

A cam producing harmonic motion of the follower is composed of one or more circular arcs (see Art. 6·24) and hence is easy and cheap to manufacture accurately. Where the speed is low and inertia forces are not important, this type of cam would be more economical to make than the other forms.

CAM PROFILE CONSTRUCTION

6·12 General method So far we have discussed only the method of drawing displacement diagrams for required follower motions. The next step to be considered is that of finding the cam profiles necessary to produce these movements. The construction is altered in detail with different types of followers, but we may outline a general method which is applicable to all cases irrespective of the form of the displacement curve or the variety of follower in use. It can be applied to disk cams, cylinder cams, and translation cams and comprises the following steps:

(*a*) The cam is considered as being the fixed link in the mechanism instead of the frame which carries the cam shaft and follower guides. That is, we deal with an inversion of the actual mechanism. As noted in Art. 1·8, the relative motion of any pair of links remains unaltered when the mechanism is inverted. Therefore, the cam and follower will have the same relative motion whether the frame or the cam is considered as the fixed member.

(*b*) The portion of the follower that acts on the cam is then drawn in various positions which it will occupy at different instants during its cycle of motion relative to the stationary cam. The contact surface of the follower may consist of the surface of a roller; a knife edge; a flat, convex, or concave sliding face; etc. In Fig. 6·14, in dashed lines, is shown the position of the follower corresponding to angular displacements of 30°, 60°, 90°, etc., from an arbitrary zero radius. The choice of the angular intervals depends on the number of points it is desirable to locate on the cam profile.

(*c*) The cam profile is found by drawing a smooth curve tangent to the follower contact surface in all its various positions.

The contact surface of the follower is located as required in *b* by first finding the position of some selected point on the follower. The point chosen, which we shall call the **"reference point,"** should be one that is easily located from data furnished by the displacement curve and also one from which the working face of the follower can be conveniently drawn. For example, where a roller is used, the roller center is the best point for the purpose; where the follower is flat-faced, the point where the follower axis intersects the contact face is satisfactory.

It may be noted that the constructions described in the following articles differ from one another only because of variations in the form of follower employed and differences in the way in which it is constrained to move with reference to the frame and cam.

DISK CAMS

6·13 Knife-edge follower In this mechanism, the follower has contact with the cam along a line represented by the point *A* in Fig. 6·14, in all positions. This style of follower is suitable only for very light service because the edge cannot be effectively lubricated, pressure is concentrated on this portion, and wear is likely to be excessive.

Assuming that data are given whereby the displacement diagram (Fig. 6·13) can be plotted by methods already outlined, we shall proceed to discuss the method of drawing the cam profile. The diameter of the base circle is taken as 2 in. and the lift 1 in. Distances x, y, z, etc., in Fig. 6·13, represent the follower displacements after 30°, 60°, 90°, etc., of cam movement. Any other convenient angles may, of course, be used. The base circle is first drawn (Fig. 6·14), and a 0° radiant is chosen as a reference line representing the initial position of the follower axis. In the initial position, shown in solid lines, the knife edge of the follower touches the base circle.

In accordance with the general plan outlined in Art. 6·12, we consider the cam as the fixed link and move the follower around it. Point *A* is the most convenient "reference" point, and its successive positions are first located. To find the position of *A* after 30° of cam movement, we set off the distance x from *A*

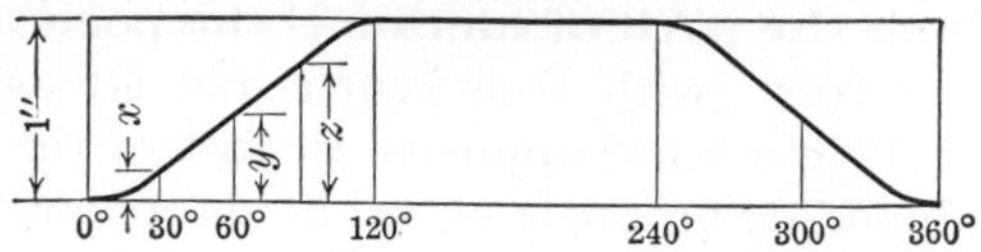

FIG. 6·13.

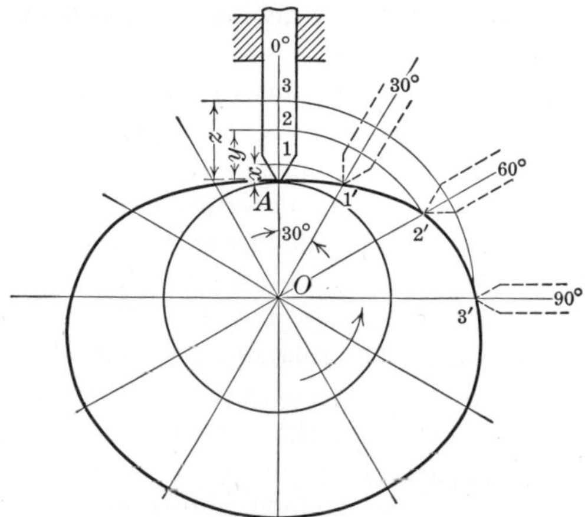

FIG. 6·14.

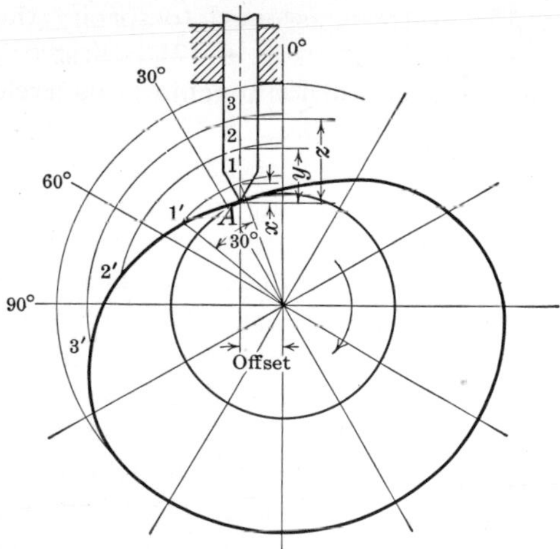

FIG. 6·15.

outwardly **along the path of motion** of this point; thus point 1 is determined. Next, with O as center and $O1$ as radius, we swing an arc 1–1′ in a sense **opposite** to that of the cam movement, and subtending an angle of 30° at the point O. Then 1′ will be the new position of A corresponding to 30° angular motion. Using y, z, etc., as displacements, we find points 2′, 3′, etc., in the same way. As the cam always touches the follower at A, we complete the construction by drawing a smooth curve through A, 1′, 2′, 3′, etc.

The follower edge does not always move in a straight path passing through the cam axis; Fig. 6·15 shows the case where the follower is offset; that is, A moves along a line passing to one side of the cam center. The description of the construction required to obtain the cam profile in Fig. 6·14 will apply without change to Fig. 6·15.

6·14 Roller follower The follower is usually either guided so as to move with rectilinear motion or pivoted so as to swing about a fixed point. The general method outlined in Art. 6·12 applies in either case. The center of the roller is used as a reference point whose path is first determined, and from which the follower contact surface, namely, the circumference of the roller, is located in various positions.

(a) Roller follower with rectilinear motion The displacement diagram, Fig. 6·16, is assumed to specify the motion requirements. The base circle (Fig. 6·17) is first drawn and the roller located in its initial position touching this circle. The path of the roller center, AA', is drawn. A 0° radiant, for convenience, parallel to AA', is next located, and angular intervals of 30° are laid off from it about O. Keeping the cam stationary, we then find the position of the roller center A, after 30° displacement of the follower. The displacement diagram indicates a displacement x at 30°; this distance is set off along AA', giving point 1. With center O and radius $O1$, an arc 1–1′ is described in a sense opposite to that of the cam movement, and of such length as to subtend an angle of 30° at O. Point 1′ can most easily be located by making chord 1–1′ equal to chord LM or $1L$ equal to $1'M$.

Points 2′, 3′, 4′, etc., are found in a similar way. By using these points as centers and with the roller radius, corresponding outlines of the follower contact surface are drawn. The required cam profile is evidently a curve drawn tangent to each of these circles. This curve is made as smooth as possible.

In Fig. 6·17, the line AA' does not pass through the cam axis; hence the follower is said to be "offset." An offset is sometimes provided to reduce side thrust during the lift period.

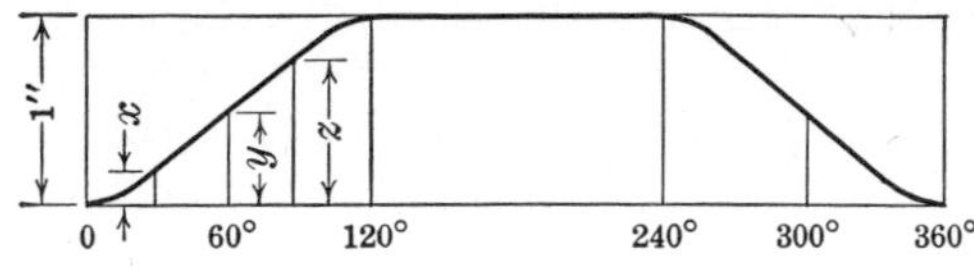

Fig. 6·16.

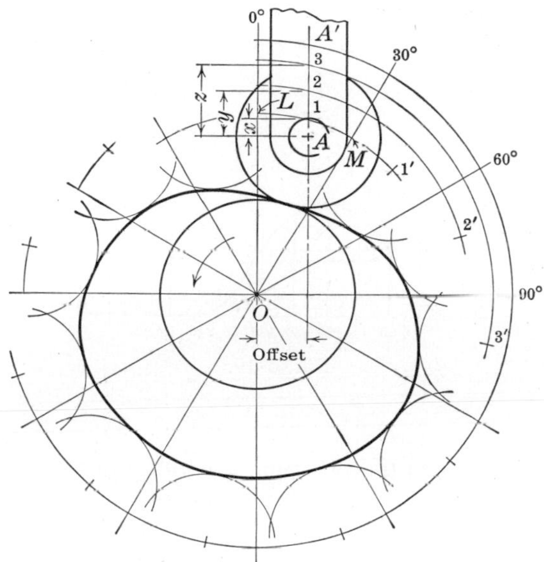

Fig. 6·17.

Figure 6·18 illustrates the cam obtained when the follower has no offset, that is, when AA' passes through O. Points 1′, 2′, 3′ then fall, respectively, on the 30°, 60°, 90° radiants.

(b) Pivoted roller follower Here the angular motion of the follower is assumed to be specified, the total displacement being $\phi°$. A displacement diagram drawn for the angular motion of the follower will also serve as a linear-displacement diagram for the motion of the roller center A, since the two quantities are

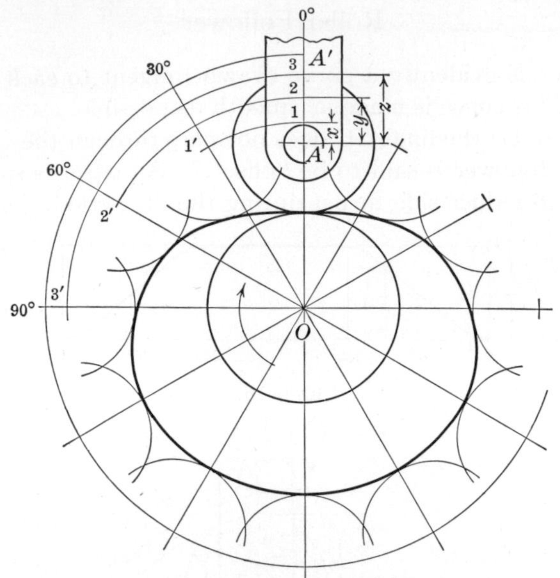

FIG. 6·18.

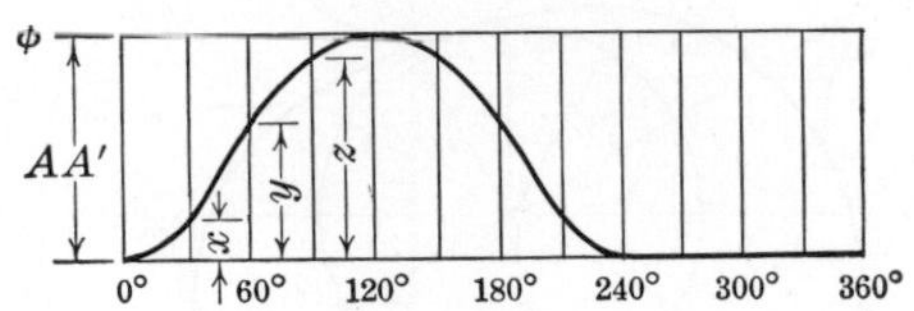

FIG. 6·19.

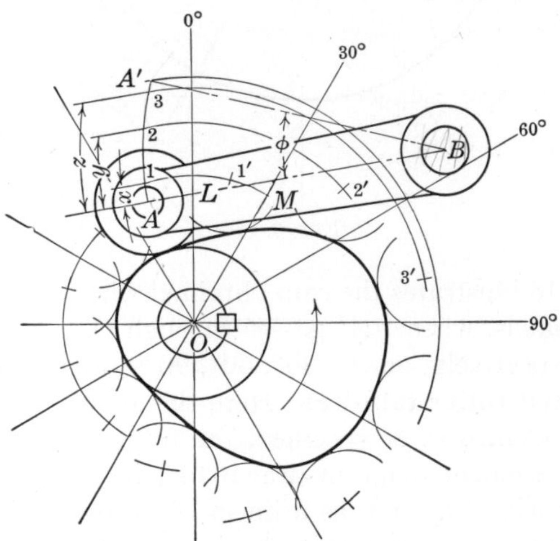

FIG. 6·20.

directly proportional to each other ($\mathbf{s} = \phi r$). This consideration is the basis for the construction that follows. It is assumed that the base circle, roller diameter, length of follower, and position of pivot are known. In Fig. 6·20 the mechanism is first drawn with the roller touching the base circle. An arc AA', with center B and radius BA, of such a length as to subtend an angle of $\phi°$ at B, is the path of motion of the roller center.

The displacement diagram, Fig. 6·19, is next drawn, the rectified length of AA' being used to represent the angle ϕ. The method of doing this is exactly the same whether the follower displacements are linear or angular. From this point on, the construction is identical with that used for Fig. 6·17. Distance x, representing the displacement at 30°, is set off along the arc AA', giving point 1. With O as center and radius $O1$ an arc is constructed, and a chord 1–1′ is laid off on it, of length equal to chord LM (or $1L = 1'M$). Points 2′, 3′, etc., are found in the same way. Roller circles are drawn with 1′, 2′, 3′ as centers, and finally the cam profile is formed so as to touch all these circles.

6·15 Follower with convex sliding face (See Fig. 6·21.) Such followers usually have contact surfaces formed by circular arcs. If we take a roller follower and fasten the roller so that it cannot rotate on the follower, the motion of the latter remains unchanged. A sliding follower is therefore equivalent kinematically to a roller follower having a contact face of the same shape, as far as the follower motion is concerned. The reference point used with a roller follower in constructing the cam profile is the roller center. If the center of curvature (A, Fig. 6·21) for the sliding follower is used as the reference point, the construction as outlined in Art. 6·14 may be applied without change.

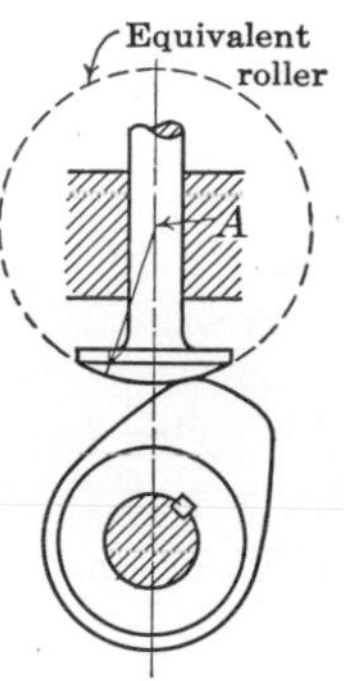

FIG. 6·21.

6·16 Cam pressure angle As a cam rotates and acts on its follower, it exerts a force on the follower through the point of contact and normal to the surface of the cam, as shown in Fig. 6·22. This force may be broken into two components, one normal to and the other in the direction of motion of the follower. The component perpendicular to the motion, F_n, is obviously undesirable since it not only does no useful work but also tends to snap off the follower stem and cause excessive wear in the follower guide bearings.

A measure of the relative magnitude of the undesirable component may be had from the cam pressure angle **α**. **The pressure angle has one side in the direction of motion of the follower and the other normal to the cam surface at the point of contact,** as illustrated in Fig. 6·22.

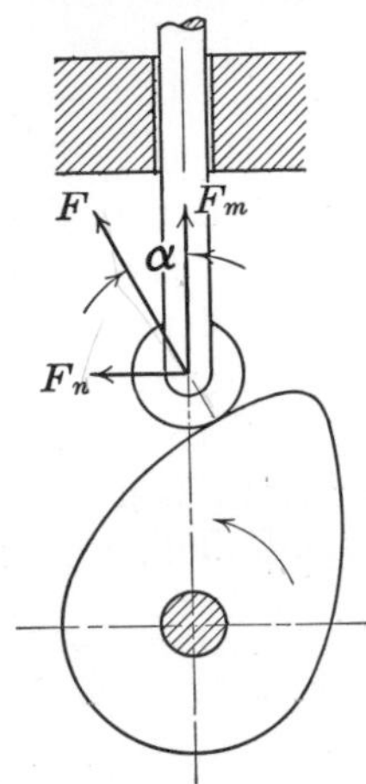

Fig. 6·22 Cam Pressure Angle.

The maximum value of the angle should be as small as possible and, in general, should not exceed about 30°. The magnitude of the undesirable component is a function not only of the pressure angle, but also of the total force involved. This, in turn, depends on the cam speed, coefficient of friction, radius of the cam, resisting or spring load on the follower, etc. In view of these factors, it is not possible to set an absolute maximum value of the maximum pressure angle for all conditions.

The pressure angle is a function of the radius of the base circle plus the radius of the roller follower, the offset, the lift of the follower, the angle turned through by the cam while the lift is occurring, and the follower motion employed.

6·17 Flat-faced follower Here two cases are considered: (*a*) where the follower has rectilinear motion, and (*b*) where the follower has angular movement about a pivot.

(a) Flat-faced follower with rectilinear motion Figure 6·24 illustrates this case. Assuming that the displacement diagram has been obtained and is of the form shown in Fig. 6·23, we proceed as follows:

Draw the base circle for the cam, and divide it into convenient angular divisions. Draw the follower in its initial position BC, tangent to the base circle. Point A where the follower centerline intersects the flat face BC is chosen as the reference point. Set off distances x, y, z, etc., obtained from the displacement diagram, along the path of motion of A, obtaining points 1, 2, 3, etc. With

O as center and $O1$ as radius, swing an arc 1–1′. Point 1′ is the position of A after 30° displacement. Points 2′, 3′, etc., are found in the same way from displacements y, z, etc. Through 1′ draw a line perpendicular to the radius $O1'$; this represents the follower face for 30° displacement. Draw similar lines through 2′, 3′, etc., each perpendicular to the corresponding radius. The

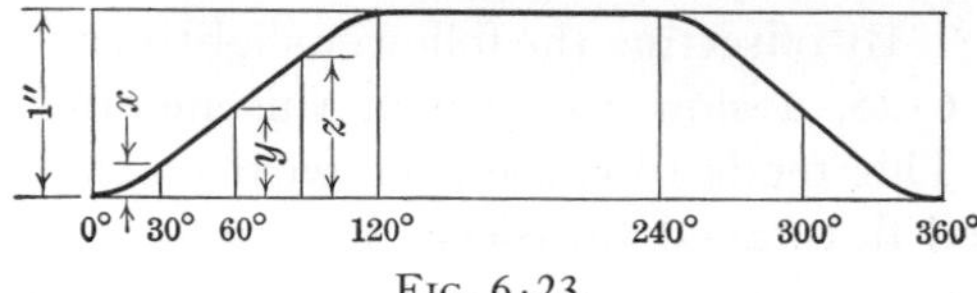

FIG. 6·23.

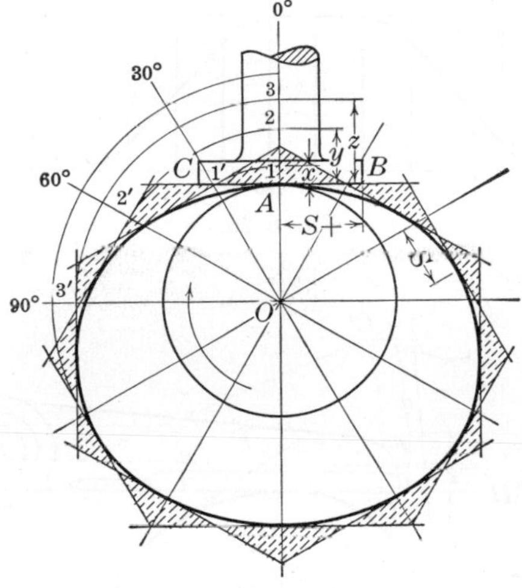

FIG. 6·24.

cam profile is found by drawing a curve tangent to each of these lines. It may be noted that the intersections of these lines form triangles, shown by the cross-hatched surfaces in the figure. The drawing of the cam profile will be facilitated if it is remembered that the required curve touches the bases of each of the triangles at about their midpoint.

The necessary **length of follower face** BC in Fig. 6·24 can readily be determined by inspection of the figure. The face is usually a circular disk, free to rotate about the follower axis. The point of contact is only on the axis in "rest" positions and

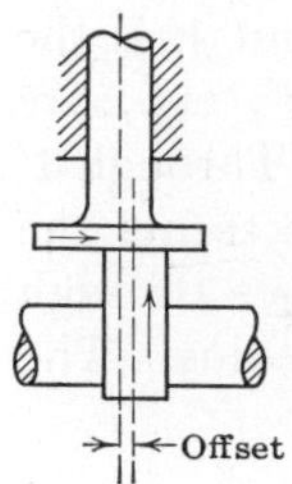

FIG. 6·25.

moves out toward B or C as the follower velocity increases. The distances AB and AC must be great enough so that the contact point never passes B or C. By inspection of the diagram, the length of the longest tangent S can be found; AB and AC should be at least equal to S, and preferably slightly greater.

By offsetting the follower slightly, as shown in Fig. 6·25, a slow rotation of this member is induced. This tends to cause even wear on the contact face.

(b) Pivoted flat-faced follower Figure 6·27 illustrates this mechanism, the follower turning about a fixed pivot at B. To

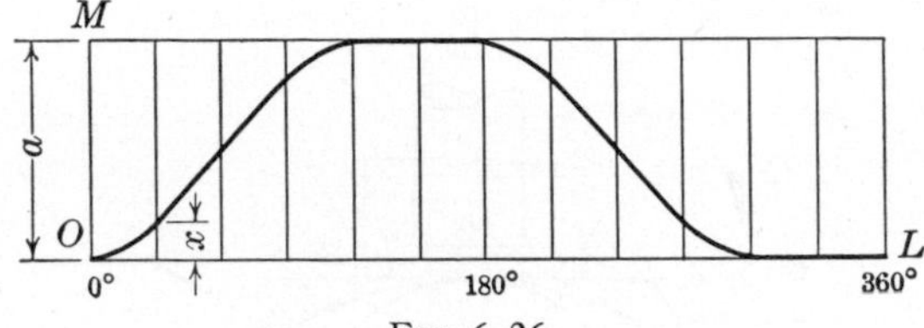

FIG. 6·26.

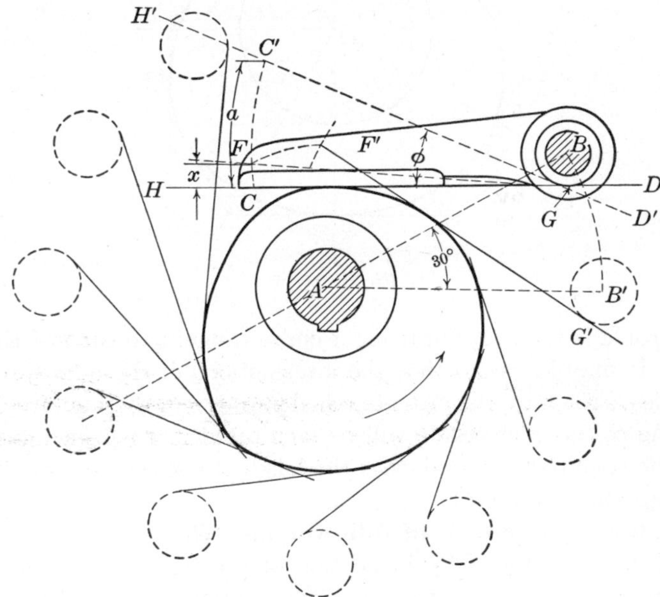

FIG. 6·27.

construct the cam profile, any point, such as C, on the follower face is selected as a reference point. Arc CC', with center B, is the path of motion of C, assuming that the follower is to have a total displacement of $\phi°$. The displacement diagram, Fig. 6·26, is drawn in the usual manner, the rectified length of CC', or a, being used to represent follower displacement. The form of the curve depends on the motion specifications. The construction for a point on the cam profile at 30° cam displacement is indicated in the figure. Distance x represents the angular displacement of the follower at this instant; this distance is set off along the arc CC', thus giving point F. The follower is next rotated 30° in a sense opposite to that of the cam movement, which causes F to move to F' and B to B'. F' is easily located, since the angle $BAB' = 30°$ and $BF = B'F'$. By drawing, with B' as center, a circle of radius BG, the tangent $F'G'$ will represent the new position of the follower face. Repetition of this construction for other cam angles gives the series of lines shown in the figure, to which the cam profile must be tangent.

6·18 Base-circle diameter In assuming the diameter of the base circle, it is important to keep certain factors in mind.

For a given lift $\mathbf{s}$ during a specified cam angular displacement $\boldsymbol{\theta}$, a larger base circle will result in a smaller pressure angle $\boldsymbol{\alpha}$. This is illustrated in Fig. 6·28, in which a lift $\mathbf{s}$ is desired in a cam angle $\boldsymbol{\theta}$. A knife-edge follower is used; and, for simplicity, the

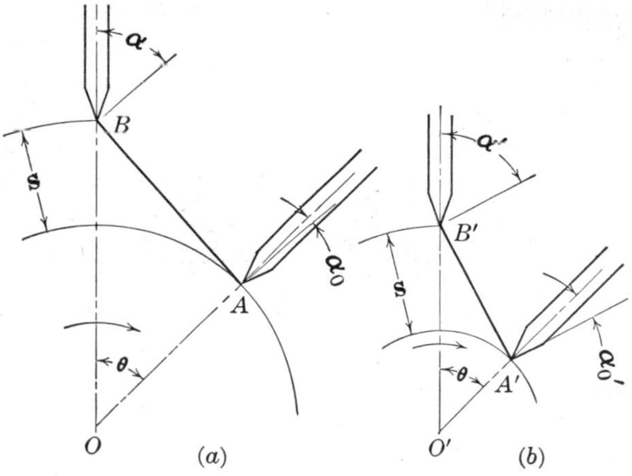

FIG. 6·28 Effect of Base-Circle Size on Pressure Angle for Cams.

shape of the cam profile during the motion is assumed to be a straight line. In part *a* of the figure the base-circle diameter is twice as large as in part *b*, with all other factors held constant. The pressure angle in part *a* is considerably smaller than in part *b* for corresponding positions of the knife-edge follower.

If the base-circle diameter is too small, it may result in a condition where it is impossible to draw a curve to touch all the positions of the follower. Thus, for the flat-faced follower shown in Fig. 6·24, a small base circle may result in a situation shown in Fig. 6·29 where it is impossible to draw a curve to touch all lines, such as 1–1′, 2–2′, 3–3′, etc. The cause is too rapid acceleration or deceleration of the follower, and the remedy is to increase the base-circle diameter. When the base circle is enlarged a certain amount, three of the lines will meet at a point; then the profile will have a sharp corner which is liable to wear away rapidly. Further increase in the base-circle diameter will cause this corner to disappear.

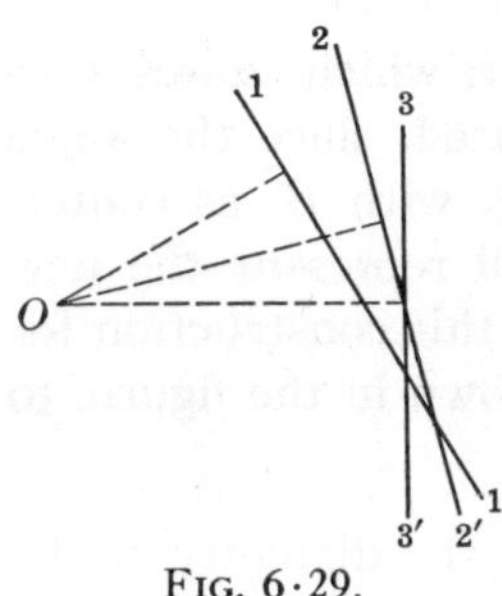

FIG. 6·29.

In general, the diameter of the base circle should be made as large as possible within the limitations of space available. It should also be larger in diameter than the cam hub or shaft to insure that the follower does not ride on the hub or shaft rather than the cam profile.

6·19 Primary and secondary follower

The mechanism of Fig. 6·31 has a pivoted follower, on the back of which a second follower with rectilinear motion makes contact. We shall refer to these, respectively, as the "primary" and "secondary" followers. The advantages of such an arrangement are: (*a*) the secondary follower is relieved of most of the side thrust, (*b*) a large multiplying or reduction ratio of the primary displacement is obtainable with a given cam, and (*c*) the axis of the secondary follower may be offset a considerable amount from the cam axis to accommodate the mechanism in a given machine.

It may be assumed that the motion of the secondary follower is definitely specified, so that a displacement diagram (as in Fig. 6·30) can be drawn; also, that sufficient data are given to enable the mechanism to be drawn in the position shown by the full lines of Fig. 6·31 with the roller in contact with the base circle.

Roller center E moves in an arc EF with its center at the pivot point D. The straight line GY is the path of the point G, the

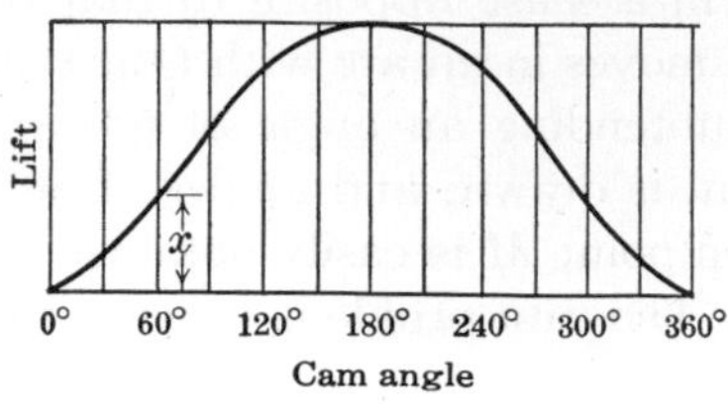

FIG. 6·30.

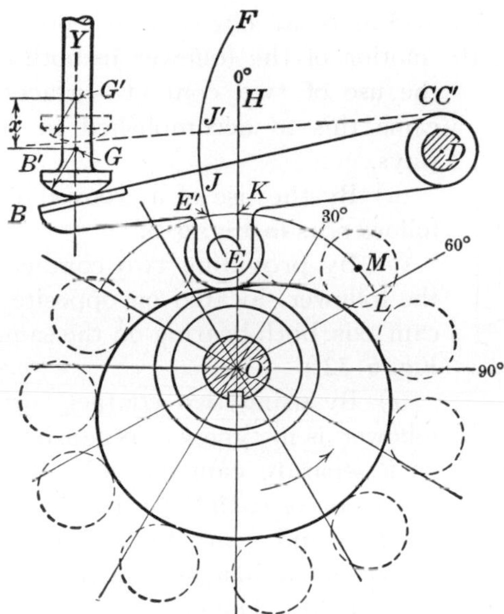

FIG. 6·31.

reference point on the secondary follower. The construction for the roller position corresponding to 60° displacement from initial position is shown in the figure. The displacement diagram shows a follower displacement of x at this instant. This distance is set off along GY, thus giving the point G'. The follower in its new position is drawn as shown, in dashed lines, G' being used to locate the arc forming the contact surface. We next draw $B'C'$

touching this arc, representing the new position of the top face of the primary follower. $B'C'$ crosses the arc EF at J'. If $J'E'$, equal to JE, is set off along EF, evidently E' is the new location of the roller center. Our next step is to rotate the primary follower 60° in a sense opposite to that of the motion of the cam. Point E' moves in an arc with O as center to the point M, the arc $E'M$ subtending an angle of 60° at O. If OH, an arbitrary 0° radiant, is drawn, and angles of 30°, 60°, 90°, etc., laid off from it, then point M is easily obtained by making chord LM equal to KE'. The cam profile is tangent to the roller circle with M as center.

6·20 Positive-motion cam mechanisms This variety was mentioned in Art. 6·3 as being one in which provision is made for controlling the motion of the follower in both directions by the use of two contact surfaces. For disk cams this is accomplished in the following ways.

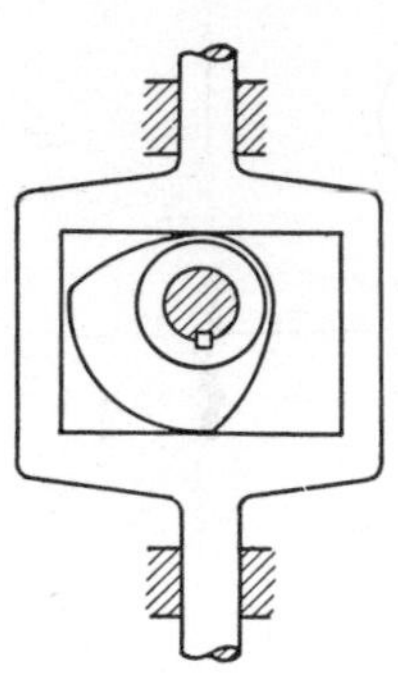
Fig. 6·32

(*a*) By the use of a grooved disk and roller follower, as in Fig. 6·5.

(*b*) By providing two contact surfaces on the follower, located on opposite sides of the cam axis, both bearing on the same cam. (See Fig. 6·32.)

(*c*) By using two contact surfaces on the follower as in type *b*, but causing each to bear on a separate cam (see Fig. 6·34). A brief discussion of each type follows.

Type a In Fig. 6·5, *a* and *b* are the two contact surfaces. The inner one *a* is constructed just as though the cam were of the ordinary nonpositive kind. Then circles of diameter equal to that of the roller are drawn at convenient angular intervals, touching the surface *a*. A curve drawn to touch each of these circles on the outside will outline the surface *b*. A certain amount of clearance is necessary, the groove being made slightly wider than the roller.

It may be observed that, when the roller rolls against *a*, it turns counterclockwise, whereas, when rolling against *b*, it turns clockwise. Each of these conditions exists at least once during a revolution; hence the roller must reverse its angular movement at least twice per revolution. This is bound to cause slippage, which may produce excessive wear at some points on the contact surfaces.

Type b When a flat-faced follower with reciprocating motion is used and the mechanism has the form shown in Fig. 6·32, the mechanism can be designed to give any required motion for 180°, subject only to limitations that apply to any cam with a flat-faced

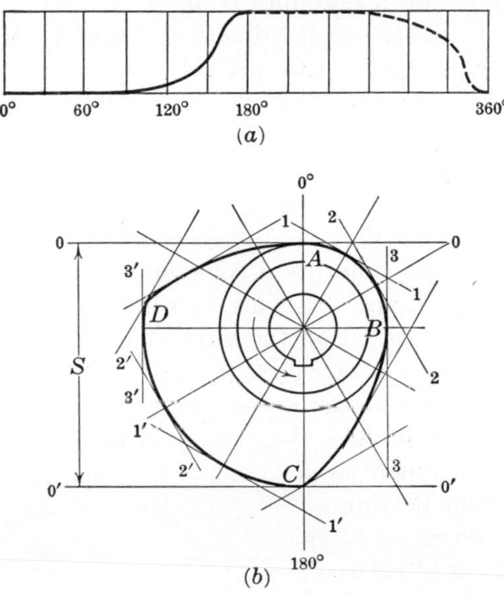

Fig. 6·33.

follower. The motion during the other half of the revolution, however, will be the same as that obtained during the first half, since it is caused by contact between the same cam profile and a follower face of the same shape, the only difference being that the direction is reversed. This type is not suitable, therefore, for an application in which the follower motion must be different on the lift and return strokes.

Where the follower has angular motion about a pivot, the motion can be specified for 180° plus the angular displacement of the follower.

In Fig. 6·33*a* is shown an assumed lift diagram for 180° of motion. The details of construction for a cam mechanism are given in Fig. 6·33*b*. The half cam surface *ABC* is found by the construction of Art. 6·17*a*. The lines 0–0, 1–1, 2–2, etc., show the positions occupied by the upper face at the ends of equal angular intervals of 30°. The necessary distance *S* from the upper to the lower face of the follower is evidently equal to base-circle diameter + lift.

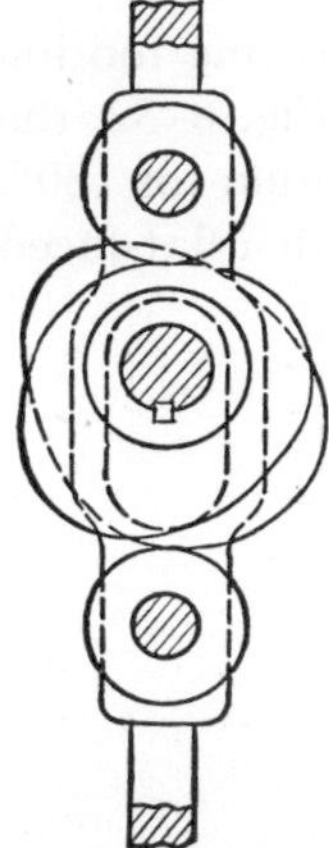

Fig. 6·34.

To find the profile of the portion *CDA* of the cam, draw lines 0′–0′, 1′–1′, 2′–2′, etc., respectively parallel to and at distance *S* from 0–0, 1–1, 2–2, etc. Curve *CDA* is then drawn tangent to these lines. Clearance is provided by making the distance between the follower faces somewhat larger than *S*.

The preceding construction produces a profile such that the distance between any pair of parallel tangents is constant.

Type c This consists of two disk cams, mounted on the same shaft, acting on a follower with two contact faces or rollers placed on opposite sides of the cam shaft, each bearing on one of the cams (see Fig. 6·34). In designing the cam profiles, the first or "**motion**" cam is drawn in the same manner as a nonpositive cam bearing on one of the rollers or faces. The second or "**return**" cam is then drawn so that its profile will maintain contact with the other roller or face of the follower. It is usually most convenient to make both the base circles of the same size. In this case the distance *S*, in Fig. 6·35, from center to center of rollers is equal to 2 × roller radius + base-circle diameter + lift.

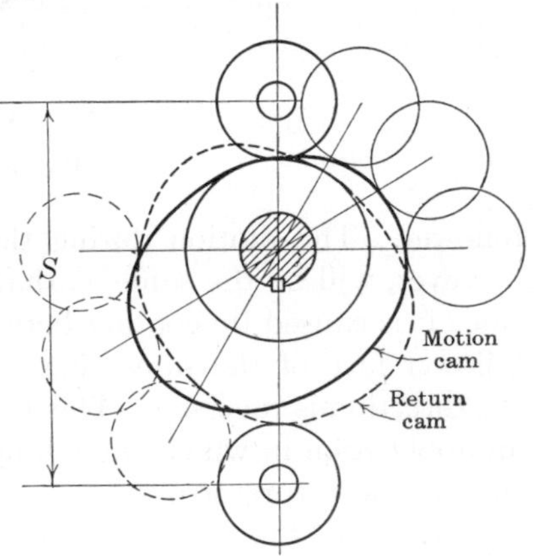

Fig. 6·35.

Figure 6·35 shows the construction. The roller circles drawn in dashed lines, to which the profile of the return cam is tangent, are located diametrically opposite the circles in solid lines, tangent to the motion cam, the distances between the centers of each pair on the same diameter being equal to S.

Although more complicated and expensive to make, this type imposes no limitations on the motion as does type *b* with single disk. Neither does it have the undesirable reversal of roller rotation that occurs in type *a*.

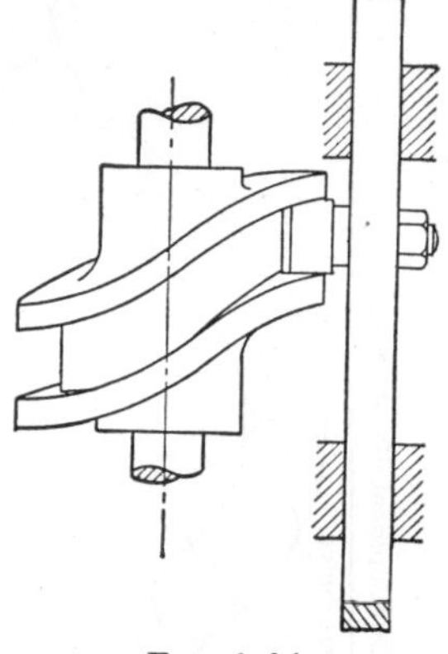

FIG. 6·36.

CYLINDER CAMS

6·21 Types These may have followers guided so as to move in a straight line along an element of the cylinder (Fig. 6·36) or followers pivoted so as to move about an axis perpendicular to the cam axis (Fig. 6·37). The roller, if cylindrical, cannot have pure rolling contact because of the difference in the surface speed at the top and bottom of the groove. Consequently it is sometimes made in the form of the frustum of a cone (Fig. 6·38) with the apex on the axis of revolution of the cam. Although this promotes pure rolling action, it also introduces an undesirable thrust, tending to move the roller away from the cam.

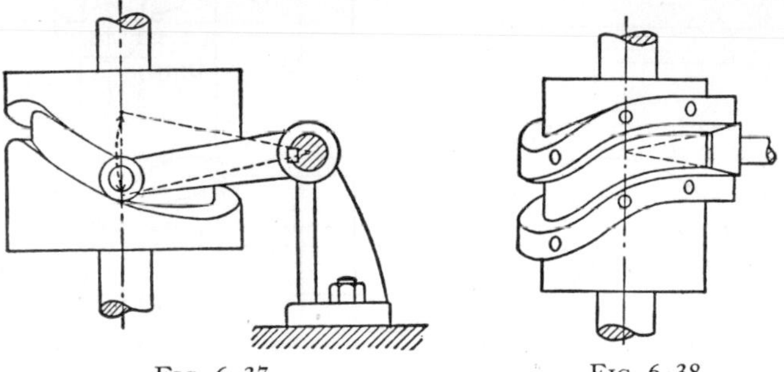

FIG. 6·37. FIG. 6·38.

6·22 Cylinder cam with rectilinear motion of follower Figure 6·39 shows the construction of a cylinder cam which meets the following specifications:

Cylinder diameter...........	6 in.
Roller diameter.............	$1\frac{1}{4}$ in.
Groove depth...............	$\frac{13}{16}$ in.

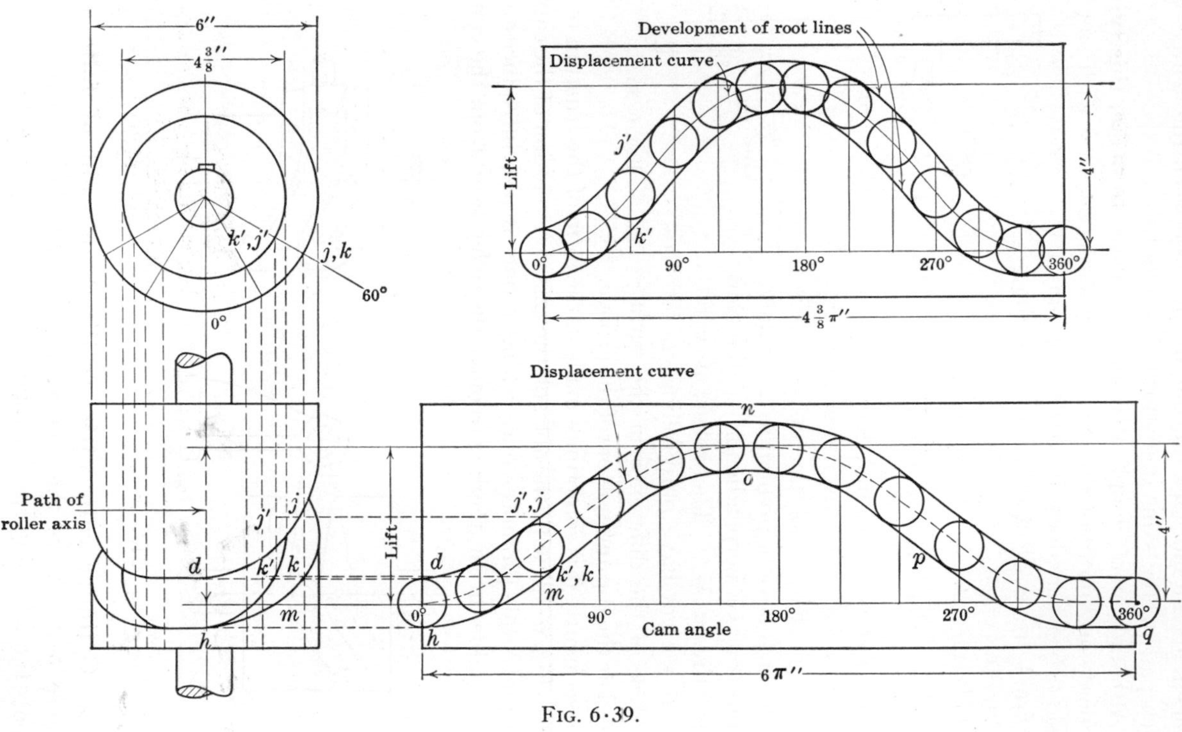

6″
$4\frac{3}{8}''$
k′, j′
j, k
60°
0°
Path of roller axis
j′
j
d
k′
k
m
h
Development of root lines
Displacement curve
j′
k′
Lift
4″
0°
90°
180°
270°
360°
$4\frac{3}{8}\pi''$
Displacement curve
n
o
j′, j
d
k′, k
m
p
Lift
4″
0°
90°
180°
270°
360°
Cam angle
h
q
$6\pi''$

Fig. 6·39.

The roller is cylindrical. The follower moves in a straight line along a cylinder element, rising from initial position with constant acceleration for 45°, with constant velocity for 60°, with constant deceleration for 45° to top position. It then rests for 30° and returns with the same motion as on the lift. The total lift is 4 in.

A cam angle-displacement diagram is first drawn (Fig. 6·39), the base being taken of such length that it represents the cylinder circumference (6π in.) to a convenient scale. Taking centers at a number of points along the curve, and with roller radius, draw circles as indicated in the figure. Draw curves tangent to these circles above and below; they will be the developed outline of the groove on the cylinder surface. If a templet of this form is made and wrapped around the cylinder, the required profile can be marked on the latter. The development of the root cylinder, of length $4\frac{3}{8}\pi$ in., is also shown in the figure. For strictly accurate results this is needed for drawing the elevation of the root lines. The shorter method adopted in Fig. 6·39, using only the outer cylinder development, is approximately correct for the root lines.

Figure 6·40 shows a Fay automatic lathe, which is completely automatic in its cycle. The operator simply places the work in the unit and pulls the starting lever, and the machine goes through the complete cycle of operations to produce an internal-

Jones & Lamson Machine Co.

FIG. 6·40 Fay Automatic Lathe.

combustion-engine piston or airplane-engine cylinder, etc., and stops automatically. Naturally this is an ideal application for the use of cams, translation and cylinder cams being employed. In the figure G points to a translation cam which varies the pressure on the cutting tool. Various shapes of these cams may be used, and they may be moved to various positions depending on the product being manufactured. The movements of the carriage, back arm and auxiliary facing attachment are controlled by the cylinder cams shown at M and the corresponding right end of the unit (see also Fig. 6·41). These cams consist of

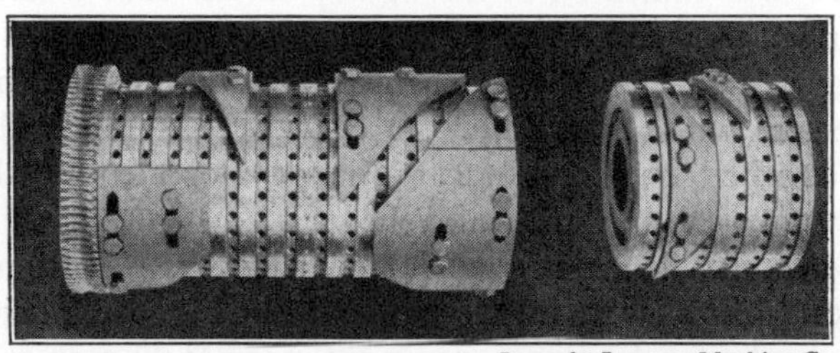

Jones & Lamson Machine Co.

FIG. 6·41.

drums, which have numerous tapped holes as shown, to which are attached curved plates to act as cylinder cam surfaces and give the desired motion. Sets of plates are made for each product to be manufactured and may be attached as required.

CIRCULAR-ARC CAMS

6·23 General Many cams have profiles formed by circular arcs. There are three reasons for using such outlines in preference to other curves: (1) the drawing office specifications are more easily made for the use of the shop; (2) the process of manufacture is cheaper; (3) the completed cam can be checked more easily and with greater accuracy. Valve cams used in automobile and other internal-combustion engines, as well as many others, are usually of this class.

By proper choice of the radii and centers of the arcs, theoretical requirements as to follower movements can be approximated very closely. The process of design can be carried out by first drawing a displacement diagram of the desired motion to a large scale and from it laying out the cam. Then, by trial, arcs and radii are chosen which will approximate the true form. Finally, the resulting cam is checked by working back to a displacement diagram which is compared with the original one. If the revision of the cam is found to have altered the displacement curve to an unsatisfactory form, a further revision may be necessary.

For high-speed cams it is necessary to draw an acceleration curve for the follower, since the spring pressure needed in the nonpositive type is dependent to a large extent on the weight of the follower and attached parts and on the acceleration. Starting with the displacement diagram and treating it as a displacement-time curve, by the method of Art. 2·12, we may construct a velocity-time and an acceleration-time curve, the latter giving the desired information for calculation of the spring. The image method of Chapter 4 can also be used (see Arts. 4·6 to 4·8). Other methods of arriving at the velocity and acceleration of the follower are described in the article that follows. These have been found to give accurate results with little labor.

6·24 Circular-arc cams with flat-faced follower In Fig. 6·42 is shown a simple form of cam of this type, consisting of a circular disk rotating about a point O other than its geometric center A. The distance r from the center A to the face of the follower is evidently constant for any position of the cam. Therefore, the vertical motions of point A and the follower are the same. The vertical motion of A is simple harmonic when the cam rotates at constant angular velocity, since it is then moving in a circle about O at constant speed. It may be observed that B, the point of contact, is at the foot of a perpendicular from A on the cam face. If a perpendicular OC is drawn from O to AB and the angle CAO or AOD is called θ', the following relationships hold by Art. 2·8.

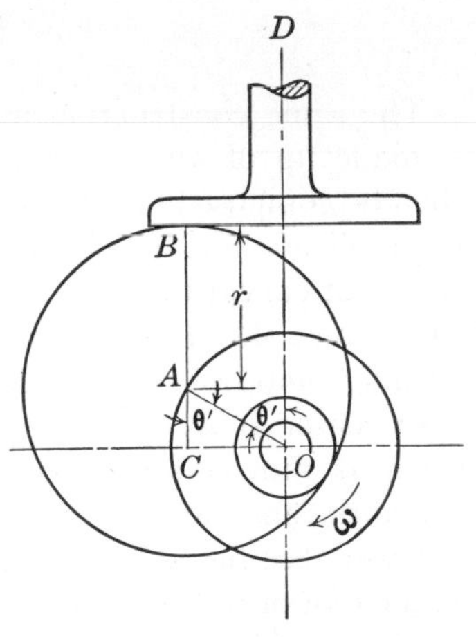

FIG. 6·42.

$$\text{Follower displacement} = \text{vertical displacement of } A = OA \cos \theta' = AC$$

$$\text{Follower velocity} = \text{vertical velocity of } A = \omega\, OA \sin \theta' = \omega\, OC$$

$$\text{Follower acceleration} = \text{vertical acceleration of } A = \omega^2\, OA \cos \theta' = \omega^2\, AC$$

where ω is the angular velocity of the cam

Plotting the lengths OC and AC on a base representing cam angles will therefore determine points on the velocity and acceleration curves for the follower motion, as shown in Fig. 6·43. These are evidently sine and cosine curves.

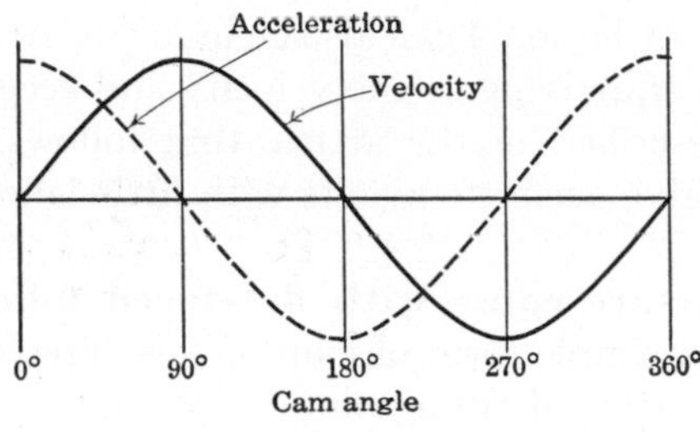

FIG. 6·43.

The same construction may be used for a cam whose profile is made up of several circular curves; the follower motion will then be composed of corresponding sections of harmonics varying in amplitude and phase in accordance with the locations of the center of curvature.

Figure 6·44 illustrates the application to a portion of a cam outline composed of a circular arc KL with center at A', and LM with center at A. Here the cam is kept stationary and the follower is moved around it, as in previous cam constructions. When the angular displacement is θ from a reference position, the follower face lies along XY and touches the cam at the point B at the foot of the perpendicular AB. OC is drawn from O perpendicular to AB. From the foregoing discussion it is evident that OC ($= \mathbf{v}$) and AC ($= \mathbf{a}$) represent graphically the velocity and acceleration of the follower at cam displacement θ. These distances are therefore transferred to the velocity and acceleration diagrams of Figs. 6·45 and 6·46 and plotted as ordinates at angle θ. Other points on the curves are obtained in a similar manner. The follower begins contact with the arc LM at cam angle α and terminates contact at angle β when the cam is

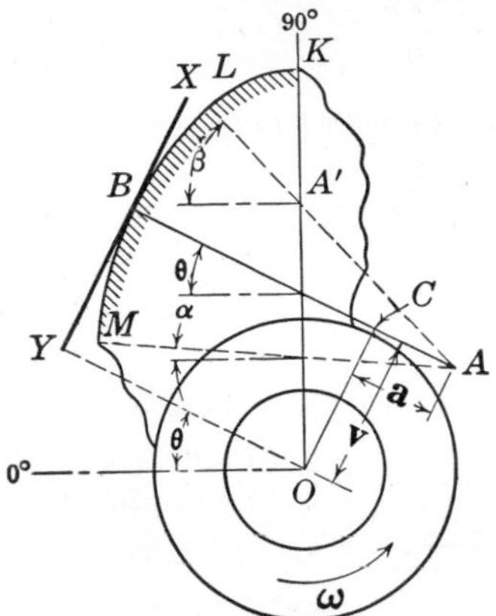

FIG. 6·44.

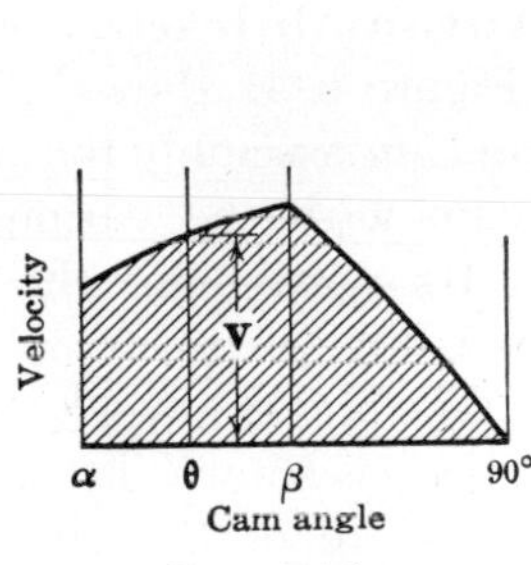

FIG. 6·45.

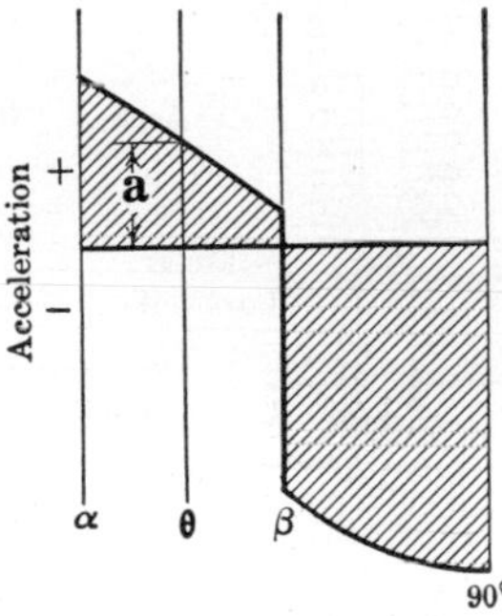

FIG. 6·46.

assumed to have counterclockwise rotation. In this event the acceleration represented by AC is positive and has consequently been plotted above the base line. If C should fall on AB produced, the sign would be the opposite.

If it is assumed that the cam turns at 900 rpm and that the cam is drawn twice full size, the velocity and acceleration scales can be found as follows:

Angular velocity of the cam (ω) $= 2\pi \times \frac{900}{60} = 94.2$ rad per sec

$$\text{Follower velocity} = \omega \times CO \quad \text{where } CO \text{ is actual size}$$

$$= \omega \times \frac{CO}{2} \quad \text{where } CO \text{ is twice full size}$$

$$= \frac{94.2}{2} \times CO \text{ in. per sec} \quad \text{where } CO \text{ is in inches}$$

$$= 3.92 \times CO \text{ fps}$$

For the velocity curve, therefore, 1 in. = 3.92 fps. Similarly, for the acceleration curve, 1 in. $= \dfrac{\omega^2}{2 \times 12} = 369$ fps^2.

Specialized graphical methods for determining the velocity and acceleration of roller and flat-faced followers with circular arc cams may be found in papers by G. L. Guillet in "Graphical Analysis of Circular Arc Cams" in the *American Machinist*, October 21 and 28, 1926, and June 16, 1927, and by H. Schreck in "Kinematics of Cams" in the *ASME Transactions*, 1926.

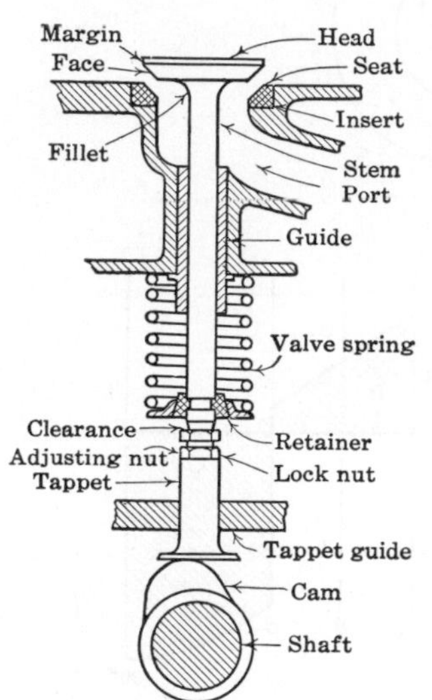

Reprinted from July 1948 Lubrication, published by The Texas Company

FIG. 6·47. Valve-Assembly Nomenclature.

6·25 Automobile-engine valve cams Figure 6·47 shows a typical valve and cam assembly for an automobile cam with the various parts named. Its position in the engine is shown in Fig. 1·1.

The intake and exhaust valve cam used in a jeep is shown in Fig. 6·48. These cams are of the circular-arc variety and are designed to operate with a flat-faced follower. The cam is symmetrical about the vertical centerline, each half being composed of four sections. Each section fulfills a definite function in the movement of the valve, as follows:

(*a*) The valve is closed, and there is a clearance of 0.020 in. between the follower and cam over the portion *ab*.

(*b*) The cam profile is a regular curve for portion *bc*, subtending an angle of 35°, during which the radial distances to the profile increase uniformly at the rate of 0.00057 in. per degree. The total lift of the follower during this period is thus equal to 0.020 in. for the whole interval. This slow lift at nearly constant velocity closes up the clearance between the follower and the valve stem without noise.

(*c*) The portion of the cam profile *cd*, which is a circular arc with center along *LM* and radius as indicated, produces a high acceleration of follower and valve, resulting in rapid lift.

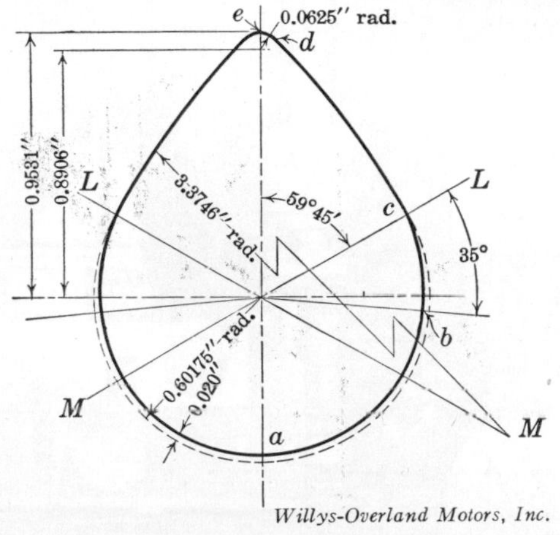

Fig. 6·48.

(*d*) The "toe" portion of the cam *de*, a circular arc of small radius, produces a comparatively low deceleration of the follower at the end of which the valve velocity is decreased to zero at the top of its travel.

The cam is symmetrical about *ea*. The acceleration during *cd* is usually three to four times the deceleration during *de*. The valve spring keeps the follower in contact with the cam during the latter period, and by designing for a low deceleration it is possible to avoid the use of a heavy spring.

6·26 Cam manufacture Cams may be manufactured by the generating process described in Art. 8·16 for gear teeth, or by a milling process. If only one cam is required, it may be laid out directly on the metal and worked to final shape by machining and hand filing.

When many identical cams are to be manufactured, special machine tools are used. Figure 6·49 illustrates such a machine to cut cylinder cams. A master cam or former (labeled *A* on the figure) is worked to its correct shape and mounted on the unit. As it rotates it raises or lowers the head *C*, carrying the end-milling cutter *D*, by means of the former roll or follower *B*. The cam blank *E* is mounted vertically on an arbor and is rotated about its axis by a gear train and shaft *F*, at the correct speed to give the desired groove shape. Generally a roughing cut is followed by one or more finishing cuts, and then a grinding wheel may replace the milling cutter.

Rowbottom Machine Co.

FIG. 6·49. Cam Milling Machine.

The same principle may be used in cutting disk cams by substituting a horizontal arbor to hold the work.

QUESTIONS

6·1 Plot displacement diagrams for the follower motions as specified in *a* to *e*. Show in each case sufficient construction lines, points, and notation to indicate the methods employed.

(*a*) A follower lifts 1 in. with constant velocity to highest position during 120° of cam displacement, rests for 60°, and falls with cycloidal motion during 45° to initial position, where it rests for the remainder of the revolution.

(*b*) A follower lifts 2 in. with constant and equal acceleration and deceleration to the top of its travel during 180° of cam movement, rests for 30°, returns to its initial position with constant velocity during 120°, and rests for the remainder of the revolution.

(*c*) A follower lifts 1 in. with modified constant velocity during 120° of cam rotation with a 60° acceleration period and a 30° deceleration period. It then rests while the cam rotates from 120° to 150°, and then rises 1 in. additional with simple harmonic motion while the cam turns from 150° to 240°. While the cam rotates from 240° to 360°, the follower drops 2 in. to its original position with constant acceleration and deceleration in a ratio of 3:1.

(*d*) A follower lifts $1\frac{1}{4}$ in. with constant acceleration and deceleration in a ratio of 2:3 during a cam rotation of 150°; and then an additional $\frac{3}{4}$ in. with modified constant velocity while the cam rotates from 150° to 270°. The acceleration period during this latter motion occurs during a cam turn of 30°; the deceleration is accomplished during the last 45° of cam angle. The follower then drops 2 in. to its initial position with cycloidal motion while the cam turns through the angle from 270° to 330°. The last 30° of cam angle are taken up by a rest period.

(*e*) A pivoted follower, starting from the extreme outward position, moves in with constant and equal acceleration and deceleration to the other end of its travel, the total displacement being 25° during a cam movement of 90°. It then rests for 45° and returns to its initial position during 60° with motion of the same character as on the other stroke. A rest period makes up the remainder of the revolution. The radius of the follower arm is 4 in.

6·2 Why is it impracticable to use an unmodified constant-velocity cam at high speeds? How should it be modified in order to obtain best results?

6·3 A follower lifts $\frac{1}{2}$ in. during a cam displacement of 90°, the cam rotating at a constant speed of 120 rpm. (*a*) Find the velocity of the follower if it is constant. (*b*) If the follower lifts with constant and equal acceleration and deceleration, find the value of the acceleration and the maximum velocity attained.

Ans. (*a*) 4 in. per sec. (*b*) 128 in. per sec^2; 8 in. per sec.

6·4 A follower lifts $\frac{3}{4}$ in. during a half revolution of the cam, the latter rotating at a constant speed of 480 rpm. The constant acceleration for the first part of the lift period is three times as great as the constant deceleration during the latter part of this period. Find the value of the acceleration and the cam displacement during which it takes place.

6·5 Calculate the maximum velocity and acceleration of a follower which moves through a distance of 1 in. with simple harmonic motion during 120° of cam displacement, the cam rotating at 200 rpm.

Ans. 15.7 in. per sec, 492 in. per sec^2.

6·6 In each of the following cases, *a* to *i*, assume a displacement diagram to be given, and show how to plot the cam profile which will give the required motion to the follower. Show sufficient construction lines and notation to indicate the method employed in each case.

(*a*) Disk cam rotating clockwise with knife-edge follower, the edge moving in a straight line passing through the cam axis.

(*b*) Disk cam rotating clockwise with knife-edge follower moving in a straight line passing to the left of the cam axis.

(*c*) Disk cam rotating counterclockwise with roller follower having rectilinear motion, the roller center moving in a straight line which intersects the cam axis.

(*d*) Disk cam rotating counterclockwise with roller follower having rectilinear motion, the roller center moving along a straight line passing somewhat to the right of the cam axis.

(*e*) Disk cam rotating clockwise with roller follower pivoted to the left and somewhat above the cam axis.

(*f*) Disk cam turning clockwise with follower having convex sliding face. Follower moves without angular displacement, its axis passing through the cam axis.

(*g*) Disk cam turning counterclockwise, having flat-faced follower with rectilinear motion. How is the necessary breadth of the follower face determined in this case?

(*h*) Disk cam turning counterclockwise with flat-faced follower pivoted to the right and somewhat above the cam axis.

(*i*) Disk cam with roller-type, pivoted primary follower and convex-faced secondary follower having rectilinear motion.

6·7 Sketch and explain the action in the three types of positive-motion cam mechanisms.

6·8 (*a*) Where a positive-motion cam mechanism has a single cam acting on two faces of a yoke follower, what limitation is imposed on the motion of the follower? (*b*) What is the main objection to the use of positive-motion cam mechanisms with a single roller acting on two cam faces?

6·9 Assuming that the form of the displacement curve is known, show how to find the cam profiles in each of the following positive-motion cam mechanisms.

(*a*) Single-disk cam turning clockwise with yoke-type follower having two parallel, flat contact faces. Follower has rectilinear motion.

(*b*) Single-disk cam turning clockwise with yoke-type follower carrying two rollers. Roller centers move in a straight line passing through the cam axis.

(*c*) Single-disk cam turning clockwise with yoke-type follower carrying two rollers. Follower pivots about a point on the right side of the cam axis.

(*d*) Slotted disk cam with two contact faces acting on a roller-type follower. The follower reciprocates along a straight line passing through the cam axis.

(*e*) Mechanism with motion and return cams each bearing on one of two parallel flat faces of yoke follower with rectilinear motion.

6·10 State one advantage and one disadvantage of using a conical roller in a cylinder-cam mechanism as compared with the use of a cylindrical roller.

6·11 Show how to draw a development of the profile of a cylinder cam when the form of the displacement curve is known. Show the construction for obtaining the elevation of the cam. Assume that the follower has recilinear motion along an element of the cam cylinder and that the roller is cylindrical.

6·12 State three practical advantages of circular-arc profiles over curves of other kinds.

6·13 Show how to find graphically the velocity and acceleration of a flat-faced follower moving with rectilinear motion. It is in contact with a circular arc disk cam, whose dimensions and speed are known. State the velocity and acceleration scales.

6·14 A cam for a four-cycle internal-combustion engine exhaust valve is designed to have a period of valve opening that lasts for 110° of crankshaft rotation. As is usual, the cam rotates at one-half crankshaft speed. If the cam is designed for constant acceleration and deceleration with an acceleration-deceleration ratio of 3:1, find (*a*) the maximum velocity of the valve during the opening period, and (*b*) the maximum acceleration of the valve. The engine speed is 3600 rpm and the valve lift $\frac{1}{4}$ in.

6·15 How would you alter a cam mechanism in order to overcome the following difficulties? (*a*) Too much side thrust on the follower. (*b*) Inability to secure sufficiently rapid lift with a flat-faced follower. How would you avoid (*c*) the necessity of using a spring, (*d*) difficulties in specifying the form of cam profile?

6·16 List the factors that enter into the determination of the size of the base circle of a cam.

6·17 Define and illustrate with a sketch the pressure angle of a cam. Why is it important in cam design? Upon what factors does it depend?

7 Rolling Contact

7·1 Conditions for rolling contact When two bodies in contact move with respect to each other in such a way that there is no relative motion at the point of contact, the bodies are said to have **pure rolling contact.** It follows that the points in contact have, for the instant, the same velocity relative to a third body. Moreover, by Art. 3·3*d*, the instant center of the two bodies is located at the contact point.

When two bodies with pure rolling contact turn about instant or permanent centers on a third body, the point of contact must always lie on the straight line joining these centers. This may be shown by reference to Fig. 7·1, in which 2 and 3 have rolling contact and turn respectively about centers O_{21} and O_{31}. P is the point of contact at the instant, and, since at this point no relative motion exists, P is the instant center O_{23}. By Kennedy's theorem (Art. 3·4), O_{21}, O_{31}, and O_{23} lie on one straight line.

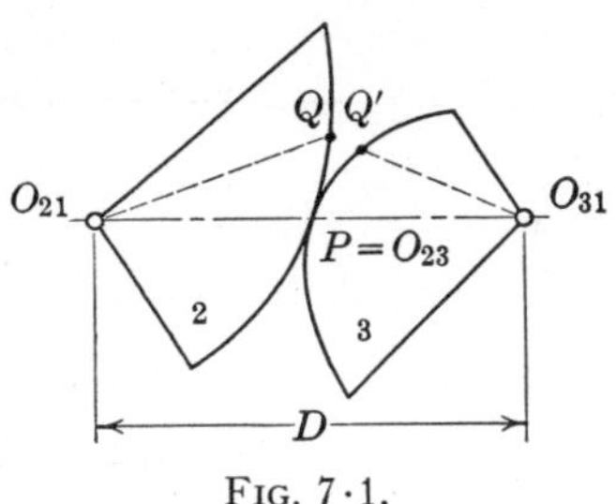

FIG. 7·1.

It has been shown that the point of contact of a pair of rolling bodies is on the line joining their instant centers or pivots. We shall consider the case where two bodies with pure rolling contact turn about fixed pivots. In Fig. 7·1, O_{21} and O_{31} now become permanent centers as well as instant centers. If we select any point Q on the profile of body 2, measure the length of the profile from P to Q, and lay off an equal length PQ' along the profile of 3, then evidently, when the bodies rotate, at some time Q and Q' will coincide; otherwise slippage will have taken place. Since Q and Q' meet on the line $O_{21}O_{31}$,

$$O_{21}Q + Q'O_{31} = O_{21}P + PO_{31} = D \qquad (7\cdot1)$$

where D is the distance between the permanent centers. Thus, bodies of any form may have pure rolling contact; but they will have a fixed distance between their centers of rotation and will therefore be capable of turning about permanent centers on a third body, only when the condition stated by equation 7·1 holds true. This condition is that the **sum of the radiants** to any pair of points that pure rolling will bring in contact **must be constant.**

7·2 Angular velocity ratio In Fig. 7·2 two bodies in rolling contact make contact for the instant at a point P. If $\mathbf{v}_P$ is the linear velocity of the common point and we consider P as a point on 2, $\mathbf{v}_P = \boldsymbol{\omega}_{21} \times OP$.

Regarding P as a point on 3, we find $\mathbf{v}_P = \boldsymbol{\omega}_{31} \times O'P$. Thus, $\boldsymbol{\omega}_{21} \times OP = \boldsymbol{\omega}_{31} \times O'P$, or

$$\frac{\boldsymbol{\omega}_{31}}{\boldsymbol{\omega}_{21}} = \frac{OP}{O'P} \tag{7·2}$$

In the case considered it is obvious that the bodies 2 and 3 rotate in opposite senses. If the two rotations are considered as positive and negative, respectively, the velocity ratio should bear a negative sign.

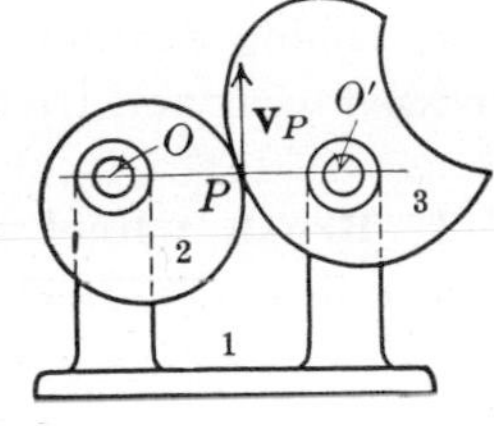

FIG. 7·2.

Instantaneous conditions only were considered; consequently, points O and O' in Fig. 7·2 need only be instant pivots and not necessarily fixed pivots.

The foregoing equation, stated in words, means that **the velocity ratio of a pair of bodies in rolling contact is inversely proportional to the distance from their point of contact to their respective pivots.** When the point of contact falls between their pivots, they must rotate in opposite senses. When it falls to one side of both pivots, the reverse is true.

For constant velocity ratio, OP and $O'P$ must have a constant ratio, which is true only when P occupies a fixed position on the line of centers. A pair of circles are the only curves that fulfill this condition; consequently, bodies that roll together with constant velocity ratio must have circular sections perpendicular to their axes of revolution, and such bodies will have velocities inversely proportional to their radii.

7·3 Friction drives may be defined as being those in which power is transmitted by the rolling contact of driving and driven members, friction at the contact surfaces being depended on to avoid appreciable slippage. They are practical applications of mechanisms having rolling contact. **Cylindrical wheels** with internal or external contact are commonly employed to connect parallel shafts. Wheels taking the form of **frustums of cones** are used for connecting intersecting shafts. These may have external contact (as in Fig. 7·8) or internal contact (as in Fig. 7·9). The frustums must be those of cones having a common apex in order that pure rolling conditions may be approached.

Practically, a certain amount of slippage is bound to take place in a friction drive when power is being transmitted. This type of drive is most serviceable for light duty. A heavy contact pressure is necessary when transmitting a large amount of power; this tends to cause friction losses and wear on the bearings of the wheel axles as well as on the contact surfaces.

For the purpose of increasing the power that may be transmitted by friction wheels for a given contact pressure, the wheels are sometimes provided with V-shaped circumferential grooves. It can easily be shown, however, that such construction renders pure rolling contact impossible and therefore tends toward increased wear and friction losses.

7·4 Brush wheel and plate A friction drive of the form shown in Fig. 7·3 is sometimes used where it is desired to obtain a speed ratio that can be varied at will. The brush wheel 2 is usually the driver, making frictional contact with the driven plate 3. Wheel 2 is mounted so that it may be shifted in an axial direction, thus moving in a line parallel to the surface of the plate. The speed ratio of driven and driving wheels depends on its position. Reversal of the sense of rotation is effected by moving 2 to the opposite side of the plate axis. A recess at the center of the plate causes the two members to break contact when 2 is in mid-position, giving a "neutral" point in which no drive is obtained.

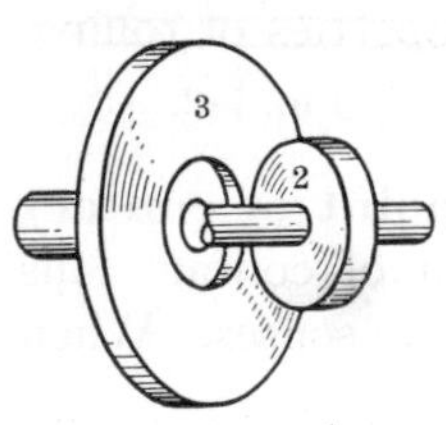

Fig. 7·3.

Pure rolling takes place only when 2 has no sensible thickness and consequently makes point contact. Such a condition in the practical machine could be approached if the power transmitted were very small. A wide brush wheel with line contact will have pure rolling contact at or near its center point, with increasing sliding velocity as the edges are approached. This tends to cause rapid wear at the sides.

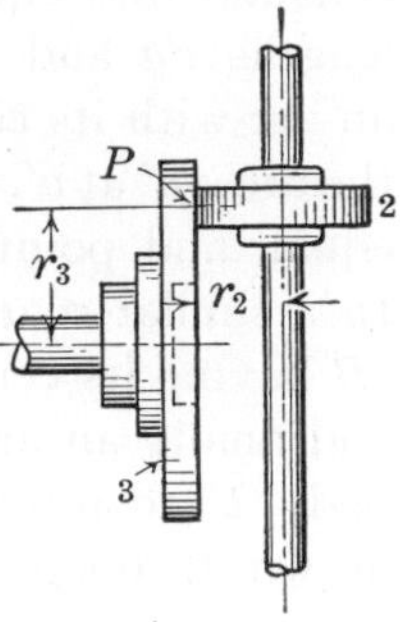

If P (Fig. 7·4) is the point at which pure rolling takes place, then $\mathbf{v}_P$ is the same when calculated from the angular velocity of either body. Therefore,

$$\mathbf{v}_P = \boldsymbol{\omega}_2 \times r_2 = \boldsymbol{\omega}_3 \times r_3$$

or

$$\frac{\boldsymbol{\omega}_2}{\boldsymbol{\omega}_3} = \frac{r_3}{r_2}$$

Fig. 7·4.

When $\boldsymbol{\omega}_2$ is constant, $\boldsymbol{\omega}_3$ will have its maximum value when r_3 is least, and its minimum value when r_3 is largest. These radii may be selected to give the desired range of speeds. P, the point of pure rolling, is generally assumed to be located at the middle of the face of the wheel 2.

7·5 Profile construction The following approximate construction may be used to find the profile of a body which is required to have pure rolling contact with a second body of known form, both bodies being assumed to oscillate about permanent centers.

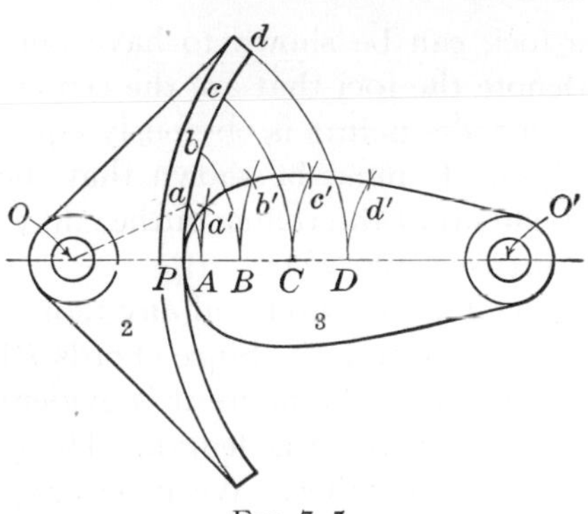

Fig. 7·5.

The construction is based on the properties of rolling bodies discussed in Art. 7·1. Let 2 (Fig. 7·5) be the body of known form oscillating about O, and suppose it is required to find the profile of a second body 3 oscillating about O' which will roll with the given body 2. By joining O and O' we find P, which must be the contact point in the position given. A convenient number of points a, b, c, etc., are selected on the profile of 2. To find a point a' on 3 that will come into contact with a as the bodies roll together, we draw an arc with O as a center and a radius Oa which intersects OO' at A. Then with O' as a center and a radius $O'A$ we strike an arc Aa', which satisfies the condition that the sum of the radiants to mating points should be constant and equal to OO'. A second condition is that the arc lengths Pa and Pa' should be equal to avoid slippage. Hence an arc with its center at P and a radius Pa is drawn to intersect the arc Aa' at a'. Then arc lengths Pa and Pa' are approximately equal, and points a and a' will coincide during the oscillation. In a similar manner point b' may be found by drawing the arc bB having its center at O, then the arc Bb' with its center at O', and finally an arc with its center at a' and a radius of ab (from body 2) to intersect arc Bb' at b'. Finally a smooth curve is drawn through P, a', b', c', etc. This construction becomes exact when points a, b, c are an infinitesimal distance apart.

7·6 Rolling ellipses Two equal ellipses, initially placed as in Fig. 7·6, with all foci lying along the same straight line, and

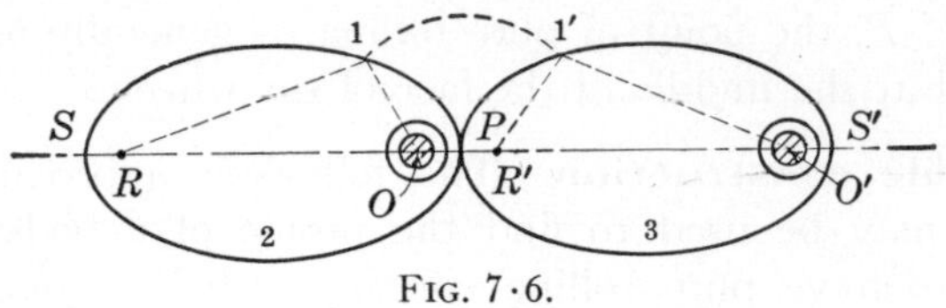

FIG. 7·6.

each turning about one of its foci, can be shown to have pure rolling contact. If O and O' denote the foci that are the centers of rotation, the distance between these points is obviously equal to the major axis of either ellipse. It must be shown that the sum of the radii to any pair of points that the rolling of the curves will bring into contact is constant (see Art. 7·1).

Using the initial point of contact P as a center and any radius, we strike an arc cutting the curves at 1 and 1'. Since chords $P1$ and $P1'$ are equal, from the symmetry of the figure it is evident that the elliptical arcs $P1$ and $P1'$ are of the same length. Therefore, pure rolling will bring 1 and 1' together. We must show that $O1 + O'1'$ equals OO'. If R, R' are the other two foci, from the properties of the ellipse we know that $O1 + 1R$ equals the major axis. But, since the ellipses are equal in all respects, $1R = O'1'$. Therefore,

$$O1 + O'1' = O1 + 1R = \text{major axis} = OO'$$

Thus the requirement of equation 7·1 is complied with.

The angular velocity ratio ω_3/ω_2 of the ellipses in the relative position shown in Fig. 7·6 is equal to $OP/O'P$, by Art. 7·2. When ellipse 2 has rotated 180°, S and S' will come in contact, and at that instant the velocity ratio will be $OS/O'S' = O'P/OP$. These are, respectively, minimum and maximum values of the velocity ratio, the latter being the reciprocal of the former. During each half revolution of the ellipses, the ratio changes from one value to the other.

7·7 Ellipses for desired velocity ratios It is possible to construct ellipses that will give any desired variation in velocity ratio. Figure 7·7 illustrates the construction for a case where the driven ellipse is to have, as a maximum, three times the angular velocity of the driver. It follows that the minimum velocity of the driven member is one-third that of the driver. The distance OO', between the centers of rotation, is assumed to be known.

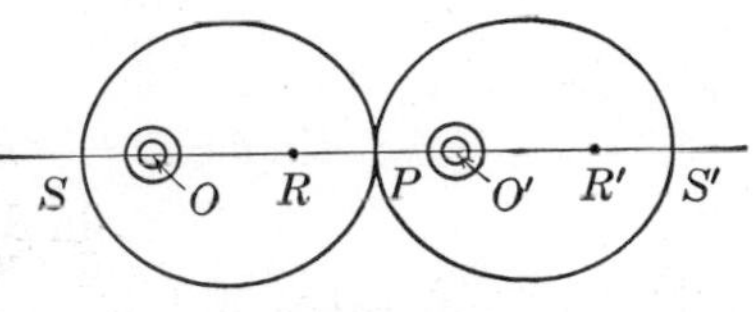

Fig. 7·7.

In Fig. 7·7, OO' is first divided into two parts OP and PO', such that $OP/O'P = 3/1$. If OS, equal to $O'P$, is laid off along OO' produced, then PS will be the major axis of one ellipse. PS' equal to PS is the major axis of the second ellipse. The foci R and R' are located by making RP and $R'S'$ equal to PO'. Knowing the foci and major axes, we may draw the ellipses by any of the usual methods.

7·8 Velocity ratio of rolling cones Figure 7·8 shows two cones used to connect shafts meeting at an angle θ. The distances BC and CD are the radii of the circular bases. At C the cones have a common velocity $\mathbf{v}_C$. Then,

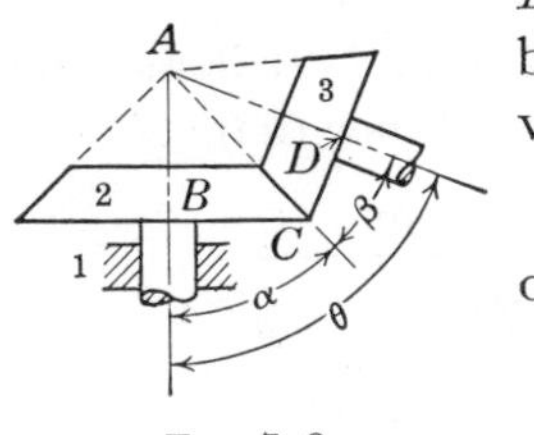

Fig. 7·8.

$$\mathbf{v}_C = \omega_{21} \times BC = \omega_{31} \times CD$$

or

$$\frac{\omega_{31}}{\omega_{21}} = \frac{BC}{CD}$$

The velocities are therefore inversely proportional to the radii or diameters of the bases.

Let α and β be the angles of the cones. From the figure,

$$\sin \alpha = \frac{BC}{AC} \tag{A}$$

$$\sin \beta = \frac{CD}{AC} \tag{B}$$

Dividing equation A by equation B gives

$$\frac{\sin \alpha}{\sin \beta} = \frac{BC}{CD} = \frac{\omega_{31}}{\omega_{21}}$$

But

$$\alpha = \theta - \beta$$

Therefore,

$$\frac{\sin (\theta - \beta)}{\sin \beta} = \frac{\omega_{31}}{\omega_{21}}$$

or

$$\frac{\sin \theta \cos \beta - \cos \theta \sin \beta}{\sin \beta} = \frac{\omega_{31}}{\omega_{21}}$$

Dividing numerator and denominator by $\cos \beta$, we have

$$\frac{\sin \theta}{\tan \beta} - \cos \theta = \frac{\omega_{31}}{\omega_{21}}$$

or

$$\tan \beta = \frac{\sin \theta}{\dfrac{\omega_{31}}{\omega_{21}} + \cos \theta} \tag{7·3}$$

In the same way it can be proved that

$$\tan \alpha = \frac{\sin \theta}{\dfrac{\omega_{21}}{\omega_{31}} + \cos \theta} \tag{7·4}$$

For rolling cones with internal contact (see Fig. 7·9) it may be proved in a similar manner that

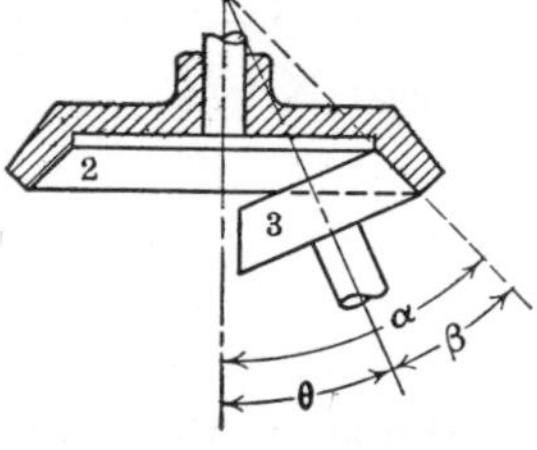

Fig. 7·9.

$$\tan \beta = \frac{\sin \theta}{\dfrac{\omega_{31}}{\omega_{21}} - \cos \theta} \tag{7·5}$$

$$\tan \alpha = \frac{-\sin \theta}{\dfrac{\omega_{21}}{\omega_{31}} - \cos \theta} \tag{7·6}$$

These formulas enable us to calculate the cone angles when the angle between shafts and the velocity ratio are known.

7·9 Rolling cones. Graphical method As an alternative to the calculation of the angles of rolling cones, a graphical solution can easily be made.

OA and *OB* (Fig. 7·10) represent the axes of intersecting shafts to be connected by rolling cones with a speed ratio of 5:2. These may have either external or internal contact; the former is considered first.

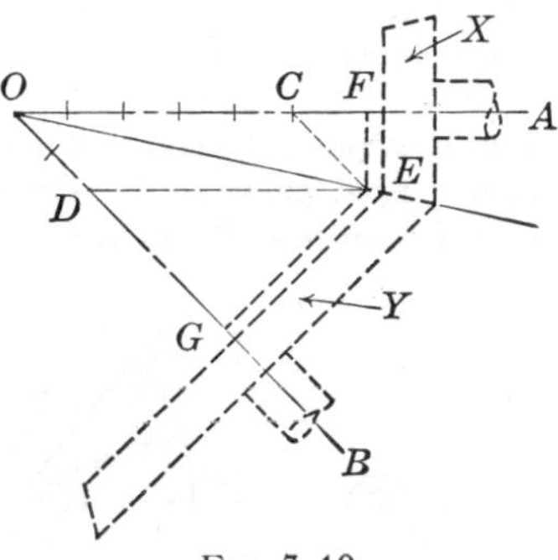

FIG. 7·10.

A distance of five units is laid off along *OA*, thus locating the point *C*. Similarly, point *D* on *OB* is found by making *OD* equal two units. From *C*, *CE* is drawn parallel to *OB*, and, from *D*, *DE* parallel to *AO*. The intersection *E* is a point on the contact line of cones that give the desired speed ratio.

Join *OE* and drop perpendiculars *EF* and *EG* to the axes *AO* and *OB*. From the geometry of the figure, it can be shown that

$$EF : EG = OD : OC = 2 : 5$$

Furthermore, a pair of perpendiculars drawn from any point on *OE* on the two axes will have the same ratio of lengths. At *X* and *Y* (Fig. 7·10) are shown two cone frustums drawn with a pair of these perpendiculars as base radii. The speed ratio is

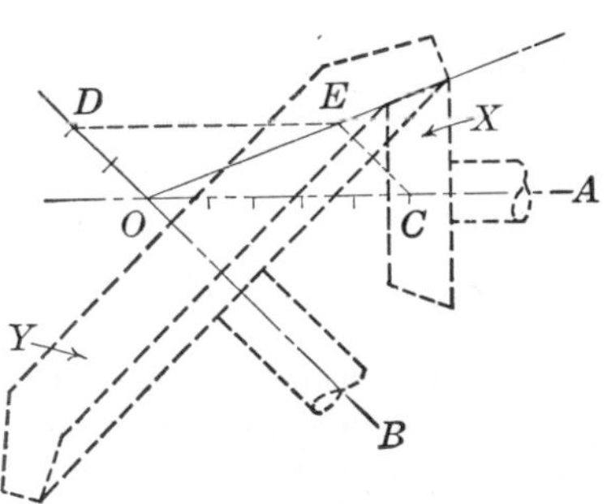

FIG. 7·11.

$$\omega_Y : \omega_X = EF : EG = 2 : 5$$

The **cone angles** to give the speed ratio specified are *AOE* and *EOB*.

Figure 7·11 illustrates the case where cones with internal contact are desired with the same speed ratio as before. The construction differs from that of Fig. 7·10 only to the extent that OD is laid off along BO produced. It should be noted that the use of internal instead of external contact reverses the sense of rotation of the driven member.

QUESTIONS

7·1 (*a*) What is meant by pure rolling contact? (*b*) When any two bodies have pure rolling contact, what can be said regarding the location of the contact point? (*c*) When two bodies turn about fixed pivots and have pure rolling contact with one another, what conditions must be satisfied in regard to their profiles? Prove this statement.

7·2 In Figs. P7·2*a* to *c* show how to find the profile of a body rotating about fixed pivot B which will have pure rolling contact with the body turning about a fixed pivot at A. Calculate the angular velocity ratios when the contact point is at P and at Q.

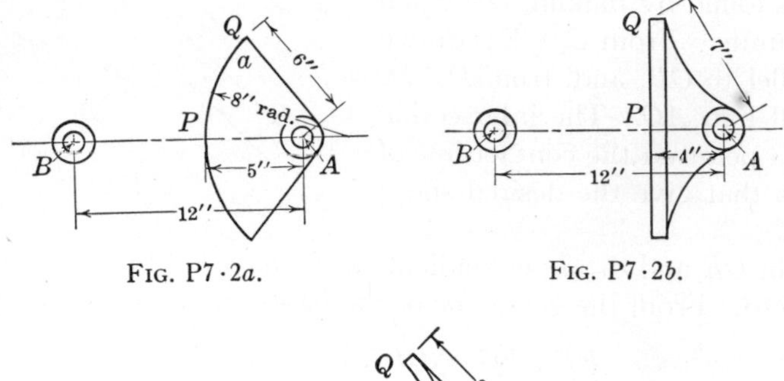

FIG. P7·2*a*. FIG. P7·2*b*.

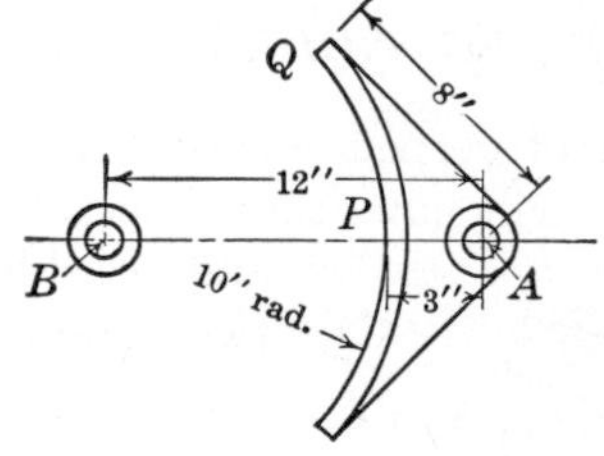

FIG. P7·2*c*.

7·3 Prove that a pair of equal ellipses rotating about fixed centers at their foci may have pure rolling contact.

7·4 Two parallel shafts are at a distance of 15 in. center to center. They are to be connected by rolling ellipses so as to obtain a maximum velocity ratio of 4:1. (*a*) Find the lengths of their major axes and the distances between their foci. (*b*) What is the minimum velocity ratio of the shafts?

7·5 Rolling cones with external contact are required to connect two shafts at 60°, the velocity ratio to be 3:2. Show how to find graphically the cone angles.

7·6 Rolling cones with internal contact are required to connect two shafts at 30°, the velocity ratio to be 3:1. Show how to find graphically the cone angles.

7·7 Two shafts intersecting at an angle of 60° are connected by means of rolling cones with external contact. One cone has a center angle of 20° and rotates at 300 rpm. Find the center angle of the other cone and its rpm.

Ans. 40°; 160 rpm.

7·8 A rolling cone with a center angle of 15° turning at 240 rpm makes external contact with a second cone which turns at 360 rpm. Find the angle between the shafts and the apex angle of the second cone.

7·9 Rolling cones with internal contact are to be used to secure a speed ratio of 4:1. The smaller cone has a center angle of 10°. What is the center angle of the larger cone, and what is the angle between the shafts?

7·10 A pair of equal rolling ellipses have a distance between their foci of 4 in. The major axes are 7 in. long. Find the maximum and minimum speed ratios. *Ans.* 1:3.67, 3.67:1.

7·11 A large bucket elevator has a head sprocket with six teeth, the arrangement requiring a speed variation of the sprocket from a minimum of 10 rpm to a maximum of $11\frac{1}{2}$ rpm in order to secure a uniform bucket speed. This variation in the sprocket speed is obtained by means of a pair of non-circular gears with elliptical pitch surfaces. If the center-to-center distance of the gears is 30 in., find the length of the major axes and the distance between the foci.

7·12 What is a friction drive? Sketch a form of friction drive that permits alteration of the velocity ratio when in service. How can it be arranged to reverse the direction of motion of the driven member? Why is pure rolling impossible in this device?

7·13 A brush-wheel-and-plate friction drive is required to connect two shafts, the driver turning at 300 rpm, and the driven plate to turn at a maximum speed of 100 rpm and a minimum of 25 rpm. The driving wheel is 5 in. in diameter and 1 in. wide. Find the maximum and minimum diameter required for the plate.

7·14 What maximum and minimum speeds are obtainable at the driven shaft in a brush-wheel-and-disk friction drive in which the wheel, 8 in. in diameter and $1\frac{1}{2}$ in. wide, rotates at 400 rpm and in which the disk has a maximum diameter on the contact surface of 26 in., the minimum diameter being 14 in.? Allow 3 per cent for slippage.

7·15 Two cylinders with rolling contact rotate in the *same* direction with a velocity ratio of 5. The center distance is 10 in. What is the diameter of each cylinder?

8 Gears

8·1 Gears are commonly employed for transmitting power from one rotating shaft to another. In comparison with friction or belt drives, they are especially adapted where an exact velocity ratio is required or where driving and driven members must maintain definite phase relationships.

Since the interlocking action of the teeth makes the drive positive, and friction is not depended on to avoid slippage, the force required to hold the gears in position when power is being transmitted is much less than in an equivalent friction drive. This results in lower bearing pressures, less wear on the bearing surfaces, and greater efficiency.

Pitch surfaces The pitch surfaces of gears may be defined as imaginary surfaces which roll together without slipping, similar to those of friction bodies. For any gear the form and dimensions of the pitch surface must be known before the teeth can be properly designed. Figure 8·1 shows the cylindrical pitch surface for a spur gear.

Tooth element A gear tooth may be regarded as composed of surfaces swept by a line moving through space. The line is

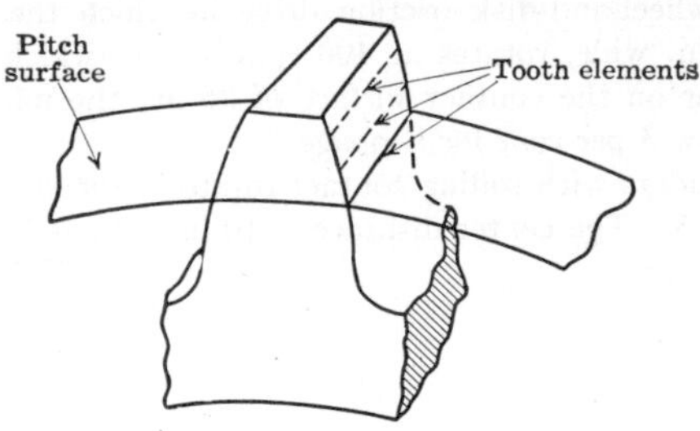

FIG. 8·1.

not always straight or even of constant shape. This surface generator in any one of its consecutive positions is known as a tooth element. Tooth elements always connect corresponding points on tooth sections taken perpendicular to the pitch surfaces. In Fig. 8·1 are shown tooth elements for a spur gear, which are straight lines parallel to one another.

Pitch surfaces of mating gears may have either (*a*) **pure rolling contact** or (*b*) **sliding contact.** This matter is important, since it determines whether or not the teeth have relative sliding along the tooth elements. When this kind of sliding action occurs, it places certain limitations on the form of the elements.

Gear wheels are illustrations of **higher pairing,** because line or point contact only is obtained.

8·2 Gear classification Gears may be classified according to the relative position of the axes of revolution. The axes may be (*a*) parallel, (*b*) intersecting, (*c*) neither parallel nor intersecting. We shall first make a brief survey of the common forms and later discuss each in more detail.

(a) Gears for connecting parallel shafts Here we may employ the common **spur gears** as shown in Fig. 8·2 or the **helical gears with parallel axes** of Fig. 8·3. In both, the

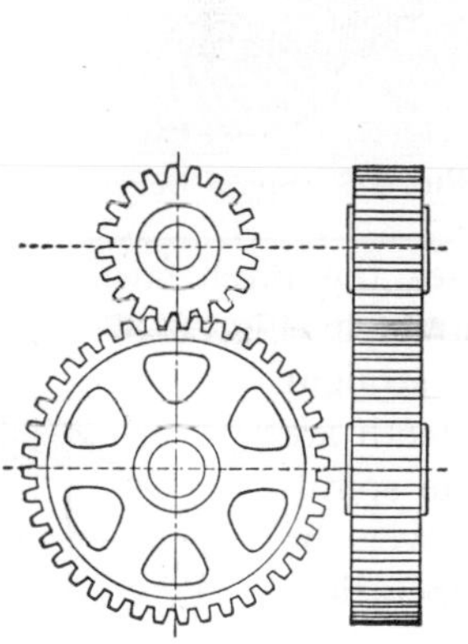

FIG. 8·2 Spur Gears.

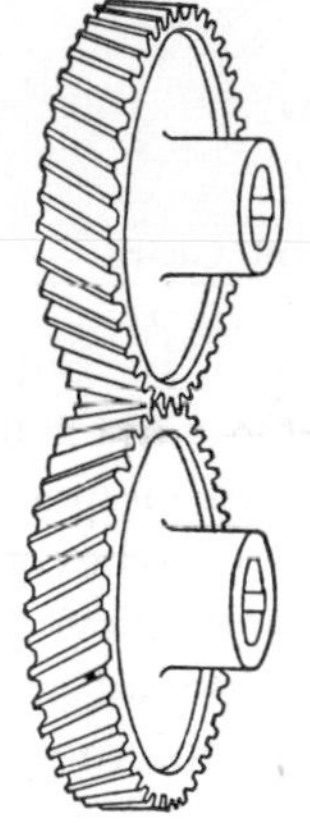

FIG. 8·3 Helical Gears with Parallel Axes.

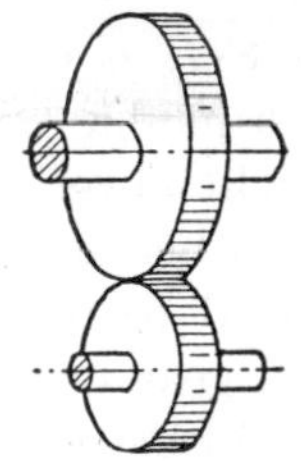

FIG. 8·4 Pitch Surfaces of Gears with Parallel Axes.

pitch surfaces are cylindrical with pure rolling contact as illustrated in Fig. 8·4. The helical gear operates more quietly than the other type, the difference in this respect being particularly

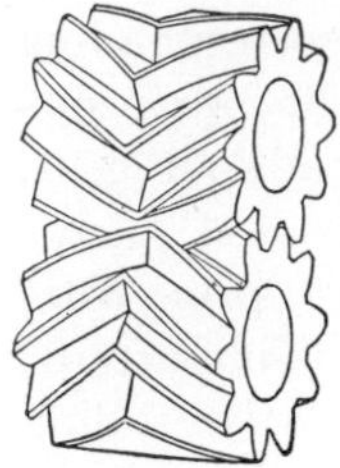

FIG. 8·5 Herringbone Gears.

noticeable at high speed. The disadvantage of the helical gear lies in the end thrust produced when the gear is transmitting power.

In the **herringbone gears** of Fig. 8·5 the end thrust set up by one side is balanced by an equal and opposite thrust caused by the action on the other side. These gears can be regarded as composed of two helical gears of similar dimensions, one having a right-handed and the other a left-handed helix.

(b) Gears for intersecting shafts In this case the **straight-bevel gear,** illustrated in Fig. 8·6, or the **spiral bevel** shown in

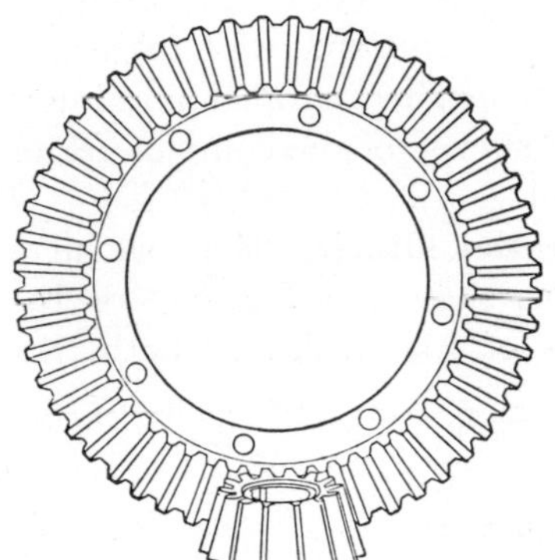

FIG. 8·6 Straight-Bevel Gears.

FIG. 8·7 Spiral-Bevel Gears.

Fig. 8·7, is employed. In both cases the pitch surfaces are cones having a common apex as shown in Fig. 8·8. In the straight bevel the tooth elements are straight lines, whereas in the spiral bevel the teeth are inclined to the axis and curved. The spiral-bevel gear has a decided advantage over the straight-bevel gear in quietness of operation, similar to that of helical gears over spur gears.

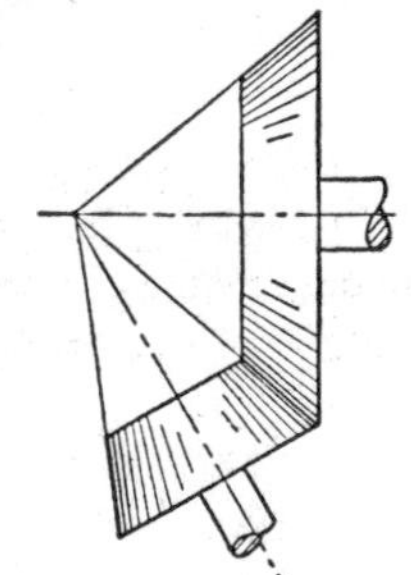

FIG. 8·8 Bevel-Gear Pitch Surfaces.

A pair of bevel gears that are the same size and whose shafts intersect at right angles are known as **miter gears.** Their chief use is to transmit motion around a corner without altering the angular velocity.

(c) Gears for connecting shafts neither intersecting nor parallel Here **helical gears with crossed axes** or **worm** or **hypoid gears** are suitable.

Helical gears with crossed axes (Fig. 8·9) are used to connect shafts that are not parallel or intersecting. Their pitch surfaces are cylindrical (Fig. 8·10). They touch at a point and have sliding contact; hence the teeth also make point contact and have a component of sliding along the tooth helix.

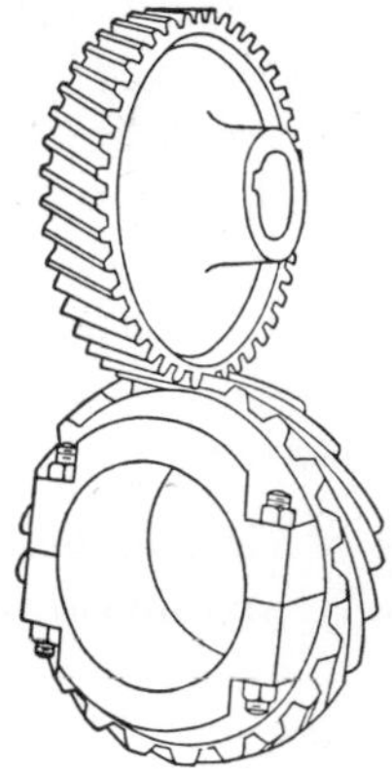

Fig. 8·9 Helical Gears with Crossed Axes.

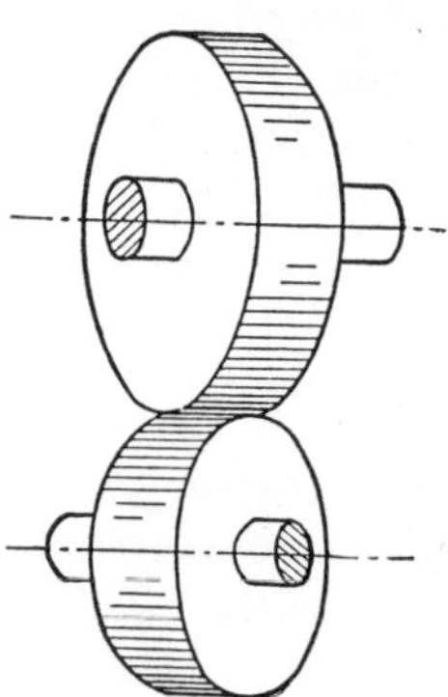

Fig. 8·10 Pitch Cylinders for Helical Gears with Crossed Axes.

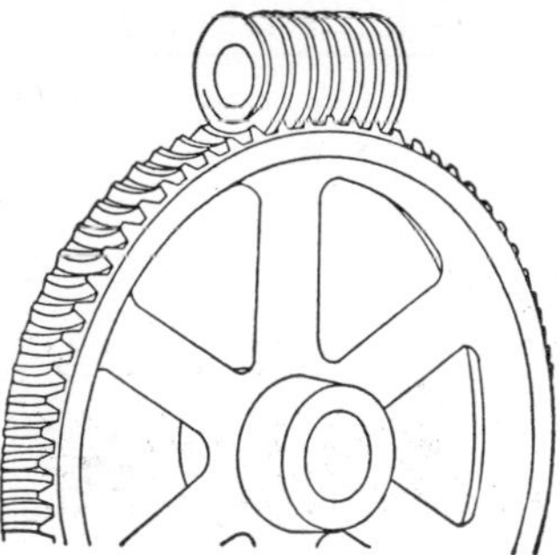

Fig. 8·11 Worm Gear.

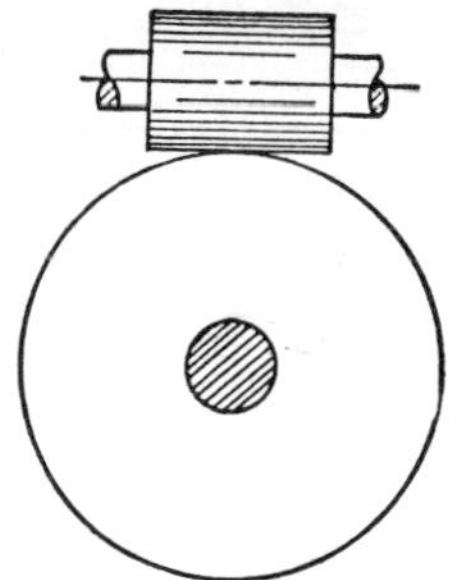

Fig. 8·12 Worm-Gear Pitch Surfaces.

The **worm gear,** shown in Fig. 8·11, is a special form of helical gear, the two members being known as the **worm** and the **worm wheel.** The worm, as compared with the helical gear, has a large helix angle, with the result that each tooth extends a long distance around the circumference. It is customary to speak of worm teeth as "threads" because of the resemblance the worm bears to a threaded bolt. Hence we refer to a "single-threaded worm," a "double-threaded worm," etc., depending on the number of teeth formed on the cylindrical surface. The worm wheel may have the tooth surface concaved as shown in Fig. 8·11, for the purpose of obtaining line instead of point contact of the teeth. The shape of the pitch surfaces of a worm gear is shown in Fig. 8·12.

Hypoid gears somewhat resemble spiral bevel gears in general appearance. Contact between the two pitch surfaces takes place along a line common to the two rotations.

8·3 Velocity ratio A rule for pairs of circular gears is that **the angular velocity ratio is inversely proportional to the numbers of teeth.** This rule applies to all common classes of gears, such as spur, bevel, and helical gears.

When two gears are in motion, it is evident that equal numbers of teeth on each gear pass any fixed point in a definite time interval, since the teeth on one gear mesh in consecutive order with the tooth spaces on the other gear. A gear having N_2 teeth makes one turn while N_2 teeth pass the fixed point. A meshing gear with N_3 teeth will therefore make N_2/N_3 turns during the same interval.

If $\boldsymbol{\omega}_2$ and $\boldsymbol{\omega}_3$ are, respectively, the angular velocities of the two gears, then

$$\frac{\omega_2}{\omega_3} = \frac{1}{N_2/N_3} = \frac{N_3}{N_2} \tag{8·1}$$

which proves the foregoing rule.

SPUR GEARS

8·4 Gear terms Figure 8·13 illustrates most of the definitions that follow (see also Fig. 8·37).

Pitch diameter The diameter of the cylinder which is the pitch surface of a spur gear is known as the pitch diameter. Since the pitch cylinders of two spur gears roll together, the angular-velocity ratio is the inverse ratio of the pitch diameters, by Art. 7·2. A pair of mating spur gears have numbers of teeth proportional to their pitch circumferences, because both must have the same spacing of the teeth in order to obtain pure rolling of the pitch circles. Thus, for two such gears, 2 and 3,

$$\frac{\omega_2}{\omega_3} = \frac{D_3}{D_2} = \frac{N_3}{N_2} \tag{8·2}$$

where N, D, and ω represent, respectively, number of teeth, pitch diameter, and angular velocity.

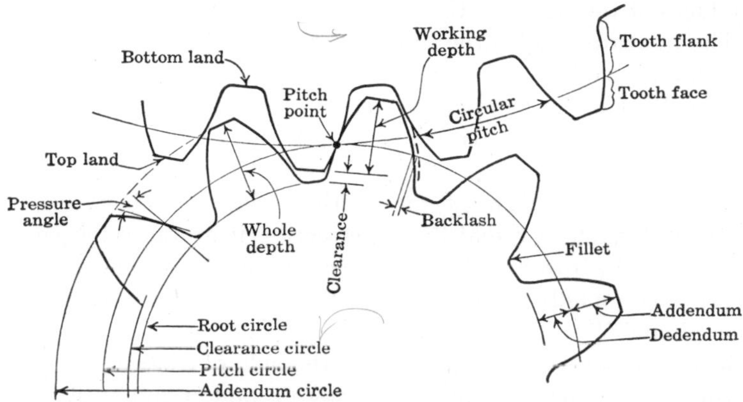

FIG. 8·13 Gear Nomenclature.

Pitch point That point on the line joining the centers of two gears at which the pitch circles touch is called the pitch point.

Addendum The distance from the pitch circle to the outer end of the tooth, measured radially, is known as the addendum.

Clearance The clearance is the amount by which the tips of the teeth on one gear clear the roots of the teeth on the mating gear. This is measured along the line of centers.

Dedendum The radial distance from the pitch circle to the root circle is called the dedendum.

The **whole depth** is the sum of the addendum and dedendum.

The **working depth** is the whole depth minus the clearance.

Backlash The minimum distance between the nondriving side of a tooth and the adjacent side of the mating tooth is called the backlash. It is measured at the pitch circle (see Fig. 8·13).

The **face of the tooth** is the surface of the tooth between the pitch and addendum circles.

The **face width** is the width of the gear measured on the pitch surface in a plane containing the axis of rotation. The face of the tooth should not be confused with the face width, for the two are entirely different. The former is a surface and the latter a dimension.

The **flank of the tooth** is the surface of the tooth between the pitch and root circles.

The **top land** is the surface of the top of the tooth between the faces of the same tooth.

The **bottom land** is the surface of the gear between the flanks of adjacent teeth.

The **fillet** is the curved surface of the tooth flank joining it to the bottom land. It lies between the clearance and root circles.

The **pressure angle** of the tooth is the angle between the tooth profile and a radial line intersecting it at the pitch circle.

Gear and pinion When two gears mesh with each other, the larger is commonly referred to as "the gear" and the smaller as "the pinion."

Rack When teeth are cut along the side of a straight bar, it is known as a rack. Figure 8·14 shows a pinion and rack. The pitch surface of the latter is a plane.

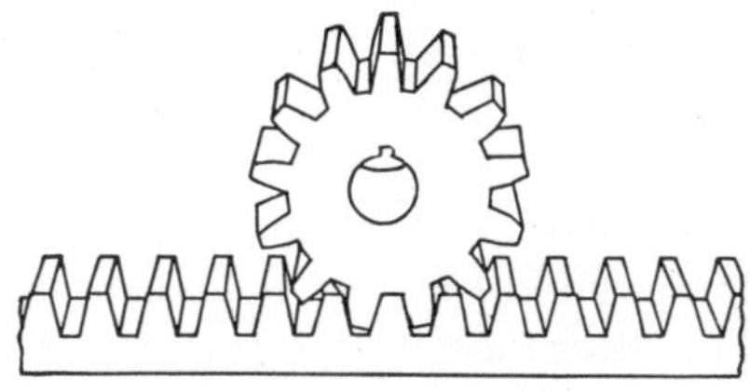

FIG. 8·14 Rack and Pinion.

Angle and arc of action The angle turned through by the driver for the period during which one of its teeth remains in contact with a mating tooth on the driven wheel is known as the **angle of action** of the driver. The angle turned through by the driven wheel in the same period is the **angle of action** of the driven wheel. The corresponding arcs on the pitch circle are called the **arcs of action.**

Evidently, the arc of action must be greater than the circular pitch; otherwise contact between one pair of teeth would cease before the next pair made contact. In general, the longer the teeth, the greater the arc of action. This consideration has been an important factor in fixing the length of standard teeth.

The **contact ratio** is a measure of the average number of teeth in contact in a pair of mating gears and equals the arc of action divided by the circular pitch.

The **angle of approach** is the angle turned through by the gear from the instant a pair of teeth make contact to the instant at which they are in contact at the pitch point.

The **angle of recess** is the angle turned through by the gear from the instant a pair of teeth are in contact at the pitch point to the instant when contact between the same teeth ceases.

The **angle of action** is equal to the sum of the angles of approach and recess.

8·5 Pitch The pitch of a gear is a measure of the size of the teeth; all tooth dimensions in standard systems are based on the pitch. Gears that are intended to run with each other must have the same pitch, as well as tooth profiles of proper form. Two common methods of stating gear pitches are as follows:

The **circular pitch** is the distance between corresponding points on adjacent teeth, this distance being measured along the circumference of the pitch circle. When p denotes the circular pitch,

$$p = \frac{\pi D}{N} \qquad (8 \cdot 3)$$

The **diametral pitch** is the result obtained by dividing the number of teeth by the pitch diameter. Stated otherwise, it is the number of teeth per inch of pitch diameter. Where P_d is this pitch,

$$P_d = \frac{N}{D} \qquad (8 \cdot 4)$$

It should be observed that the **circular pitch** is a linear dimension, ordinarily expressed as so many inches. The **diametral-pitch** units are the reciprocal of inches. It is, however, customary to state it as a number or ratio. Figure 8·15 is useful in visualizing the size of teeth having various diametral pitches.

The Barber-Colman Co.

FIG. 8·15 Tooth Size for Standard Diametral Pitches.

Relation between circular and diametral pitch Multiplying equation 8·3 by equation 8·4, we have

$$pP_d = \pi \tag{8·5}$$

The **circular-pitch** method of specifying tooth sizes is the older one, but the **diametral-pitch** method has advantages which have resulted in very general use, especially for small teeth. One advantage is shown as follows: A gear with 19 teeth of 2 DP has a pitch diameter of $19/2 = 9\frac{1}{2}$ in., by equation 8·4. A gear with 19 teeth of 2-in. circular pitch has a pitch diameter of $\dfrac{19 \times 2}{\pi} = 12.095 +$ in., by equation 8·3. The calculation is easier in the former case, and the result is always a rational number.

Generally, circular pitch is used in specifying large cast teeth and some worm-gear sizes, whereas the diametral pitch is used for all other gears.

8·6 Fundamental law of gearing Gears are generally of circular section and give a constant angular velocity ratio of the connected shafts, though noncircular gears are employed where a variable-speed ratio is desired. Whether circular or noncircular, **the teeth should be so shaped as to produce pure rolling contact of the pitch surfaces.** The pitch surfaces, therefore, comply with the laws governing bodies having pure rolling contact as discussed in Chapter 7. Thus the point of contact of two pitch profiles, known as the **pitch point,** is the common instant center for the two gears.

If gear teeth are so designed as to give pure rolling of the pitch surfaces, then the following law of gear teeth will result:

The common normal to the tooth surfaces at the point of contact must always pass through the pitch point.

This law is proved as follows: Figure 8·16 shows two teeth making contact at *C*.

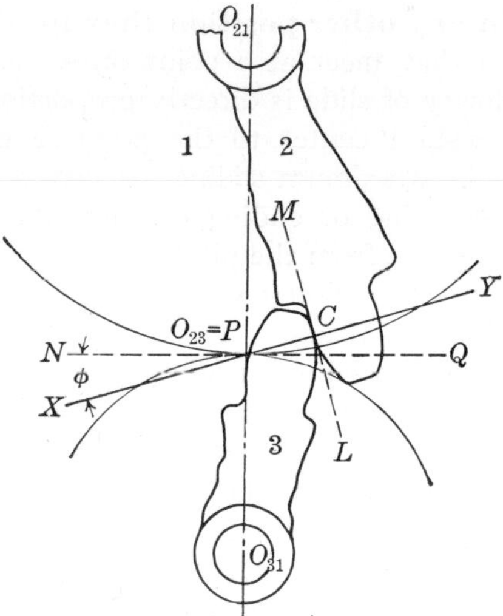

FIG. 8·16.

Considering these gears, 2 and 3, and the frame 1 in which they rotate as three bodies having relative motion, it is possible to locate their instant centers. Thus it is obvious that O_{21} and O_{31} lie at the centers of rotation of bodies 2 and 3 respectively.

The mating teeth are two bodies in sliding contact at C; hence the relative motion at the contact point is along the common tangent LM; otherwise the teeth would tend to interfere or break contact. Therefore the instant center O_{23} must lie along the common normal XY. By Kennedy's theorem it must also lie on a line through O_{21} and O_{31}. Hence the instant center O_{23} must coincide with point P.

For rolling bodies, by Art. 7·2:

$$\frac{\omega_{2/1}}{\omega_{3/1}} = \frac{O_{31}O_{23}}{O_{21}O_{23}}$$

If this ratio is to be kept constant, then the center O_{23}, or point P, must maintain a fixed position; and P must be the point of contact of the two pitch surfaces, or the pitch point.

8·7 Sliding action of teeth When a pair of teeth touch at the pitch point, they have, for the instant, pure rolling contact, since the point of contact is then the instant center for the gears. It follows that **in any other position they must slide** on one another, for then they meet at a point other than the instant center. The velocity of slide is directly proportional to the distance from the instant center to the point of contact at the instant considered. Maximum sliding velocity occurs when the teeth are just beginning or ending contact, the contact point being then most remote from the pitch point.

The magnitude of the sliding velocity at any instant can be determined graphically.

In Fig. 8·17 is illustrated a pair of conjugate teeth in contact at point C. The common normal at C is the line XY passing through the pitch point P. The linear velocity of C, considered as a point on gear 2, is represented by the vector **CE** perpendicular to the radius CA. The velocity of C, considered as a point on gear 3, is represented by the vector **CD**, perpendicular to CB. Vectors **CE** and **CD** may be resolved into components parallel and perpendicular to the normal XY. The components of each parallel to XY must be the same normal velocity $\mathbf{v}_n$, as the teeth maintain contact and yet do not cut into one another. The algebraic difference of the velocity components perpendicular to

XY, namely, **DE** = **FD** − **FE**, represents the rate of slide of one surface on the other, or the sliding velocity. Inspection of the figure will show that this velocity decreases as the contact point moves toward point P and increases when it moves in the reverse direction.

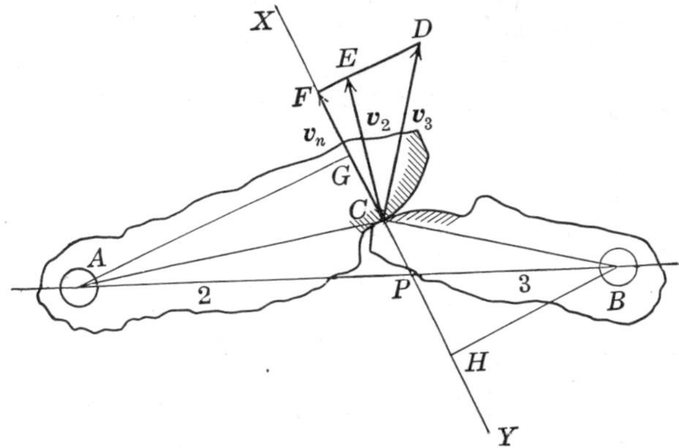

FIG. 8·17. Sliding Action of Gear Teeth.

8·8 Tooth Profiles In general, it is possible to select teeth of any shape for a gear and then proceed to form teeth on a second gear which will be conjugate to the first, satisfying the fundamental law of gearing. If the shape is selected at random, and a conjugate tooth of theoretically correct shape is formed, it does not necessarily follow that the use of such teeth would be practical.

Aside from the fact that the working faces of gear teeth must comply with the fundamental law of Art. 8·6, several other requirements have influenced the choice of standard gear-tooth forms and proportions.

(*a*) The teeth must be capable of accurate production at low cost.

(*b*) The tooth form should have good wearing qualities. Low rubbing speeds and close approach to surface contact are both favorable. The latter condition is secured when mating teeth both have large radii of curvature. Tooth pressures are distributed over a wider strip of surface when large radii are used. The result is a lower intensity of pressure and less wear.

(*c*) The tooth form must result in good "beam strength." In service, forces act on the tooth side tending to bend it like a beam.

Beam strength is greatest in a short tooth with a wide section across the root.

(*d*) The arc of contact must be at least equal to the circular pitch; otherwise there would not be continuous contact between gears. An arc of action greater than 1.4 times the circular pitch is generally held to be good design. Below this limit, noisy action of the gears is likely unless they are very accurately cut.

(*e*) Interchangeability of a series of gears of the same pitch is generally desirable, although it is unnecessary with many gears which are of the "special purpose" type.

The cycloid was used extensively for tooth profiles, but it has been largely replaced by the involute.

CYCLOIDAL TEETH

8·9 The cycloid is a curve described by a point on a circle which rolls internally or externally on another circle. The rolling circle is known as the **describing circle,** and in forming a gear-tooth outline it is rolled internally and externally on the pitch circle. Internal rolling forms the flank of the tooth; external rolling forms the face. In Fig. 8·18, *a* and *b* are the pitch circles of the gears. Circle *c* is rolled internally on *a*, the point *P* on *c* describing the curve *PB*, which forms the flank of the tooth on the upper wheel. Circle *c* is then rolled externally on *b*, point *P* on *c* now tracing out the curve *PC*, which is the face of the tooth on the lower gear.

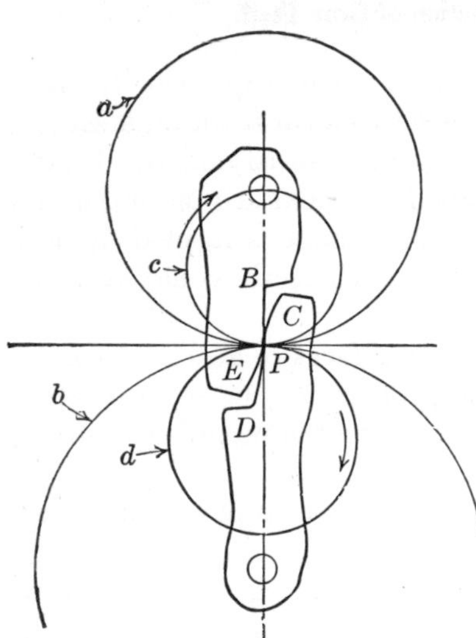

Fig. 8·18.

Likewise, curves *PD* and *PE* are obtained by rolling circle *d* internally on *b* and externally on *a*. These curves form, respectively, the flank of the lower and the face of the upper gears. The two describing circles, *c* and *d*, need not be the same size, but the same circle must be used for the face of one tooth and the flank of the other which works with it. In practice, to secure interchangeable gears, the same radius of describing circles is used throughout a series.

When the diameter of the describing circle is one-half the pitch diameter of the gear, the flank of the tooth becomes a radial straight line (see *PB*, Fig. 8·18), and the tooth is somewhat narrow at the root. If the describing circle is made larger, the tooth becomes still narrower at the root and lacks strength; also, if the describing circle is made large enough, it may be impossible to cut the gear teeth by use of a milling cutter, because the space between the teeth widens out from the pitch circle toward the root.

8·10 Proof of fundamental law for cycloids To show that cycloids may be used for gear teeth, it is necessary to prove that the normal at the point of contact of a pair of these curves, generated by the same describing circle, will always pass through the pitch point.

In Fig. 8·19, *a* and *b* are the pitch circles for a pair of spur gears, and *P* is the pitch point.

Cycloid *RM*, attached to *b*, is traced out by a point on the describing circle *c* when it rolls externally on *b*. Cycloid *RL*, attached to *a*, is described by a point on *c* as the latter circle rolls internally on *a*.

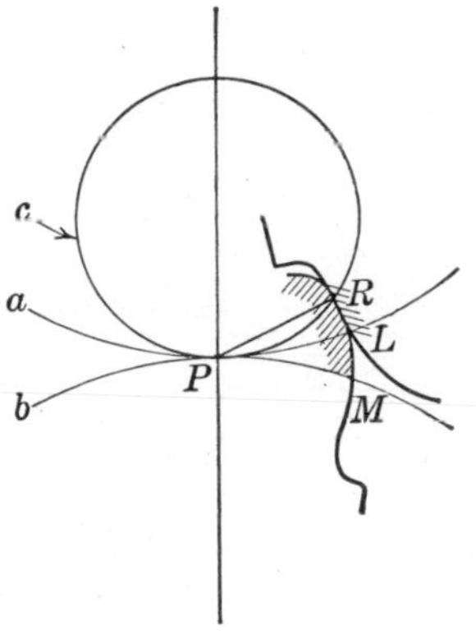

FIG. 8·19.

The two cycloids are in contact at *R* for the position of the gears shown in the figure. Point *P*, where *a*, *b*, and *c* are in contact, is the common instant center for the relative motions of these bodies, since at this point they have no relative motion. Therefore, *R*, as a point on *c*, has a motion to both *a* and *b* in a direction at right angles to *PR*. Consequently, *PR* must be the common normal to the curves *RL* and *RM*.

These statements are true for any position of the teeth, and *P* is a fixed point; therefore, the cycloids have the required property for gear-tooth profiles, as expressed by the law of Art. 8·6.

8·11 Path of contact In Fig. 8·20 a pair of mating-tooth profiles of the cycloidal type are shown in three positions: namely, a_1b_1, when just making contact; a_2b_2, when in contact at the pitch point; and a_3b_3, when about to break contact. The path

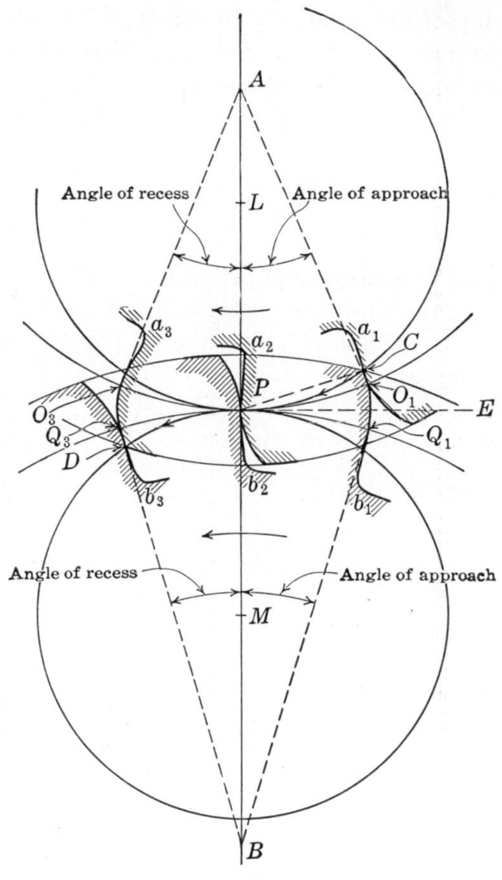

FIG. 8·20.

of the point of contact must be the curve CPD, which is composed of portions of the circumference of the two generating circles with centers at L and M.

Point C where contact begins is located at the intersection of the upper describing circle with the addendum circle of the gear, whereas D is found at the intersection of the lower describing circle with the addendum circle of the pinion. Lengthening the teeth evidently moves the points C and D further apart and increases the period of contact. By joining CP and drawing PE perpendicular to the line of centers AB, we find the pressure angle CPE for that position of the gears in which C is the contact point. This angle diminishes to zero as the point of contact approaches P and thereafter increases to another maximum at D. The cycloidal form of tooth is therefore characterized by a variable-pressure angle, which is zero when the teeth make contact at the pitch point.

8·12 Angles of approach and recess Referring once more to Fig. 8·20, since a_1, a_2, and a_3 represent three positions of the same tooth on the pinion, O_1, P, and O_3 are three positions of one point on the tooth, and the angles O_1AP and PAO_3 show the corresponding angular movements of the pinion. These angles are, respectively, the **approach** and **recess** angles for the pinion. From points Q_1PQ_3, the angles Q_1BP of approach and PBQ_3 of recess for the gear are found.

The **arcs of action** are the same for both gear and pinion and are equal to either O_1O_3 or Q_1Q_3.

INVOLUTE TEETH

8·13 Involutes In general, if we take a straight line and roll it on a curve of any form, a point on this line will describe a path known as an involute of the curve. For nearly all gears with involute teeth, the involute is formed by rolling the straight line on a circle. The only exceptions to this are gears of noncircular shape. When we speak of an involute in connection with gears, without further definition, the involute of a circle is meant. This circle is commonly called the **base circle** of the involute.

8·14 Mechanical development of involute curves A device, shown in Fig. 8·21, illustrates a method of development of conjugate involute curves. A cord CD, $C'D'$ is wrapped around two circular disks 2 and 3. Disk 2 has a transparent plate m attached to its face, and 3 has a similar plate n fastened to it. If 2 is rotated, the cord, acting as a belt, will drive 3 in the opposite sense. A point R on the cord will then trace out on the plate m an involute KL, and on the plate n an involute MN.

By keeping 2 and 3 in fixed position and then cutting the cord at R, the same curves may be traced out by the two ends when the loose portions are wound on and unwound from the disks to which they are attached.

Considering the above methods for obtaining the curves, two facts are evident: (*a*) that the point of contact always lies along the line of the cord: namely, along CD; (*b*) that, since the tangent portion of the cord is always swinging with reference to a disk about its point of tangency with the disk in question, the relative motion is always perpendicular to the tangent line. CD is therefore the common normal to the two curves at all times, and it crosses the line of centers at a fixed point P. Moreover, the line of action makes a constant angle DPQ with a normal PQ to the line of centers of the disks. For the given disk diameters and center distance, this angle DPQ is the pressure angle.

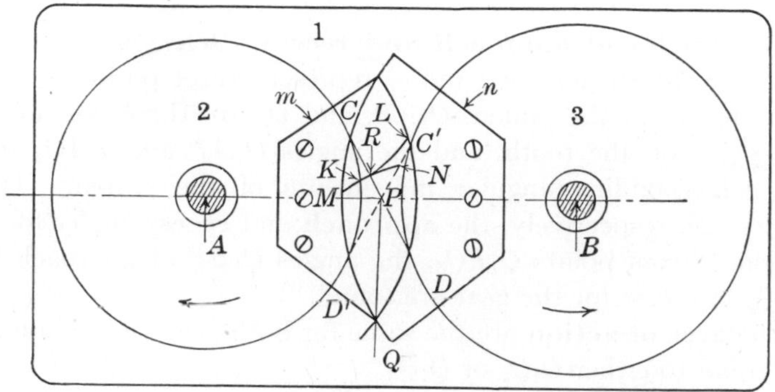

FIG. 8·21.

To summarize, it has been shown that involute profiles:

(*a*) Follow the requirements of the fundamental law of gearing.

(*b*) Have a straight-line path of contact.

(*c*) Have a constant pressure angle for a given installation.

Point P (Fig. 8·21) where the line CD intersects the line of centers is the instant center of wheels 2 and 3. Hence the angular-velocity ratio ω_2/ω_3 is equal to BP/AP, and P is therefore the pitch point by Art. 8·6.

When the pitch point P and the pressure angle are known, the base circles may be found, since they are tangent to the line CD, whose position is fixed by these data.

Tooth action In Fig. 8·22 is shown a pair of involute gear profiles in three positions. We shall assume that the gears rotate as indicated by the arrows on the diagram. At a_1, b_1 the teeth are just beginning to make contact; at a_2, b_2 the teeth are in contact at the pitch point; and at a_3, b_3 contact is just about to cease.

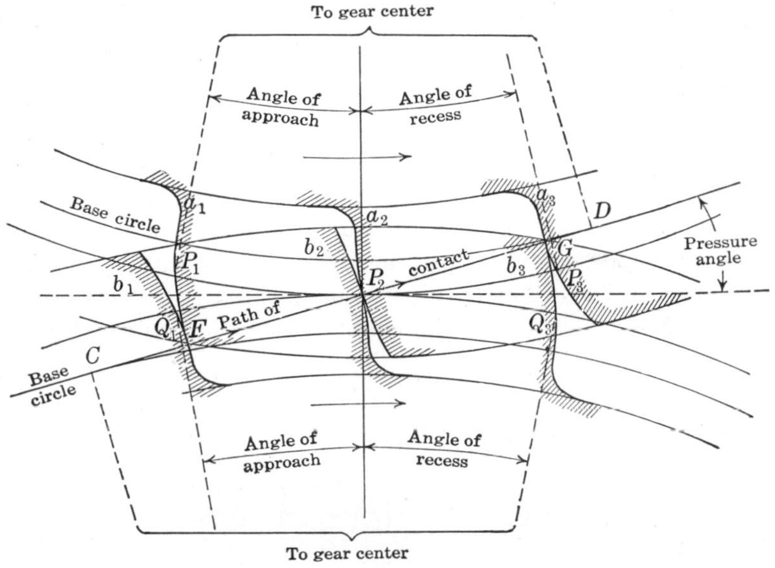

FIG. 8·22 Involute Tooth Action.

The point of contact must lie at all times on the straight line CD, this line being the common tangent to the base circles. Contact begins at F and ends at G. P_1, P_2, P_3 on the pitch circle of the upper gear are corresponding positions of one point on this gear, whereas Q_1, P_2, Q_3 are similarly the three positions occupied by one point on the lower gear. Since the pitch circles have pure rolling contact, arcs $P_1P_2P_3$ and $Q_1P_2Q_3$ are of equal length. Also, by definition, P_1P_2 is the arc of approach and P_2P_3 the arc of recess for the upper gear, while arcs Q_1P_2 and P_2Q_3 have the same values for the lower gear. The angles of approach and recess for the former are found by joining P_1 and P_3 to the center of the upper gear as indicated on the figure. A similar construction locates the angles of approach and recess for the lower gear. The pressure angle is noted in the figure.

It may be observed that points F and G, where contact begins and ends, are found at the intersections of the addendum circles with the pressure line CD. F and G are located between points C and D in this figure, but with other tooth proportions and numbers of teeth on the gears it may happen that either F or G or both F and G fall on line CD produced. This leads to interference of the teeth (see Art. 8·19).

8·15 Properties of the involute Involute curves have an outstanding advantage over cycloidal or other curves which might be employed for working profiles in circular gears: namely, that **the center-to-center distance can be changed without destroying conjugate tooth action or changing the angular velocity ratio.** That is, a pair of these curves will comply with the fundamental law, no matter what the center-to-center distance may be. Proof of this statement can be seen by reference to Fig. 8·23. When the gear centers A and B are moved farther

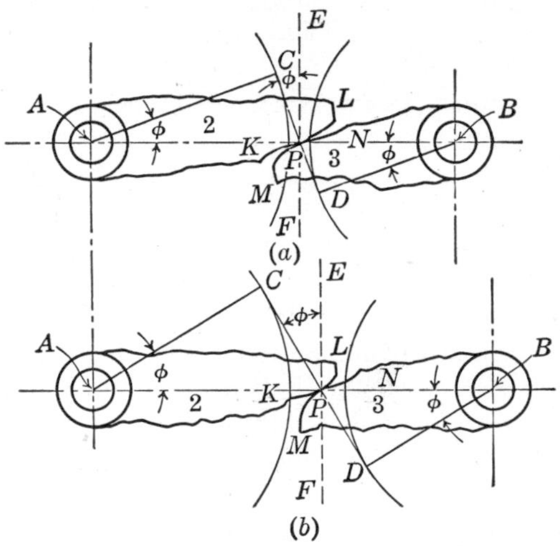

FIG. 8·23.

apart, the common tangent CD to the base circles will incline at a greater angle with EF, hence increasing the pressure angle ϕ. As before, the common tangent will cross the line of centers at a fixed point because we are still dealing with contact of involutes. The pitch radii AP and BP become larger, but the ratio of BP

to AP remains unchanged as the base circle diameters are unchanged, and hence the speed ratio is unaltered. For, by reference to the figure,

$$AP = AC/\cos\phi \quad \text{and} \quad BP = BD/\cos\phi$$

Now

$$\frac{\omega_2}{\omega_3} = \frac{BP}{AP} = \frac{BD/\cos\phi}{AC/\cos\phi} = \frac{BD}{AC}$$

But BD/AC is independent of the center-to-center distance. **The speed ratio is in consequence dependent only on the relative diameters of the base circles** and does not change when the center-to-center distance is varied.

A second deduction that can be made from Fig. 8·23 is that **an involute profile has neither pitch circle nor pressure angle peculiar to itself, but obtains both of these by virtue of its location in regard to a second involute.** Thus a gear which meshes with two others may have two pitch circles of different diameters, each corresponding to one contact. Improved tooth forms are sometimes made possible by taking advantage of this property.

A third deduction easily made from the geometry of Fig. 8·23 is that **the diameter of the base circle is equal to the diameter of the pitch circle multiplied by the cosine of the pressure angle.**

Since a rack can be regarded as a portion of a gear wheel with infinite pitch radius, the base circle for the rack involute is also of infinite radius, and the involute itself is a straight line. Rack teeth on the involute system therefore have straight working surfaces. Figure 8·24 illustrates a rack tooth of this kind. The angle between the side of a tooth and the perpendicular to the pitch line is equal to the pressure angle.

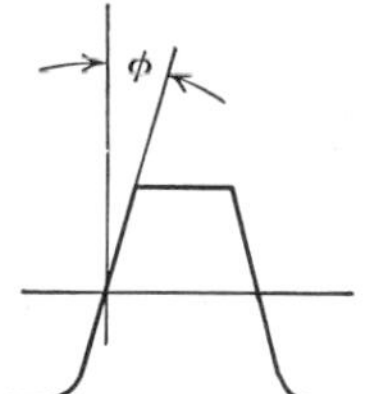

FIG. 8·24 Involute Rack Tooth.

A pressure angle of $14\frac{1}{2}°$ was early adopted for involute gear teeth. The sine of this angle is approximately 0.25, which simplifies the work of laying out the teeth. The same pressure angle is still extensively used since it usually results in satisfactory tooth forms. Larger angles, up to 25°, are not uncommon, particularly where small tooth numbers are required.

The following conclusions * concerning the involute and its application to gear teeth may be summarized as:

1. The involute is wholly determined by the diameter of its base circle.
2. An involute moving about its base-circle center imparts rotative motion to a contacting involute in the exact ratio of the diameters of their respective base circles.
3. An involute has no pressure angle until brought into intimate contact with another involute or a rack.
4. The pressure angle is determined by the center distance and the base-circle diameters.
5. The pressure angle once established is constant for a fixed center distance.
6. An involute has no pitch diameter until brought into intimate contact with another involute or a rack.
7. The pitch diameter of an involute contacting another involute is determined by the center distance and the ratio.
8. The pressure angle of an involute contacting a rack is unchanged when the base-circle center is moved toward or away from the rack.
9. The pitch diameter of an involute contacting a rack is unchanged when the base circle is moved toward or away from the rack.
10. The pitch-line position of an engaging involute and rack is determined by the intersection of the line of action and a line passing through the base-circle center and perpendicular to the direction of rack travel.

The student should satisfy himself as to the validity of the foregoing statements and thoroughly understand them, as they form the basis of involute-gear design.

Practical advantages resulting from the use of involute profiles may be summarized as follows:

(*a*) Involute gears may be mounted with small initial inaccuracies in the center-to-center distance, or this distance may change as the result of bearing wear, tooth contact still complying with the fundamental gear-tooth law.

(*b*) Involute gears may be used for applications such as driving rolls in steel mills, where the center-to-center distance constantly varies.

(*c*) The working surface of the involute rack is of the simplest possible form: a plane. This reduces to a minimum the difficulty of producing accurate conjugate teeth—a manufacturing advantage.

* Taken with permission from "The Involute Curve and Involute Gearing," 6th Ed., 1950, published by The Fellows Gear Shaper Company.

(*d*) Where the teeth are cut by formed milling cutters, the number of cutters needed in covering the range from the smallest pinion to rack is less than would be necessary for cycloidal profiles. This is due to the slow change in tooth curvature as the tooth numbers are increased.

The main disadvantage of involute teeth lies in the fact that interference is obtained with pinions having small tooth numbers, but this may be eliminated by varying the heights of the addendum and dedendum of the mating teeth.

8·16 Production of gear teeth Before continuing the discussion of spur-gear profiles, it is desirable to consider the manner in which the teeth are produced.

One of the earliest processes was to sand-**cast** the gear and teeth. This method is still used for slow-speed gears which are to be exposed to the weather. The tooth surfaces are sure to be rusted and corroded so that initial inaccuracies can have little effect on the action.

The second method of producing the surfaces is by **milling** out the space between the teeth. A milling cutter having a cutting shape the same as the space between the teeth (see Fig. 8·25) is fed across the blank, and the blank then indexed for the next cut.

FIG. 8·25 Formed Milling Cutter.

An examination of the figures in this chapter showing gears having different numbers of teeth in mesh discloses that the shape of the teeth varies with the number of teeth in the gear, even though the pitch is constant. This may be verified by reviewing the method of generating cycloids as given in Art. 8·9, or that used to generate involutes given in Art. 8·14. As an extreme case, an involute rack tooth has straight sides. This is of importance since the strength of the tooth is a function of its shape. Since the shape of the tooth varies with the number of teeth in the gear, a different milling cutter should be used for each gear size, even though the pitch remains constant. Actually cutters are used over a range of tooth numbers, a typical example of this being shown in Table 8·1 for one tooth system. Each cutter is correct for the smallest number in the range and somewhat in error for the higher numbers. However, errors introduced in this

TABLE 8·1

Composite tooth milling cutters

Standard $14\frac{1}{2}$° system

Cutter Number	Tooth Numbers	Cutter Number	Tooth Numbers
1	135 to rack	5	21 to 22
$1\frac{1}{2}$	80 to 134	$5\frac{1}{2}$	19 to 20
2	55 to 79	6	17 to 18
$2\frac{1}{2}$	42 to 54	$6\frac{1}{2}$	15 to 16
3	35 to 41	7	14
$3\frac{1}{2}$	30 to 34	$7\frac{1}{2}$	13
4	26 to 29	8	12
$4\frac{1}{2}$	23 to 25		

way can be partially corrected for by slightly varying the depth of cut in the blank. As it is difficult to attain high standards of accuracy in the teeth cut by formed cutters, this type is most satisfactory when the loads and speeds are moderate.

For high-speed accurate gears the **generating** principle is now used almost entirely. If a rack or gear having teeth of desired shape is used as a cutter, it is possible to form teeth on a blank which will be conjugate. The process whereby the teeth are formed on the second gear might be carried out as follows: Suppose the blank to be made of a plastic material. The gear and blank are mounted on shafts and run together so that the pitch surfaces have the same linear velocity. Teeth are thus "rolled in" the surface of the soft blank. These teeth will have the correct outline. "Generating" processes of gear cutting, often used in commercial production, are carried out along similar lines. For example, in the Fellows gear shaper, the cutting tool takes the form of a gear wheel and is reciprocated across the blank (see Fig. 8·26). Between strokes the cutter and blank are both rotated slightly, the relative motion being equivalent to the rolling of the pitch surfaces. The resulting teeth will have

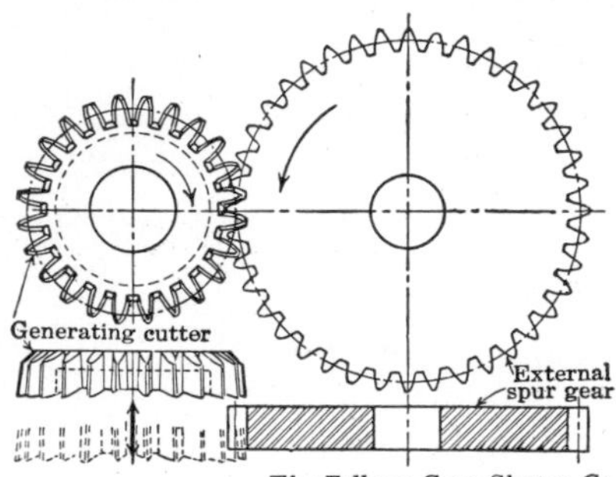

FIG. 8·26 Generating a Spur Gear with a Gear Shaper Cutter.

the same form as obtained by the "rolling-in" process described previously without requiring the use of a plastic blank.

A simple device which will draw a gear tooth of proper form to work with a rack tooth of any selected shape is shown in Fig. 8·27. This also serves to illustrate the principle of operation of spur-gear-tooth generators which use a rack-tooth cutter. A frame A has a slot on its upper side in which the rack B slides.

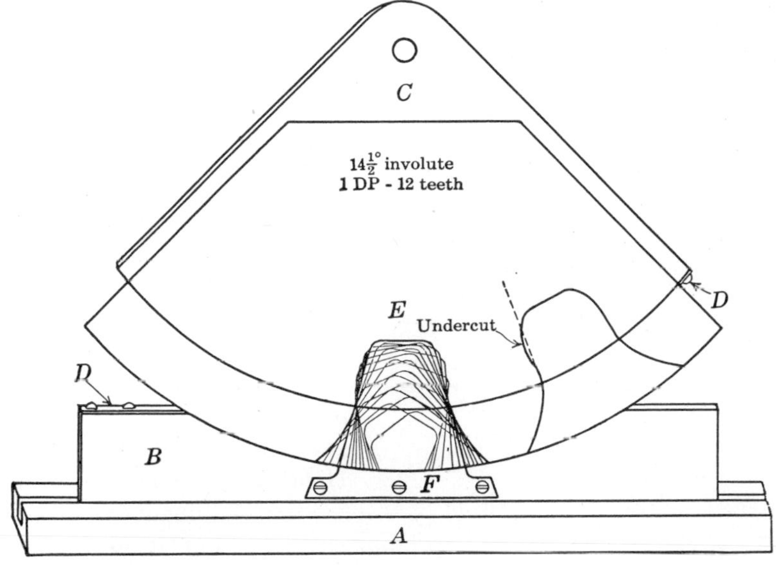

Fig. 8·27.

The frame also has a vertical bar in the rear, not visible, which carries a pivot about which the pitch-surface sector C swings. Parts B and C are connected by means of a flexible steel strip D so as to cause B to have rolling contact with C. The tooth is generated on a paper sector E which is pinned to the face of C. The rack tooth F is preferably made of Celluloid or other transparent material. The tooth form is determined by moving the rack along by small displacements and in each position drawing the outline of the rack tooth on the paper sector. The tooth profile is the tangent curve or envelope of the rack-tooth outlines.

The tooth form shown in the figure is that for a twelve-tooth pinion of $14\frac{1}{2}°$ full-depth involute type. The standard rack tooth has been lengthened by an amount $0.157/P_d$, in order to provide clearance at the root of the pinion tooth. Considerable undercutting is noticeable, part of the involute between base and pitch circle being removed as well as the material lower on the flank. This gives a short arc of action which is characteristic of the $14\frac{1}{2}°$ involute full-depth tooth when the tooth numbers are small.

The rack-type cutting tool is quite satisfactory since its sides are straight, hence are easily made accurate, and can be easily reground. The outstanding advantage of the generating method is that the same cutter can be used to form gears with any number of teeth, and with greater accuracy than in methods in which the tooth profile must be ground on the cutter. If the cutter is made to reciprocate across the blank at an angle, a helical gear will result.

The Barber-Coleman Co.

FIG. 8·28 Hobbing a Helical Gear.

A second method of generating teeth is with the use of a **hob**. As noted in Art. 8·2, a worm is really a helical gear with a large helix angle. Hence a worm may be used to generate teeth on a spur or helical gear by slotting or "gashing" it to form cutting edges, hardening, and grinding it to provide clearance back of the cutting edges. The hob and blank are then mounted on arbors (see Fig. 8·28), and both are driven so that their relative motion is similar to that of a worm and worm wheel. By varying the angle at which the worm is set relative to the blank, spur or helical gears of any desired helix angle may be generated. During the cutting process the hob is slowly fed across the blank as both are rotating.

After the teeth have been cut, they may be finished by shaving, burnishing, grinding, or lapping.

8·17 Construction of involute teeth As pointed out in Art. 8·14, the involute can be thought of as the path traced out by the end of a string which is unwound from a cylinder, the motion being, of course, in a plane perpendicular to the cylinder axis. The length of the unwound or tangent portion of the string is, in any position, equal to the length of the arc on the base circle from which it was unwrapped. Putting it another way, the tangent to the base circle from any point on an involute is equal in length to the arc from the point of tangency to the starting point of the curve. We make use of this property in constructing the curve. In Fig. 8·29 we shall suppose that a is the base circle and that we wish to draw an involute to pass through a given point A.

From A draw AB, tangent to circle a. Obtain an arc BC equal in length to AB. This can be done approximately in the drafting room by dividing AB into any number of equal parts, four being used in the diagram. Taking one of these equal lengths on our dividers, we step off four divisions, starting from B around the arc, thus locating C. The point C is the inner end of the involute curve. To obtain a point between A and C, take point D on the arc at the second division, draw DF tangent at D, and step off on it two lengths with the same divider setting as before, obtaining E, a third point on the involute. Other points are found in a similar manner. A smooth curve is finally drawn through the points, and this forms the required involute. The curve is continued outward until the addendum circle is reached.

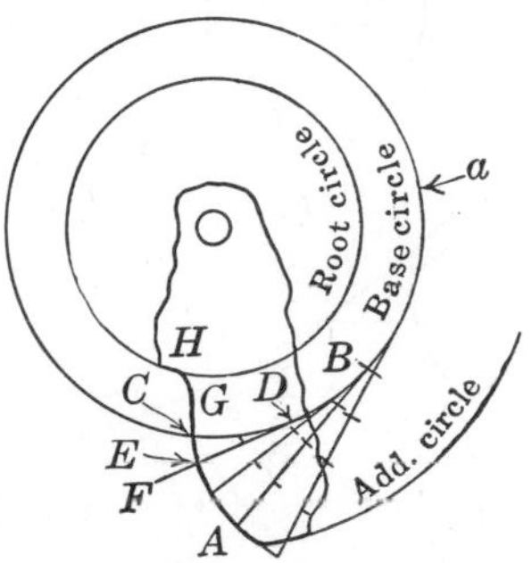

FIG. 8·29.

In completing the tooth flank, the curve must be extended inside the base circle to allow space for the mating tooth, plus a clearance. As the involute cannot penetrate the base circle, a different form is necessary for this portion. Generally we use a radial straight line CG, terminating in a small circular arc GH at the junction with the root circle. Contact does not take place on CG: its outline is determined by considerations of strength and ease of production. The purpose of the arc GH is to strengthen the tooth at the root, and it should be of as large radius as possible without causing interference with the teeth on the mating gear.

The profile shown in Fig. 8·29 is the type generally used with a formed milling cutter. As noted in Art. 8·16, this type of profile has been largely replaced by those based on the generating process. They may be drawn by the method and with the apparatus illustrated in Fig. 8·27. In many instances such apparatus is not available, so that the procedure shown in Fig. 8·30 may be employed. The principle is the same as that of Fig. 8·27, except that the pitch line of the rack is rolled on the pitch circle of the gear. A thin Celluloid template is used in the construction.*

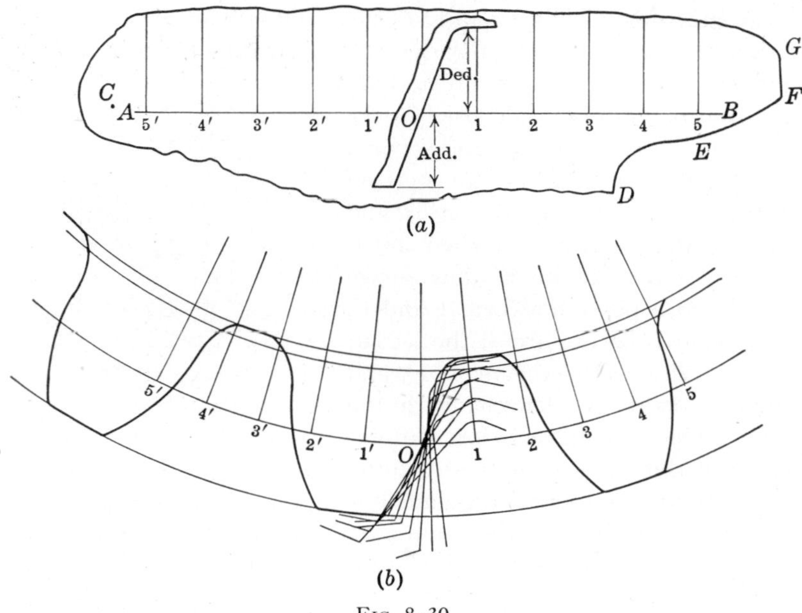

Fig. 8·30.

A line AB, representing the pitch line of the rack is scratched on the surface of the Celluloid (see Fig. 8·30a). One side of the rack tooth is drawn by laying off a line inclined with AB at an angle equal to 90° minus the pressure angle, at about the midpoint of line AB. This is extended upward an amount equal to the dedendum, and downward an amount equal to the addendum of the gear. After drawing in a fillet at the top, a portion of the Celluloid adjacent to this shape is cut away with a sharp knife. Starting from point O, equal distances are stepped off

* Dietzgen, Matte Surface, Acetate Film No. 157M-5 is suggested for this purpose.

along line AB. These are numbered 1, 2, etc., and 1′, 2′, etc., and perpendiculars to line AB are scratched on the Celluloid at these points.

The pitch, addendum, and dedendum circles of the gear are now drawn, and an arbitrary point O through which the tooth profile is to pass is selected on the pitch circle as shown in Fig. 8·30*b*. Distances equal to those used on the template are then stepped off along the pitch circle and labeled as 1, 2, etc., and 1′, 2′, etc. Short radial lines are drawn from these points. The Celluloid template is placed on the gear drawing so that points O coincide, and the normal line on the template lies on the radial line on the drawing, i.e., so that the pitch line of the rack is tangent to the pitch circle of the gear. The shape of the rack-tooth side is then traced on the drawing. The template is then moved so that point 1 coincides with point 1 on the gear drawing, and the normal line of the template coincides with the radial line of the gear drawing. The shape of the rack tooth is again traced on the drawing. This process is repeated for all the points, both primed and unprimed, until the rack tooth leaves the gear-tooth profile. The successive positions of the rack-tooth profile form an envelope which defines the shape of the gear tooth.

Then the celluloid template is placed so that a point C coincides with the gear center, and the profile of the gear tooth $DEFG$, found from the envelope previously obtained, is cut on the template. The tooth thickness and circular pitch, measured along the pitch circle, are laid off from point O. The profile may now be drawn through these points by swinging the template about point C, which coincides with the gear center, and tracing the curve $DEFG$. To obtain the curve for the opposite side of the tooth, the template is merely placed on its face with point C again coinciding with the gear center.

The purpose of this construction is to investigate the amount of undercutting of the tooth, if any, and to investigate the strength of the tooth. The latter step is outside the scope of a course on kinematics and is not considered here. The construction shown in Fig. 8·30 is for a spur gear having 16 full-depth teeth, a diametral pitch of 1, and a pressure angle of 20°.

8·18 Standard tooth forms In view of the requirements for gear-tooth forms, four types of teeth have been standardized by the American Standards Association * and the American Gear Manufacturers Association. These are known as:

(*a*) The $14\frac{1}{2}°$ composite system.
(*b*) The $14\frac{1}{2}°$ full-depth involute system.
(*c*) The 20° full-depth involute system.
(*d*) The 20° stub involute system.

Tooth proportions for these systems are given in Table 8·2. It will be noted that the composite, the $14\frac{1}{2}°$ full-depth and the 20° full-depth systems all have teeth of the same proportions. These proportions are exactly the same as those used in the earlier "Brown & Sharpe Standard" system.

TABLE 8·2

Proportions of standard teeth

	$14\frac{1}{2}°$ Composite	$14\frac{1}{2}°$ Full-Depth Involute	20° Full-Depth Involute	20° Stub Involute
Addendum	$\frac{1}{P_d}$	$\frac{1}{P_d}$	$\frac{1}{P_d}$	$\frac{0.8}{P_d}$
Minimum dedendum	$\frac{1.157}{P_d}$	$\frac{1.157}{P_d}$	$\frac{1.157}{P_d}$	$\frac{1}{P_d}$
Whole depth = addendum and dedendum	$\frac{2.157}{P_d}$	$\frac{2.157}{P_d}$	$\frac{2.157}{P_d}$	$\frac{1.8}{P_d}$
Clearance	$\frac{0.157}{P_d}$	$\frac{0.157}{P_d}$	$\frac{0.157}{P_d}$	$\frac{0.2}{P_d}$

P_d = diametral pitch.

Each of the four standard systems has gear teeth which are conjugate to a "basic rack." The basic rack is therefore the standard or reference form in cutting teeth on gears of any size.

The $14\frac{1}{2}°$ composite system This system was developed from the cycloidal tooth forms which were at one time in universal use. Approximately the middle third of the profile has an involute shape while the remainder is cycloidal in nature. These teeth are usually produced by formed milling cutters, although they may also be made by hobbing. Table 8·1 gives the cutter size required for various numbers of teeth in these

* "American Standard Spur Gear Tooth Form," American Standard B6.1-1932.

gears. Although possessing some of the advantages of the involute system, it avoids interference and undercutting of small pinions which are characteristic of that system when standard tooth proportions are used.

The $14\frac{1}{2}°$ full-depth involute system The basic rack of this system is shown in Fig. 8·31. It is straight sided, except for

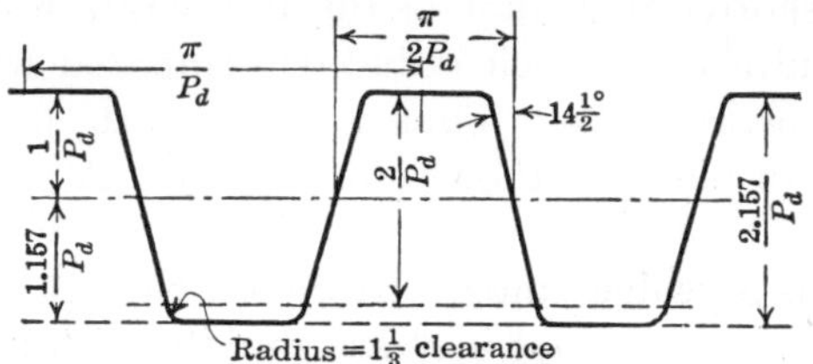

Fig. 8·31.

a fillet arc at the root to strengthen the tooth. This system is widely used for generated teeth, although the present tendency is to standardize on the 20° full-depth involute system.

Interference occurs when the tooth number of equal pinions is less than 23 or when a rack engages a gear with less than 32 teeth. Undercutting is therefore necessary with small tooth numbers, and as a result the arc of action then becomes unsatisfactory. For example, with two 12-toothed pinions the arc of contact is 0.034 times the circular pitch, an unusable value. The desired arc of action, namely, 1.4 times the circular pitch, is obtainable with gears having 20, 21, or 22 teeth, the exact value depending on the tooth number of the mating gear. This type of tooth is very satisfactory, however, when tooth numbers are large.

20° full-depth involute system The basic rack (Fig. 8·32) is the same as that for the $14\frac{1}{2}°$ system except for the pressure angle. The use of a larger pressure angle leads to better tooth

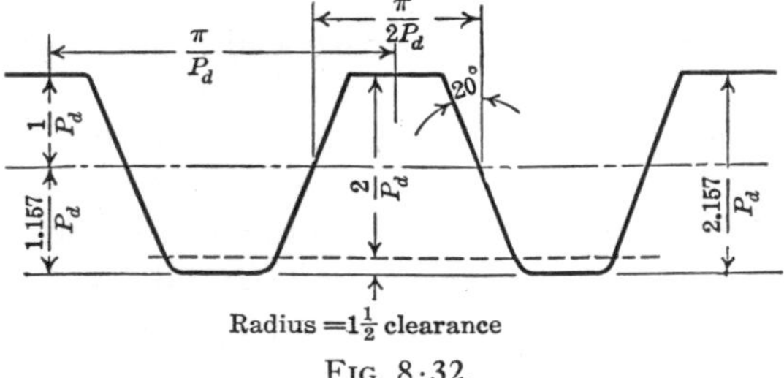

Fig. 8·32.

action when the tooth numbers are small. For example, an arc of action equal to 1.4 times the circular pitch is obtainable with equal gears of 14 teeth. In this respect, this type of tooth gives the best results of any of the four standard types with low tooth numbers. It is used for generated teeth.

20° stub involute system The basic rack has a tooth about 18 per cent shorter than that of the full-depth systems. Interference difficulties are much reduced, compared with the other standard involute teeth. Thus a stub-tooth rack will mesh with a 17-tooth pinion without interference. A pair of 12-tooth pinions gives an arc of action equal to 1.19 times the circular pitch. This is a usable value. However, the arc of action does not increase rapidly with the increase in tooth numbers, a 27–30 combination having a value only 1.35 times the circular pitch. On this account accuracy of cutting is especially important if noisy action is to be avoided.

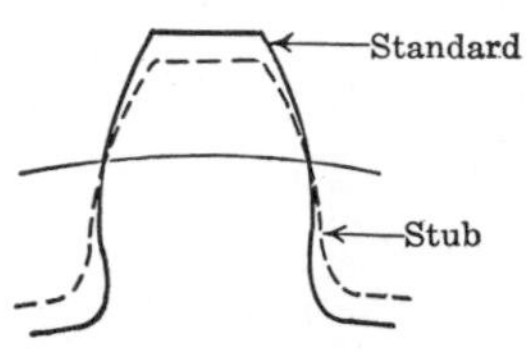

FIG. 8·33 Comparison of 20° Stub Tooth and Full-Depth $14\frac{1}{2}$° Tooth.

Figure 8·33 shows a graphical comparison of 20° stub and $14\frac{1}{2}$° full-depth teeth of the same pitch for gears of equal size. The short tooth with wide root, characteristic of the former, gives high beam strength and accounts for its suitability for use where subject to heavy shocks.

Although the 20° stub tooth was designed primarily for use in automobile transmissions, it has been supplanted by the 20° full-depth tooth. Full-depth teeth are longer and hence have a longer arc of action, and more teeth are in contact to carry the load. Although the beam strength of each tooth is less, the greater number of teeth in action permits higher loads to be carried.

8·19 Interference Gear teeth are said to interfere when they tend to overlap or cut into the mating teeth. Under certain conditions interference will take place when formed cutter teeth have true involute profiles. Such a situation is illustrated in Fig. 8·34. Here point G, the intersection of the addendum circle of the lower gear with the contact line CD, falls on CD produced. This condition is always accompanied by interference, as may be seen from the following discussion.

Considering the two gears in Fig. 8·34 to turn in the sense indicated by the arrows, and observing a pair of teeth, 2, 3, initially in contact at *F*, we note that the contact point traces out the line *FD* as the gears revolve. Contact does not cease at *D*, but thereafter it must take place between the involute portion *LM* of the tooth on the lower gear and the radial flank *QR*, inside the base circle of the upper gear. This flank is not of

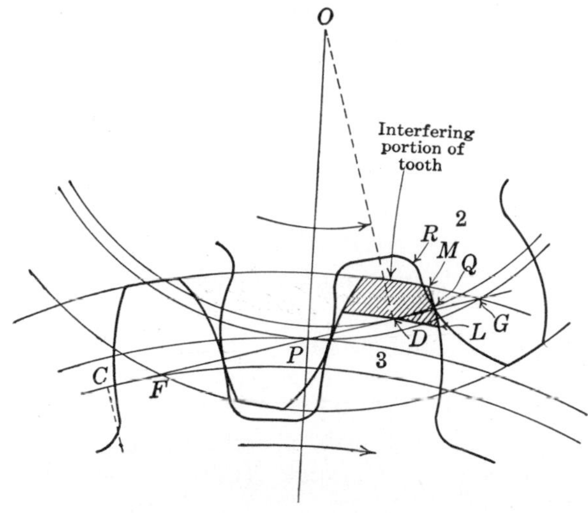

FIG. 8·34.

involute form, since the involute cannot be extended inside the base circle. If *QR* is a radial flat profile, overlapping or "interference" will take place. Modification of the tooth forms is then necessary. The following methods are possible:

(*a*) The height of the teeth may be reduced.

(*b*) The pressure angle may be increased.

(*c*) The radial flank of the pinion may be cut back. This is technically known as "undercutting" when any material is removed inside a radial line from the junction point of the involute and its base circle. (See Fig. 8·27.)

(*d*) The face of the gear tooth may be relieved.

Methods *a* and *b* are employed in conjunction with each other in stub-tooth gears.

Method *c* is often undesirable for two reasons: first that it weakens the pinion tooth, and second that it may result in a short arc of action, since excessive undercutting may remove the inner portion of the involute as well as the straight part of the tooth below the base circle.

Method *d* is satisfactory where manufacturing methods permit of its use.

8·20 Maximum radius of addendum circle without interference It is evident that the interference encountered in the gears of Fig. 8·34 could be eliminated if the teeth on the lower gear were shortened by cutting off the portion which is shown cross-hatched. This tooth would then have its **maximum addendum without interference.** In Fig. 8·35, gears with centers at A and B have pressure angle ϕ and base circle radii AC and BD. The maximum addenda radii that can be used for the gears without introducing interference are, respectively, AD and CB, the circles then passing through the interference points C and D.

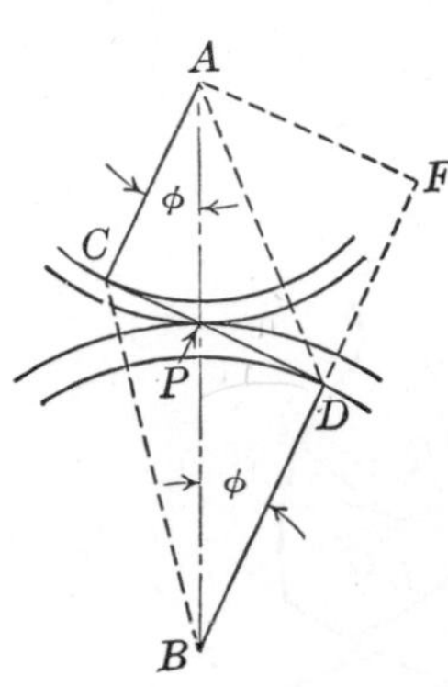

FIG. 8·35.

Since AC and BD are perpendicular to CD, we may complete a rectangle $ACDF$. From the geometry of the figure,

$$CD = AF = AB \sin \phi$$

$$AD = \sqrt{(AC)^2 + (CD)^2} = \sqrt{(AC)^2 + (AB)^2 \times \sin^2 \phi}$$

$$BC = \sqrt{(BD)^2 + (CD)^2} = \sqrt{(BD)^2 + (AB)^2 \times \sin^2 \phi}$$

Hence the maximum addendum radius without interference is equal to $\sqrt{(\text{base circle radius})^2 + (\text{center distance})^2 \times \sin^2 \phi}$.

Example Find the maximum addendum radius of two equal gears having 23 teeth of 1 diametral pitch, the pressure angle being $14\frac{1}{2}°$.

Solution

Pitch radius of gear	$= 11.5$ in.
Base circle radius	$= 11.5 \times \cos 14\frac{1}{2}°$
	$= 11.5 \times 0.968 = 11.13$
Center-to-center distance	$= 23$ in.

Hence,

Maximum addendum radius

$$= \sqrt{(11.13)^2 + (23)^2 \times (0.2504)^2} = 12.5 \text{ in.}$$

Therefore the maximum addendum = 12.5 − 11.5 = 1.0 in. If the gears are made with full-depth proportions, the addendum is $1/P_d = 1$ in. This indicates that two equal gears having 23 teeth of standard $14\frac{1}{2}°$ involute form will not interfere but are just at the limit of addendum length. Gears with fewer teeth will show interference.

8·21 Long and short addendum teeth When there are few teeth on the pinion, a flexible system of long and short addendum teeth is used to produce a stronger tooth and reduce or eliminate the amount of undercut resulting from a generating method of cutting the teeth. If formed milling cutters are used, interference may be avoided or reduced by this system. It also increases the length of the path of contact, making for smoother action and a lowered load per tooth.

The height of the addendum of the pinion is made longer than the standard value of $1/P_d$, and the addendum of the gear tooth is decreased a corresponding amount. The over-all height of the tooth, the pitch diameters, and the base-circle diameters of the gears are unchanged. The pressure angle is well standardized at 20°.

This system is only used when undercuts or a large base-circle diameter limit the length of the line of contact. The amount of the change in the length of the addendums is flexible and designed to just overcome the difficulties mentioned. Generally this change is in the neighborhood of 50 per cent of the standard height. If the teeth are cut by the generating process (as the vast majority are), the tooth proportions may be varied by changing the position of the rack-cutting tool or hob, without the use of special tools.

When the pinion teeth are undercut (as in Fig. 8·36*a*) the last point of involute action along the line of contact is at point *D*, where the line is tangent to the base circle, and the portion of the gear tooth beyond the dashed line is ineffective. By varying the heights of the addendums as shown in part *b* of Fig. 8·36, involute action will take place over the entire line of con-

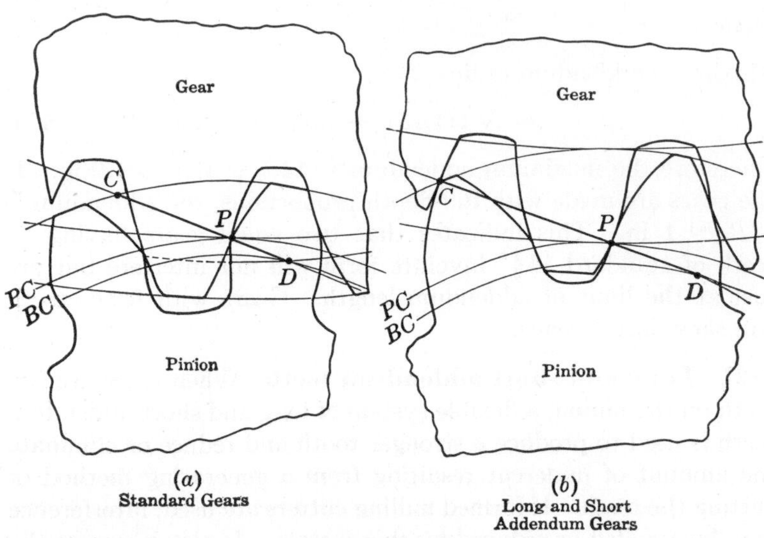

FIG. 8·36.

tact, and it may be noted that this line *CD* is considerably longer than in part *a*. Also the pinion teeth in part *b* are wider at the base and therefore stronger, and the undercut is eliminated.

8·22 Internal or annular gears One of these gears is shown in Fig. 8·37, the teeth being cut internally on a hollow cylinder or ring by either the generating principle with a shaper or with formed milling cutters. It is the opposite of an external gear in that the teeth are pointed inward rather than away from the center. Figure 8·37 illustrates the nomenclature, and from it the method of design may be deduced.

The drive is more compact than when external gears with the same velocity ratio are used. They are frequently used when the driving and driven members must rotate in the same direction and it is not convenient to employ an idler.

8·23 Problem To outline the general procedure of laying out a gear and pinion, consider the following specifications:

	Gear	Pinion
Number of teeth, N	24	12
Diametral pitch, P_d	2	2
$14\frac{1}{2}°$ full-depth involute teeth		

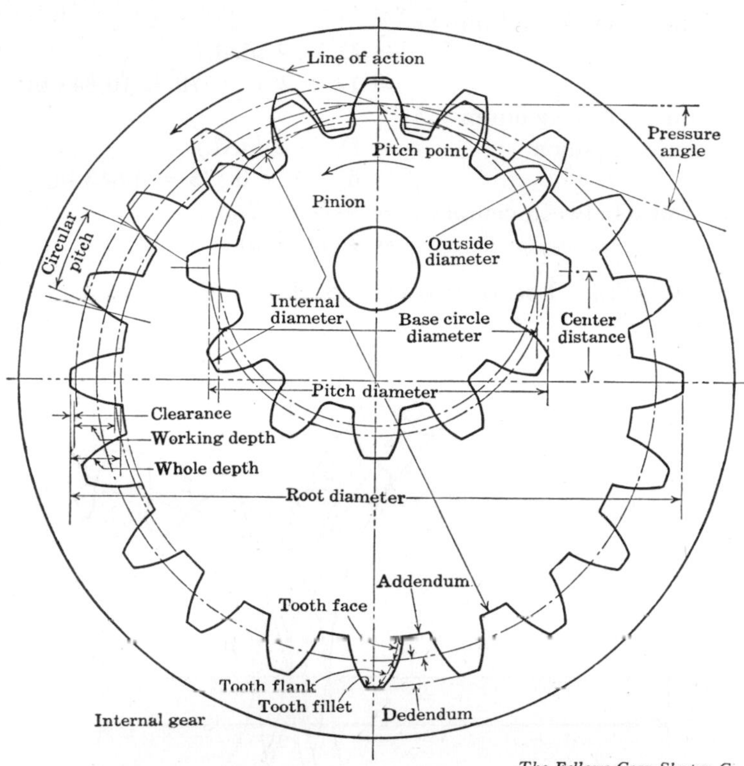

The Fellows Gear Shaper Co.

FIG. 8·37. Nomenclature of an Internal Gear Meshing with a Pinion.

From the preceding data, we make the following calculations:

Pitch diameter of gear $= N_g/P_d = 24/2 = 12$ in.
Pitch diameter of pinion $= N_p/P_d = 12/2 = 6$ in.
Addendum $= 1/P_d = 1/2 = 0.5$ in.
Dedendum $= 1.157/P_d = 1.157/2$
$= 0.578$ in.

Diameter of addendum circle of gear $= D_g + 2$ (add.)
$= 12 + 2 \times 0.5 = 13$ in.

Diameter of addendum circle of pinion $= D_p + 2$ (add.)
$= 6 + 2 \times 0.5 = 7$ in.

Diameter of dedendum circle of gear $= D_g - 2\text{ (ded.)}$
$= 12 - 2 \times 0.578 = 10.843$ in.

Diameter of dedendum circle of pinion $= D_p - 2\text{ (ded.)}$
$= 6 - 2 \times 0.578 = 4.843$ in.

Distance between centers $= \frac{1}{2}(D_g + D_p)$
$= \frac{1}{2}(12 + 6) = 9$ in.

Construction. Locate two centers A and B, 9 in. apart (see Fig. 8·38).

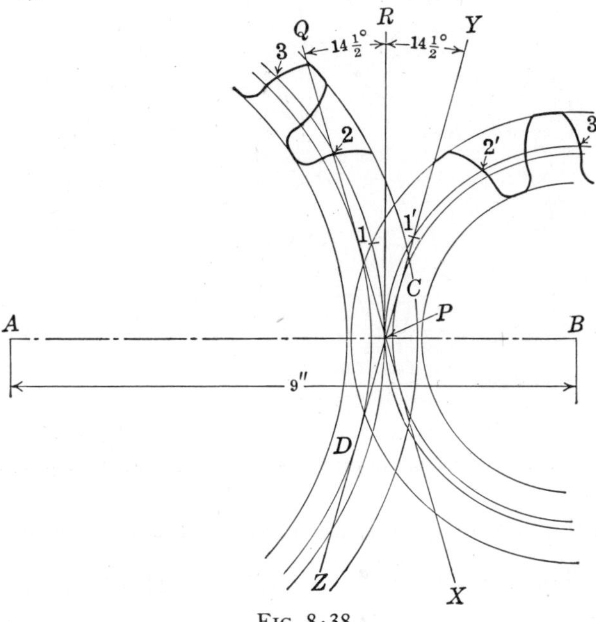

Fig. 8·38.

Using A and B as centers draw two pitch circles touching at the pitch point P. Also draw the addendum and dedendum circles for the gear and pinion.

Draw PR perpendicular to the line AB at the pitch point.

Lay off $14\frac{1}{2}°$ angles from PR, thus obtaining QX and YZ.

With centers A and B, draw circles tangent to QX and YZ. These are the base circles for the involutes.

Starting from the pitch point P, divide the pitch circumference of the gear into 24 equal parts. This can be done by calculating the angles subtended at the center by the pitch arcs and then laying off the arcs from the angles. In the case of the gear, the pitch arc subtends an angle of $360°/24 = 15°$. Points 1, 2, 3, etc., are thus found. The pitch circumference of the pinion is similarly divided into 12 equal parts, and we thus obtain points 1′, 2′, 3′, etc.

We now have the base circles for the involutes and one point on each involute where it crosses the pitch circle. Selecting any one of the points on the gear pitch circle, we now draw in the tooth outline by either of the methods described in Art. 8·17, depending upon the manner in which the tooth is to be produced. We duplicate this curve through each of the other points 1, 2, 3, etc., taking care that each of these curves has the same angular relationship to a radius through its starting point. Assuming there is no backlash, we may bisect the distances 0–1, 1–2, 2–3, etc. Through the points of bisection we draw the curves already obtained but in the reversed position, so as to form the other sides of the teeth. The same construction is employed for the pinion teeth.

8·24 Helical gears with parallel axes (Fig. 8·3) A plain spur gear may ideally be converted into a helical gear by first cutting it into an infinite number of thin sections by passing through it planes perpendicular to the axis of rotation, and then rotating these sections so that each is somewhat in advance of the adjacent one. By making these increments of angular advance of equal value, elements of the resultant teeth become true helices.

Thus, if a plane is passed through a pair of meshing helical gears with parallel axes, it will cut a profile from each gear, corresponding to one of the infinite steps, entirely similar to that of a pair of meshing spur gears. Hence the action, interference possibilities, etc., discussed previously for spur gears apply equally well for helical gears with parallel axes. Any of the tooth systems discussed for spur gears may also be used for helical gears.

The superiority of the helical gear in quiet action has already been pointed out. Noise in gear operation is due to the impact of the teeth as they come into contact. In the plain spur gear, contact takes place along the whole length of a tooth at the same instant, whereas in the helical gear contact begins at one end of the tooth and progresses to the other during an appreciable time interval. The latter action produces little noise.

The **helix angle** is the angle between the helical-pitch element and a parallel to the axis of revolution. The helix angle is usually made so large that there is always one pair of teeth in contact at the pitch point. This means that the helix must advance at least one pitch in the width of the gear. Too large an angle causes excessive end thrust. In practice the angle ranges from 15 to 30°.

8·25 Normal pitch A helix, such as AB, Fig. 8·39, drawn on the pitch surface, normal to the tooth elements, is known as the normal helix. The circular pitches of a mating pair of helical gears must be equal when these pitches are measured along the normal helix. This pitch we call the **normal circular pitch.** The **normal diametral pitch** is found by dividing the normal circular pitch into π, diametral and circular pitch therefore bearing the same relationship to one another as in common spur gears.

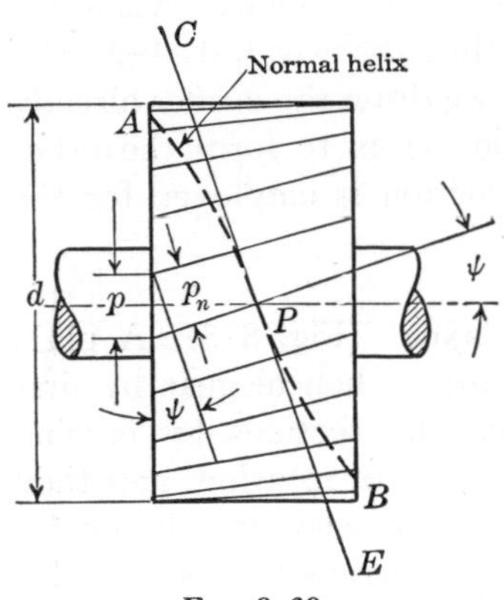

FIG. 8·39.

The normal pitch is the pitch of the cutter that must be used to produce the teeth. Thus a helical gear of 10 normal diametral pitch and a plain spur gear of 10 diametral pitch are both produced by the use of 10 DP cutters. The same shape of cutter cannot be used in both cases if the two gears referred to have equal numbers of teeth. This is due to the fact that the profiles on the normal plane are different.

We shall next proceed to express the relationship among normal pitch, pitch diameter, and numbers of teeth for the helical gear. In Fig. 8·39, let

p_n = normal circular pitch
p = circular pitch measured in the plane of revolution (known as the circumferential pitch)

P_n = normal diametral pitch ($= \pi/p_n$)
N = number of teeth
d = pitch diameter
ψ = helix angle

From the figure,

$$p = \frac{p_n}{\cos \psi} \tag{8·6}$$

$$\text{The pitch circumference} = \pi d = pN = \frac{p_n N}{\cos \psi} = \frac{\pi N}{P_n \cos \psi}$$

or

$$d = \frac{N}{P_n \cos \psi} \tag{8·7}$$

HELICAL GEARS WITH CROSSED AXES

8·26 Tooth action. Sliding velocity Gears of this type are used to connect nonintersecting shafts at any angle (see Fig. 8·9). Whether a helical gear has parallel or crossed axes depends entirely upon its use, and the same method of design and manufacture applies to both. Helical gears with crossed axes are suitable only for light loads as they have point contact and consequently high contact stresses. For heavy loads, spiral-bevel or hypoid gears are more satisfactory.

When the axes of the shafts are parallel, the pitch surfaces touch along a line. When they are not parallel, the pitch surfaces touch at a point (Fig. 8·10), and consequently the teeth have point contact. Two cylinders cannot have pure rolling contact unless their axes are parallel. Thus in helical gears with crossed axes there is a component of slide in the direction of the tooth elements.

In Fig. 8·40, 2 and 3 represent the pitch surfaces of a pair of helical gears with axes AB and CD, crossed at an angle θ. The pitch cylinders make contact at a point P, and the line LM is the common tangent to the helical tooth elements through P.

Point P, regarded as a point on 2, has a velocity represented by a vector **PQ** ($= \mathbf{v}_2$) perpendicular to AB. Point P considered as a point on 3 has a velocity represented by a vector **PR** ($= \mathbf{v}_3$) at 90° to CD. Vectors **PQ** and **PR** must have a common component **PS** ($= \mathbf{v}_n$) in a direction normal to the common tangent

ML. If this were not true, the teeth would either come out of contact or interfere. The algebraic difference of the components of **PQ** and **PR** in a direction parallel to ML, namely, **QS** plus **SR**, represents the sliding velocity at the pitch surface along the tooth elements.

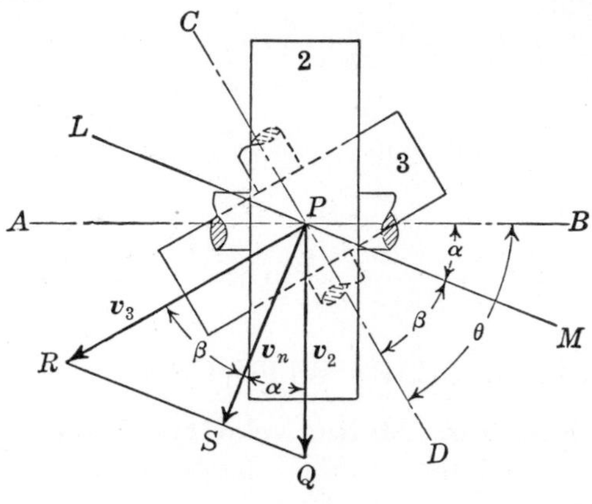

FIG. 8·40.

8·27 Angular velocity ratio The **helix angle** of the teeth is the angle between a tangent to the helix at a point on the pitch surface and a line parallel to the gear axis. In Fig. 8·40, α is the helix angle for the gear 2, and β for the gear 3. Evidently, from the figure,

$$\alpha + \beta = \theta$$

Also, by construction,

$$\text{Angle } SPQ = \alpha \qquad \text{Angle } SPR = \beta$$

and therefore

$$\mathbf{v}_2 \cos\alpha = \mathbf{SP} = \mathbf{v}_3 \cos\beta \quad \text{or} \quad \frac{\mathbf{v}_2}{\mathbf{v}_3} = \frac{\cos\beta}{\cos\alpha}$$

Now,

$$\boldsymbol{\omega}_2 = \frac{\mathbf{v}_2}{r_2} \quad \text{and} \quad \boldsymbol{\omega}_3 = \frac{\mathbf{v}_3}{r_3}$$

Therefore, the angular velocity ratio is

$$\frac{\boldsymbol{\omega}_2}{\boldsymbol{\omega}_3} = \frac{\mathbf{v}_2 r_3}{\mathbf{v}_3 r_2} = \frac{r_3 \cos\beta}{r_2 \cos\alpha} \tag{8·8}$$

It may be noted that the velocity ratio depends not only on the pitch diameters but also on the helix angles of the teeth. With unchanged diameters a different speed ratio can be obtained from a pair of these gears by altering the helix angles.

Equation 8·8 expresses the angular velocity ratio of helical gears in terms of the pitch diameters and helix angles. For two gears 2 and 3,

$$\frac{\omega_2}{\omega_3} = \frac{d_3 \cos \beta}{d_2 \cos \alpha}$$

where α and β are the helix angles.

By equation 8·7,

$$d_3 = \frac{N_3}{P_n \cos \beta} \quad \text{and} \quad d_2 = \frac{N_2}{P_n \cos \alpha}$$

Substituting these values of d_3 and d_2 in the above gives

$$\frac{\omega_2}{\omega_3} = \frac{N_3}{N_2}$$

In helical as in spur gears, therefore, the angular velocities are inversely proportional to the numbers of teeth.

WORM GEARS

8·28 Properties and uses The vast majority of worm gears are used to connect shafts that are perpendicular to each other, although they are not limited to this angle. They may be designed for high reduction ratios with great compactness. Under certain conditions (when the efficiency is less than 50 per cent) the drive is "irreversible"; that is, although the worm can drive the wheel, the wheel cannot drive the worm. This is an advantage in certain applications such as hoists. When properly constructed they will operate with little noise and show good efficiency.

A simple form of worm wheel, illustrated at *a*, Fig. 8·41, is just a helical gear. The pitch surfaces are cylindrical, and the teeth have point contact. It is suitable for light loads only.

Line contact, with a consequent improvement in wearing qualities and load-carrying capacity, is secured in the conventional gear shown at *b*, Fig. 8·41. Here the worm-wheel surface is concaved so as to conform with the worm outline, and the active section is not confined to the central plane.

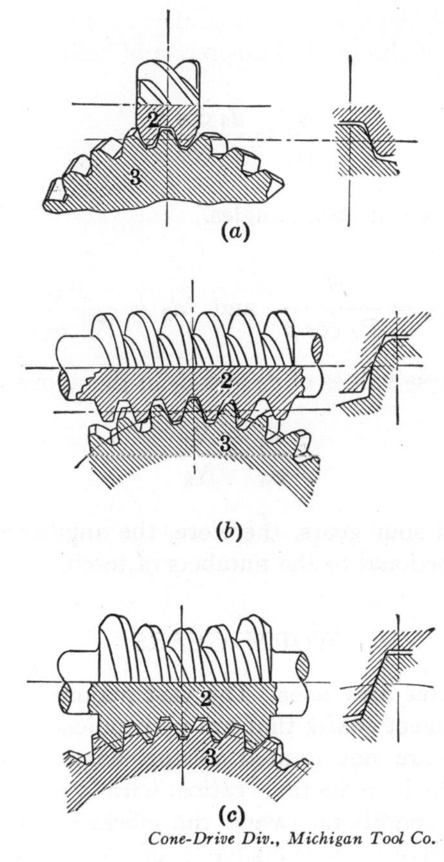

Cone-Drive Div., Michigan Tool Co.

Fig. 8·41.

A special type of worm, which is throated to conform with the worm wheel, as shown in Fig. 8·41*c*, provides a large number of worm teeth in contact with the wheel, thus increasing the load-carrying capacity. Proper action requires that accurate endwise adjustment of the worm be maintained. In the United States it is known as a Cone drive, whereas in England it is called a Hindley worm.

8·29 Worm-gear terms Figure 8·42 illustrates certain worm-gear terms.

The **pitch** of the **worm** is the distance from a point on one thread or tooth to the corresponding point on the next tooth,

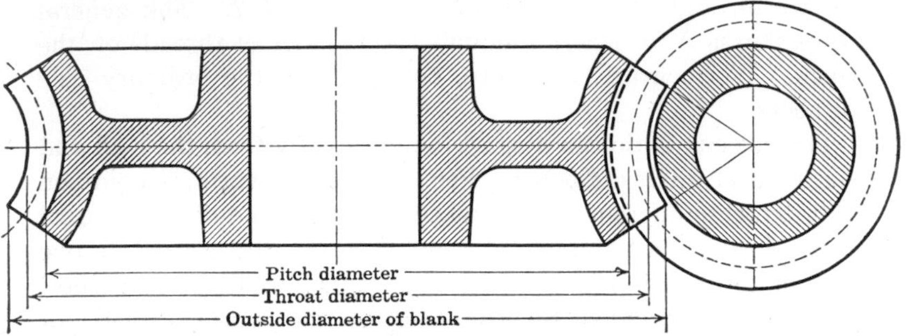

FIG. 8·42 Worm-Gear Terms.

measured in a direction parallel to the axis of revolution. The **pitch** of the **worm wheel** is the distance from a point on one tooth to a similar point on the next tooth, measured on the pitch surface in the plane of revolution.

The **lead** is the distance the worm helix advances along the axis per turn. When a worm is "single threaded," the pitch and lead are equal to one another; when "double threaded," the lead is twice the pitch. In general, where the worm has n threads, the lead is n times the pitch.

Figure 8·43 shows three worms, all having the same circular pitch p, but different leads since they are single-, double- and triple-threaded, respectively.

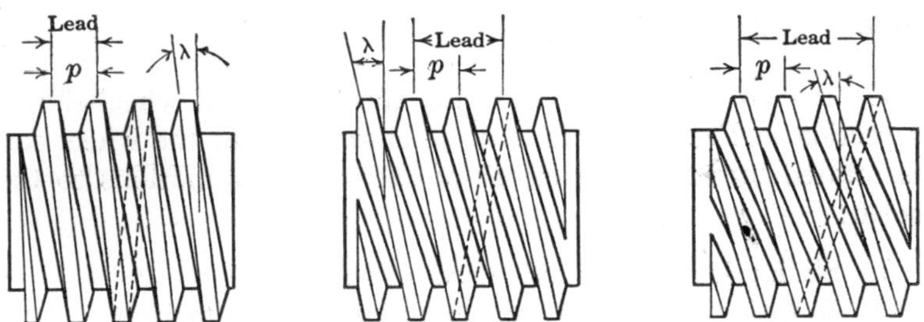

FIG. 8·43 Single-, Double-, and Triple-Threaded Worms.

Velocity ratio When the worm has a single thread, the worm wheel is advanced one tooth per turn of the worm; hence if the worm wheel has N teeth, the worm must make N revolutions per turn of the worm wheel. The velocity ratio of worm to wheel is therefore $N/1$, or N. When the worm is double threaded, the worm wheel is advanced two teeth per turn of the worm, and the velocity ratio becomes $N/2$. The general expression is N/n, where n equals the number of threads on the worm. Worm gears, therefore, comply with the ordinary rule for gears.

The velocity ratio can also be found directly from the lead and worm-wheel pitch diameter. Per turn of the worm, a point on the pitch circumference of the wheel is advanced a distance equal to the lead. The number of revolutions of the worm for one turn of the worm wheel is therefore equal to the worm-wheel circumference divided by the lead of the worm thread, or πd_{ww}/lead. This is the **velocity ratio.**

It should be observed that the velocity ratio is independent of the diameter of the worm. The worm diameter is chosen primarily on the basis of strength, deflection and available hob sizes.

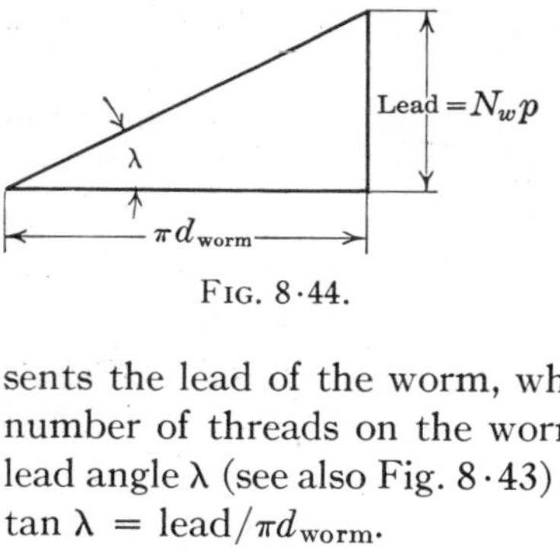

FIG. 8·44.

Figure 8·44 shows the pitch surface of one thread of a worm developed onto a plane. The base of the triangle equals πd_{worm}, the pitch circumference of the worm; whereas the altitude represents the lead of the worm, which is the circular pitch times the number of threads on the worm (i.e., single, double, etc.). The lead angle λ (see also Fig. 8·43) may be found from the expression: $\tan \lambda = \text{lead}/\pi d_{\text{worm}}$.

8·30 Tooth action Considering the worm and wheel shown in section in Fig. 8·41*b*, it may be observed that the wheel can be rotated by imparting either of the following motions to the worm:

(*a*) Sliding it along its axis without rotation.
(*b*) Rotating it about its axis without endwise motion.

The action of the teeth on one another is the same in both *a* and *b*, except that in *b* the teeth have relative sliding along the tooth elements. Both motions require teeth of the same shape.

We may therefore regard the worm as a rack and the worm wheel as a special form of gear meshing with it.

The conditions for constant velocity ratio are satisfied when section 2, Fig. 8·41*b*, found by passing a plane through the worm axis, has the form of a spur rack, and section 3 of the worm wheel in the same plane has the form of a conjugate spur-gear tooth.

The teeth on the worm wheel are cut by the hobbing process, while the threads on the worm are cut by a milling cutter or a lathe tool.

BEVEL GEARS

8·31 General Bevel gears may be used to connect intersecting shafts making any angle with one another. The pitch cones

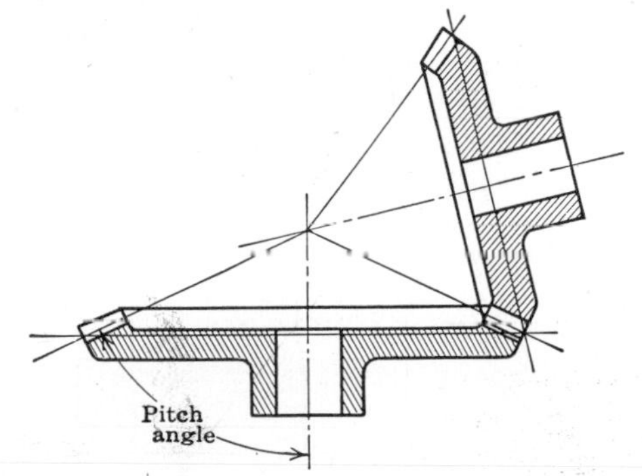

Fig. 8·45 External Bevel Gears.

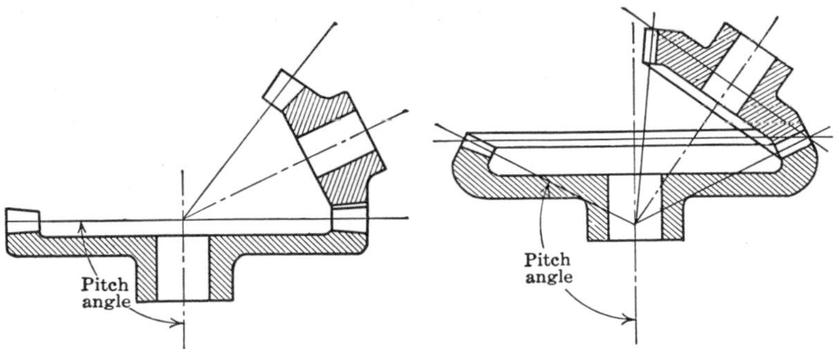

Fig. 8·46 Crown Gear and Pinion. Fig. 8·47 Internal Bevel Gear and Pinion.

of conjugate bevel gears of the ordinary type must have a common apex to secure pure rolling contact of the pitch cones along their elements. All the cone elements are straight and radiate from the common apex.

Bevel gears may be classified according to the size of their pitch angle. Those having a pitch angle less than 90° are known as **external bevels** (Fig. 8·45). In a **crown gear** (Fig. 8·46) the pitch angle of the gear is 90°, and the cone becomes a plane surface. **Internal bevels** (Fig. 8·47) have a pitch angle greater than 90°, the cone being inverted. Equal bevel gears connecting shafts at 90° are known as **miter gears.**

8·32 Bevel-gear terms Figure 8·48 indicates the meanings of the terms **pitch angle, face angle, pitch diameter, out-**

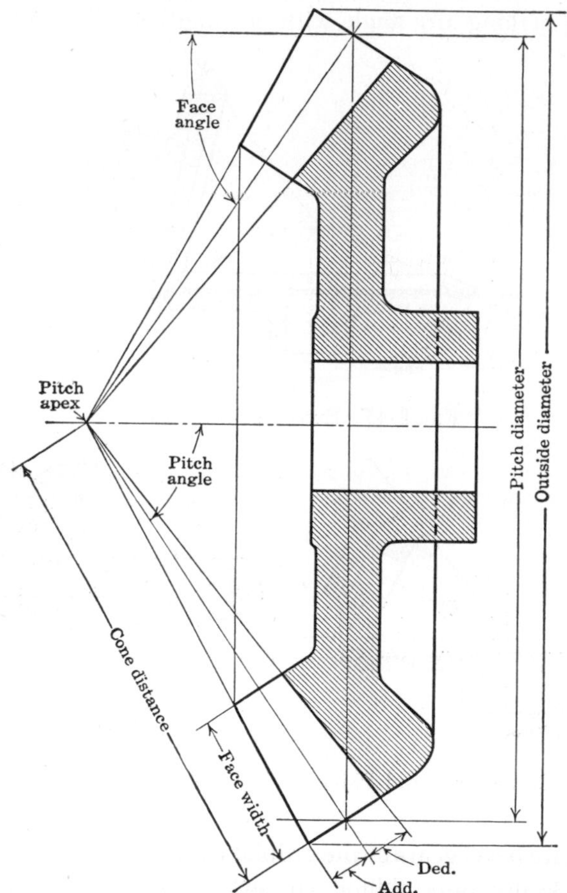

FIG. 8·48 Bevel-Gear Nomenclature.

side diameter, cone distance, face width, and **pitch apex** as applied to bevel gears.

Pitch The **circular pitch** of the teeth in a bevel gear diminishes as we pass along the surface toward the apex of the pitch cone. Strictly speaking, a statement regarding the pitch of a gear of this kind should be supplemented by information as to where it is measured. In accordance with common usage, however, the circular pitch, unless otherwise specified, means the pitch measured at the outer ends of the teeth. The same statement applies to the pitch diameter, diametral pitch, addendum, dedendum, etc.

The **velocity ratio** of bevel gears follows the usual rule for toothed gearing, the angular velocity ratio of a pair being inversely proportional to the numbers of teeth. For a given pitch, the numbers of teeth vary directly as the pitch diameters, that is, as the diameters of the bases of the pitch cones. Diameters are dependent on the pitch angles. When the angle between the gear axes and the velocity ratio are known, the proper pitch angles may be determined by the method of Art. 7·8, which applies to rolling cones.

In view of the fact that different speed ratios require different pitch angles, bevel gears must be designed in pairs for a particular ratio, and interchangeability does not exist to the same extent as in spur gears.

8·33 Spiral angle Bevel-gear teeth may be classified by the angle at which the teeth are curved relative to the elements of the pitch cone as straight, Zerol,* and spiral, as illustrated in Figs. 8·49 and 8·50.

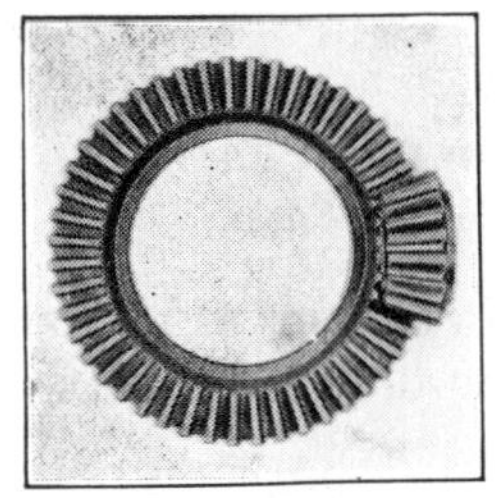

(*a*)

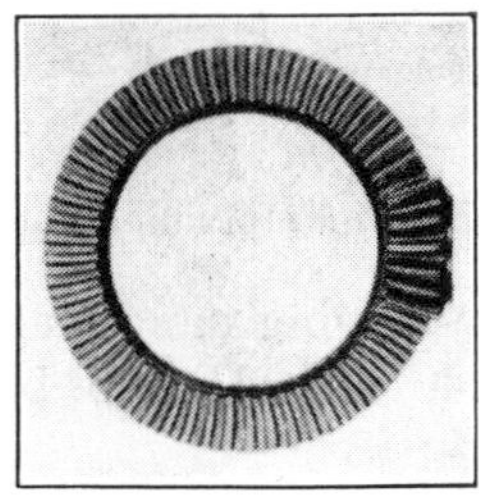

(*b*)

Gleason Works

(*c*)

FIG. 8·49 Straight-Bevel, Zerol, and Spiral-Bevel Gears.

* Name trademarked by Gleason Works, Rochester, N. Y.

The oldest and simplest form of tooth is the **straight tooth,** whose elements make a zero angle with the elements of the pitch cone. It is illustrated in Fig. 8·49*a*. It is generally satisfactory for pitch line speeds below 1000 fpm.

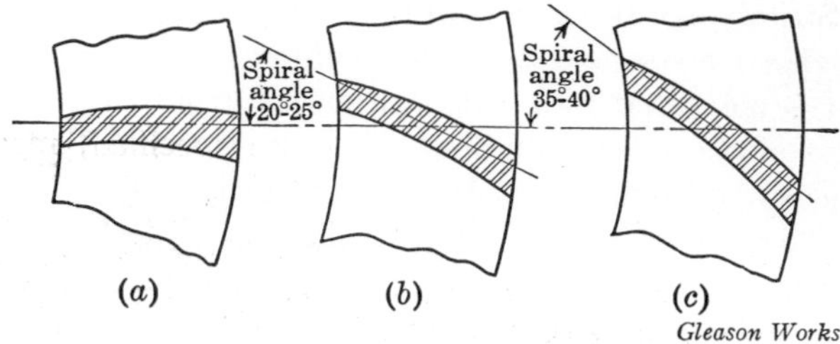

FIG. 8·50 Spiral Angles for Bevel Gears. (*a*) Zerol for low axial thrust. (*b*) Low spiral angle for moderate axial thrust. (*c*) Large spiral angle for high axial thrust.

Zerol gear teeth are curved, but have a zero spiral angle as shown in Figs. 8·49*b* and 8·50*a*. The thrust forces in these gears are the same as for straight bevel gears.

Spiral-bevel gear teeth (Fig. 8·49*c* and 8·50*b* and *c*) have the same advantage over the straight bevels that helical gears have over spur gears. They are used for speeds greater than 1000 fpm and for higher loads. The **face advance** should be at least 1.25 times the circular pitch (see Fig. 8·51) to insure

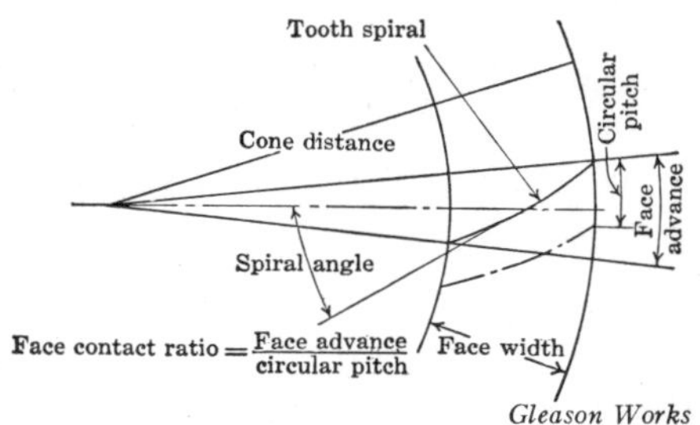

FIG. 8·51 Diagram for Obtaining Face Contact Ratio.

smooth, quiet action by having more teeth in contact at a given time. The spiral angle is generally kept below 40 to 45° as shown in Fig. 8·50*b* and *c*.

Standards have been adopted by the American Gear Manufacturers Association governing the tooth proportions as a function of the velocity ratio. These proportions are selected to eliminate undercutting and to make the pinion and gear teeth of equal strength. The pressure angle is standardized at 20° for these teeth.

8·34 Tooth action Bevel gears have **relative spherical motion,** since all points remain at fixed distances from the common apex of the pitch cones. The teeth should in consequence be laid out on spherical surfaces for the same reason that spur-gear teeth are laid out on plane surfaces. It is convenient to consider a bevel gear to be composed of a large number of thin laminae, each having the form of a portion of a thin, hollow sphere as shown in Fig. 8·52. Each of these laminae makes contact with a corresponding lamina on the mating gear, the tooth form of one member being conjugate to that of the other.

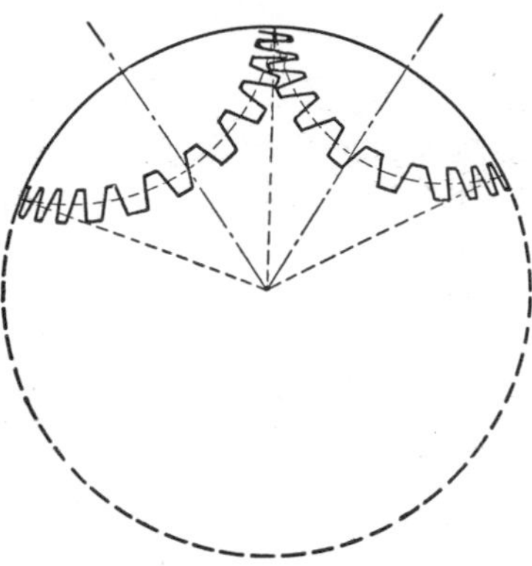

Fig. 8·52.

Figure 8·53 shows the formation of a pair of bevels from a sphere which is intersected by two planes *EC* and *CD*, touching one another at *C*. The pair of circular intersections, represented by lines *EC* and *CD*, may be used as the bases of pitch cones *OEC* and *OCD* for the bevel gears. These gears will revolve about axes *OB* and *OA*, touching one another along cone elements. The surfaces of sections *EMC* and *CND* may be regarded as the exteriors of a pair of mating spherical laminae referred to above. Instead of attempting to find the proper forms of the teeth on these spherical surfaces, which is somewhat difficult, we resort to a simplified method known as **Tredgold's approximation.** By this method we find two cones *BEC* and *ACD*, tangent to the sphere along the circumferences of the circles represented by lines *CD* and *CE*. These are known as the **back cones,** and each has elements which are normal to intersecting elements on the corresponding pitch cones. We observe that these cones very nearly coincide with the spherical surface near their points of tangency around the circles *CD* and *CE*. Teeth laid out on the conical surfaces, using *CD* and *CE* as pitch circles, will closely resemble

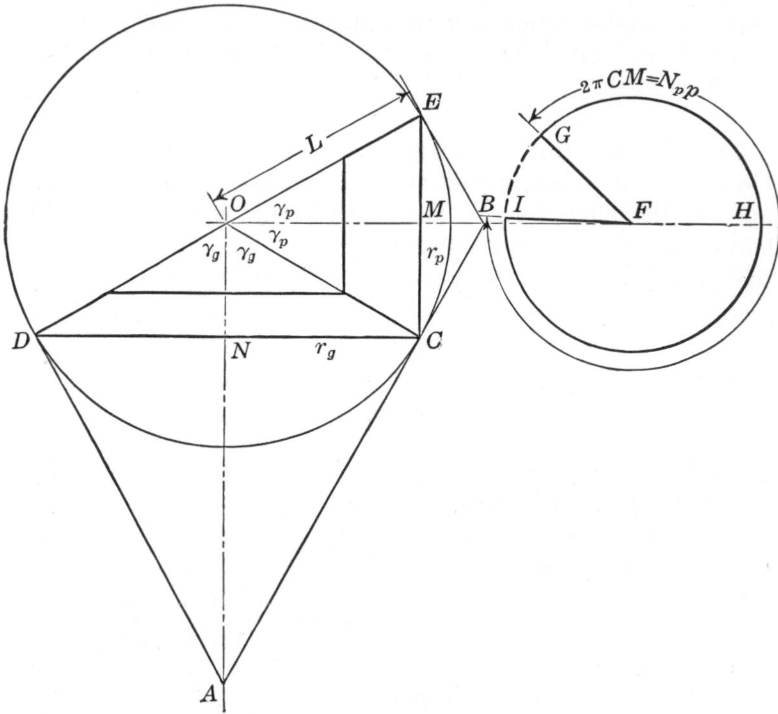

FIG. 8·53.

in their action the teeth of ordinary spur gears. Hence the profiles on the back cones may be made the same as those of spur gears of the same circular pitch, little error being introduced in so doing.

To draw the tooth sections on the back cones, we first develop the cone surfaces and thus reduce the problem to one of drawing spur-gear teeth of known pitch. Hence these equivalent gears can be investigated for their tooth action, undercut, interference, etc., as though they were spur gears. The radius of these equivalent spur gears will be equal to the length of the element of the back cone, or back-cone distance, rather than the pitch radius of the bevel gear. The shape of the teeth will not be that corresponding to the actual number of teeth on the bevel gear, but rather that found by dividing the circumference of the equivalent spur gear by the circular pitch. Generally this is a decimal value.

When the back cone is developed, the sector *FGHI*, having

a radius FG or BE (the **back-cone distance**) results. The length of the arc of this sector equals the pitch circumference of the gear, which may be expressed as either $2\pi CM$ or $N_p p$, where N_p is the actual number of teeth on the pinion and p is the circular pitch of these teeth. If this sector is completed to make a full circle as shown by the dashed arc, that is, made into a complete spur gear rather than a partial one, the circumference will be either $2\pi FG$ or $N_{e_p} p$, where N_{e_p} is the equivalent number of teeth on the pinion. By proportion of the circumference of the full circle to the arc length of the sector we may write

$$\frac{N_{e_p} p}{N_p p} = \frac{2\pi FG}{2\pi CM} \quad \text{or} \quad N_{e_p} = N_p \frac{FG}{CM} \tag{8·9}$$

Stated in words: **The equivalent number of teeth equals the actual number of teeth on the bevel pinion times the back-cone distance divided by the pitch radius of the bevel pinion.** Thus, while the bevel pinion has actually N_p teeth, the shape of those teeth is the same as those on a spur gear having N_{e_p} teeth, the circular pitch being the same in both cases.

If the shafts intersect at right angles, equation 8·9 may be written in other forms. The triangles OMC and CMB are similar as their sides are mutually perpendicular. Calling L the length of the cone element OE or OC, we have, by proportion,

$$\frac{BC}{OC} = \frac{MC}{OM} \quad \text{or} \quad \frac{BC}{L} = \frac{r_p}{r_g}$$

where r_p and r_g are the radii of the pinion and gear, respectively. Hence, the back-cone distance BC equals Lr_p/r_g. The equivalent number of teeth on the pinion is $N_{e_p} = 2\pi BC/p$, and the actual number of teeth is $N_p = 2\pi MC/p = 2\pi r_p/p$. Combining these three equations yields

$$N_{e_p} = \frac{2\pi BC}{p} = \frac{2\pi L r_p}{p r_g} = \frac{N_p L}{r_g} \tag{8·10}$$

It may be noted that r_g/L equals $\cos \gamma_p$, where γ_p is the pitch angle of the pinion. Hence equation 8·10 may be written

$$N_{e_p} = \frac{N_p}{\cos \gamma_p} \tag{8·11}$$

Similar equations may be found for the gear using the other back cone of the pair. For shafts intersecting at right angles, these are

$$N_{e_g} = \frac{N_g L}{r_p} = \frac{N_g}{\cos \gamma_g} \tag{8·12}$$

where γ_g is the pitch angle of the gear.

The back-cone distance may be used as the pitch radius of the equivalent gear and the teeth drawn in the usual manner. This is illustrated in the example that follows.

Example In Fig. 8·54 is shown the tooth development by Tredgold's method for a standard involute gear of 24 teeth, 5 diametral pitch, meshing with an 18-tooth pinion, for connecting two shafts at 90°. The construction is as follows:

The axes *OA* and *OB* are drawn making an angle *AOB* equal to 90°.

Pitch diameter of the gear $= 24/5 = 4.8$ in.
Pitch diameter of the pinion $= 18/5 = 3.6$ in.

Draw *OC* = (3.6/2) in., and set off *CD* = (4.8/2) in. parallel to *OB*. *D* is a point on the pitch cones. Connect *OD*,

Addendum of the teeth $= \frac{1}{5} = 0.2$ in.
Clearance $= 0.1571/5 = 0.0314$ in.

Draw *DE* at 90° to *OD* = 0.2 in.

Draw *DF* at 90° to *OD* = 0.2 in. + 0.0314 in. = 0.2314 in.

Join *OE* and *OF*. These are the addendum and root lines of the gear tooth.

Produce *DFE* to *A* and *B*.

Then *A* is the apex of the back cone for the gear.

With center *A* and radius *AD*, draw arc *DM*.

With center *A* and radii *AE* and *AF*, draw arcs defining tips and roots of teeth on the back cone.

The circular pitch of the teeth $= \pi/5 = 0.628$ in.

Lay off distances *DG*, *GH*, *HM* on the pitch arc, equal to 0.628 in.

Draw involute tooth profiles through *G*, *H*, *M*, etc., as for a spur gear of pitch radius *AD* and 5 DP.

Bisect *DG*, *GH*, *HM*, obtaining points *P*, *Q*, *R*. Draw involute profiles through these points as before, to form the other sides of the teeth.

To draw the tooth development on the back cone at the inside of the gear, use A as center once more and $A'D'$ as radius, and draw the arc $D_1G_1M_1$.

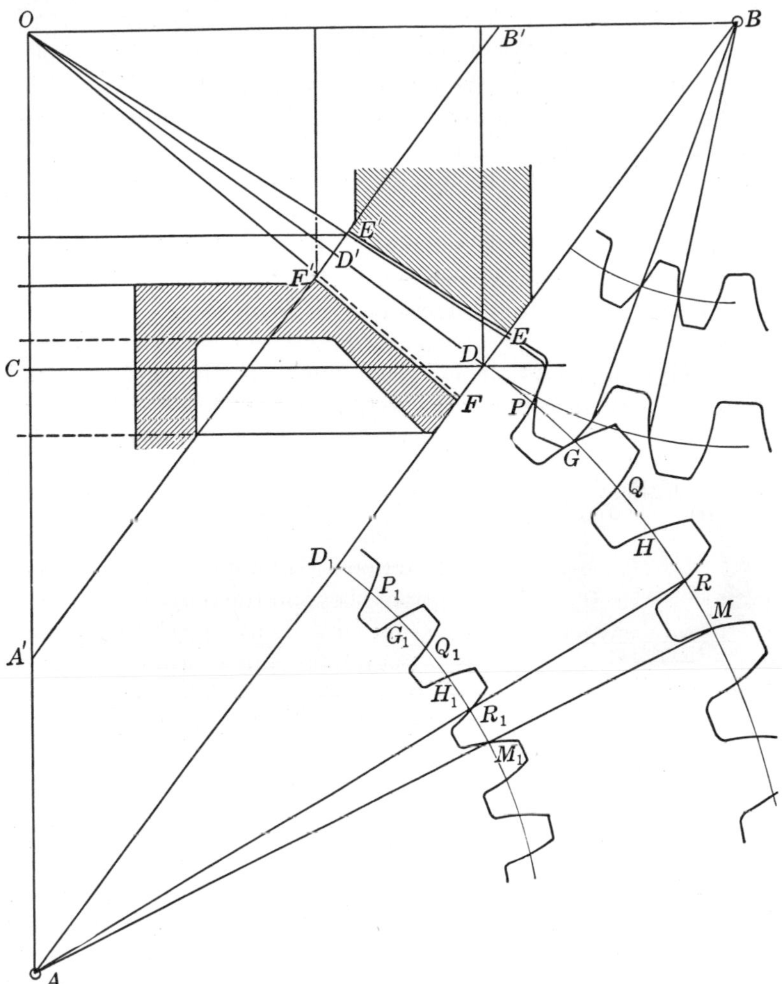

FIG. 8·54 Development of Bevel-Gear Teeth on the Back Cones.

Join MA and RA. These lines intersect the arc at M_1 and R_1. Space off distances around the arc equal to M_1R_1, obtaining points $P_1G_1Q_1$, etc.

Draw circles with A as center and radii $A'E'$ and $A'F'$. These define the addenda and roots of the teeth.

Construct involute tooth profiles passing through D_1, P_1, G_1, Q_1, etc., as for a spur gear of pitch radius $A'D'$ and circular pitch D_1G_1.

We have now obtained the shape of the teeth as they appear on the development of the normal cones at the outside and inside of the gear. It may be noted that the tooth forms are **similar figures** at the two sections.

The construction for the pinion teeth is carried out in the same manner.

Interference and undercutting of teeth can be investigated from the normal cone developments, as for the spur gear, and modifications of the tooth faces may be made if necessary.

8·35 Hypoid gears These gears, illustrated in Figs. 8·55 and 8·56, are used to connect shafts that are not intersecting. The tooth elements are of spiral shape to give progressive contact leading to quiet operation. They do not have pitch surfaces in the same sense that spur or bevel gears do, and the action is so complex that a detailed description is beyond the scope of this text.*

Gleason Works

FIG. 8·55 Hypoid Gears.

They are suited for pitch-line speeds greater than 1000 fpm or rotative speeds greater than 1000 rpm. They are stronger and quieter than spiral-bevel gears and may be used to secure large reduction ratios in a small space. As the shafts do not intersect, bearings may be placed on both sides of both the gear and pinion to secure greater rigidity. They are widely used as automobile-axle gears. For this application the drive shaft may be offset below the center of the axle, rendering possible a lower body design of the car.

Reduction ratios as high as 60 to 1 have been made, and higher ratios are possible. Figure 8·56 shows two pairs of such gears.

* See "Design, Production, and Application of the Hypoid Rear-Axle Gear," by A. L. Stewart and E. Wildhaber, *SAE Journal*, June, 1926. Also "Basic Relationship of Hypoid Gears," by E. Wildhaber, *American Machinist*, February 14, 28; March 14; June 6, 20; July 18; August 1, 15; all 1946.

One has a combination of 2 to 38 teeth, with a gear $4\frac{3}{8}$ in. in diameter and a tapered pinion; and the other a 2-to-90-tooth combination, with a gear 9 in. in diameter and the pinion of parallel form.

Gleason Works

FIG. 8·56 Hypoid Gears.

QUESTIONS

8·1 What are the advantages of a gear drive compared with a friction-wheel drive?

8·2 Explain the meaning of the following terms as applied to gear wheels: (*a*) pitch circle, (*b*) circular pitch, (*c*) diametral pitch, (*d*) pitch point.

8·3 Derive an expression for the relationship between the circular and diametral pitch of a spur gear.

8·4 Define the following terms as applied to gears: (*a*) addendum, (*b*) dedendum, (*c*) face of tooth, (*d*) flank of tooth, (*e*) face width, (*f*) backlash.

8·5 What are conjugate gears? What is the fundamental law governing the shape of conjugate teeth?

8·6 What are (*a*) the clearance of gear teeth, (*b*) the arc of action, (*c*) the angle of approach, (*d*) the angle of recess? How is the arc of action affected by lengthening the teeth?

8·7 What are the forms of the pitch surfaces in the following varieties of gears: (*a*) helical, (*b*) plain spur, (*c*) bevel, (*d*) worm?

8·8 What three common kinds of gears are used for connecting parallel shafts? Sketch.

8·9 When shafts intersect, what two types of gears are used to connect them? Sketch.

8·10 What two kinds of gears are used to connect shafts that are neither parallel nor intersecting?

8·11 Sketch (*a*) a spur gear, (*b*) a helical gear, (*c*) a straight-bevel gear, (*d*) a spiral-bevel gear.

8·12 Sketch (*a*) a herringbone gear, (*b*) a worm gear.

8·13 What are the geometrical forms of pitch surfaces for (*a*) a spur gear, (*b*) a herringbone gear, (*c*) a straight-bevel gear, (*d*) a spiral-bevel gear, (*e*) a worm gear?

8·14 Why is it necessary that the teeth on mating gears be so formed that a constant velocity ratio is obtained? What must be true of the tooth profiles to produce this result?

8·15 Prove that in conjugate gears the normal to the tooth surfaces at the point of contact must pass through the pitch point.

8·16 Why are cycloids and involutes used for tooth profiles in gear wheels? Can other curves be used?

8·17 What is the "describing" circle in a cycloidal gear? What is a cycloid, and how are the flanks and faces of a cycloidal gear formed?

8·18 In standard cycloidal gears, what is the size of the describing circle? Why is this size used instead of a larger one?

8·19 What is an involute? Show how to draw an involute when one point on it and the diameter of the base circle are given.

8·20 What are the proportions of the standard full-depth involute teeth?

8·21 What is the path of contact of a pair of involute gears? What is meant by interference of gear teeth? Show by sketch how a pair of gear teeth may be examined for interference.

8·22 What four modifications may be made in involute gear teeth of standard proportions to avoid interference? What method is commonly employed?

8·23 Under what conditions is interference obtained in two equal gears with standard $14\frac{1}{2}°$ involute teeth? With a rack and pinion?

8·24 Why is it impossible to modify an involute rack for interference so that it will have a profile of theoretically correct form to work with more than one size of pinion?

8·25 What relationship must exist between the arc of action and the circular pitch? Why?

8·26 What two considerations fix the size of the fillet arc at the root of a spur-gear tooth?

8·27 What is a stub tooth? What are its advantages and disadvantages compared with standard teeth, and for what kind of service is it used?

8·28 What is the pressure angle of a pair of involute gears? Does it change during the period of contact of a pair of mating teeth? What values are used (*a*) for standard involute gears, (*b*) for stub-tooth gears? What is the effect on the shape of tooth when the pressure angle is increased? On the bearing pressure?

8·29 What are the practical advantages of involute compared with cycloidal gears? How are the pressure angle and backlash in involute gears affected by using a greater center-to-center distance than standard?

8·30 A gear with standard $14\frac{1}{2}°$ full-depth involute teeth has a pitch diameter of 6 in. and a diametral pitch of 4. Calculate the following: (*a*) number of teeth, (*b*) addendum, (*c*) working depth, (*d*) clearance, (*e*) root diameter, (*f*) outside diameter, (*g*) base-circle diameter.

8·31 Same as Problem 8·30 but teeth are of standard AGMA stub-tooth form.

8·32 Same as Problem 8·30 except that gear diameter is 4 in. and diametral pitch is 5.

8·33 A gear has 20 teeth of 2-in. circular pitch, the teeth being of standard $14\frac{1}{2}°$ involute form. Calculate (*a*) the pitch diameter, (*b*) the addendum, (*c*) the clearance, (*d*) the working depth, (*e*) the root diameter, (*f*) the outside diameter, (*g*) the base-circle diameter.

8·34 Two shafts 10 in. apart are to be connected by spur gears with external teeth, one shaft running at 400 rpm, and the other at 600 rpm. Find the pitch diameters of the gears and the number of teeth if the diametral pitch is 4. What is the value of the circular pitch?

Ans. 12 in., 8 in., 48, 32, 0.7854 in.

8·35 *A* and *B* are two mating spur gears. *A* has 30 teeth of 3 diametral pitch and *B* has a pitch diameter of 15 in. The teeth are of standard $14\frac{1}{2}°$ involute form. Find: (*a*) number of teeth on *B*; (*b*) center-to-center distance of shafts; (*c*) circular pitch; (*d*) addendum; (*e*) dedendum; (*f*) root diameter of *A*; (*g*) outside diameter of *A*; (*h*) diameter of base circle of *A*; (*i*) speed ratio of *A* to *B*.

8·36 Spur gear *A* has 20 teeth of 2-in. circular pitch and meshes with gear *B* having 28 teeth. Find the center-to-center distance of the shafts and the speed ratio. *Ans.* 15.27 in.; 1.4.

8·37 Shaft *A* carries a spur gear with internal teeth. Its pitch diameter is 20 in., and the diametral pitch is 3. Shaft *B* carries a mating gear with 12 teeth. Find the center-to-center distance and the speed ratio of the shafts.

8·38 A pair of gears having teeth of 20° stub involute form makes internal contact. The shafts are 10 in. from center to center, and the angular velocity ratio is 3:1. The diametral pitch is 4. Find: (*a*) pitch diameters of the gears; (*b*) number of teeth on each gear; (*c*) addendum for each gear; (*d*) dedendum for each gear; (*e*) diameter of base circle for the pinion.

8·39 What is an annular gear? What relationship exists between the teeth of a spur gear and those of an annular gear of an equal pitch and diameter?

8·40 A pair of spur gears 2 and 3 have internal contact on 3. The number of teeth on 2 is 20, and the angular velocity ratio of 2 to 3 is 5:2. The center-to-center distance is $7\frac{1}{2}$ in. Teeth are $14\frac{1}{2}°$ involute form. Find: (*a*) number of teeth on 3; (*b*) pitch diameter of 2 and 3; (*c*) diametral pitch; (*d*) outside diameter of 2; (*e*) height of teeth.

8·41 How do the tooth actions of pairs of helical gears differ from one another: (*a*) when the shafts are parallel, (*b*) when the shafts are not parallel?

8·42 Show that in a pair of helical gears with crossed axes, 2 and 3:

$$\frac{\omega_2}{\omega_3} = \frac{d_3 \cos \beta}{d_2 \cos \alpha}$$

where ω_2 and ω_3 are the angular velocities, d_2 and d_3 the pitch diameters, and α and β the helix angles.

8·43 Justify each of the ten statements regarding the involute and its application to gear teeth given in Art. 8·15.

8·44 A helical gear of 6-in. pitch diameter has a helix angle of 25°, and there are 24 teeth. Find the values of the circular and diametral pitches measured both circumferentially and normal to the teeth.

Ans. $P_d = 4$; $p = 0.7854$ in.; $P_n = 4.42$; $p_n = 0.712$ in.

8·45 A helical gear of 10-in. pitch diameter has a normal diametral pitch of 4. The helix angle is 20°. Find the normal circular pitch, and also the diametral and circular pitches measured circumferentially.

8·46 The outside diameter of a 48-tooth spur gear having $14\frac{1}{2}°$ full-depth involute teeth is 5 in. What is the circular pitch?

8·47 A helical gear of 10-in. pitch diameter has a helix angle of 30°, and there are 30 teeth. Find values of the circular and diametral pitches measured both circumferentially and normal to the teeth.

8·48 A helical gear with 26 teeth, pitch diameter 6 in., has a normal diametral pitch of 5. Find the helix angle.

8·49 A helical gear of 8-in. pitch diameter has 47 teeth, the helix angle being 21°. Find the normal circular pitch.

8·50 A pair of helical gears are used to connect two shafts at 60°. One gear has a pitch diameter of 8 in. and a helix angle of 35°. Its angular velocity is 1.1 times that of the other. Find for the second gear (*a*) helix angle, (*b*) pitch diameter. *Ans.* (*a*) 25°; (*b*) 7.94 in.

8·51 A pair of helical gears connect two shafts at an angle of 45°. The pitch diameters are, respectively, 8 in. and 12 in., and the speed ratio 4:3. Find the helix angles of the teeth. *Ans.* 14°; 31°.

8·52 Two helical gears having 21 teeth and 63 teeth, respectively, are used to connect a pair of shafts at an angle of 60°. The pitch diameters of the gears are 7 in. and 14 in. Find the helix angles of the teeth.

8·53 A pair of helical gears 2 and 3 connect shafts located at 90°. Gear 2 has a helix angle of 30° and a pitch diameter of 10 in. Gear 2 rotates at 1200 rpm and 3 at 800 rpm. Determine the pitch diameter of 3.

8·54 Helical gears of 6-in. and 8-in. pitch diameters, respectively, have a speed ratio of 3:2. The shafts meet at an angle of 60°. Find graphically the helix angles of the teeth.

8·55 Two helical gears 2 and 3 are mounted on shafts intersecting at an angle of 75°. Gear 2 has a pitch diameter of 8 in., and 3 of 12 in. Gear 2 has a helix angle of 30°. Find the speed ratio of the gears.

8·56 Show by sketch the meaning of the following terms: pitch, lead, and lead angle of a worm. How would you calculate the lead angle when the pitch diameter and lead are known?

8·57 Indicate by a sketch the general form of three types of worm wheels. Which is most commonly used, and why?

8·58 What is the nature of an axial section of a worm? Of a worm wheel?

8·59 A quadruple-threaded worm has two threads per inch. When it is mated with a certain worm wheel, the angular velocity ratio is 20:1. Determine the pitch diameter and number of teeth on the worm wheel.

8·60 A worm gear consists of a worm with triple thread driving a worm wheel with 48 teeth, to which is attached a 24-in. pulley. The worm is driven at 900 rpm. Find the linear speed at the pulley face. *Ans.* 353 fpm.

8·61 A worm has a lead of $\frac{1}{4}$ in. and meshes with a worm wheel of 8-in. pitch diameter. Determine the number of turns required on the worm shaft to revolve the worm wheel one turn.

8·62 A worm has a pitch diameter of 2 in. and is triple threaded. It meshes with a worm wheel of 12-in. pitch diameter, and the speed ratio is 30:1. What is the axial pitch of the worm?

8·63 A double-threaded worm has an axial pitch of $\frac{1}{2}$ in. and meshes with a worm wheel with a pitch diameter of 6 in. Find the speed ratio.

8·64 In a worm-gear drive the worm wheel is 12.73-in. pitch diameter and is driven by a worm which is double threaded. The axial pitch of the worm is $\frac{1}{2}$ in. If the worm rotates at 800 rpm, what is the speed of the worm wheel?

8·65 Explain the meaning of the following terms as applied to a bevel gear: (*a*) pitch diameter, (*b*) face width, (*c*) addendum, (*d*) dedendum.

8·66 A pair of bevel gears connect two shafts at 60° and have a speed ratio of 3:5. If the larger gear has 45 teeth of 5 diametral pitch, find the pitch diameter and number of teeth on the smaller gear. Also, find the pitch angles.

8·67 Explain why the diametral pitch is different at the inside and outside of the teeth in a bevel gear.

8·68 What do we mean by the "back cone"? For what is it used?

8·69 What is Tredgold's approximation as applied to bevel gears?

8·70 A pair of bevel gears connecting two shafts at 90° have a speed ratio of 3:2. Find the pitch angle for both. If the larger wheel has 30 teeth of 4 diametral pitch, find the pitch diameter and the number of teeth on the smaller gear. *Ans.* 33° 40′; 56° 20′; 5 in., 20.

8·71 A bevel gear of 8-in. diameter, 6 diametral pitch, has a pitch angle of 60°. Find the number of teeth on the spur gear whose tooth form is the same as that of the bevel gear on the back-cone development. *Ans.* 96.

8·72 A bevel gear, with a pitch angle of 30°, has 32 teeth of 4 diametral pitch. What is the number of teeth on a spur gear with teeth of the same form?

8·73 A bevel gear with 50 teeth and 5 diametral pitch has a pitch angle of 60°. Determine the number of teeth on the corresponding spur gear.

8·74 A pair of bevel gears used to connect shafts at 90° have a speed ratio of 4.5:1. The smaller gear has a 2-in. pitch diameter, and the teeth have a diametral pitch of 5. The teeth are of 20° full-depth involute form. Find the pitch diameter and number of teeth on the larger gear and also the center angles of both gears. What are the values of the addendum and whole depth of the teeth?

8·75 A pair of bevel gears having shafts intersecting at 75° give a velocity ratio of 2:1. The larger gear has a diameter of 14 in. The diametral pitch of the teeth is 5. Find the center angles. Determine the number of teeth on the spur gear whose tooth form is the same as that of the smaller gear.

8·76 Why is it necessary to find the equivalent number of teeth of bevel gears?

8·77 A pair of miter gears have pitch diameters of 6 in., and each has 20 teeth. What is the equivalent number of teeth of these gears?

9 Gear Trains

9·1 Train value A mechanism that transmits motion from a driving to a driven shaft by means of two or more gear wheels is called a **gear train.** Problems involving the calculation of the velocity ratios of such trains will be considered in this chapter.

The **train value** we shall define as the ratio

$$\frac{\text{Angular velocity of the last wheel (driven)}}{\text{Angular velocity of the first wheel (driver)}}$$

These velocities are measured in the ordinary gear train with reference to the fixed frame that supports the gear shafts.

A positive sign for the train value indicates that the first and last wheels turn in the same sense; a negative sign indicates rotation in the opposite senses.

In Art. 8·3 it was shown that the same general law for the velocity ratio applies to any pair of toothed gears, whether spur, helical, or bevel, etc. This law states that the velocity ratio of a pair of gears is the inverse ratio of the numbers of teeth. Hence the method of finding the train value in terms of the numbers of teeth is the same for all gear trains, no matter what varieties of gears they contain.

9·2 A simple gear train is one in which no two wheels are rigidly fastened to the same shaft so as to rotate at the same angular velocity. Figure 9·1 shows a train of this kind. Here motion is transmitted from 2 to 5 through intermediate wheels 3 and 4. By definition, the train value is ω_{51}/ω_{21}. The pitch circles of the gears roll together without slipping; therefore the pitch-line velocity is

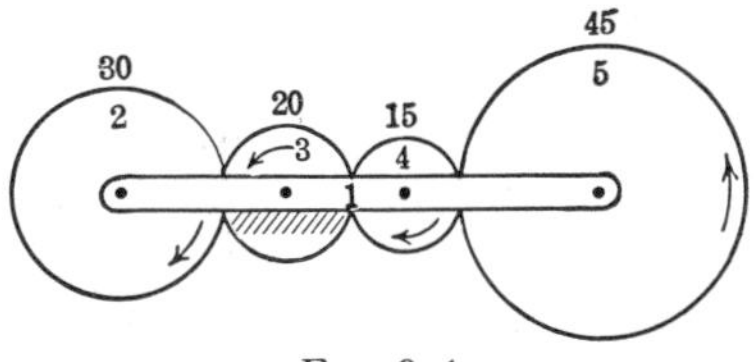

FIG. 9·1.

the same for all. It follows that wheel 5, through contact with 4, will turn at the same pitch-line speed as though it meshed with 2. The sizes of intermediate wheels 3 and 4 or the numbers of teeth they contain have no effect on the train value. For this reason, 3 and 4 are usually termed **idlers.** This is somewhat of a misnomer, since these wheels transmit power as well as 2 and 5 do.

If wheel 4 were removed from the train and 5 then driven from 3, 5 would still have the same speed but in the reverse sense. Thus the number of idlers controls the sign of the train value.

In view of the foregoing it is evident that the train value for a simple gear train is equal to the inverse ratio of the numbers of teeth on the first and last wheels. For the train of Fig. 9·1,

$$\frac{\omega_{51}}{\omega_{21}} = -\frac{N_2}{N_5} \tag{9·1}$$

where N_2 and N_5 are the numbers of teeth.

By inspection, wheels 2 and 5 are observed to rotate in opposite senses, which accounts for the negative sign. Substituting the numbers of teeth indicated in the figure yields

$$\frac{\omega_{51}}{\omega_{21}} = -\frac{30}{45} = -\frac{2}{3}$$

Figure 9·2 shows a simple gear train containing an annular or

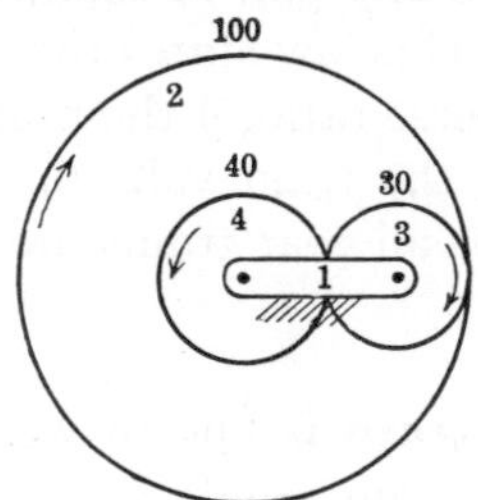

FIG. 9·2.

internal gear 2, driving an idler 3 which in turn drives wheel 4. The train ratio is

$$\frac{\omega_{41}}{\omega_{21}} = -\frac{100}{40} = -2\tfrac{1}{2}$$

We use the minus sign, since the driving wheel turns clockwise when the driven wheel turns counterclockwise.

9·3 A compound gear train is one in which at least one pair of wheels are rigidly attached to the same shaft so that both revolve at the same angular speed. One of these trains is shown in Fig. 9·3. In this train the drive is through 2, 3, 4, 5, in order,

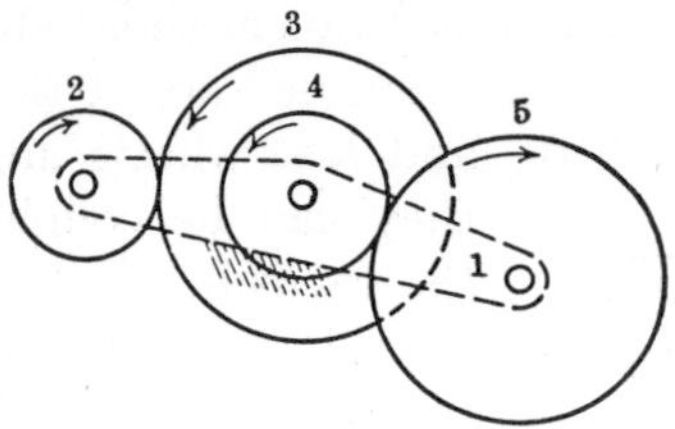

FIG. 9·3.

and wheels 3 and 4 are keyed to the same shaft. To find the train ratio we may proceed as follows:

Considering wheels 2 and 3,

$$\frac{\omega_{31}}{\omega_{21}} = \frac{N_2}{N_3} \tag{A}$$

Also, considering wheels 4 and 5,

$$\frac{\omega_{51}}{\omega_{41}} = \frac{N_4}{N_5} \tag{B}$$

Multiplying equations A and B, we have

$$\frac{\omega_{31}}{\omega_{21}} \times \frac{\omega_{51}}{\omega_{41}} = \frac{N_2 \times N_4}{N_3 \times N_5}$$

But $\omega_{31} = \omega_{41}$ since these wheels are keyed to the same shaft. Therefore,

$$\frac{\omega_{51}}{\omega_{21}} = \frac{N_2 \times N_4}{N_3 \times N_5} \tag{9·2}$$

Calling the first wheel in each pair of meshing gears a **driver** and the second a **driven** wheel, we may write

$$\text{Train value} = \pm \frac{\text{product of numbers of teeth on drivers}}{\text{product of numbers of teeth on drivens}}$$

The sign, as before, depends on whether rotation at the driven end of the train is the same or opposite to that at the driving end. Compound trains are often used where the speed reduction is large. In such cases a simple train with the same speed ratio might require the use of one very large gear.

9·4 Reverted gear trains A gear train is said to be reverted when the first and last gears turn about the same axis. The gear trains in an automobile transmission which are in use on "low," "intermediate," or "reverse" are of this type. The first and last wheels are coaxial, so that they can be coupled together when the car is in "high." The back gears of a lathe form part of a reverted train. In Fig. 9·4 is shown a reverted train of four spur gears, 3 and 4 being keyed to the same shaft. The distance from center to center of the shafts is $R_2 + R_3 = R_4 + R_5$. If all wheels have teeth of the same pitch, the numbers of teeth are proportional to the pitch radii. Hence, if $R_2 = C \times N_2$ then $R_3 = C \times N_3$, $R_4 = C \times N_4$, $R_5 = C \times N_5$, where C is a constant. Substituting these values in the above equation, we have

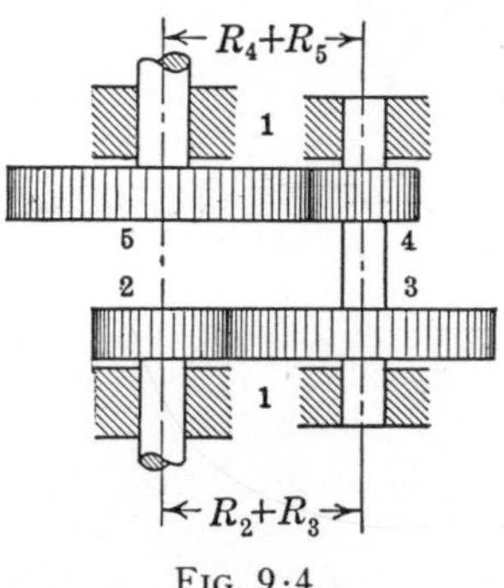

FIG. 9·4.

$$N_2 + N_3 = N_4 + N_5 \tag{9·3}$$

Example A reverted gear train of four gears, arranged as shown in Fig. 9·4, has a train value of $\frac{1}{6}$. Wheel 2 has 20 teeth; wheel 3, 40 teeth. Find the number of teeth for 4 and 5, assuming that the pitch of the teeth is the same for all wheels.

The train value is

$$\frac{\omega_{51}}{\omega_{21}} = \frac{1}{6} = \frac{N_2 \times N_4}{N_3 \times N_5} = \frac{20 \times N_4}{40 \times N_5}$$

Therefore,

$$\frac{N_4}{N_5} = \frac{1}{3} \quad \text{or} \quad N_4 = \frac{N_5}{3} \tag{A}$$

Also, from equation 9·3,

$$N_2 + N_3 = N_4 + N_5 \tag{B}$$
$$20 + 40 = N_4 + N_5$$

Equations A and B may be solved for N_4 and N_5. We thus find $N_4 = 15$, $N_5 = 45$.

9·5 Automobile transmission Figure 9·5 illustrates a common form of automobile transmission which provides three speeds: forward, neutral, and reverse. The more important

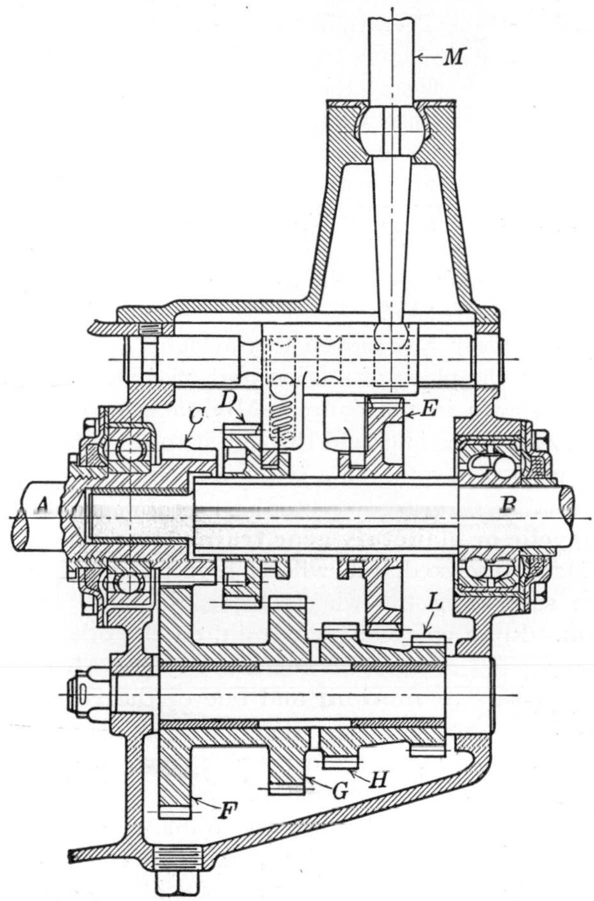

FIG. 9·5 Sliding-Gear Automobile Transmission.

members consist of driving shaft A and coaxial driven shaft B, sliding gears D and E which turn with B, and gears F, G, H, L, rigidly connected together and rotating on a lay shaft. The illustration shows the transmission in neutral position. Gears C and F are always in mesh, so that unit F, G, H, I is always in motion.

The gear system is controlled by lever M which slides gears D or E to right or left as desired. The transmission operates as follows:

(*a*) *Third speed* (*direct drive*) Gear D is moved to the left, the internal teeth on D engaging with C. Shafts A and B now rotate at the same speed.

(*b*) *Second speed* Gear D is shifted to the right, engaging gear G. The reverted gear train C, F, G, D causes B to rotate in the same sense as A but at a reduced speed.

(*c*) *First speed* Gear E is moved to the left, engaging H. The gear train C, F, H, E drives B in the same sense as A with a speed reduction of larger value than in the second speed position on account of the decrease in the ratio of tooth numbers, $N_H:N_E$ as compared with $N_G:N_D$.

(*d*) *Reverse* Gear E is moved to the right, engaging an idler located behind the plane of section and meshing with L. This idler is not shown in the figure. Motion is now transmitted through C, F, L to the idler and through it to E. The addition of the idler causes B to rotate in a sense opposite to that of A.

9·6 Epicyclic or planetary gear trains In the ordinary gear trains already discussed, the wheels revolve about fixed axes, the frame supporting the wheels being the fixed link in the mechanism. In an epicyclic gear train, on the other hand, the **axes of certain of the wheels are in motion,** and one of the gears generally becomes the fixed link. An ordinary gear train may be converted into an epicyclic train by fixing one of the wheels and causing the frame carrying the wheel axles to revolve. The epicyclic train of Fig. 9·6 has a stationary wheel 1, and frame 3 revolves about the pin at A with the result that 2 rolls around on 1.

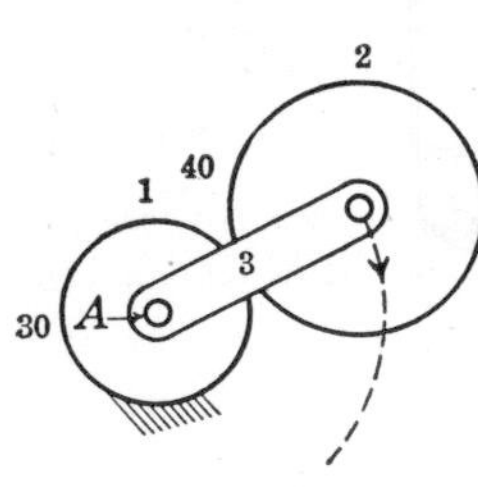

FIG. 9·6.

What we often want to know about an epicyclic is the ratio of the angular velocity of the driven wheel to the angular velocity of the frame carrying the wheel axles. In Fig. 9·6 this is ω_{21}/ω_{31}, both velocities being measured with respect to the fixed wheel. This quantity we may call the **epicyclic value,** and we will consider two methods of calculating it.

9·7 First method The evaluation of the epicyclic value may be made by applying two fundamental principles concerning the motion of any three bodies.

1. If we have three moving bodies, the angular velocity of the third relative to the first is equal to the angular velocity of the second relative to the first plus the angular velocity of the third relative to the second (see Art. 2·13). Thus, if 1, 3, 2, in Fig. 9·6, are the three bodies, then,

$$\omega_{21} = \omega_{31} + \omega_{23} \tag{A}$$

2. If we have two bodies, the angular velocity of the first relative to the second is equal numerically to the angular velocity of the second relative to the first, but of opposite sign. Hence,

$$\omega_{31} = -\omega_{13} \tag{B}$$

With reference to Fig. 9·6, the epicyclic value equals

$$\frac{\omega_{21}}{\omega_{31}} = \frac{\omega_{31} + \omega_{23}}{\omega_{31}} \quad \text{by equation } A$$

$$= 1 + \frac{\omega_{23}}{\omega_{31}} = 1 - \frac{\omega_{23}}{\omega_{13}} \quad \text{by equation } B$$

But ω_{23}/ω_{13} is the train value when the frame 3 is the fixed link. If we call this train value T,

$$\textbf{Epicyclic value} = 1 - T \tag{9·4}$$

Care must be exercised in two directions: (*a*) in obtaining the proper sign for T and (*b*) in calculating its value. The **denominator** in the fraction expressing the train value is the **angular velocity of the wheel which becomes the fixed link in the epicyclic.**

Example 1 Suppose 3, Fig. 9·6, makes one turn clockwise; find the number of turns made by 2. Wheel 1 has 30 teeth and wheel 2 has 40 teeth.

The train value $T = \omega_{23}/\omega_{13} = -30/40$. The minus sign is required, since 1 and 2 rotate in opposite senses.

By equation 9·4, the epicyclic value $\omega_{21}/\omega_{31} = 1 - T = 1 - (-\frac{3}{4}) = +1\frac{3}{4}$. While 3 makes +1 turn, 2 makes $+1\frac{3}{4}$ turns.

Example 2 An epicyclic gear train (Fig. 9·7) has a stationary wheel 1. Arm 5 turns at 50 rpm clockwise. Find the speed and direction of rotation of 4.

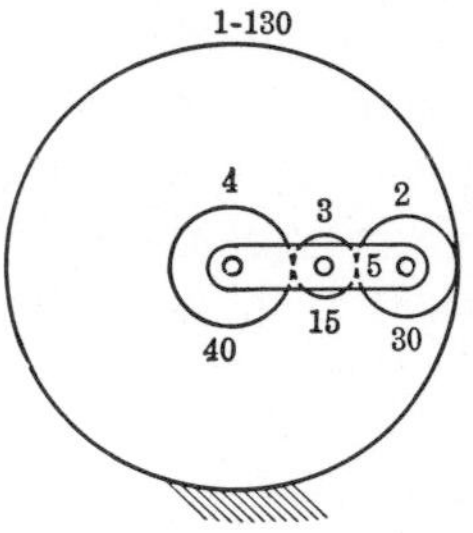

Wheels 2 and 3 are evidently idlers.

$$\text{Train value } \frac{\omega_{45}}{\omega_{15}} = +\frac{130}{40}$$

$$\text{Epicyclic value } \frac{\omega_{41}}{\omega_{51}} = 1 - T = 1 - \frac{130}{40} = -2\tfrac{1}{4}$$

FIG. 9·7.

If 5 makes 50 revolutions clockwise, 4 makes $50 \times (-2\frac{1}{4}) = -112.5$ rpm.

The minus sign indicates counterclockwise rotation.

9·8 Second method A more general method of calculating the velocity ratio of epicyclic trains that may be used when no member is held fixed will now be described. It consists of three steps:

1. The whole train is locked so that there can be no relative motion of the parts, and it is then rotated one revolution clockwise. As a result each member of the train will rotate one revolution clockwise. This may be clarified by slowly rotating this book one revolution and noting that every member in a picture of a train makes one revolution about its own axis.

2. The epicyclic train is now converted into an ordinary train by locking the arm on which the gears are mounted and at the same time releasing the fixed gear. The gear formerly fixed is now rotated one turn counterclockwise, and the number of turns made by all the members recorded on a table.

3. The net result of the previous operations may be found by adding algebraically the number of revolutions made by each member of the train. The resultant movement of the "fixed" gear is always zero; hence the angular displacements of the other gears are the same as though the train had remained an epicyclic. From these angular displacements, the velocity ratio of the train can be calculated.

Example 1 Applying the above method to the epicyclic train of Fig. 9·8, we have: (1) the train is locked and the whole mechanism is rotated one revolution clockwise; (2) arm 4 is locked and gear 1 rotated one turn in a counterclockwise or negative direction, and the number of turns of the other gears are noted on the table; (3) the resultant motion of the members concerned is found by adding algebraically the values set up in the table for steps *1* and *2*. This is shown in Table 9·1. Thus, while the

TABLE 9·1

Step	Turns 1	2	3	4
1	+1	+1	+1	+1
2	−1	...	+4	0
3	0	...	+5	+1

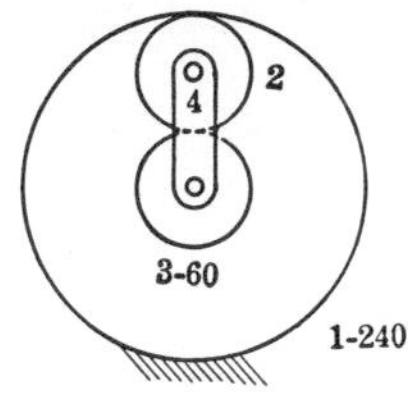

FIG. 9·8.

arm 4 makes +1 turn, gear 3 makes +5 turns, and the ratio ω_{31}/ω_{41} equals +5.

Example 2 In Fig. 9·9 is illustrated a compound epicyclic train in which the arm 6 carrying gears 3 and 4 is neither the driver nor the driven link. Driver 2 engages gear 3, which in turn meshes with the stationary annular gear 1. Gears 3 and 4 are keyed to a shaft supported by arm 6, which is free to turn on shaft *A*. Gear 4 engages annular gear 5, which is keyed to the driven shaft *B*.

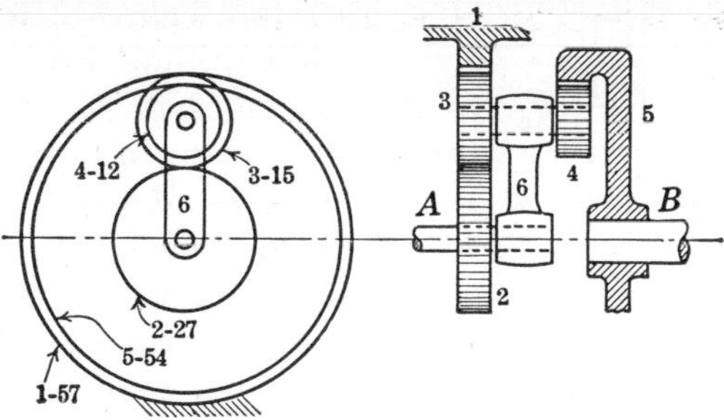

FIG. 9·9.

The first step in finding the train ratio is to lock the train and rotate the whole mechanism one turn in a positive (clockwise) direction. The second step is to fix the arm 6, rotate the fixed gear 1 one revolution in a negative (counterclockwise) direction, and tabulate the turns of the other gears. The third step is to add algebraically the motions obtained in the steps already taken to find the resultant motion. This is done in Table 9·2.

TABLE 9·2

	Turns					
Step	1	2	3	4	5	6
1	+1	+1	+1	+1	+1	+1
2	−1	$+\frac{57}{27}$	$-\frac{57}{15}$	$-\frac{57}{15}$	$-\frac{57}{15}\cdot\frac{12}{54}$	0
3	0	$+\frac{28}{9}$	.....	.....	$+\frac{7}{45}$	+1

Thus, while gear 2 makes +28/9 turns, gear 5 makes +7/45 turns. The speed ratio $\omega_{51}/\omega_{21} = \dfrac{7/45}{28/9} = +1/20$. Hence, while shaft A makes 20 turns, shaft B makes 1 turn in the same direction.

Example 3 Figure 9·10 shows a compound reverted epicyclic train arranged to give a large speed reduction from the driving shaft A to the driven shaft C. Shaft A drives an arm 5, which supports shaft B to which are keyed gear wheels 2 and 3. Wheel 1 is fixed. Rotation of A therefore causes 2 to roll on 1; 3 meanwhile driving 4, which is keyed to the driven shaft C. Suppose that the numbers of teeth on the gears are: 1—60 teeth, 2−61 teeth, 3—60 teeth, 4—61 teeth. Shaft A turns 100 rpm clockwise. Find the speed and direction of rotation of shaft C.

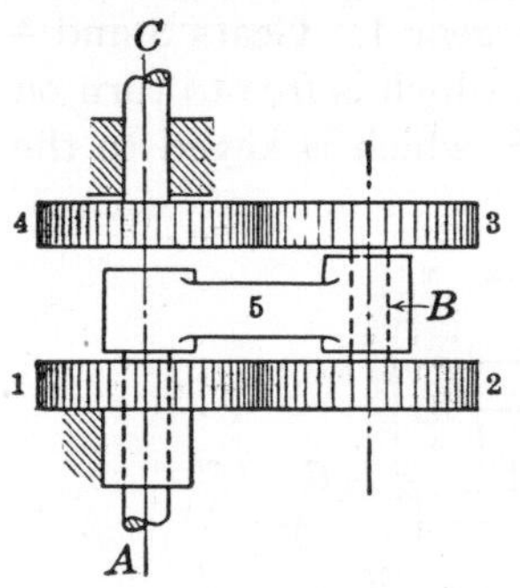

FIG. 9·10.

Following the usual procedure, we first rotate the entire train one turn clockwise (+1). Then we hold the arm 5 fixed, rotate the fixed gear 1 one turn in the opposite direction, and find the number of turns made by the other gears, as shown in step *2* of the table. Finally, the resultant motion is obtained in step *3* by adding steps *1* and *2* algebraically, as shown in Table 9·3. From this it may be seen that, if shaft A makes 100 rpm clockwise, C makes 100(121/3721) = 3.25 rpm in the same direction.

This case illustrates the method by which a large speed reduction can be obtained by means of an epicyclic train, using gears which are all about the same size. The train may thus be made in a compact form.

TABLE 9·3

	Turns				
Step	1	2	3	4	5
1	+1	+1	+1	+1	+1
2	−1	$+\frac{60}{61}$	$+\frac{60}{61}$	$-\frac{60}{61}\cdot\frac{60}{61}$	0
3	0	.....	.....	$+\frac{121}{3721}$	+1

It will be instructive to investigate this example further by interchanging the two pairs of gears. Then the numbers of teeth on the gears are: 1—61 teeth, 2—60 teeth, 3—61 teeth, 4—60 teeth. Shaft *A* again turns 100 rpm clockwise, and it is desired to find the speed and direction of rotation of shaft *C*.

The procedure is exactly the same as before, and is summarized in Table 9·4.

TABLE 9·4

	Turns				
Step	1	2	3	4	5
1	+1	+1	+1	+1	+1
2	−1	$+\frac{61}{60}$	$+\frac{61}{60}$	$-\frac{61}{60}\cdot\frac{61}{60}$	0
3	0	.....	.....	$-\frac{121}{3600}$	+1

From this it may be seen that, if shaft *A* rotates 100 rpm clockwise, shaft *C* rotates 100(121/3600) = 3.36 rpm in the opposite direction.

Hence, merely interchanging the two sets of gears is sufficient to cause the direction of rotation of the driven shaft to be reversed, the size of the train and the length of the arm 5 being unaltered.

9·9 Epicyclic trains with no gear fixed Occasionally an epicyclic gear train may be used in which no gear is held fixed.

The most common example of this is an automobile differential when the car is turning a corner, which will be considered later.

The procedure in problems of this type is similar to the second method outlined in Art. 9·8, except that in the first step, instead of the locked train being rotated one revolution, it is rotated as many revolutions as the arm makes per unit of time; and in the second step, when the arm is locked, the gear whose absolute speed is known must be rotated in the direction a number of times which, when added to the turns of the whole train in the first step will give the correct algebraic total. It is perhaps best illustrated by an example.

Example 1 In Fig. 9·11, shaft A, rotating 100 rpm clockwise, drives an epicyclic gear train by the meshing of gear 2 with 3, and 4 with 5. It should be realized that gears 2 and 4 on shaft A do not form part of the epicyclic train but merely drive it. The numbers of teeth on each gear are shown on the figure. It is desired to know the direction of rotation and speed of shaft B.

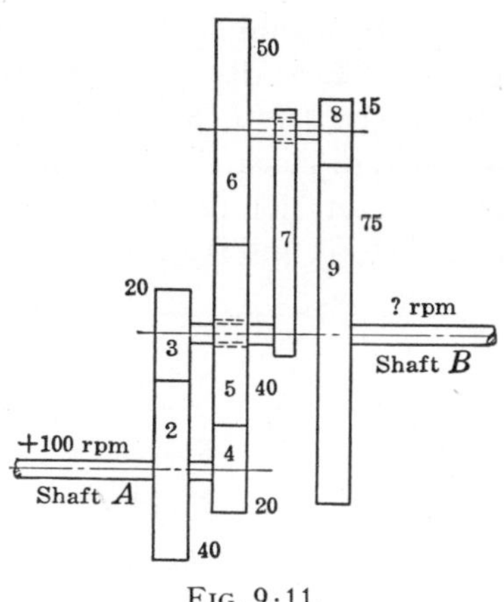

Fig. 9·11.

The speed of gear 3, or the arm 7 which is keyed to 3, is $100 \times \frac{40}{20} = -200$ rpm. The speed of gear 5 is $100 \times \frac{20}{40} = -50$ rpm. Table 9·5 may now be set up listing the gears in the epicyclic train. For step *1* the entire train is rotated 200 revolutions counterclockwise, which is the speed and direction of rotation

TABLE 9·5

	Turns				
Step	3 or 7	5	6	8	9
1	−200	−200	−200	−200	−200
2	0	+150	$-150 \cdot \frac{40}{50}$	$-150 \cdot \frac{40}{50}$	$+150 \cdot \frac{40}{50} \cdot \frac{15}{75}$
3	−200	−50	−320	−320	−176

of the arm 7. For step *2* the arm 7 is held fixed, and gear 5 revolved a number of turns in the proper direction so that its resultant motion will be that actually occurring, or −50 rpm. The required value is evidently +150 rpm. With the arm 7 fixed and gear 5 rotated +150 revolutions, the revolutions of the other gears may be found and listed. In step *3* the resultant motion is found by algebraic addition, and it is found that gear 9, or shaft *B*, rotates −176 rpm, that is, counterclockwise.

Example 2 Figure 9·12 shows a diagrammatic sketch of an automobile differential. Power is received along the drive shaft from the engine via the transmission and transmitted through the bevel gears 2 and 3. On gear 3 are lugs which support bevel gears 4 and 4′ meshing with gears 5 and 6. Gears 5 and 6 are keyed to the axles to which the wheels are also keyed.

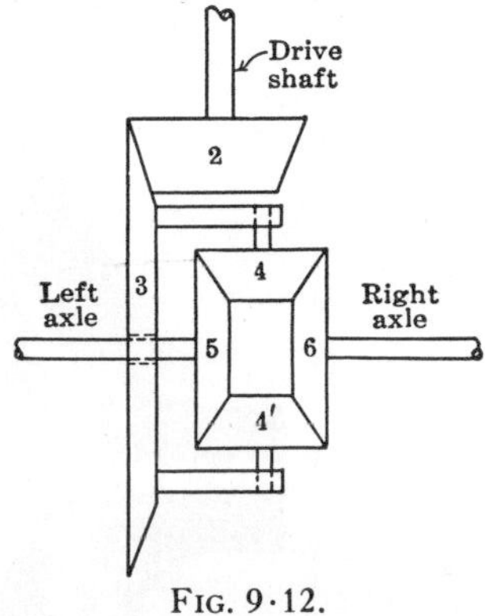

FIG. 9·12.

When the car is traveling along a straight road, the differential turns "end over end"; that is, there is no relative motion between gears 4 or 4′ and gears 5 and 6. However, when the auto turns a corner, one wheel and axle must travel slower and the other speed up to prevent slippage of the tire on the road. This causes relative motion of the gears in the epicyclic train of which 3 is the arm, and the other gears are 4 or 4′, 5 and 6. Assume that on a straight road each axle turns 100 rpm, but that on a curve the speed of the right wheel drops to 50 rpm. What will be the speed of the left axle, assuming that the drive-shaft speed is unchanged?

Following the method outlined above (see Table 9·6), it is known that the speed of the gear or arm 3 is +100 rpm. Hence, in step *1* we rotate the train +100 revolutions. In step *2* the arm, or gear 3, is held fixed and gear 6 revolved a number of turns in the proper direction so that its resultant motion will be that actually occurring, or +50 rpm. This value is −50 turns. With the arm 3 fixed and gear 6 rotated −50 turns, it is apparent that gear 5 will rotate +50 turns. This is true since gears 5 and 6 are the same size, and gears 4 and 4′ merely act as idlers. When the values are entered in the table, the resultant motion is found in step *3*. It may be observed that the speed of one wheel will increase the same amount that the other decreases. If the rear end is jacked up and one wheel held fixed, the other

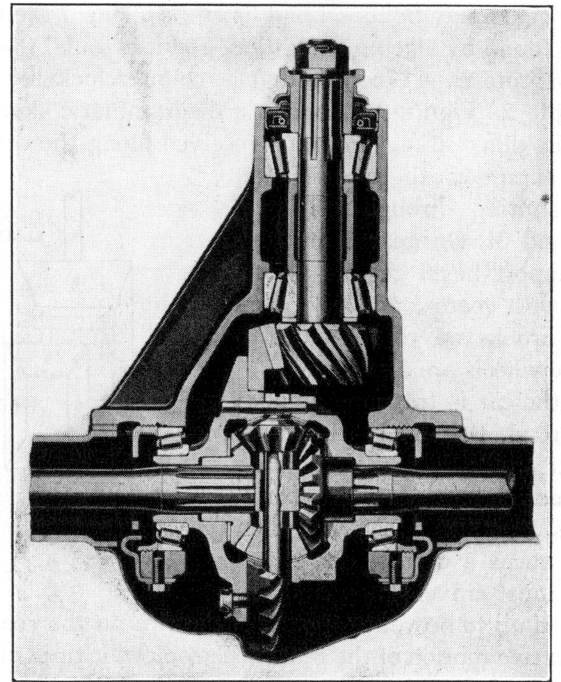

Plymouth Div., Chrysler Corp.

FIG. 9·13 Differential and Rear Axle.

rotates twice as fast. This situation occurs frequently in the winter when one wheel of an auto is resting on ice having a low coefficient of friction and the other is on a dry road having a

TABLE 9·6

	Turns		
Step	3	5	6
1	+100	+100	+100
2	0	+50	−50
3	+100	+150	+50

high coefficient of friction. In such cases the car must be pushed away from this condition before it can be driven.

Figure 9·13 shows an actual differential of a Plymouth.

9·10 Applications of epicyclic trains Although epicyclic trains are apt to be noisy, they are used in automobile differentials (Fig. 9·13), electric motors with integral reduction gears, hoisting blocks (Fig. 9·14), and some speed reducers (Fig. 9·15).

Figure 9·14 shows an application of a compound reverted epicyclic gear train to a hoisting block. The device is operated by a hand chain on the right, which runs on a sprocket of comparatively large diameter. This sprocket is connected to a shaft which transmits motion to the gear train on the left. This train is an epicyclic with fixed internal gear, having as a driven member a cage supporting the small revolving pinions. This cage is keyed to a sleeve which also carries the hoisting-chain sprocket at the middle of the block. An automatic clutch in the right-hand side of the case holds the load until the hand chain is pulled in the lowering direction.

Yale and Towne Mfg. Co.

FIG. 9·14 Spur-Geared Hoisting Block.

By proper choice of the sprocket diameters and gear sizes the device is designed for any desired speed ratio of hoisting chain to hand chain. Neglecting friction losses, the ratio of the load-chain pull to the hand-chain pull is the reciprocal of their speed ratio, since the work done by both is the same (see also Fig. P9·19).

Where a reduction in the rate of revolution must be made between the prime mover and the driven machine, as for example where an electric motor is used to drive a slow-speed machine, a speed reducer of the epicyclic type shown in Fig. 9·15 is often employed as a substitute for belts, chains, or exposed gears. An annular gear is the fixed member.

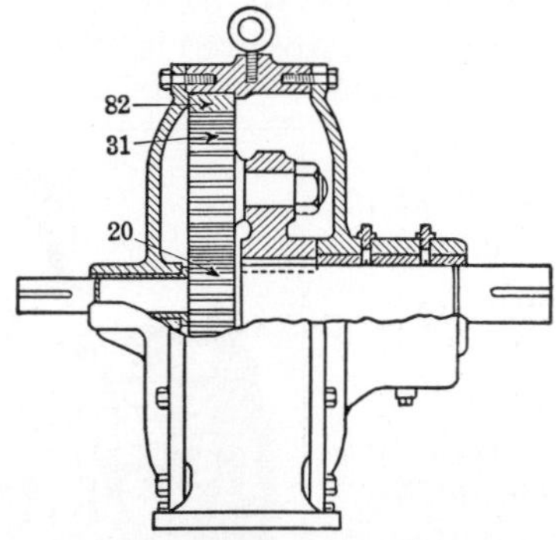

FIG. 9·15 Speed Reducer with Epicyclic Gear Train.

QUESTIONS

9·1 Define the following terms as applied to gear trains: (*a*) train value, (*b*) simple gear train, (*c*) compound gear train, (*d*) reverted gear train.

9·2 A gear train consists of an internal or annular spur gear 2 and a gear 3 meshing with it. The two wheels revolve about fixed centers 6 in. apart. Wheel 2 turns at 30 rpm and 3 at 120 rpm. Find (*a*) the pitch diameters of both gears, (*b*) the number of teeth on each if the diametral pitch is 4.

Ans. (*a*) 16 in., 4 in. (*b*) 64, 16.

9·3 Find the train value in the following train of gears:

15 teeth
30 teeth
20 teeth
45 teeth

9·4 Find the train value in the following train:

30 teeth
75 teeth—10-in. pitch diameter
12-in. pitch diameter—50 teeth
60 teeth *Ans.* $\frac{5}{18}$.

9·5 Find the train value in the following gear train:

10-tooth spur gear
30-tooth spur gear—40-tooth spur gear
120-tooth spur gear—single-threaded worm
40-tooth worm wheel
Ans. $\frac{1}{360}$.

9·6 A compound reverted spur-gear train with four wheels, 2, 3, 4, 5, has a train value of $1:4\frac{1}{2}$, all gear teeth having the same pitch. 2 has 40 teeth, 3 has 60 teeth. Find the number of teeth in 4 and 5. If the diametral pitch is 3, find the distance between shaft centers.

Ans. $N_4 = 25$; $N_5 = 75$; 16.667 in.

9·7 The back gear train of a lathe is made up as follows: Wheel 2 on the cone pulley with 16 teeth drives 3 with 72 teeth. Wheel 4 is rigidly connected to 3 and drives 5, connected to the live spindle of the machine. The train value is $1:13\frac{1}{2}$. Find the numbers of teeth on 4 and 5.

9·8 Determine the numbers of teeth for the four helical gears of a compound reverted gear train if all the teeth have a diametral pitch of 12, the distance between the shaft centerlines is $2\frac{1}{2}$ in., and the train value is 1:6.

9·9 It is desired to connect two parallel shafts having their centerlines 6 in. apart by a pair of spur gears. The diametral pitch should be one of those given in Fig. 8·15. Determine the number of teeth on each gear for a train value of 5:1. Specify the diametral pitch used. What other factor would probably be considered in making a final selection of the numbers of teeth to be used?

9·10 A compound triple-reduction gear train is to reduce the speed of the driving shaft from 1250 to 10 rpm in equal steps. If the distance between successive shaft centerlines is to be 12 in. and the number of teeth on each driven gear is 28, determine the diametral pitch of the gear teeth.

9·11 When an auto is in intermediate gear, the gear train in use is composed of the following gears, the first one being directly connected to the engine:

24 teeth
41 teeth—34 teeth
31 teeth—11-tooth bevel pinion
56-tooth bevel gear

(*a*) Find the ratio of the rear-axle speed to the engine speed.

(*b*) If the tires are 30 in. in diameter, find the engine speed corresponding to a car speed of 20 mph. *Ans.* (*a*) 1:7.93. (*b*) 1775 rpm.

9·12 In the automobile transmission shown in Fig. 9·5, calculate the four possible speed ratios of shaft B to shaft A when the numbers of teeth on the gears are as follows:

C—22, F—39, G—32, D—29, E—38, H—23, L—18

9·13 What is an epicyclic gear train? How may an ordinary gear train be converted into an epicyclic?

9·14 An epicyclic train consists of a simple train of three wheels, 1, 2, and 3, carried on a frame 4. Wheel 1 is fixed and 4 turns clockwise at 75 rpm. Wheel 1 has 60 teeth, 2—20 teeth, 3—30 teeth. Find the speed and sense of the motion of 3. *Ans.* 75 rpm counterclockwise.

9·15 An epicyclic gear consists of a simple gear train of two wheels 1 and 2, carried on a frame 3. Wheel 1 is fixed; 2 turns counterclockwise at 100 rpm. Wheel 1 has 40 teeth, 2—50 teeth. Find the speed and direction of motion of 3. *Ans.* 55.56 rpm counterclockwise.

9·16 In a reverted epicyclic train the gears in order are 1, 2, 3, 4. Arm 5 pivots about the center of 1 and carries the wheels 2 and 3, keyed together at its outer end. Wheel 1 has 30 teeth, 2—50, 3—20, 4—60. The arm 5 is driven at 150 rpm. Find the speed of 4 when 1 is fixed. *Ans.* 120 rpm.

9·17 An epicyclic train is composed of a fixed annular wheel 1, with 150 teeth. Meshing with 1 is a wheel 2 which drives wheel 4 through an idler 3, 4 being concentric with 1. Wheels 2 and 3 are carried on an arm which revolves clockwise at 100 rpm. Wheel 2 has 25 teeth, 3—30 teeth, 4—40 teeth. Find the speed and sense of rotation of 4.

9·18 An epicyclic train contains a fixed annular wheel 1, with 200 teeth. Meshing with 1 is wheel 2 with 90 teeth, which drives 3 with 20 teeth. Wheel 3 is concentric with 1. Wheel 2 is carried on an arm 4 which revolves about the axis of 1. Wheel 3 is the driver, and it rotates at 100 rpm clockwise. Find the speed of arm 4.

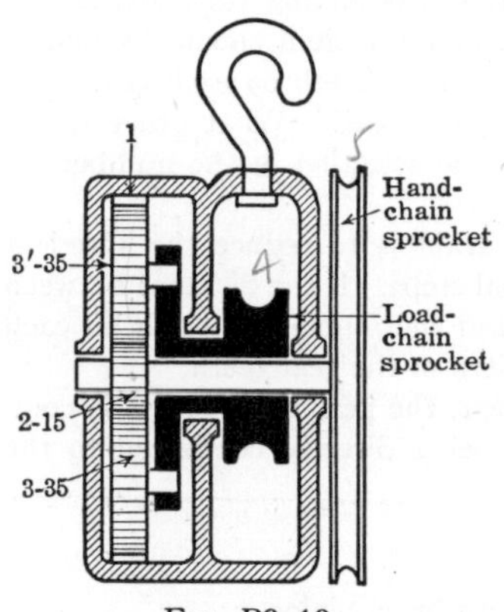

FIG. P9·19.

9·19 The epicyclic train used in a hoisting block is shown diagrammatically in Fig. P9·19. The hand-chain sprocket is 12 in. in diameter and the load-chain sprocket is 6 in. in diameter. Gear 2 is keyed to the hand-chain sprocket shaft. Gears 3, 3′ are pivoted on arms attached to the load-chain sprocket. Annular gear 1 is stationary. The numbers of teeth are as indicated in the figure. Find (*a*) ratio of the chain speeds, (*b*) the load that can be lifted by a pull of 100 lb on the hand chain (friction neglected).

Ans. (*a*) 1:13$\frac{1}{3}$. (*b*) 1333 lb.

9·20 Make the calculation for the speed ratio of the epicyclic train shown in Fig. 9·15.

9·21 Find the speed ratio obtained by use of the gear train shown in Fig. P9·21.

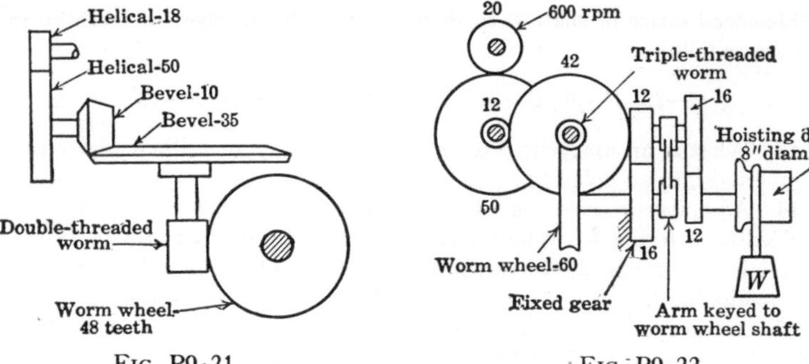

FIG. P9·21. FIG. P9·22.

9·22 Determine the rate at which the weight W is raised by use of the gear train shown in Fig. P9·22.

9·23 In the epicyclic gear train shown in Fig. P9·23 shaft A is rotated at 350 rpm in a clockwise sense. Gear 2 has 20 teeth, 3 has 28 teeth, and 4, 35 teeth. Gears 2 and 3 are attached to arm 5. Find the number of teeth on the fixed gear 1 and the speed and sense of rotation of shaft B.

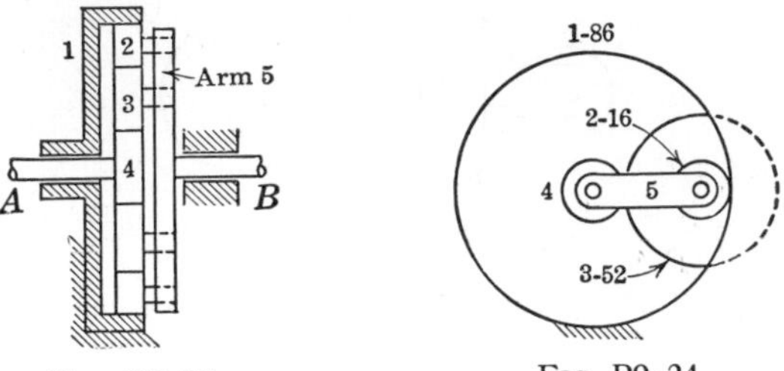

FIG. P9·23. FIG. P9·24.

9·24 In the epicyclic train shown in Fig. P9·24, gears 2 and 3 are keyed to a shaft carried on revolving arm 5. Arm 5 turns about the axis of gears 1 and 4. (*a*) If all the gear teeth have the same pitch, find the number of teeth on 4. (*b*) If 4 rotates at 600 rpm clockwise, find the angular velocity and sense of rotation of arm 5. *Ans.* 18 *t*, 36.3 rpm clockwise.

9·25 In Fig. P9·25, 1 is a fixed internal gear. Shafts A and B are coaxial. Arm 6 is keyed to A and carries at its outer end gears 2, 3, 4. Gear 2 has 40 teeth; 3, 18; 4, 20; 5, 50. (*a*) If all gears have the same pitch, find the number of teeth on 1. (*b*) If shaft A rotates at 200 rpm clockwise, find the speed and sense of rotation of shaft B.

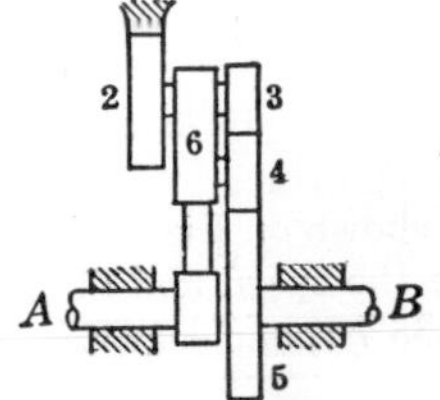

FIG. P9·25.

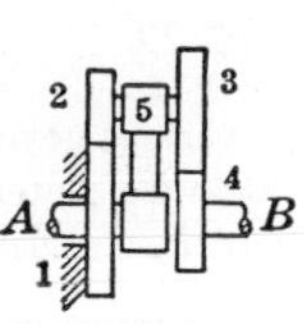

FIG. P9·26.

9·26 In the epicyclic shown in Fig. P9·26 all gears have the same pitch. Gear 1 has 80 teeth, and 2 has 40 teeth. Shaft A with arm 5 rotates at 100 rpm clockwise, and shaft B rotates at 180 rpm counterclockwise. Determine the number of teeth on gears 3 and 4.

9·27 Gear 10, Fig. P9·27, is rotated at a speed of 200 rpm. Find the speed at which weight W is raised.

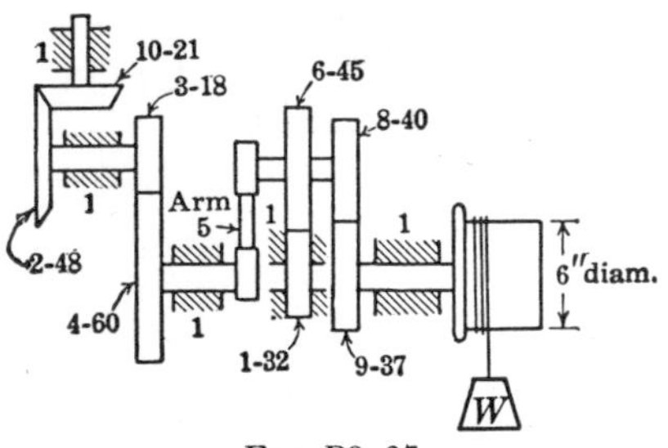

FIG. P9·27.

9·28 In Fig. P9·28 gear 2 has 20 teeth, 3 has 40 teeth and 4 has 30 teeth. (*a*) If gear 2 is held fixed and gear 4 turns +25 rpm, find the rpm of the arm 5. (*b*) If gear 2 turns −5 rpm and the arm +3 rpm, find the rpm of gears 3 and 4.

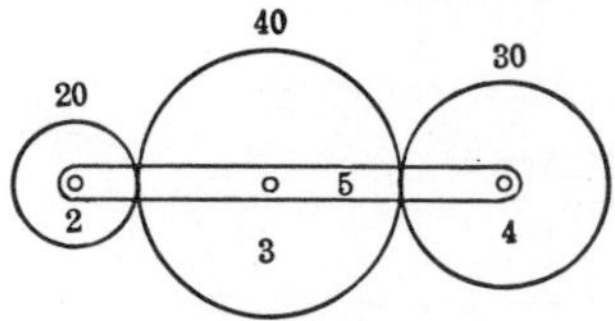

FIG. P9·28.

9·29 In Fig. P9·29 the numbers of teeth on the various gears are shown. If shaft *A* rotates 100 rpm clockwise, determine the speed and direction of rotation of shaft *B*.

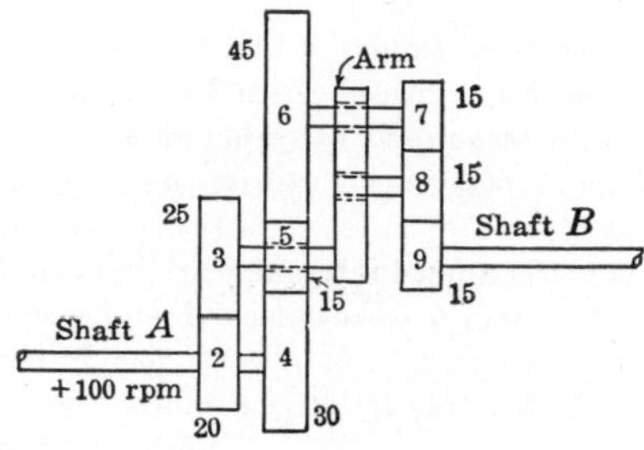

FIG. P9·29.

9·30 The numbers of teeth on the various gears are shown on Fig. P9·30. If shaft *A* rotates 100 rpm counterclockwise, determine the speed and direction of rotation of the arm, or shaft *B*. *Ans.* 135.7 rpm clockwise.

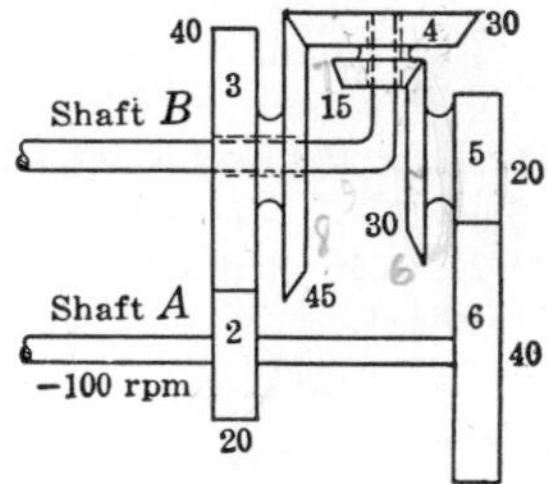

FIG. P9·30.

10 Flexible Connectors

10·1 Belts, ropes, and **chains** are the important members of the class of links that we term nonrigid or flexible, since their form changes while in motion. They are adapted for transmitting a pull but are incapable of carrying a thrust.

Ropes and belts do not give a positive drive, because their ability to transmit power depends on friction between the band and pulleys. Thus they must be given an initial tension, which causes a pressure on the bearings much higher than in equivalent chain or gear drives.

BELT DRIVES

10·2 Belts run with greatest economy at 3000 to 5000 fpm. Their operation is affected by exposure to the weather and by the presence of water, oil, grease, etc., which alter the frictional forces at the contact surfaces.

The drive not being positive, a definite phase relationship cannot be maintained between driver and driven unit. This precludes the use of belts for many purposes, as, for example, for the operation of cam shafts and timing devices in internal-combustion engines, for driving the lead screw in lathes when thread cutting, and for connecting moving parts of many automatic machines.

10·3 Speed ratio in belt drives We shall assume that no slippage takes place and that the material is inextensible. Neither of these assumptions is correct in practice, and therefore our calculated theoretical speed must be modified to take care of these factors.

In Fig. 10·1 we have a belt drive in which R_2, R_3 are the radii of the driving and driven pulleys, respectively, and t is the belt thickness. Evidently, when the belt is bent round a pulley, the outside fibers will stretch and the inside fibers contract. There will be a neutral surface at the center of the belt at which neither extension nor contraction will take place. The speed ratio of the drive will, therefore, be equal to that of a pair of pulleys of radius $R_2 + t/2$ and $R_3 + t/2$ connected by a belt of infinitesimal thickness.

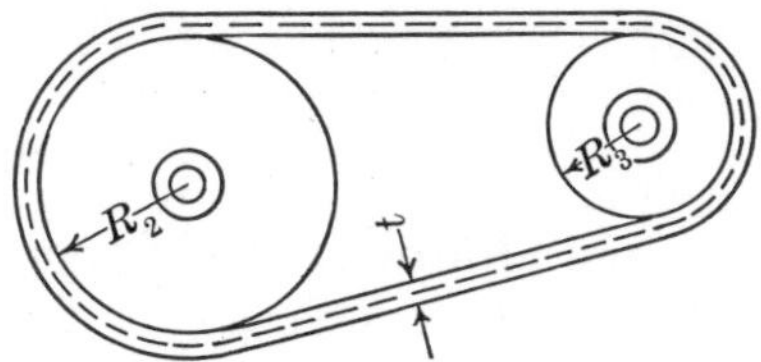

FIG. 10·1 Open Belt Drive.

Let $\mathbf{v}$ = belt speed = linear velocity at the neutral surface. Then,

$$\omega_2 = \frac{\mathbf{v}}{R_2 + \frac{t}{2}} \qquad \omega_3 = \frac{\mathbf{v}}{R_3 + \frac{t}{2}}$$

Therefore,

$$\frac{\omega_3}{\omega_2} = \frac{R_2 + \frac{t}{2}}{R_3 + \frac{t}{2}} \tag{10·1}$$

Usually t is small in comparison with R_2 and R_3. Therefore we may write as a close approximation,

$$\frac{\omega_3}{\omega_2} = \frac{R_2}{R_3} \tag{10·2}$$

When the speed of a driven shaft is calculated from that of the driver by one of the above equations, the result is known as the **ideal speed.** The **actual speed** of the driven shaft will always be somewhat less, the difference being due to "slip," which in practice amounts to 2 to 4 per cent of the ideal speed. Thus

$$\text{Actual rpm} = \text{ideal rpm}\left(1 - \frac{\text{per cent slip}}{100}\right)$$

A belt of given size will transmit maximum power if run at a linear speed of 4000 to 5000 fpm. It is therefore desirable to design the drive so as to keep within this range, unless the rpm of the driver is low, in which event a lower belt speed may be necessary in order to avoid the use of large and expensive pulleys.

Exact speeds may be unobtainable if stock pulleys are to be used because such pulleys are made only in certain sizes, usually of even-inch diameters. A close approximation is secured by proper selection.

Example A line shaft is to be driven at 500 rpm from an electric motor turning at 1750 rpm. The belt speed should be about 4000 fpm. Provide for a slip of 4 per cent. Find suitable diameters of stock pulleys, which are obtainable in even-inch diameters.

Solution

$$\text{Belt speed} = \pi D_2 n_2$$

where D_2 = driver diameter, and n_2 = rpm

$$4000 \times 12 = \pi D_2 \times 1750$$

or

$$D_2 = \frac{4000 \times 12}{\pi \times 1750} = 8.75 \text{ in.}$$

Also,

$$\text{Ideal rpm} = \frac{\text{actual rpm}}{1 - \text{slip}} = \frac{500}{1 - 0.04} = 521$$

Hence, by equation 10·2,

$$\frac{D_2}{D_3} = \frac{521}{1750} \quad \text{or} \quad D_3 = D_2 \times 3.36$$

If

$$D_2 = 7 \quad 8 \quad 9 \quad 10 \text{ in.}$$

then

$$D_3 = 23.5 \quad 26.8 \quad 30.2 \quad 33.6 \text{ in.}$$
$$(23) \quad (27) \quad (30) \quad (34)$$

Final choice might be influenced by relative cost of pulleys, but, considering desired belt and driven pulley speeds, the values D_2 = 8 in. and D_3 = 27 in. should be selected as giving closest approximation to requirements.

10·4 Crossed and open belt drives The drive of Fig. 10·1, in which both pulleys turn in the same sense, is known as an

open belt drive. In Fig. 10·2 is shown the **crossed belt drive;** here the pulleys turn in opposite senses.

Both forms give satisfactory service, though the crossed drive tends to wear out sooner on account of the rubbing action where

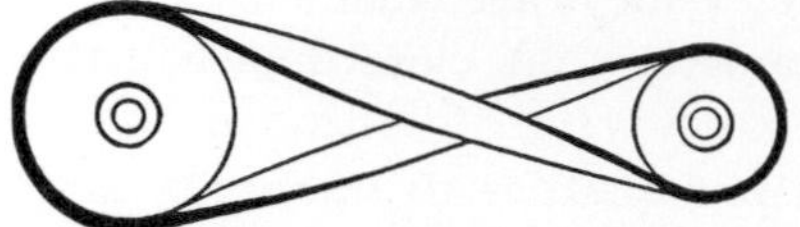

FIG. 10·2 Crossed Belt Drive.

the belt crosses itself. This is more pronounced when the belt is wide and the drive a short one. The larger arcs of contact between belt and pulleys in the crossed drive are advantageous.

A combination consisting of one open and one crossed belt in conjunction with loose pulleys (see Fig. 10·3) is used as a means of driving a machine in either direction, or of stopping its motion. The belts are moved sidewise by means of a belt shifter *S*. The belts run on loose pulleys *a* and *c* when the shifter is in its midposition; then the driven shaft is stationary. Moving the shifter to the right throws the open belt on the keyed pulley *b*, whereas moving it to the left brings the crossed belt on the keyed pulley *b*. The motion of the driven shaft may, therefore, be clockwise or counterclockwise, depending on the position of the shifter. The shifter should act on the slack side of the belt, near the driven pulley. This drive is quite common in connection with machine tools.

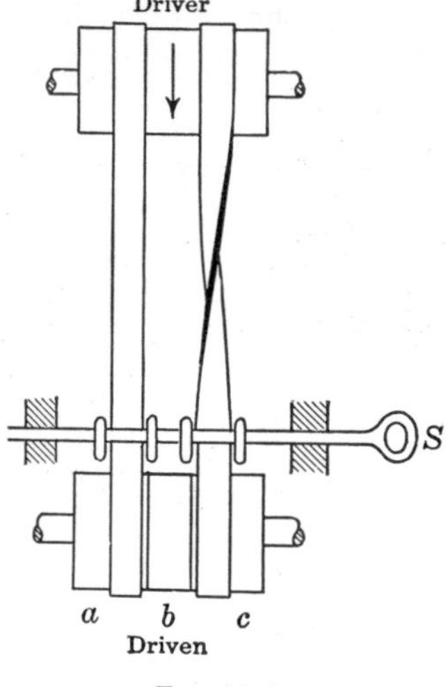

FIG. 10·3.

10·5 Crowned and flat pulleys A crowned pulley has a larger diameter at the middle of the face than at the ends, whereas a **flat pulley** has the same diameter throughout. When flat pulleys are used, a very slight misalignment of the shafts or a small defect in the belt will cause the belt to run off the pulleys. This can be avoided by means of a belt guide which has arms to hold the belt in the required position, by flanging the pulleys, or by using crowned pulleys. Guides and flanges cause wear on the edges of the belt; hence crowned pulleys are preferable.

The reason why the crown pulley causes the belt to run centrally may be seen by reference to Fig. 10·4. Here the belt is shown in a position at one side of the pulley. The belt tends to stretch more on the side *BD* than on the side *AC*; it therefore assumes a curved form. As the pulley rotates, section *AB* will move along the paths indicated by the dashed lines *AE* and *BF*. The belt therefore runs toward the central plane of the pulley and takes up a position where its centerline coincides with the ridge of the crowned surface.

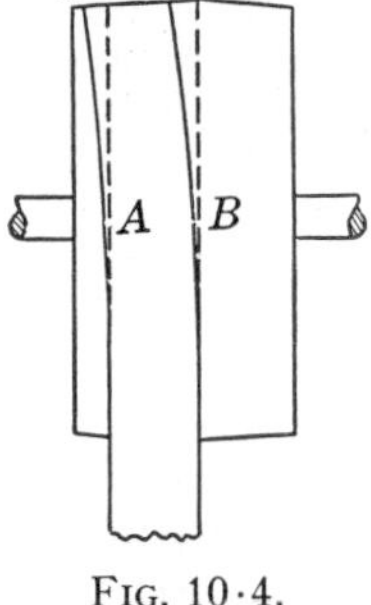

FIG. 10·4.

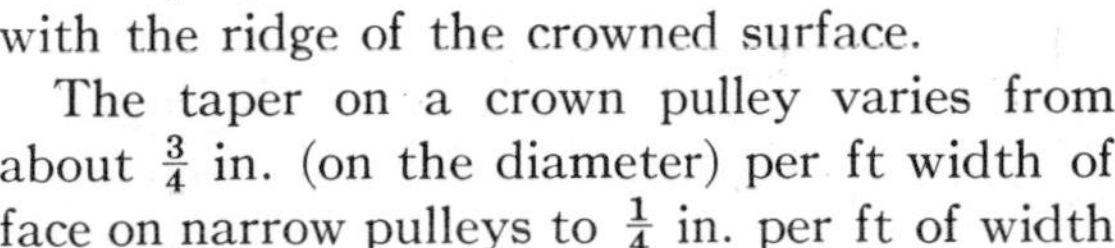

The taper on a crown pulley varies from about $\frac{3}{4}$ in. (on the diameter) per ft width of face on narrow pulleys to $\frac{1}{4}$ in. per ft of width on wide ones. The taper may be uniform as shown in the rim section of Fig. 10·5, or the profile may be a circular arc as in Fig. 10·6.

FIG. 10·5. FIG. 10·6.

The face of the pulley is usually a little wider than the belt in order to prevent overhang if the belt is not running exactly central.

10·6 Nonparallel shaft drives. Quarter-twist drives Belts are most commonly employed for connecting parallel shafts, but they may be used to connect nonparallel shafts as well. In any belt drive the following condition must be observed in regard to the location of the pulleys in order to keep the belt from running off.

The belt must leave each pulley in the central plane of the pulley face toward which it moves.

A drive connecting two shafts at 90° is known as a **quarter-twist** belt drive. One form is shown in Fig. 10·7. The pulleys are located to conform to the law just stated. Note the plan view of the drive, in which the pulleys intersect at *A*, the mid-point of both faces.

Evidently the belt can be run only in the direction indicated by the arrows. The point X, where the belt leaves the upper pulley, is in the plane XY passing through the middle of the lower pulley; also, point R, where the belt leaves the lower pulley, is in the plane RS passing through the middle of the upper pulley. This form of drive can also be used for connecting shafts at any angle between 0° and 180°. When the angle is 0° we have an ordinary open belt drive; at the other extreme it becomes a crossed belt drive.

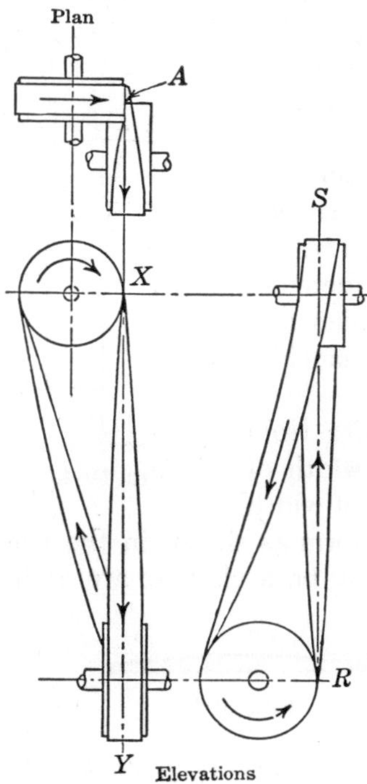

Fig. 10·7 Quarter-Twist Belt Drive.

An alternative variety of quarter-twist drive is shown in Fig. 10·8. This has a guide pulley, or **mule pulley,** on the slack side of the drive. The mule pulley incidentally increases the arc of contact of the driving pulley; its main object is to bring the belt leaving this pulley into the plane passing through the middle of the driven pulley face. In this drive, a uniform tension is obtained across the belt section on the tight side, since the center of the belt is always in the plane passing through the middle of the driven pulley. This is not true of the drive of Fig. 10·7. By tilting the forward end of the mule-pulley shaft upward to the proper angle, the tension can be made uniform across the section on the slack side also. This drive is suitable for rotation in one direction only, because reversal would put the guide pulley on the tight side of the belt.

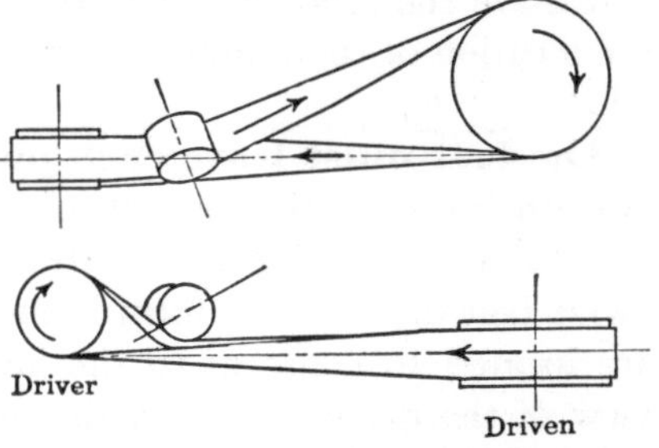

Fig. 10·8 Belt Drive Using Mule Pulley.

Quarter-twist belts should be avoided wherever possible, as the wear on such belts is excessive. They give fairly good service with narrow belts on long drives.

10·7 Calculation of belt length Knowing the center-to-center distance L and the pulley radii R_2 and R_3, we can calculate the ideal belt length (see Figs. 10·9 and 10·10). In both figures we draw DE parallel with AB, meeting CA at E. The total length of belt $= FG + DC +$ arc $FHD +$ arc CJG.

Now,

$$FG + DC = 2(DC) = 2\sqrt{(DE)^2 - (CE)^2} \qquad (\text{angle } DCE = 90°)$$

$$= 2\sqrt{L^2 - (R_2 \pm R_3)^2} \qquad (10·3)$$

The positive sign is used for crossed belts, and the negative for open belts.

Let θ be the angle made by the straight portion of the belt with the line of centers.

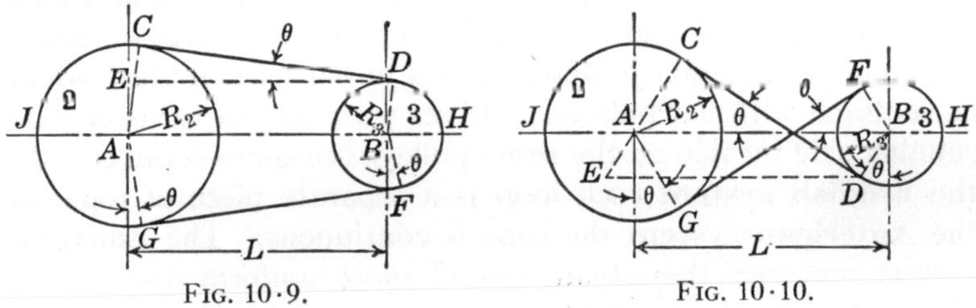

Fig. 10·9. Fig. 10·10.

(a) Open belts From Fig. 10·9, where the angles are expressed in radians,

$$\text{Arc } CJG = (\pi + 2\theta)R_2 \quad \text{and} \quad \text{Arc } FHD = (\pi - 2\theta)R_3$$

The total length of the open belt,

$$FG + DC + \text{arc } CJG + \text{arc } FHD$$

is therefore equal to

$$2\sqrt{L^2 - (R_2 - R_3)^2} + \pi(R_2 + R_3) + 2\theta(R_2 - R_3)$$

$$= 2\sqrt{L^2 - (R_2 - R_3)^2} + \pi(R_2 + R_3) + 2(R_2 - R_3)\sin^{-1}\left(\frac{R_2 - R_3}{L}\right) \qquad (10·4)$$

(b) Crossed belts It can be shown by Fig. 10·10 that the exact length of these belts is given by the expression

$$2\sqrt{L^2 - (R_2 + R_3)^2} + \pi(R_2 + R_3) + 2\theta(R_2 + R_3)$$
$$= 2\sqrt{L^2 - (R_2 + R_3)^2}$$
$$+ (R_2 + R_3)\left[\pi + 2\sin^{-1}\left(\frac{R_2 + R_3}{L}\right)\right] \qquad (10\cdot5)$$

The value of this expression is constant as long as $(R_2 + R_3)$ and L are constant. We reach the important conclusion that the length of a crossed belt is constant when the center-to-center distance and sum of the radii of the pulleys are constant.

ROPE DRIVES

10·8 Ropes are run on grooved pulleys. The groove acts as a guide for the ropes, and the wedging action in the groove makes it possible to transmit power with less initial tension than would be required with flat pulleys. Drives with several turns of rope running side by side on the same pulleys are quite common. In the **English system** each loop is a separate piece of rope; in the **American system** the rope is continuous. The American system possesses the advantages of more uniform distribution of tension over the different turns and permits of the use of one tightener for the drive. On the other hand, in the English system, breakage of one turn does not put the whole drive out of commission, but much splicing of ends is necessary and no convenient way of properly taking up the stretch is possible.

Rope drives are practically always used in preference to other mechanical drives for long-distance transmission of power, on the ground of both cost and suitability. However, the general adoption of electric power, accompanied by the practice of driving each machine or group of machines by a separate motor, has rendered the rope drive almost obsolete.

The calculation of the speed ratio for a rope drive differs in no way from that of a belt drive. Kinematically, the two drives are identical.

V-BELTS

10·9 Belts of trapezoidal section, known as V-belts, have become a popular form of mechanical drive during the past few years, and for some purposes they have entirely replaced the older type of flat belt.

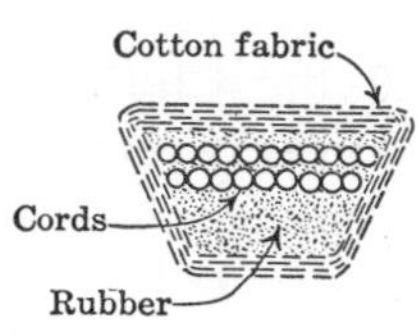

Fig. 10·11 Section through V-Belt.

The V-belt is almost always of the endless type constructed of canvas, cotton cords, and rubber, the whole being molded and vulcanized together. Figure 10·11 shows a typical section. The sides of the belt are slightly concave, and the included angle is usually 42°. The belts run in grooved pulleys, the angle of the groove being about 36° in the smaller-diameter pulleys and 38° to 40° in larger pulleys. Pulley-groove angles are made less than belt angles, which become smaller when the belt is bent around the pulley.

V-belts possess two valuable characteristics. First, they may be operated very satisfactorily with a short center-to-center distance. This distance need not be greater than the diameter of the larger pulley. Second, they require little adjustment to compensate for wear or stretch, since, owing to the wedging action in the groove, this style of belt will transmit a considerable amount of power without excessive slip even when the initial tension is practically nil.

L. H. Gilmer Co., Div. U. S. Rubber Co.
Fig. 10·12 V-Belt Drive.

It is usual for a V-belt drive to consist of several belts run in parallel grooves, which is an example of the English system (see Fig. 10·12), where the power to be transmitted exceeds the capacity of a single belt. The belts should then be "matched," particularly in length; otherwise the load will not be equally distributed among the belts, and uneven wear will result.

For similar reasons it has not been found satisfactory to attempt to run old and new belts in parallel.

CHAIN DRIVES

10·10 Chains are made of a series of jointed metal links in a variety of forms. They may be classified in accordance with their uses as (*a*) hoisting and hauling chains, (*b*) elevator and conveyer chains, and (*c*) power-transmission chains.

The **coil chain** (Fig. 10·13) is the usual form of hoisting chain. It is made of iron of circular section bent to the proper form and welded at the joint. The **sprocket wheels** for this chain are shown in Figs. 10·14 and 10·15. The plain **grooved sheave** is

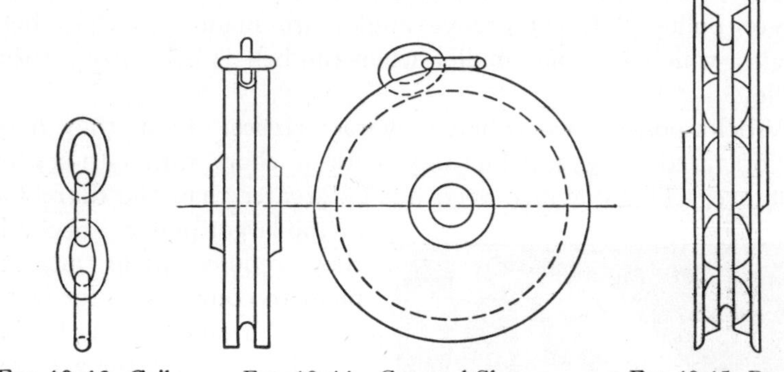

FIG. 10·13 Coil Chain. FIG. 10·14 Grooved Sheave. FIG. 10·15 Pocket Sheave.

suitable only as a guide and not as a means of transmitting energy to or from the chain. The **pocket sheave** (Fig. 10·15) has a central groove and depressions which conform to the profile of the links, a liberal clearance being allowed at the end of these depressions to provide for stretching of the chain or irregularities in the pitch.

Conveyer chains The **Ewart chain** (Fig. 10·16), which has easily detachable links, and the **pintle chain** (Fig. 10·17) are two of a large class of chains employed in mills, mines, and factories for elevators and conveyers handling a variety of materials. For such purposes, buckets, flights, etc., are connected to the chains by various kinds of attachment links. These chains are generally of malleable iron and are run on cast sprockets.

This construction is suitable for rough service and slow speeds. These chains are operated at about 100 fpm.

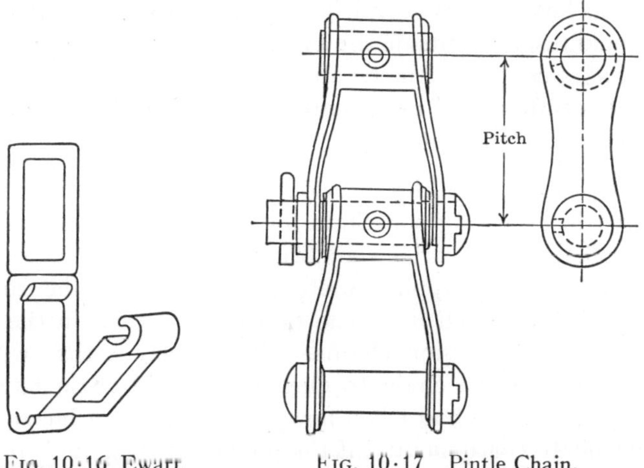

Fig. 10·16 Ewart Chain.

Fig. 10·17 Pintle Chain.

Power-transmission chains These are generally of stronger materials and more accurately made than the classes of chains described above. Wearing surfaces are of steel, hardened and ground, and the chains are run on sprockets with cut teeth. Consequently, they are more costly but may be operated at higher speeds.

The **roller chain,** illustrated in Fig. 10·18, is used mainly as a power-transmission chain. The construction at the joints is

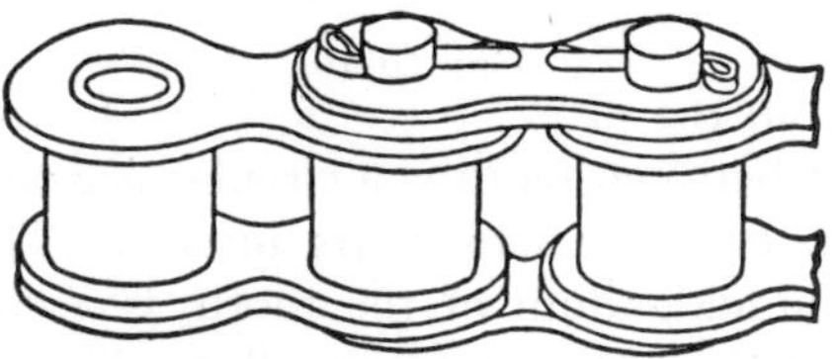

Fig. 10·18 Roller Chain.

such as to obtain as large bearing surfaces as possible. The pin connecting two sections is either riveted to the outer pair of links or fastened in such a way that it cannot turn relative to them. The bushing through which this pin passes is riveted to the inner pair of links. When the chain bends in passing on or off a sprocket, the pin and bushing form a turning pair and their contact surfaces slide on one another. Here the area is large, extending nearly the full width of the chain. The area of contact of pin and links is small, and if they had relative motion rapid wear would result. Outside the bushing is a hardened-steel roller which makes contact with the sprocket teeth.

Silent chains are used entirely for power transmission. These are considered later.

10·11 Sprocket profiles Two practical difficulties are encountered in designing sprockets for chain drives. The first is that the chain pitch varies somewhat because of inaccuracies in manufacture. This applies more particularly to the rougher forms of chain, though it is true to a minor extent in the high-grade power-transmission chains. The second is that wear at the joints causes the chain to elongate, an old chain having a greater pitch than it had when new. Wear does not increase the sprocket pitch; consequently, if the pitches of chain and sprocket were originally the same, after service they will differ somewhat. For both the reasons just given, the design must be such as to permit of satisfactory operation when the pitches are not equal.

Let us first consider the form of sprocket tooth for roller chains we might use if no pitch difference existed. The profile of such a tooth is shown by the solid lines in Fig. 10·19. The portion

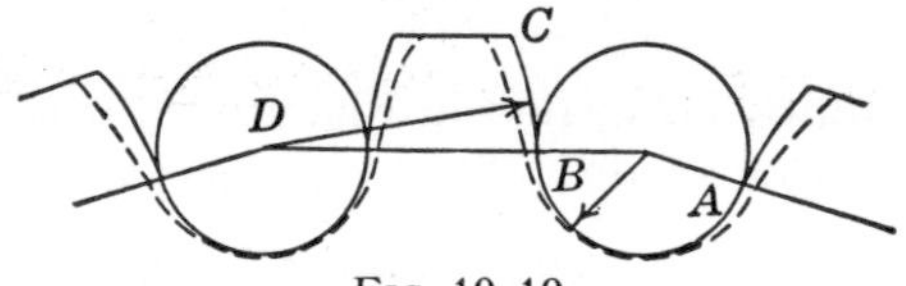

FIG. 10·19.

AB of the space between teeth is a circular arc of radius equal to that of the pin or roller which fits into it. The portion *BC*, extending to the addendum of the tooth, is a circular arc with center at the axis *D* of the adjacent roller. This form causes the roller to maintain contact with the tooth when leaving the sprocket. Such a tooth would be satisfactory only so long as the chain pitch remained equal to that of the sprocket. Elongation of the chain would cause the roller to strike hard on the tooth side.

Modification of the theoretical tooth form to allow for a difference in pitch of chain and sprocket is made in two ways.

One of these, now used only on the slow-speed (conveyer) type of chain, is illustrated by the dashed lines of Fig. 10·19. The tooth is made narrower in order to obtain "pitch-line" clearance; also the addendum is rounded off to reduce the friction as the rollers move in and out of contact. Figures 10·20 and 10·21 illustrate in an exaggerated form the effect of these modifications on the chain action. Figure 10·20 shows the engagement of a new chain and sprocket, the chain pitch being somewhat shorter than that of the sprocket. It is evident that roller A, just about

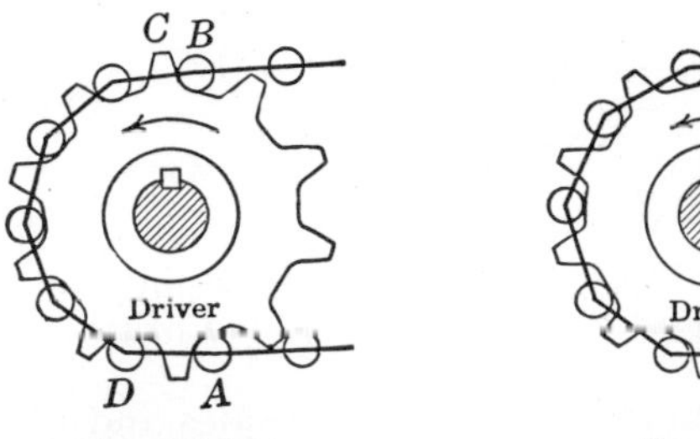

FIG. 10·20. FIG. 10·21.

to leave the driving sprocket, is carrying all the load. Roller B, which has just come into engagement, barely clears the back of the tooth C. When A goes out of engagement it rolls up the side of the tooth and allows the chain to slip back slightly on the sprocket so that roller D will take the load. At a certain point in the life of the chain, when its pitch has increased to that of the sprocket, all the rollers will bear equally against the mating teeth if the wear is uniform. Later, when it has worn so that its pitch is greater than that of the sprocket, conditions will be as illustrated in Fig. 10·21. Here the roller A, which is the last to engage the sprocket, is carrying all the load which it picked up as it rolled down the side of the tooth. During this period the whole chain would slide ahead somewhat on the sprocket. Therefore, whether the pitch of the chain is larger or smaller than that of the sprocket, the load is carried by one tooth at a time. The chain slippage leads to noise and vibration at high chain speeds.

10·12 Silent chains This type, illustrated in Fig. 10·22, is used for power transmission. Its construction is such that it can very easily be made in any width to suit the load to be carried.

Consequently it is suitable for transmission of large amounts of power. The characteristic feature is the hooked form of link, made of stampings from sheet steel.

This chain was invented by Renold in England. The Morse silent chain and that made by the Link-Belt Engineering Company are two well-known varieties manufactured in the United States. Both of these have constructions at the joint differing somewhat from the original Renold chain, the object being to improve the wearing qualities.

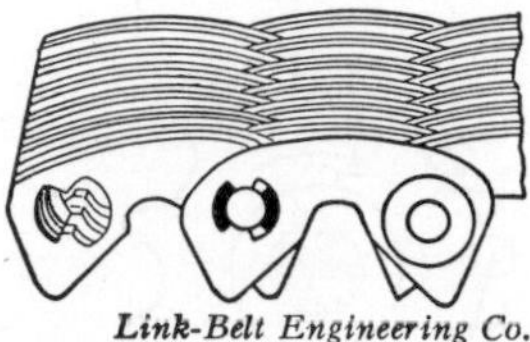

Link-Belt Engineering Co.

FIG. 10·22 Silent Chain.

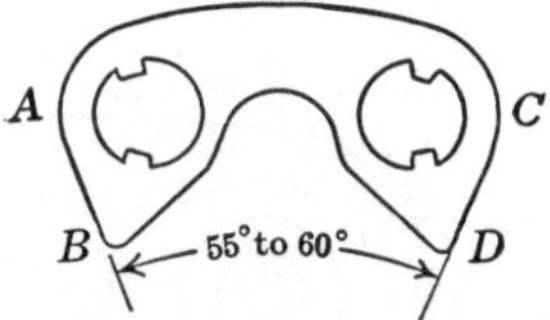

FIG. 10·23 Link for Silent Chain.

The sprocket teeth are straight on the sides and make surface contact with the straight portions *AB* and *CD* (Fig. 10·23) of the links. The angle between *AB* and *CD* is 55° to 60°. When the chain pitch increases through wear the chain rides nearer the points of the teeth, the action being the same as that of the roller chain with the standard sprocket. The comparative absence of noise can be attributed to three factors: (*a*) automatic adjustment of position on the sprockets to compensate for wear, (*b*) large surface contact with sprockets, and (*c*) sliding action during contact, due to the oblique direction of relative motion of the surfaces at the instant preceding contact.

Figures 10·22 and 10·23 show a joint construction consisting of a round pin fitted into a bushing made in two segments, each of which is keyed to one row of links, with the result that sliding motion, due to bending of the chain, takes place between the pin and segments. This construction has two advantages over a plain pin-and-hole method of connecting the links: first, it practically doubles the bearing surface; and second, it improves the lubrication on account of the long unbroken bearing surface on each segment.

In the form of chain, extensively used, illustrated in Fig. 10·24, the pin itself is made in two segments each keyed to a row of links. The segments are so shaped as to approximate rolling contact with each other, the sliding action being very slight. This tends to eliminate friction losses and results in an improvement in durability and efficiency in the transmission of power.

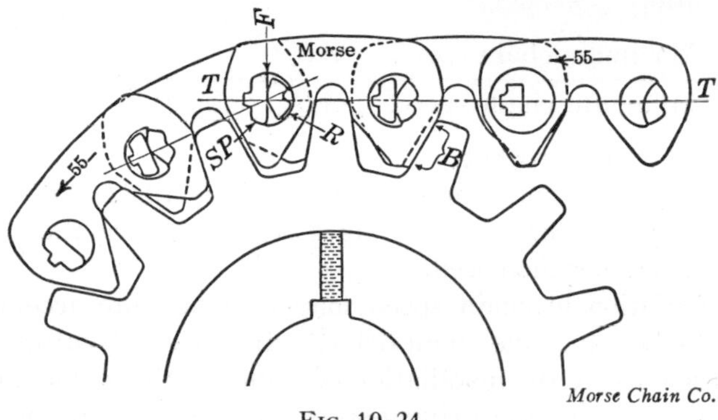

FIG. 10·24.

10·13 Speed variation in chain drives When a chain passes around a sprocket, it takes the form of a polygon whose sides have a length equal to the chain pitch. Suppose that the driving sprocket is rotating at uniform speed; the chain will then have a linear velocity that varies somewhat on account of the polygonal form in which it moves. This variation is small in sprockets with many teeth and becomes of importance only in applications using six- or eight-tooth sprockets in combination with a long-pitch chain.

Figure 10·25 shows a six-tooth sprocket in a position where a roller at C has just come in contact with a sprocket tooth. The

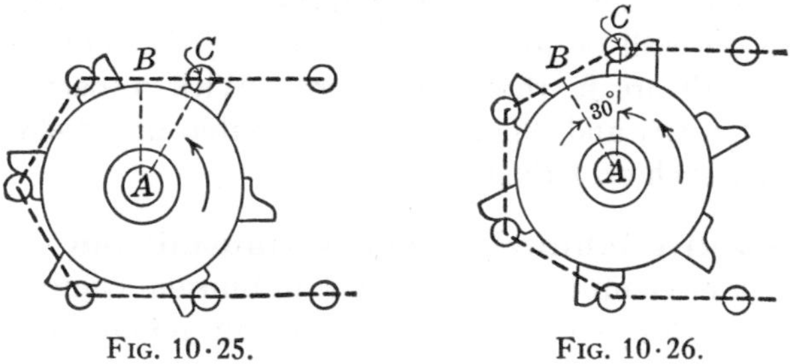

FIG. 10·25. FIG. 10·26.

chain velocity is evidently equal to $\omega \times AB$, where ω is the angular velocity of the sprocket. After the sprocket has revolved 30° the condition is that of Fig. 10·26, and the chain velocity is $\omega \times AC$. The former expression evidently fixes the value of the minimum chain velocity; the latter gives the maximum chain velocity.

The ratio,

$$\frac{\text{Maximum chain speed}}{\text{Minimum chain speed}} = \frac{AC}{AB} = \frac{1}{\cos 30^\circ} = 1.155$$

for the six-tooth sprocket.

With an eight-tooth sprocket this ratio is 1.082; with a ten-tooth, 1.051; and diminishing values are obtained as the number of teeth is further increased.

The variation in chain speed may in a measure account for noise produced in some chain drives. In bucket elevators it has on occasion led to the installation of compensating devices in the drive, which cause the driving-sprocket speed to vary in order to obtain a constant speed of the chain. In this case, however, the object is not to reduce noise but to avoid irregular motion of the elevator. Such devices are never required when the sprocket has more than eight teeth.

When power is being transmitted from one shaft to another, it is obvious that, if the driving sprocket is the same size as the driven sprocket and both have at any instant the same angular position of the teeth with reference to the tight side of the chain, then the speed variation due to the action of the chain on the driving sprocket will be neutralized by an opposite action taking place at the driven sprocket. Hence, under these conditions, the driving and driven shafts will have a constant velocity ratio.

Where the sprockets are not of the same size, a partial compensation can still be made by so adjusting the center distance that the teeth are in the same phase. With respect to noise, rapidity of wear, and efficiency, a noticeable improvement can be made by such an adjustment.

10·14 Positive infinitely variable transmission An interesting form of chain drive which has an unusual combination of properties, namely, positive drive and an infinite number of speed ratios, is shown in Fig. 10·27. The device consists essentially of two sprocket wheels and a chain of special type. The sprockets are composed of two sliding disks with fluted, conical working surfaces. The chain contains pockets filled with flat steel plates which are free to move in a direction at right angles to the length of the chain. When the chain engages the fluted sides of the sprocket, the plates are pushed over by the ridges on one side of the sprocket and enter the hollows on the opposite

Link-Belt Co.

FIG. 10·27 Positive Variable-Speed Transmission.

side of the sprocket. In effect the sprockets continuously form mating teeth on the chain as it makes contact, and thus a positive drive is secured. The sprocket sides are adjusted by a hand wheel and lever mounting in such a way that one pair move toward each other as the others move apart, the result being to change the pitch diameters at which the chain operates, and hence alter the speed ratio.

In the usual design, the speed of the driven shaft at maximum setting of the transmission is two to six times its minimum speed.

QUESTIONS

10·1 Under what conditions are belts a suitable form of drive? In what cases is it impossible to use a belt drive?

10·2 What is the relationship between the speed ratio and the pulley diameters in a belt drive? How can the exact formula be modified when the belt thickness is small compared with the pulley radius?

10·3 Find the pulley diameters that must be used on motors turning at the following revolutions per minute if the belt speeds are to be 3200 fpm: (*a*) 3600 rpm; (*b*) 1750 rpm; (*c*) 900 rpm; (*d*) 600 rpm.

10·4 Split steel pulleys are available in stock sizes varying by inch increments. What diameters should be selected for a grinder turning at 4000 rpm if the motor runs at 1750 rpm and 4 per cent slip is estimated? The belt speed is to be approximately 3300 fpm.

10·5 A multiple V-belt drive using *C* section belt is employed to connect a Diesel engine running at 1600 rpm to a line shaft running at 600 rpm. The manufacturer recommends a belt speed not higher than 5000 fpm and pulley diameters not less than 9 in. Select stock pulleys (no fractional inch sizes), allowing for 3 per cent slip.

10·6 A belt drive is to connect a motor running at 900 rpm to a line shaft which is to turn approximately at 500 rpm. The belt speed is not to exceed 3850 fpm. Standard pulleys are obtainable in even-inch diameters. Select pulley diameters (*a*) neglecting belt thickness and slip, (*b*) allowing for belt thickness of $\frac{3}{8}$ in., (*c*) allowing also for slippage of 5 per cent.

Ans. (*a*) 15 in., 27 in. (*b*) 16 in., 29 in. (*c*) 14 in., 27 in.

10·7 A machine which should run at 200 rpm is to be belt-driven through one countershaft running about 600 rpm by a motor running at 1800 rpm. The belt speed is not to be higher than 4000 fpm. The largest pulley in the drive must not be over 36 in. in diameter. Select suitable pulley of stock sizes (even-inch diameters) for the drive, allowing for a total slip of 8 per cent.

10·8 What are "crossed" and "open" belt drives? Show by sketch how a pair of belts can be used in conjunction with tight and loose pulleys to produce a reversible drive. Name a common use for an arrangement of this sort.

10·9 What three methods are used to prevent a belt from running off the pulleys? Explain why crowning the pulley tends to cause the belt to run centrally. What two forms are used for the pulley profile?

10·10 Show two methods of connecting shafts at 90° by means of a belt drive. Where a mule pulley is employed, on which side of the belt should it act?

10·11 What is the law, regarding the location of the pulleys in any belt drive, that must be observed in order to keep the belt from running off the pulleys?

10·12 Calculate the belt length in an open belt drive connecting two shafts 10 ft apart, the pulleys being, respectively, 12 in. and 24 in. in diameter.

Ans. 24 ft $8\frac{3}{4}$ in.

10·13 A V-belt drive has pulleys, respectively, 6 in. and 18 in. in diameter. The center-to-center distance should not be less than the diameter of the larger pulley. Find a satisfactory belt length for shortest drive. Stock belts are available in lengths varying by 2-in. increments.

10·14 Give two reasons for using grooved pulleys in rope drives. What are the American and English systems of rope drives? Point out the advantages and disadvantages of each.

10·15 Under what conditions are V-belt drives to be preferred to other forms of mechanical drives?

10·16 Sketch four common types of chains. State the kind of service for which each is best adapted.

10·17 What methods are employed in the design of sprocket teeth to take care of variation in chain pitch, in the case of conveyer and similar slow-speed chains?

10·18 What two forms of chains are especially adapted for power transmission? What features of construction make them suitable for operation at high speeds?

10·19 What form of tooth would be suitable for a roller chain if the pitch were perfectly uniform and the elongation due to wear could be neglected?

10·20 In designing sprocket tooth for slow-speed conveyer chains, by what means can we provide for a small difference of pitch between chain and sprocket?

10·21 How is the elongation of the chain due to wear taken care of in the standard type of sprocket for roller chains? What form of tooth is used in this sprocket?

10·22 Sketch the link used in the silent chain. What part of the link bears against the sprocket, and what is the shape of the contact surface?

10·23 When a silent chain bends, what surfaces form the turning pair? Why has the original form of silent chain been altered, in regard to the construction at the joints?

10·24 To what factors can the quiet operation of the silent chain be attributed?

10·25 Explain why a variation in the speed ratio is obtained in a chain drive during each revolution when the sprockets are of unequal size? How is this variation affected by the number of teeth on the sprockets? When the sprockets are of equal size, how must they be arranged in order to obtain a constant speed ratio?

10·26 A silent chain with $\frac{5}{8}$-in. pitch is used to connect an engine turning at 1500 rpm to a machine rotating at approximately 350 rpm. The chain speed is to be not more than 1800 fpm. The sprockets should not have less than 18 teeth nor more than 105 teeth. Find suitable tooth numbers for both sprockets.

10·27 A chain of $\frac{1}{2}$-in. pitch is driven from an 18-tooth sprocket turning at 2000 rpm. Calculate the maximum and minimum linear velocity of the chain.

10·28 In a chain drive the smaller sprocket has 12 teeth. By proper arrangement of the phase position of the larger sprocket it is possible to secure a 50 per cent compensation of the speed variation due to the smaller sprocket. Will the drive be satisfactory if the speed variation must be kept below 1 per cent?

11 Miscellaneous Mechanisms

11·1 Ratchets A ratchet mechanism in its most common form consists of a device whereby two members capable of rotation are connected so that one will rotate the other in a certain sense, but not in the opposite sense.

Its use, however, is not limited to members having rotational motion. Often the driver has a reciprocating straight-line motion and compels linear motion of the driven member in one direction only.

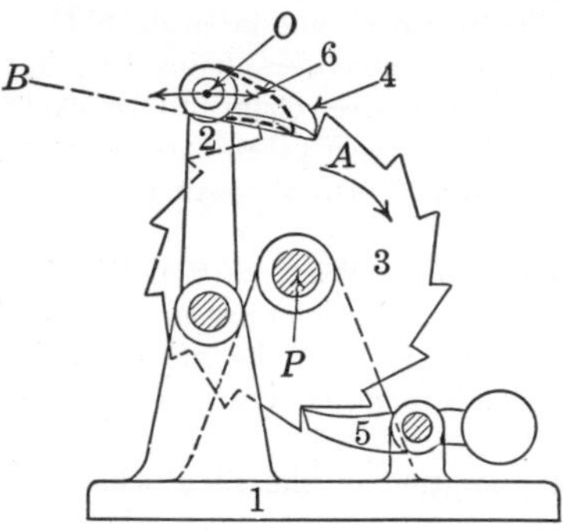

FIG. 11·1 Toothed Ratchet.

The ratchet wheel 3 of Fig. 11·1 is turned in a clockwise sense by the action of pawl 4 when driver 2 turns clockwise. When 2 turns counterclockwise, 3 remains stationary. A second pawl 5, pivoted on the frame of the mechanism, is sometimes used to prevent the ratchet wheel from running backward.

Two points should be noted in regard to the teeth on the ratchet wheel.

(*a*) The normal *AB* to the face of the tooth at the point of contact should pass between centers *O* and *P*. Otherwise the pawl tends to slip out of contact when the driving force is applied.

(*b*) A certain amount of "lost motion" may occur if the point of the pawl is not against a tooth face at the instant when the driver begins to move in the driving direction. This lost motion may vary from zero to the tooth pitch as a maximum, depending on conditions. A small pitch, therefore, insures a small amount of lost motion. By the addition of another pawl 6, of different length (see Fig. 11·1), the possible lost motion may be reduced to one-half its former value.

Figure 11·2 shows the mechanism of a lifting jack in which the driven link is given rectilinear motion when the handle is oscillated.

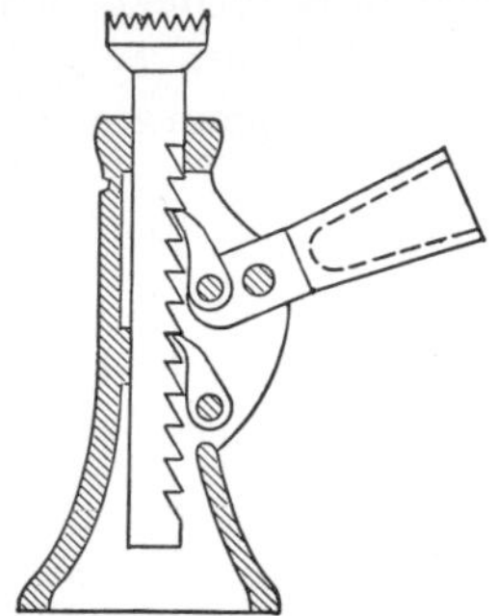

Fig. 11·2 Lifting Jack.

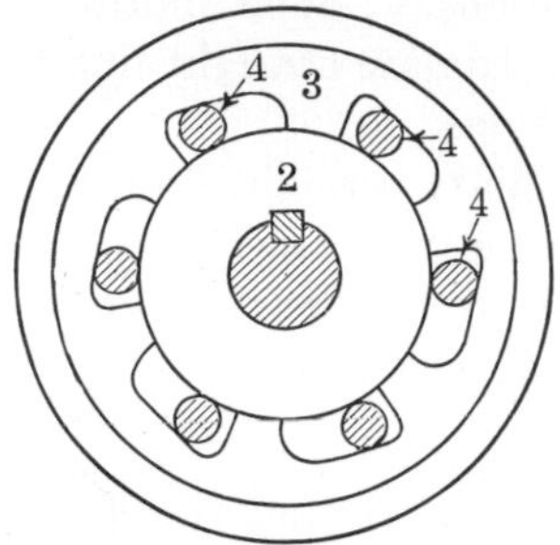

Fig. 11·3 Silent Ratchet.

Figure 11·3 shows a form of **silent ratchet.** Rollers 4 are placed in slots which taper. Rotation of the driver 2 in a clockwise sense causes the rollers to move toward the narrow ends of the slots where they wedge tightly and thus lock together driver 2 and driven member 3. This mechanism can be arranged to allow little lost motion, and the noisy action of the pawl-and-tooth type is avoided. Positive action is lacking, since friction alone is responsible for the transmission of motion to the driven member.

Figure 11·4 illustrates another form of silent ratchet with friction pawls whose action is assisted by the use of springs.

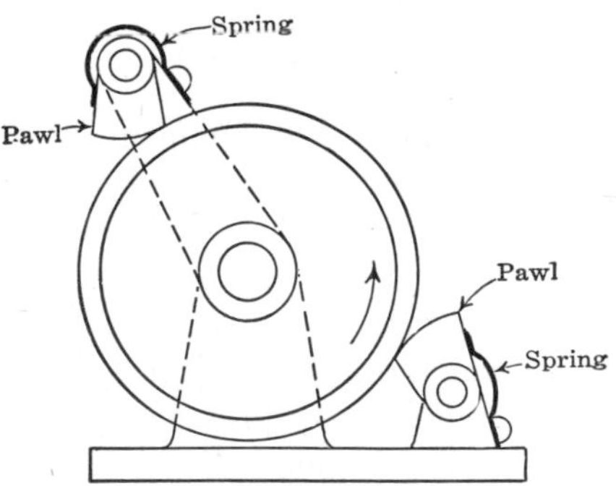

Fig. 11·4 Silent Ratchet.

11·2 Straight-line motions Where a link is required to have rectilinear motion, constraint is generally effected by the use of a "slide and guide" with plane surfaces in contact. Rectilinear motion can be obtained, however, by several mechanisms containing turning pairs only. These are generally termed "straight-line motions." Such motions can be divided into two classes: (*a*) approximate straight-line motions, and (*b*) accurate straight-line motions.

The **Watt** straight-line motion is of historical interest only, being little used nowadays. Watt employed it in his engines as a substitute for the present-day crosshead and guide, because in his day it was difficult to form accurate plane surfaces in metal.

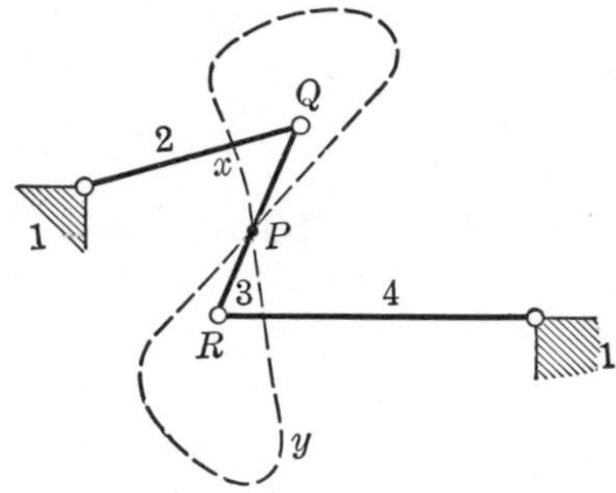

FIG. 11·5 Watt Straight-Line Motion.

The device consists of a four-bar linkage, 1, 2, 3, 4, as in Fig. 11·5. A point P on 3 traces out the dotted path shown in the figure. This will be observed to have a portion xy which is **approximately straight,** provided that point P is so selected that

$$PQ : PR = 4 : 2$$

Crosby indicator motion A mechanism shown in Fig. 11·6, composed of links connected by turning pairs, is used to connect the indicator piston rod with the recording pencil on the **Crosby engine indicator.** The pin A, connected to the end of the piston rod, is constrained to move in a vertical straight line. The pencil point at P traces out the indicator card on the drum 2. In order that the instrument may present an accurate record of the pressure changes in the engine cylinder, it is necessary that the linkage connecting the piston rod and recording point fulfill the following requirements:

(*a*) It should cause the point P to move in a straight line parallel to the direction of motion of the indicator piston.

(*b*) It should magnify the piston motion in order to draw an indicator card of reasonable size, the ratio of magnification being constant for all positions of the mechanism.

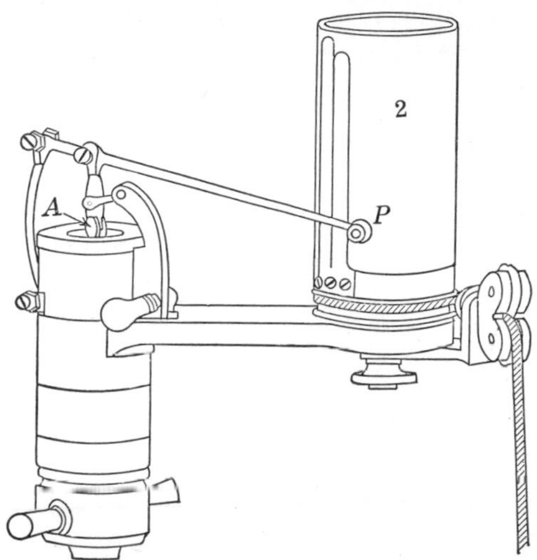

FIG. 11·6 Crosby Indicator.

Neither of these objects is accomplished with mathematical accuracy by the Crosby motion, but the errors involved are so small as to be negligible for practical uses.

The **Peaucellier** straight-line motion (Fig. 11·7) belongs to the class of **accurate straight-line motions,** since it can be shown that point C moves in a straight-line path CD, perpendicular to the centerline of the fixed link 1. The lengths of the links must have the following relative values: $2 = 3 = 4 = 5$; $6 = 1$; $7 = 8$. This mechanism has too many joints to be of great practical importance.

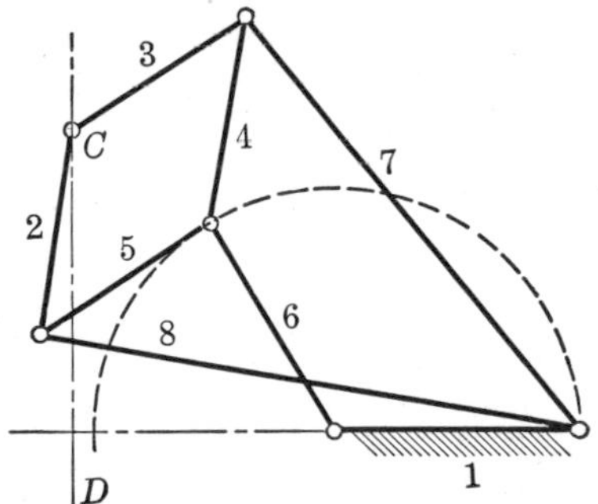

FIG. 11·7 Peaucellier Straight-Line Motion.

11·3 The pantograph is generally used as a means of reproducing drawings or maps to a smaller or larger scale. It has also been employed as a reducing motion in connection with engine indicators. Two forms are shown in Figs. 11·8 and 11·9. In both figures the length *OA* equals *BC*; also *OC* equals *AB*. The

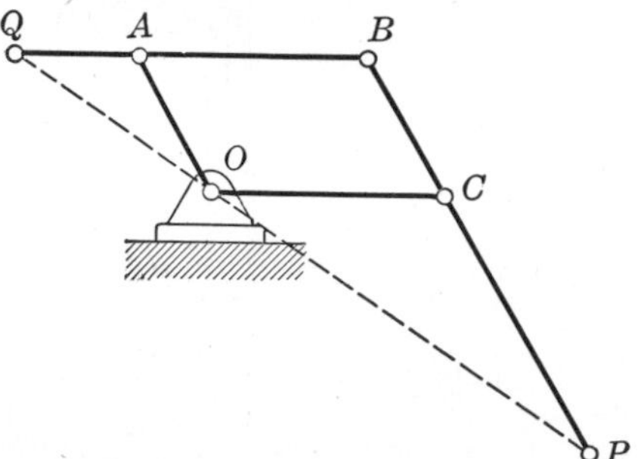

FIG. 11·8 Pantograph.

figure *OABC* is therefore a parallelogram, *O* being the fixed point or pole.

If we place the mechanism in any position, select any point *P* on *BC*, and then find a point *Q* on *AB* such that *O*, *Q*, *P* fall in the same straight line, it can be proved that points *P* and *Q* will trace out similar figures. In the practical form of the

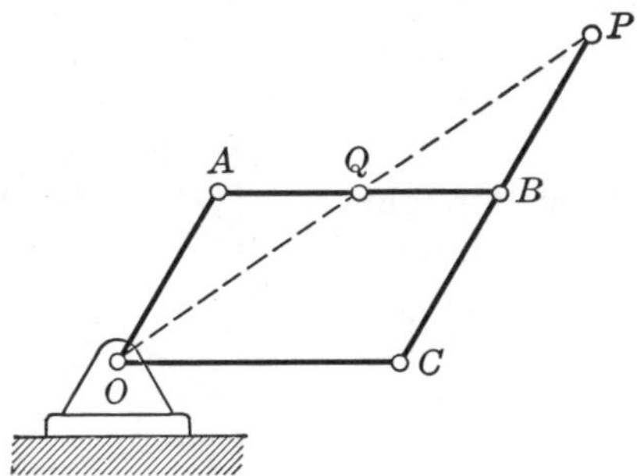

FIG. 11·9 Pantograph.

pantograph, *P* forms the tracer point, which is run around a map or figure, and a copying point at *Q* will reproduce the diagram to a smaller scale.

To prove the essential property of the pantograph, it is necessary to show (1) that *Q* remains on the straight line *OP* for any position of the mechanism, and (2) that *OQ*:*OP* is constant. The figures traced out by *P* and *Q* will then be similar, the linear dimensions being proportional to lengths *OP* and *OQ*.

In the initial position of the mechanism, in which Q lies on the straight line OP, we have similar triangles QBP and OCP and $QB:BP = OC:CP$. This holds true for any position, since QB, BP, OC, CP are fixed lengths. Also QB and OC are always parallel. Therefore, triangles QBP and OCP are always similar. It follows that Q always lies on the straight line OP and that $OQ:OP = BC:CP$ = a constant.

11·4 Elliptical trammel (Fig. 11·10) This device is serviceable in drawing ellipses. In a form somewhat different from

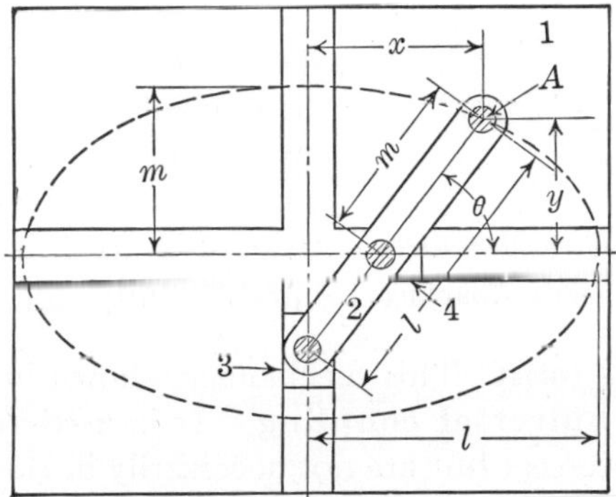

FIG. 11·10 Elliptical Trammel.

that shown in the figure, it has been employed as an **elliptical chuck** for machining parts of elliptical section. Like the **Oldham coupling** it is a four-link mechanism containing two sliding and two turning pairs. The fixed link 1 has in this case elements of two sliding pairs. Any point A on arm 2 can be shown to trace out an elliptical path on 1. This is proved as follows:

Let x and y represent the co-ordinates of point A for any position of the mechanism. From the figure,

$$y = m \sin \theta$$

$$x = l \cos \theta$$

Hence,

$$\frac{x^2}{l^2} + \frac{y^2}{m^2} = \sin^2 \theta + \cos^2 \theta = 1$$

This is the equation for an ellipse with major axis equal to $2l$ and minor axis equal to $2m$.

11·5 Oldham's coupling (Fig. 11·11) This is used to connect shafts that are parallel but not coaxial. It is a four-link mechanism, derived from the slider crank by the substitution of a sliding pair for one of the turning pairs. Link 3 has the form of a disk with a bar or key on each face, the keys being located at 90° from one another. These form sliding pairs with slots cut in the faces of disks 2 and 4.

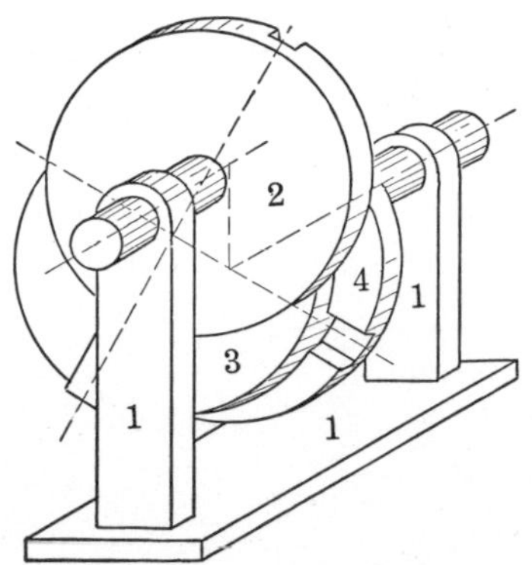

From Kinematics by R. J. Durley

FIG. 11·11 Oldham's Coupling.

The connections between 2, 3, and 4 are evidently such that all three members must turn through equal angles during the same time interval. Hence the velocity ratio of 2 to 4 is constant and equal to unity.

11·6 Hooke's joint This mechanism, shown in Fig. 11·12, is often called a **universal coupling.** It is used to connect two shafts which intersect but are not necessarily in the same straight line. A device of this kind is essential for connecting a driving and driven shaft where the angle between them changes in service. Such a condition is encountered in the transmission of power to the rear axle of an automobile. Here the drive shaft connecting the engine to the rear axle does not make a fixed angle with the axis of rotation of the engine crankshaft, because of the action of the car springs.

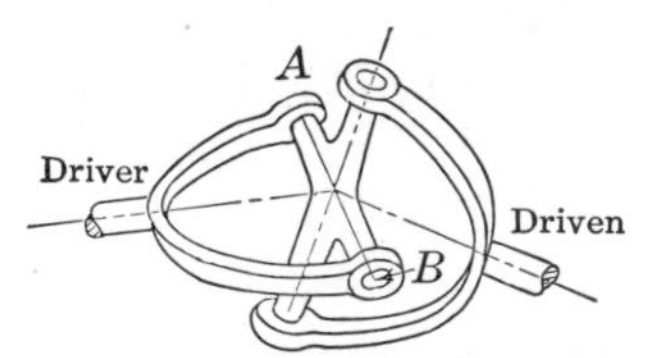

FIG. 11·12 Universal Joint.

It can be shown that a single coupling does not transmit motion with a constant angular velocity ratio, except when the shafts are in line with each other.

The velocity ratio at any instant is equal to

$$\frac{\omega_2}{\omega_1} = \frac{\cos \theta}{1 - \sin^2 \theta \sin^2 (\alpha + 90°)}$$

where θ = angle between the shafts

α = angular displacement of the driving shaft from the position where the pins on the drive shaft yoke lie in the plane of the two shafts

ω_1 = angular velocity of the driving shaft

ω_2 = angular velocity of driven shaft

The angular velocity ratio (ω_2/ω_1) varies from maximum to minimum value during an angular displacement of 90°. The maximum and minimum values of this ratio are shown by the curves of Fig. 11·13. It may be observed that the speed variation increases rapidly with the shaft angle.

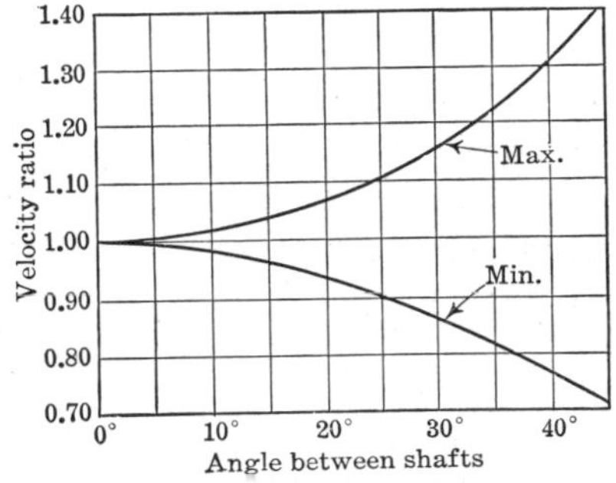

Fig. 11·13.

Constant-speed universal joints In order to avoid trouble due to the speed variation of the Hooke's joint, other forms of coupling having a constant angular velocity ratio have been developed. One of these is the Bendix-Weiss "rolling ball" universal joint shown in Fig. 11·14. This is composed of two yokes on which curved

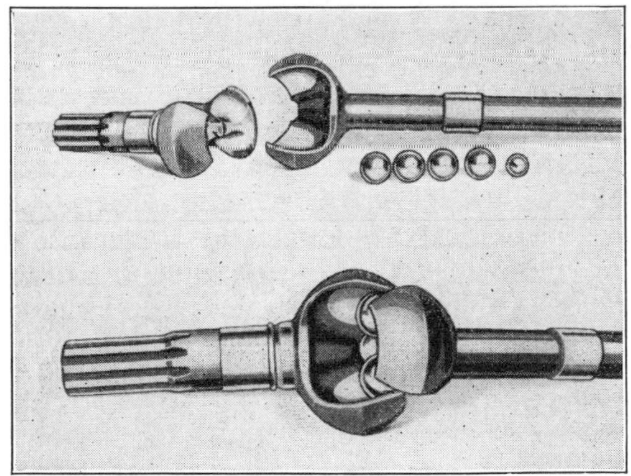

Bendix Corp.

Fig. 11·14 Constant-Speed Universal Joint.

grooves are cut, forming races on which roll four large balls. A fifth and smaller "guide" ball, centrally located, serves as a locking device to keep the assembly in position.

The geometric requirement for securing a constant angular velocity ratio is that the centers of all four balls shall lie in a plane that bisects the angle between the shafts. This requirement is met by proper design of the grooves.

A common use for this joint is in the "front-drive" automobile. Here the power must be transmitted to the front wheels, which must at the same time be capable of swinging through a large angle in order to steer the car. In this application of the universal joint, a nonconstant angular velocity ratio would be very unsatisfactory.

Constant velocity ratio by use of two universals Two shafts lying in **any** relative position may be connected by a pair of universal joints and an intermediate shaft so that they will have the **same angular velocity** at any instant. To accomplish this result, the connecting shaft is located so as to make equal angles with the main shafts, and the driving pins on the yokes attached to the connecting shaft are placed at such an angle that each lies in the plane of the adjacent shafts at the same instant. Under these conditions, a reduction or increase of the speed of the intermediate shaft, as compared with that of one of the main shafts, caused by the interposed coupling, will be exactly neutralized by an equal but opposite change of speed of the other main shaft as compared with that of the intermediate shaft, due to the second coupling. The net result is that both main shafts will have the same speed at any instant. The compensating action of the couplings is due to their symmetrical arrangement with regard to the two planes containing the adjacent shafts.

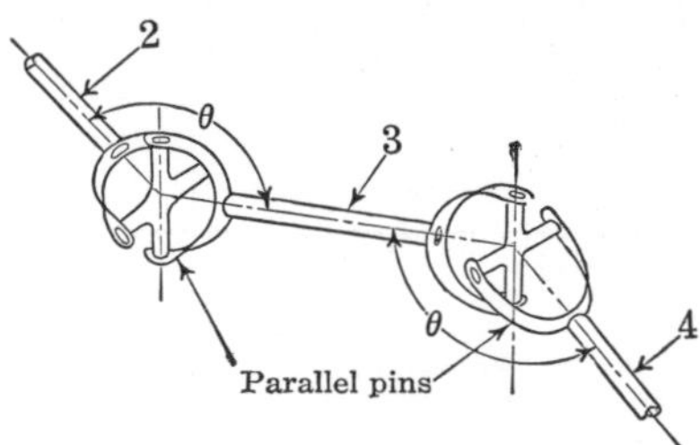

Fig. 11·15 Compensated Drive Using Two Universal Joints.

A drive for connecting parallel shafts, compensated in the manner just described, is shown in Fig. 11·15. Since the planes containing the axes of adjacent shafts are coincident, the driving pins on the connecting shaft yokes are parallel. The compensating effect of the two couplings under these particular circumstances will be clear from inspection of the figure. If the connecting shaft is cut by a transverse plane and one half of the arrangement is rotated about the axis of this shaft, the main shafts may be brought to any desired nonparallel position. When the ends of the connecting shaft are rejoined, compensation is evidently still maintained, and the relative position of the couplings is that already specified as being necessary.

11·7 Geneva stop In certain automatic machinery the **Geneva stop** is used when it is desired to obtain alternate periods of rest and angular motion for a driven member, when the driver rotates continuously in the same sense.

We find examples of it in watches, motion-picture machines, can-making machinery, and indexing devices employed in the machine shop.

It is suitable for movements of the driven link not exceeding 90° for each revolution of the driver. In Fig. 11·16 the driver 2

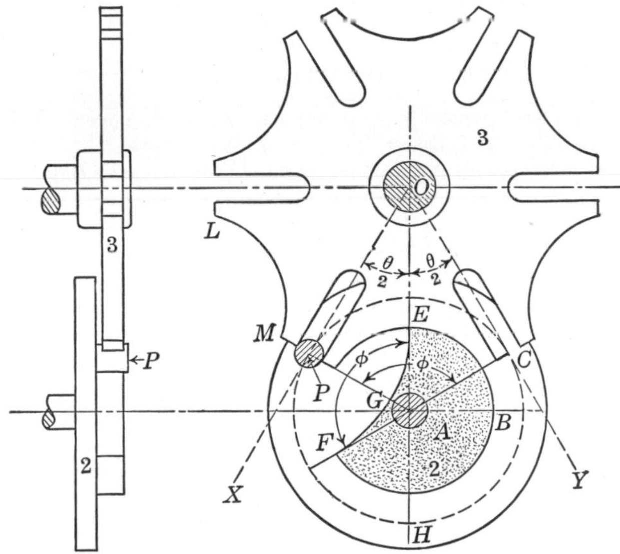

FIG. 11·16 Geneva Stop.

consists of a circular disk to which is attached a driving pin P and a second disk $EBFG$. The pin P engages for a certain portion of each revolution with radial slots in the driven member 3 which it carries forward through an angle θ. When pin P passes out of a slot, the surface EBF engages one of the geometrically similar surfaces *LM* on the driven member and holds it stationary until *P* enters the next slot.

In order that the driven member may be started and stopped without shock, it is necessary that the mechanism be designed in such a way that in the position illustrated the lines *OX*, *OY* are tangent to the circle *PCH* through the axis of the driving pin.

Thus, in laying out the mechanism, an angle $\theta/2$ is measured on each side of the line *OH*, where θ is the desired angular movement of the driven shaft.

Any circle, as *PCH*, tangent to *OX* and *OY*, may be used as the path of the driving-pin axis. The radius of this circle is the crank length for the driving pin, and its center locates the axis of the driving disk. The arc *EGF* is chosen so that the surface will clear the points of the driven disk. The angle *EAF* (ϕ) must be made equal to the angle *PAC* in order that the driven member may be alternately locked in position and released at the proper instants.

QUESTIONS

11·1 For what purpose is a ratchet mechanism employed? Sketch one form (*a*) of rachet with toothed wheel, (*b*) of silent ratchet.

11·2 Show by sketch the working parts of the ordinary lifting jack.

11·3 What two methods may be used to reduce the lost motion in a ratchet mechanism?

11·4 In a ratchet wheel, how must the teeth be shaped so that the pawl will not tend to slip out of contact?

11·5 Sketch the Oldham coupling. For what purpose is this device used?

11·6 Sketch the elliptical trammel, and prove its essential property.

11·7 Sketch one form of the pantograph mechanism. Prove that the copying and tracer points describe similar figures.

11·8 What two requirements must the link motion of an engine indicator fulfill? Sketch the linkage of the Crosby indicator.

11·9 Show by sketch the arrangement, and note the relative lengths of the links, in a Peaucellier straight-line motion.

11·10 Under what conditions is a Hooke's joint a suitable method of connecting two shafts? Show by sketch how you would arrange two such joints to maintain a constant velocity ratio.

11·11 Sketch and explain the action of the Geneva stop.

11·12 In laying out the Geneva stop, the circle, which is the path of the crankpin center, is tangent to the center lines of adjacent slots on the driven disk for one position of the mechanism. Why is this necessary?

DRAFTING-ROOM PROBLEMS *

The drawings are to be made on a 12 in. $\times$ 18 in. sheet with a border $1\frac{1}{4}$ in. wide on the left-hand side and $\frac{1}{2}$ in. wide on the other three sides. A space 2 in. $\times$ 6 in. is provided for the title in the lower right-hand corner.

In the illustrations, the dimensions shown in circles, thus ($2\frac{1}{2}''$), are distances measured from the border line. **These dimensions are always to be taken full size**, regardless of what scale is specified for the drawing.

* The author and reviser wish to acknowledge the valuable assistance of Professor J. I. Clower in the original compilation of many of these problems.

PROBLEM 1

Crosby indicator straight-line motion

The diagram on Plate 1 shows the straight-line motion mechanism used in the Crosby indicator for magnifying the motion of the indicator piston.

Plot the mechanism *four times full size* in the position shown. Then move the piston C upward in steps of $\frac{1}{16}$ in. each for a total distance of $\frac{3}{8}$ in. and plot the path of the pointer P.

Determine and note on your drawing the **ratio of magnification** of the motion of point P to C.

Data:

$AB = 1\frac{3}{4}$ in.	$CE = \frac{7}{32}$ in.
$BD = \frac{5}{8}$ in.	$EF = \frac{29}{64}$ in.
$BP = 3\frac{3}{4}$ in.	$DE = \frac{17}{32}$ in.

Lines AB and DC are parallel and vertical in the position shown.

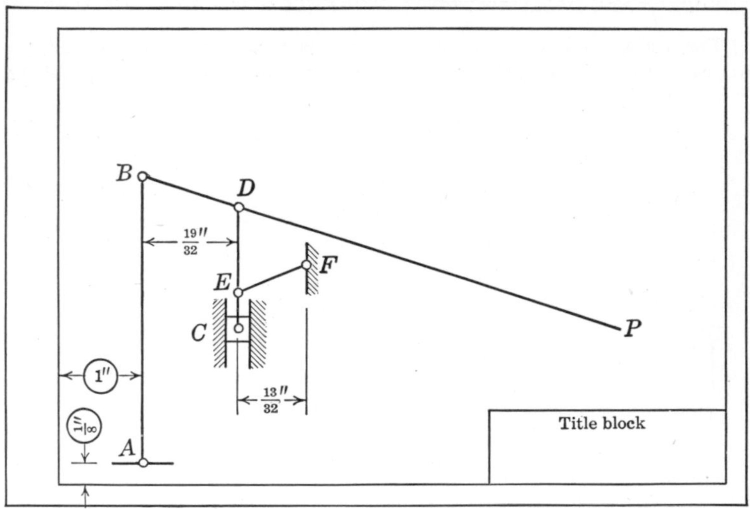

PLATE 1.

PROBLEM 2

Tabor indicator mechanism

1. Plot the linkage shown on Plate 2, *four times full size,* with BP horizontal as shown. Move the pencil point P upward, $\frac{1}{4}$ in. at a time, in a vertical line for a total travel of 2 in., starting 1 in. below the initial position. Locate the corresponding positions of points C, D, and E.

2. Determine and note on your drawing the **ratio of magnification** of the motion of point P to D.

3. Determine and indicate on the drawing the **radius and center of the circular arc** which most closely approximates the path of point E. Draw the **outline of the slot** which is required to guide the roller.

Data:

$AB = 1\frac{1}{4}$ in.	$CE = \frac{5}{8}$ in.
$BC = \frac{5}{8}$ in.	$CD = 1$ in.
$BP = 3\frac{1}{8}$ in.	Diameter of roller $= \frac{3}{16}$ in.

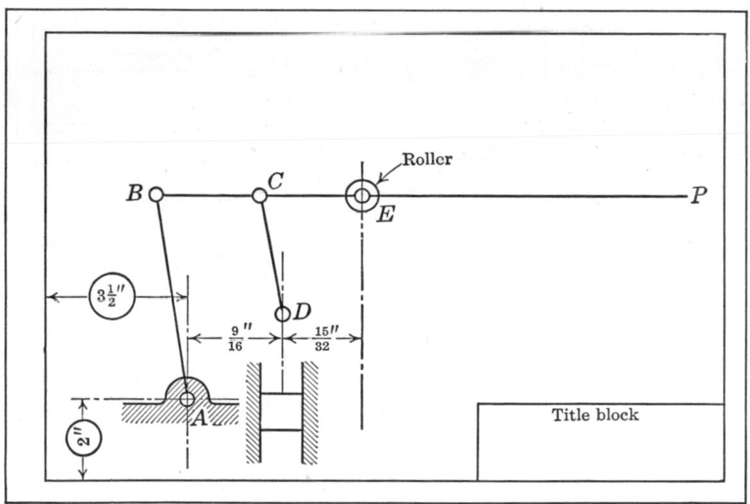

PLATE 2.

PROBLEM 3

Displacement, velocity, and acceleration curves

1. Draw the Scotch yoke shown in Plate 3, to a scale of 3 in. = 1 ft.

2. Calculate the normal and tangential acceleration of the crankpin at an instant when the crank velocity is 120 rpm and the crank acceleration is 180 rad per sec^2. Find graphically the total acceleration of the crankpin, using a scale of 1 in. = 50 fps^2.

3. Assuming that the crank rotates at a uniform rate of 300 rpm, plot polar and time curves for the displacement, velocity, and acceleration of the slotted link. For each curve make the maximum ordinate $1\frac{1}{4}$ in. long. Determine and record the scale for each curve.

4. With the same assumption as in **3,** calculate by formulas the displacement, velocity, and acceleration of the slotted link at crank angles of 0°, 30°, 60°, 90°, 120°, 150°, and 180°. Tabulate these values.

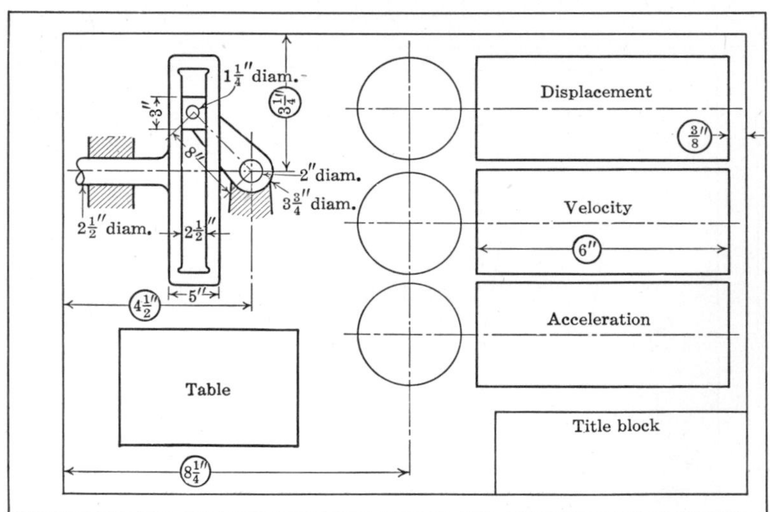

PLATE 3.

PROBLEM 4

Displacement, velocity, and acceleration-time curves

The following data relate to a moving body:

Time, sec	Distance, ft	Time, sec	Distance, ft
0	0	6	40.00
1	13.75	7	42.20
2	22.20	8	43.80
3	28.50	9	44.80
4	33.50	10	45.15
5	37.10		

Plot: (*a*) Using the above data, a **distance-time curve** on a base line located as shown on Plate 4. Scales: Distance—1 in. = 6 ft. Time—1 in. = 1 sec.

(*b*) A **velocity-time curve.** Obtain points for each 1-sec interval. Double the ordinates.

(*c*) An **acceleration-time curve.** Obtain points at intervals of 1 sec. Double the ordinates. Use *AB* as base line for this curve. Calculate velocity and acceleration scales, expressing them in foot-second units. Construct graphical scales.

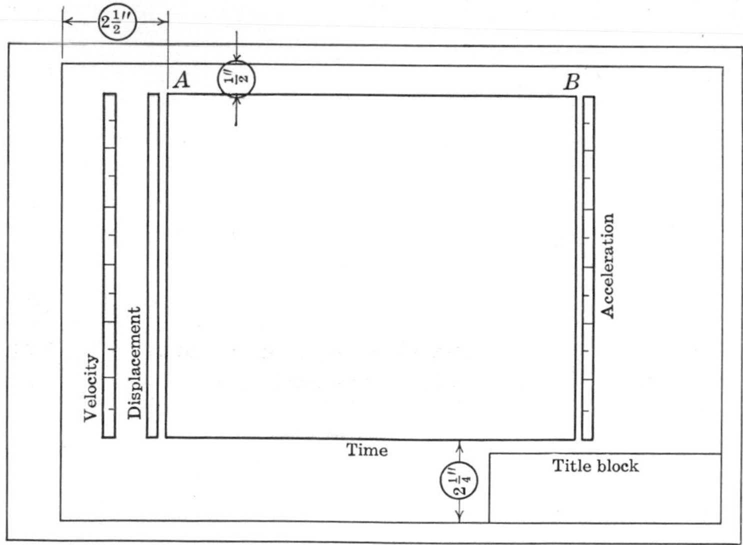

PLATE 4.

PROBLEM 5

Displacement, velocity, and acceleration-time curves

Refer to Plate 4.

The following data relate to a moving body:

Time, sec	Distance, ft	Time, sec	Distance, ft	Time, sec	Distance, ft
0	0	$3\frac{1}{2}$	9.8	7	36
$\frac{1}{2}$	0.2	4	12.8	$7\frac{1}{2}$	39.67
1	0.8	$4\frac{1}{2}$	16.2	8	42.67
$1\frac{1}{2}$	1.8	5	20	$8\frac{1}{2}$	45
2	3.2	$5\frac{1}{2}$	24	9	46.67
$2\frac{1}{2}$	5.0	6	28	$9\frac{1}{2}$	47.67
3	7.2	$6\frac{1}{2}$	32	10	48

Plot: (*a*) From above data, a **distance-time curve** on a base located as shown in Platc 4. Scales: Distance—1 in. = 6 ft. Time—1 in. = 1 sec.

(*b*) A **velocity-time curve.** Obtain points for each $\frac{1}{2}$-sec interval. Multiply ordinates by 4.

(*c*) An **acceleration-time curve.** Obtain points at intervals of $\frac{1}{2}$ sec. Use as base a horizontal line 4 in. below *AB*. Multiply the ordinates by 6.

Calculate velocity and acceleration scales, expressing them in foot-second units. Construct graphical scales.

PROBLEM 6

Centrodes

The skeleton diagrams on Plate 5 represent two four-link mechanisms. Lay them out according to the dimensions tabulated:

Slider-crank mechanism: $AB = 1\frac{1}{2}$ ft; $BC = 6$ ft
Four-bar linkage: $AB = 4\frac{1}{2}$ ft; $BC = 2\frac{1}{4}$ ft; $CD = 6$ ft; $AD = 2$ ft

1. Locate all the instant centers.

2. Plot the path of the centrodes of the instant center O_{31} as follows:

Slider-crank mechanism Holding link 1 fixed, move link 2 through four equal angles to become horizontal, locating the positions of the instant center O_{31}. Draw the resulting centrode. Then hold link 3 fixed, find the corresponding positions of the instant center O_{31}, and draw the resulting centrode.

Four-bar linkage Holding link 1 fixed, move the instant center O_{23} clockwise in six equal intervals of 6 in. each measured along the arc. Find the positions of the instant center O_{31}, and draw the centrode. Then hold link 3 fixed, find the corresponding positions of O_{31} and draw the resulting curve.

3. Print a short statement to the left of the title block, outlining how these centrodes could be used to replace links 2 and 4.

Scale: 1 in. = 1 ft.

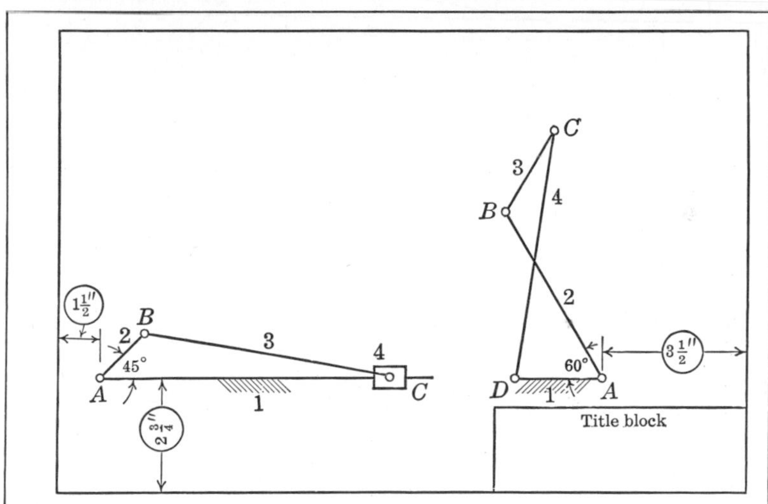

PLATE 5.

PROBLEM 7

Instant centers, linear and angular velocities

(Refer to Plate 6.)

The skeleton drawing represents a six-link quick-return mechanism. Lay out the mechanism according to the dimensions shown on the drawing.

1. Locate all the **instant centers.**

2. Determine graphically the **linear velocities** of points *P*, *Q*, *R*, and *S*, for the position of the mechanism shown in the figure when the driving link 2 makes 15 rpm in a counterclockwise direction. Tabulate the numerical values on the drawing. Velocity Scale: 1 in. = 20 fpm.

3. Representing the angular velocity of 2 by a line 1 in. long, determine graphically the corresponding **angular velocities** of links 3, 4, and 5. Tabulate the numerical values on the drawing.

Scale: 4 in. = 1 ft.

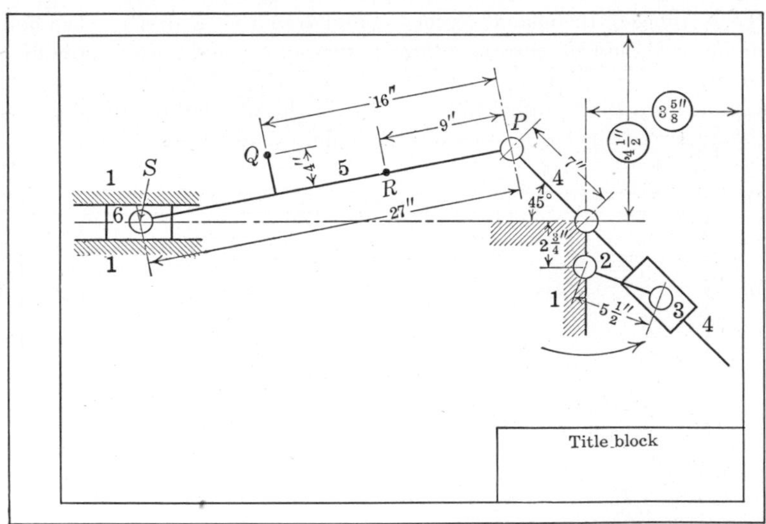

PLATE 6.

PROBLEM 8

Instant centers, linear and angular velocities

The skeleton drawing shown on Plate 7 represents a five-link cam mechanism. Lay out the mechanism according to the dimensions shown on the drawing. The velocity of point P is 10 in. per sec.

1. Locate all the **instant centers.**

2. Determine the **linear velocity** of R, S, and T by:

(*a*) The connecting-link method.

(*b*) The direct method (going from link 5 to link 3).

(*c*) The resolution method.

3. Calculate the angular velocity of link 5, and determine graphically the corresponding **angular velocities** of links 2, 3, and 4.

4. Tabulate all results in the lower left portion of the plate along with the scales used.

Scales: Space = full size; velocity 1 in. = 20 in. per sec, and 1 in. = 10 rad per sec.

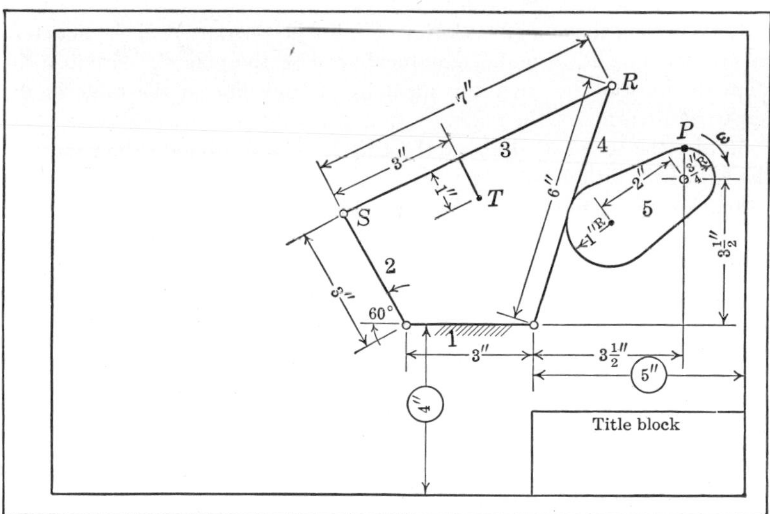

PLATE 7.

PROBLEM 9

Instant centers, linear and angular velocities, accelerations

The skeleton diagram represents a six-link mechanism in which link 2 rotates 100 rpm counterclockwise. Lay out the mechanism according to the dimensions shown on Plate 8.

1. Locate all the **instant centers.**

2. Calculate the **linear velocity** of point R, and find graphically the linear velocity of points S and T by:

(*a*) The connecting-link method.

(*b*) The direct method (going from link 2 to link 5).

(*c*) The resolution method.

(*d*) The image method. Use the pole o. Number the steps, listing the direction and meaning in the table in the upper right corner of the plate.

3. Determine graphically the **angular velocity** of links 4 and 6 from the known angular velocity of link 2.

4. Assuming the angular velocity of link 2 is constant, find the **acceleration** of points R, S, and T graphically. Use the pole o'. Number the steps, listing the direction and meaning of each line in the table in the upper right corner of the plate.

5. List the scales used above the title box, and tabulate the results to the left of the title box.

Scales: Space = full size; Velocity 1 in. = 1 fps, and 1 in. = 10 rad per sec.

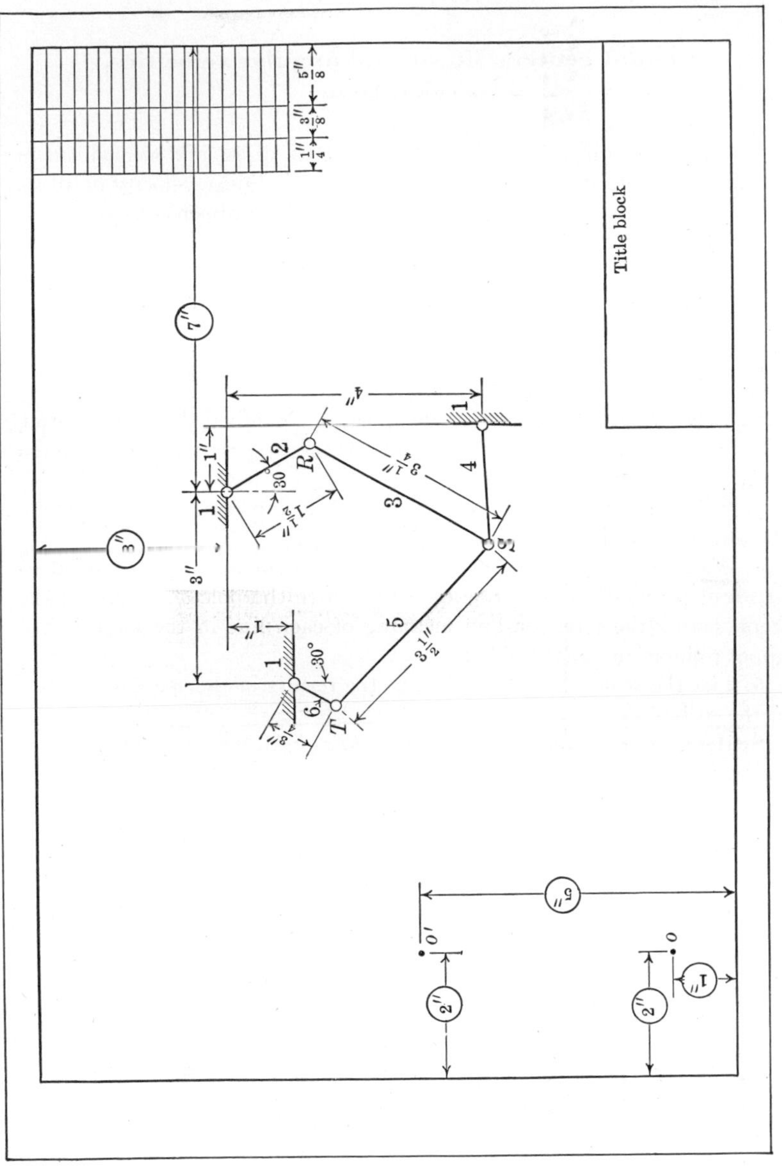

PLATE 8

PROBLEM 10

Instant centers, linear and angular velocities, accelerations

The skeleton diagram of Plate 9 represents a six-link mechanism in which link 2 rotates clockwise, point *R* having a linear velocity of 10 in. per sec. Lay out the mechanism according to the dimensions shown on Plate 9.

1. Locate all the **instant centers.**

2. Find graphically the **linear velocities** of points *S* and *T* by:

(*a*) The connecting-link method.

(*b*) The direct method (going from link 2 to link 5).

(*c*) The resolution method.

(*d*) The image method. Use the pole *o*. Number the steps, listing the direction and meaning in the table in the upper right corner of the plate.

3. Calculate the **angular velocity** of link 2, and determine graphically the angular velocity of links 3, 4, and 5.

4. Assuming the angular velocity of link 2 is constant, find the **acceleration** of points *R*, *S*, and *T* graphically. Use the pole *o′*. Number the steps, listing the direction and meaning of each line in the table in the upper right corner of the plate.

5. List the scales used and tabulate the results in the space to the left of the title block.

Scales: Space = full size; Velocity 1 in. = 5 in. per sec, and 1 in. = 5 rad per sec.

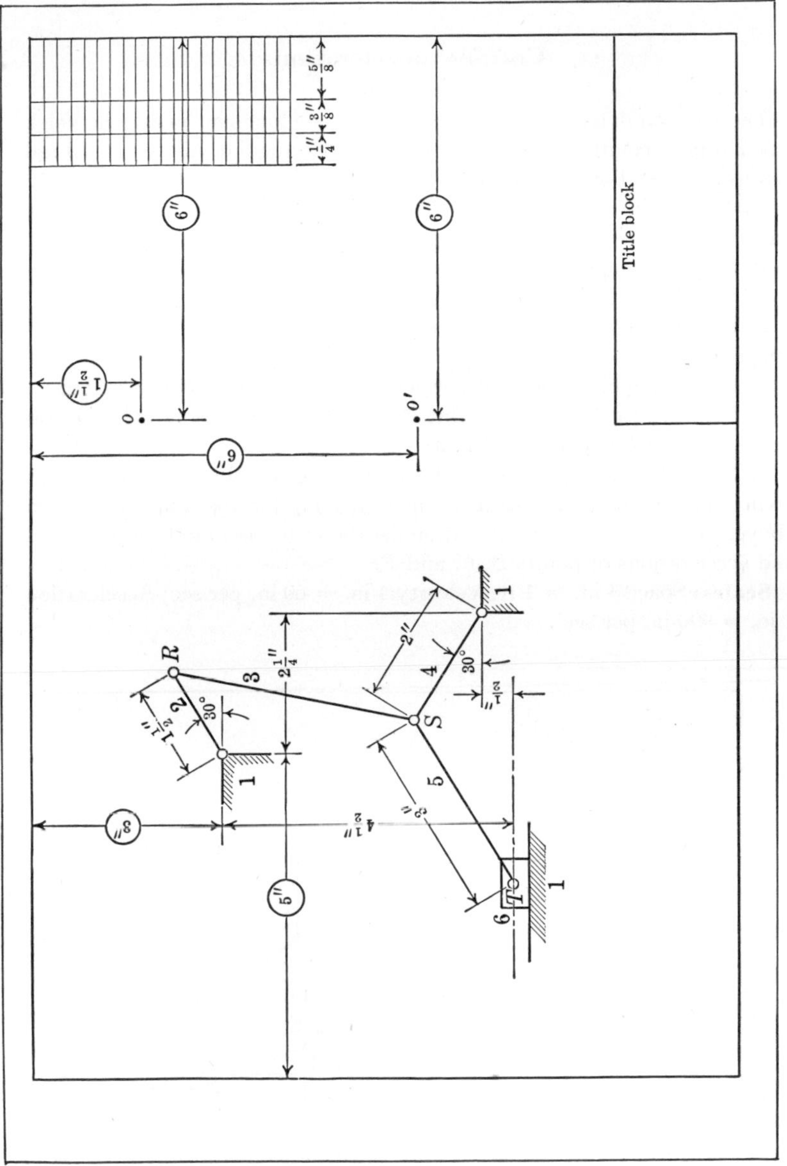

PLATE 9.

PROBLEM 11

Coriolis' acceleration

The skeleton diagram of Plate 10 represents a four-bar linkage in which link 2 rotates counterclockwise with a constant angular velocity of 10 rad per sec. The following data apply: $OO' \doteq 16$ in.; $OB = 6$ in.; $OP = 12$ in.; $BC = 6\frac{1}{2}$ in.; $O'C = 12$ in.; $O'P = 20$ in.; link 2 is perpendicular to link 1. It may be observed that point P is the instant center O_{31}.

1. Using the pole o find the velocity of points C and P from the calculated velocity of point B by the image method.

2. Using the pole o' find the acceleration of point C by the acceleration-image method.

3. Using the pole o' find the acceleration of point C by Coriolis' law.

4. Find the acceleration of point P by Coriolis' law, using the accelerations of points B and C found in **3**.

5. In the upper right corner of the drawing list the numbered steps, giving the directions and explain their meaning for the four parts given above. To the left of this tabulation list the scales used and the velocities and accelerations of points B, C, and P.

Scales: Space 3 in. = 1 ft; Velocity 1 in. = 60 in. per sec; Acceleration 1 in. = 900 in. per sec^2.

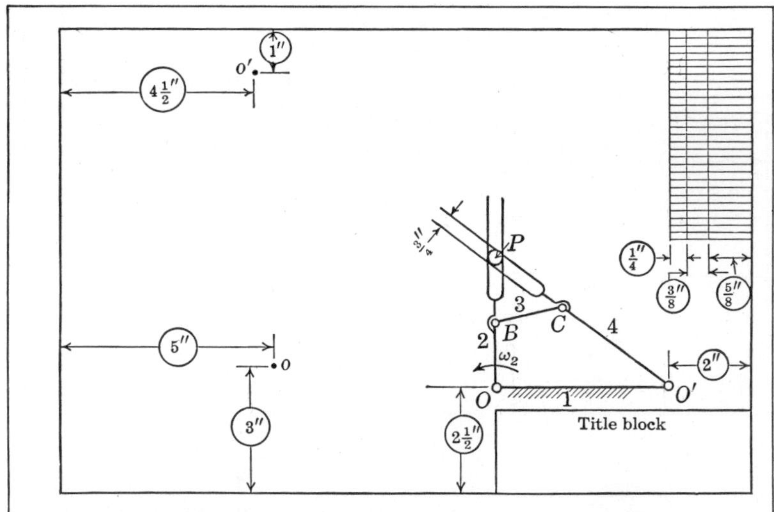

PLATE 10.

PROBLEM 12

Diagrams for slider-crank mechanism

Illustrated in Plate 11 is a skeleton diagram of the **slider-crank mechanism** used to transform rectilinear motion into rotary motion. The crosshead 4 has a stroke of 24 in. The connecting rod 3 is five times as long as the crank 2. The crank turns at a constant speed of 160 rpm in a clockwise direction.

Construct the following diagrams for a complete revolution of the crank 2; obtain points at 15° intervals.

1. Polar velocity diagram showing crosshead velocities on corresponding crank positions.

2. Velocity-displacement diagram showing crosshead velocities on positions of the crosshead pin.

3. Velocity-time curve, on a base line 9 in. long, located as shown, representing the time of one revolution of the crank 2.

4. Acceleration-displacement diagram, using same base line as **2.**

5. Acceleration-time diagram, base line same as **3.**

Label all diagrams, using notation above. Calculate and construct graphical scales for velocity and acceleration. Show the computations on the drawing.

Scale: 2 in. = 1 ft.

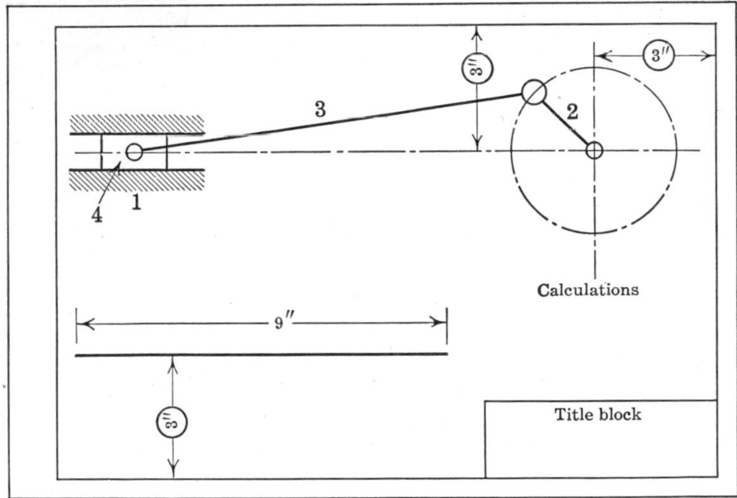

PLATE 11.

PROBLEM 13

Piston velocity and acceleration

A six-cylinder gasoline engine has a bore of $3\frac{1}{4}$ in. and a stroke of $4\frac{1}{4}$ in. It develops maximum power at a speed of 3600 rpm. The connecting rod is 8 in. long.

Locate the crankshaft center as shown in Plate 11 and construct the following diagrams, obtaining points at intervals of 15°, and assuming the engine to be turning at the speed for maximum power.

1. Polar velocity diagram, showing piston velocities on corresponding crank positions.

2. Velocity-displacement diagram, showing piston velocities on a base representing wrist-pin positions.

3. Velocity-time diagram, on a base 9 in. long, located as in Plate 11, representing the time of one revolution of the crank.

4. Acceleration-displacement diagram, using the same base as in **2.**

5. Acceleration-time diagram, on the same base as for **3.** Calculate and construct graphical scales for velocity and acceleration. Assuming that the reciprocating parts weigh 1.25 lb per cylinder, construct for the acceleration curve a graphical scale of the accelerating force.

Show all computations on the drawing.

Scale: Full size.

PROBLEM 14

Whitworth quick-return motion mechanism

Make a skeleton drawing of the mechanism according to the dimensions, Plate 12, using the following information: Length of connecting rod, DE, = 32 in.; length of $AC = 11\frac{1}{2}$ in.; $BD = 7\frac{3}{4}$ in.; $AB = 7\frac{1}{2}$ in.; and $BC = 5$ in.

1. Find the stroke of the ram.

2. Construct a full-stroke **velocity diagram** for the ram, taking as a base the line of travel of the point at which the connecting rod is attached to the ram. For the construction of this diagram, let the velocity of point C be represented by a velocity vector $1\frac{1}{8}$ in. long.

3. Calculate the **velocity scale** when crank AC turns 80 rpm. Construct a graphical scale as indicated on the sketch. Show calculations on drawing.

4. Locate all the **instant centers** for the position shown.

5. Determine the **time ratio** of the cutting stroke to the return stroke. Note this ratio on your drawing.

Scale: 3 in. = 1 ft.

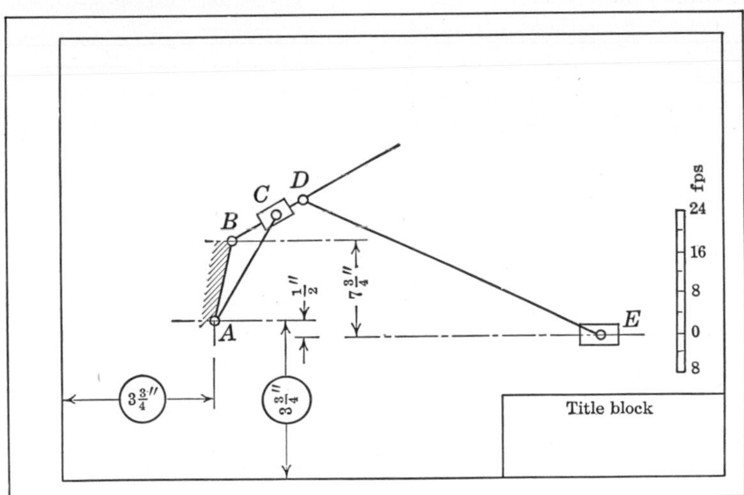

PLATE 12.

PROBLEM 15

Crank-driven quick-return motion

Draw the quick-return motion shown in Plate 13. The driving crank 2 has a length of $3\frac{3}{4}$ in. and rotates clockwise at 240 rpm. The driven slider 6 is to have a stroke of 16 in., and the time ratio of advance to return is to be 2:1.

1. Draw the mechanism as shown, with the block 6 at the left end of its stroke. Find the length of lever 4 necessary to give the proper stroke and time ratio.

2. Draw a skeleton diagram of the mechanism as indicated by the dashed lines in the figure, with crank 2 at 45° with the vertical position.

3. Locate all instant centers for the mechanism in the position specified in paragraph **2**.

4. By use of instant center O_{26}, determine the instantaneous velocity of 6. Represent the velocity of pin *M* on the driving crank by a line 2 in. long.

5. By use of instant centers O_{24} and O_{41}, determine graphically the velocity of 6 and see that it checks with the value obtained in paragraph **4**.

Scale: $\frac{1}{2}$ in. = 1 in.

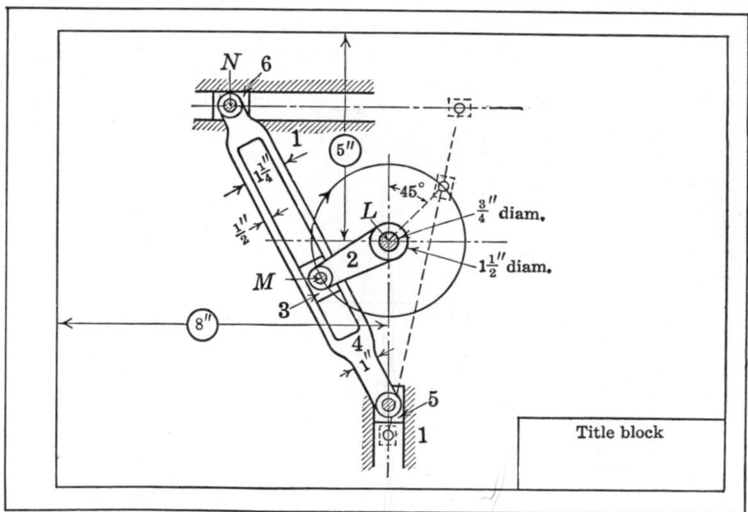

PLATE 13.

PROBLEM 16

Velocity curve for quick-return motion

1. Refer to Plate 13 and proceed as directed in paragraph **1** of Problem 15.

2. Divide the stroke of point N into eight equal parts.

3. Determine the velocity of N in the intermediate positions thus obtained, for both advance and return strokes.

4. Plot a velocity curve for sliding block 6.

The following method may be employed for determination of the velocity of 6:

Represent the constant velocity of crankpin M by a line $1\frac{1}{2}$ in. long. Find O_{41}. The absolute velocity of M on 2 is known, and the coincident point M on 4 has a movement relative to the former point in a direction along the line of slide of 3 on 4. Furthermore, M on 4 has an absolute velocity about the center O_{41} which can therefore be found graphically. From this point proceed to N.

5. Draw a graphical scale of velocity for N.

PROBLEM 17

Disk cams with roller and flat-faced followers

Design three disk cams (see Plate 14), each imparting the same motion to its follower. The right cam has a flat-faced follower, the center one a roller follower not offset, and the left one a roller follower offset $\frac{3}{8}$ in. to the right. The cams rotate clockwise. Determine points on the profiles at intervals of 30°.

CAM ANGLE	DISPLACEMENT	MOTION
0–120	+1 in.	Constant velocity with a 60° acceleration and 30° deceleration period
120–150	0	Rest
150–210	$-\frac{1}{4}$ in.	Simple harmonic
210–330	$-\frac{3}{4}$ in.	Constant acceleration : Constant deceleration = 3:1
330–360	0	Rest

Data: Diameter of base circles, $1\frac{1}{2}$ in. Diameter of roller, $\frac{3}{4}$ in.

Determine the diameter of the flat-faced follower that is required, and the maximum pressure angle (by inspection) for the two roller followers, and tell at what cam angle it occurs. Show the construction clearly on the displacement diagram. Show a sample construction for each cam.

Scale: Full size.

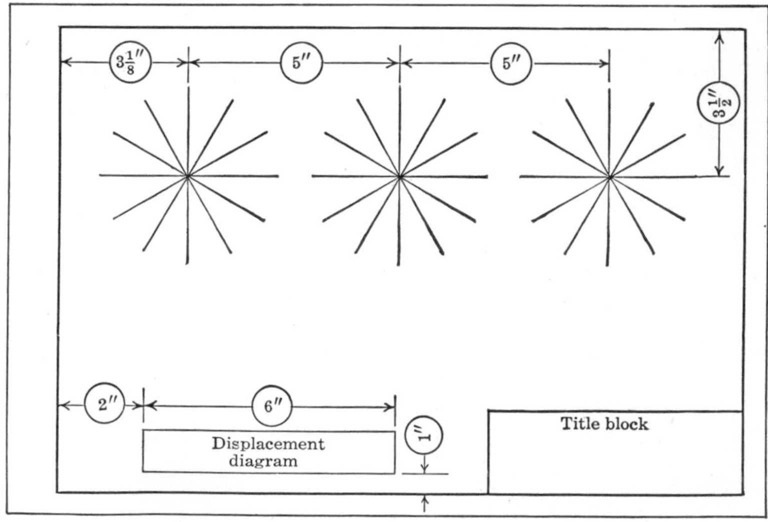

PLATE 14.

PROBLEM 18

Disk cam with pivoted roller follower

A pivoted roller follower as illustrated in Plate 15 turns through an angle of 30°. The outward motion is accomplished with constant velocity during 180° of cam displacement, except for 30° periods at the beginning and end of the movement where the acceleration and deceleration are constant. Two rest periods of equal length are provided in the extreme positions. During the return motion which requires a cam displacement of 120°, the follower is uniformly accelerated and decelerated, the acceleration-deceleration ratio being 1:2. The cam turns clockwise. Obtain points on the cam profile at 15° intervals. Determine the radius of the follower arm necessary to clear the cam.

Data:

Cam shaft diameter	$1\frac{3}{16}$ in.	Follower shaft diameter	$1\frac{1}{4}$ in.
Cam hub diameter	$2\frac{3}{8}$ in.	Follower hub diameter	$2\frac{1}{2}$ in.
Keyways	$\frac{1}{4} \times \frac{1}{8}$ in.	Roller pin diameter	$\frac{5}{8}$ in.
Roller diameter	$1\frac{5}{8}$ in.		

Scale: Full size.

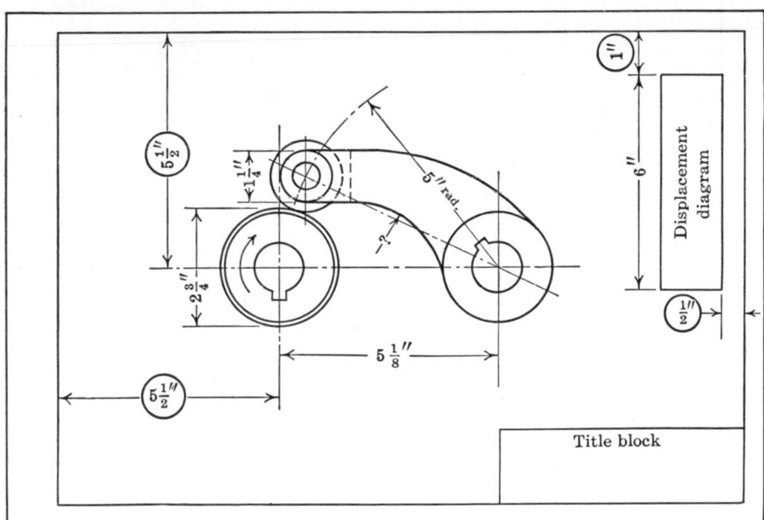

PLATE 15.

PROBLEM 19

Disk cam with pivoted flat-faced follower

(See Plate 16.)

The follower has an angular displacement of 30°. It moves outward during 12 of the 24 equal time periods required for one revolution of the cam and returns to the initial position during the following 8 time periods. Both motions are cycloidal. The cam rotates counterclockwise. The follower face when produced is tangent to the hub.

Obtain points on the cam profile at 15° intervals and determine the necessary length of the contact surface of the follower.

Data:

Cam shaft diameter	$1\frac{3}{16}$ in.	Base circle diameter	$2\frac{3}{4}$ in.
Cam hub diameter	$2\frac{3}{8}$ in.	Follower shaft diameter	$1\frac{3}{16}$ in.
Keyways	$\frac{1}{4} \times \frac{1}{8}$ in.	Follower hub diameter	$2\frac{3}{8}$ in.

Scale: Full size.

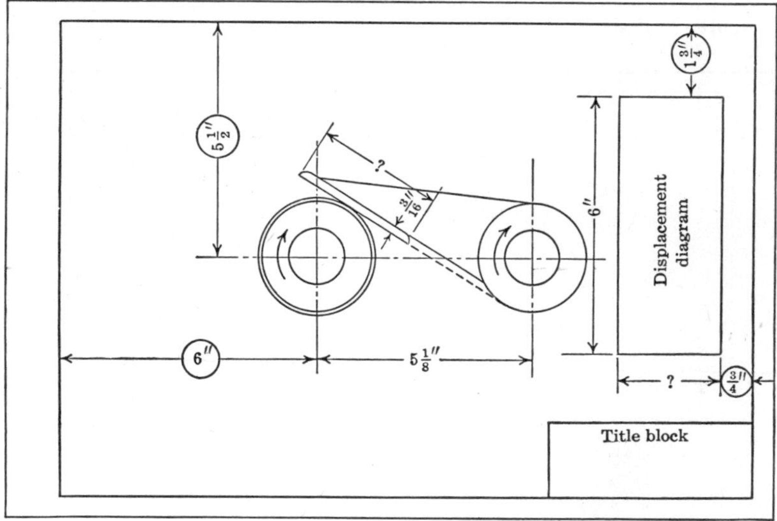

PLATE 16.

PROBLEM 20

Disk cam with primary and secondary follower

In the cam mechanism shown in Plate 17 the secondary follower has a movement of $2\frac{1}{4}$ in. Starting from the lowest position, this follower rises vertically with simple harmonic motion during 12 of the 24 equal time periods required for one revolution of the cam. It then rests for 6 time periods and falls with uniformly accelerated and decelerated motion during the remaining 6 time periods. The cam rotates clockwise. Find points on the cam profile at intervals of 15°.

Data:

Cam shaft diameter	$1\frac{1}{4}$ in.	Base circle diameter	3 in.
Cam hub diameter	$2\frac{1}{2}$ in.	Roller diameter	$1\frac{1}{2}$ in.

Scale: Full size.

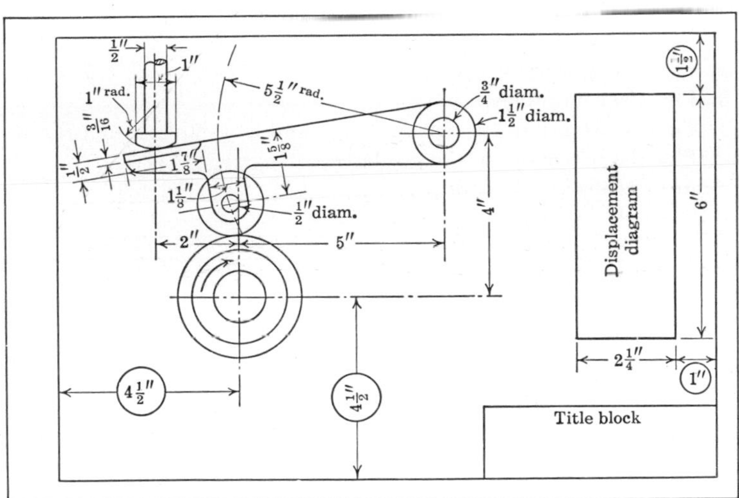

PLATE 17.

PROBLEM 21

Positive-motion cam mechanism

A yoke-type positive-motion cam mechanism of the form shown in Plate 18 has a pivoted follower which swings through a total angle of 30°. The angular motion of the follower during its clockwise displacement is composed of constant acceleration and deceleration, the acceleration-deceleration ratio being 5:2, the complete movement taking place in 210° of clockwise cam displacement.

The mechanism has the following dimensions:

Cam-shaft diameter	1 in.
Cam-hub diameter	2 in.
Follower-shaft diameter	$\frac{3}{4}$ in.
Follower-hub diameter	$1\frac{1}{2}$ in.
Base-circle diameter	3 in.

1. Find the width of the follower yoke.
2. Plot the displacement diagram from 0° to 210°.
3. Plot the cam profile.
4. Find the length of the arms on yoke and length of contact surface.
5. Plot the remainder of the displacement curve.
Scale: Full size.

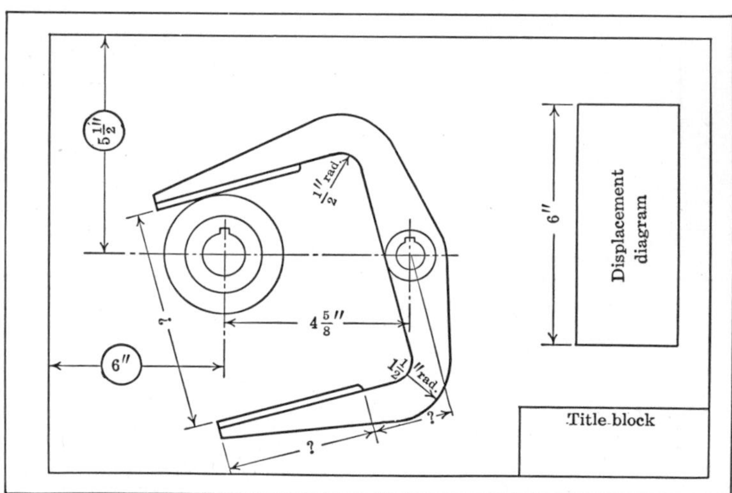

PLATE 18.

PROBLEM 22

Cylinder-cam mechanism

(See Plate 19.)

A cylinder-cam mechanism is required to move a pivoted follower through an angle of 40° (20° on each side of the horizontal position). The upward motion of the follower is accomplished during one-half revolution of the cam. This motion takes place with constant velocity except during the first and last 45° of cam displacement when the acceleration and deceleration are constant and of equal value. The follower then rests for a cam displacement of 30°. The return motion is accomplished with constant acceleration and deceleration during equal periods while the cam rotates the remaining 150°. The cam rotates clockwise. The follower is provided with a conical roller.

Draw (*a*) a displacement diagram, (*b*) a development of the cylinder, (*c*) plan and elevation of the cam.

Data:

Cam-shaft diameter	$1\frac{3}{16}$ in.	Cam-hub diameter	$2\frac{1}{4}$ in.
Maximum roller diam.	$\frac{3}{8}$ in.	Keyway	$\frac{3}{8} \times \frac{3}{16}$ in.
Depth of groove	$\frac{3}{8}$ in.	Length of cam hub	$4\frac{1}{8}$ in.
Radius of follower arm	$3\frac{1}{2}$ in.	Cam diameter	$3\frac{3}{16}$ in.

Scale: Full size.

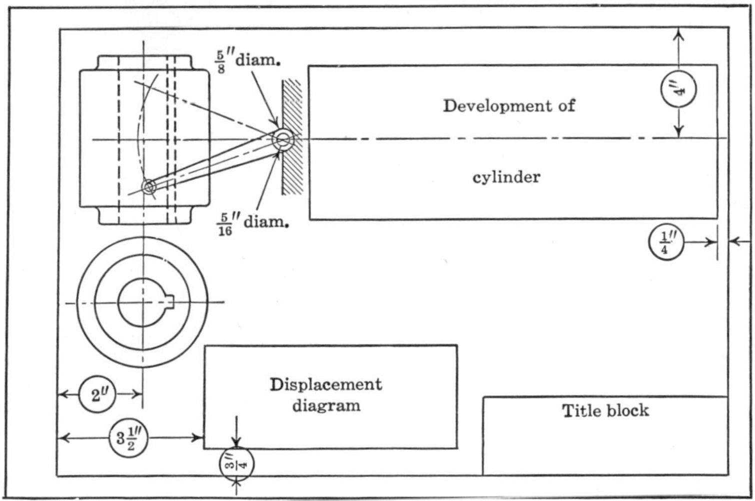

PLATE 19.

PROBLEM 23

Automobile-engine valve cam

An automobile engine has an exhaust-valve cam as shown in Plate 20, designed for use with a flat-faced follower.

1. Plot the half cam *three times full size.*

2. On a base line 9 in. long, representing 90° motion of the cam, located as shown, plot a **displacement diagram.** Obtain points at 5° intervals. Quadruple the ordinates in plotting this curve.

3. On the same base, plot a **velocity curve,** using the method of Art. 6·24, and doubling the ordinates.

4. On a base line 6 in. above the lower border line, plot an **acceleration curve.** Use the method mentioned above. Halve the ordinates.

5. Calculate the **displacement, velocity,** and **acceleration scales,** expressing them as 1 in. = —— in. (displacement); 1 in. = —— fps (velocity); 1 in. = —— fps^2 (acceleration). Assume a motor speed of 3000 rpm.

6. Construct **graphical scales,** and determine the maximum values of the acceleration, both positive and negative, and the maximum velocity. Indicate these values on the drawing.

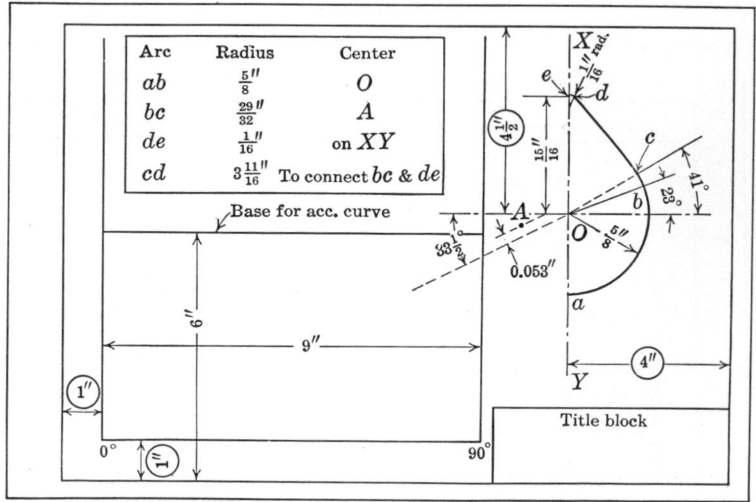

PLATE 20.

PROBLEM 24

Involute gears

(See Plate 21.)

Draw a pair of involute gears and a rack having teeth of 2 diametral pitch, zero backlash, and standard $14\frac{1}{2}°$ involute proportions to meet the following requirements:

Gear: Pitch diameter 12 in.; **Pinion:** Pitch diameter 6 in.

1. Use the generating method for drawing the tooth profiles, using a rack cutter.

2. Examine the tooth profiles for undercutting.

3. Indicate and determine the angle of action, angle of approach, and angle of recess for each gear, listing the numerical values on the drawing.

4. Indicate the path of the point of contact.

5. Completely label the drawing (not less than 35 labels) to indicate addendums, clearances, etc.

Scale: Full size.

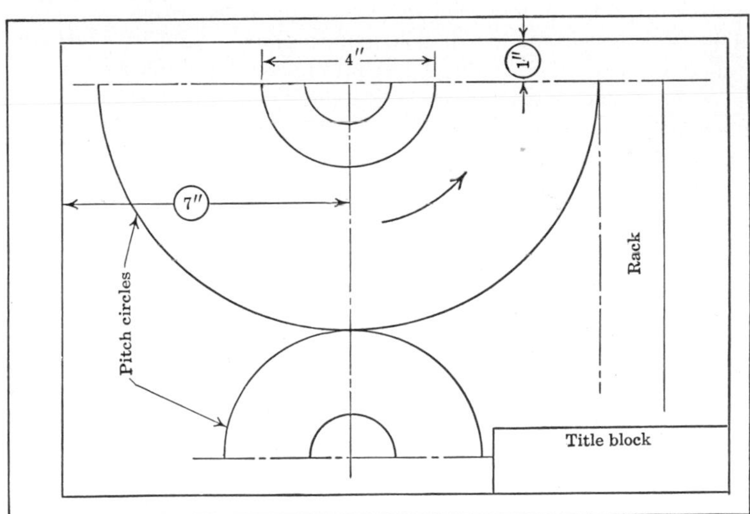

PLATE 21.

PROBLEM 25

Rack and pinion

An involute gear meshes with a rack, the teeth being in contact at the pitch point. The teeth have a diametral pitch of 1, a pressure angle of 20°, zero backlash, and are full depth. The pinion has 12 teeth, and its center is located $\frac{1}{2}$ in. below the top border and 8 in. to the right of the left border. It rotates clockwise. The pitch line of the rack is horizontal.

1. Draw two teeth on the pinion by the generating method outlined in Art. 8·17, using a Celluloid template of the rack tooth, and rolling it in $\frac{1}{2}$-in. steps on the pitch circle of the pinion.

2. Draw two teeth on the pinion with radial flanks as outlined in the first portion of Art. 8·17.

3. For each type of profile indicate on the drawing the line of involute contact, the angles of approach and recess, and the corresponding arcs.

4. Completely label the drawing (not less than 35 labels) to indicate addendums, clearances, etc.

5. Submit with the drawing a brief discussion covering the following points: (*a*) amount of tooth height affected by undercutting for profile **1**; (*b*) suggest change in addendum heights to avoid *a* and its effect on **3**; (*c*) amount of tooth height affected by interference for profile **2**; (*d*) suggest change in addendum heights to avoid *c* and its effect on **3**; (*e*) outline the basic differences and similarities between the profiles obtained by **1** and **2**.

Scale: Full size.

PROBLEM 26

Involute bevel gears

Make a drawing in section of a pair of involute bevel gears as illustrated in Plate 22. The diametral pitch is 2. The teeth have standard 20° involute proportions with no backlash.

Show the tooth forms on the developments of the normal cones at the large and small ends of the teeth by use of the generating principle of Art. 8·17.

Dimension the drawing and tabulate the following information: pitch diameter, number of teeth, diameters of blanks, angle between shafts, diametral pitch, and pitch angles.

Data:

Angular velocity ratio	10:7	Bore of pinion hub	$1\frac{3}{8}$ in.
Pitch diameter of gear	10 in.	Keyways	$\frac{3}{8} \times \frac{3}{16}$ in.
Bore of gear hub	$1\frac{1}{2}$ in.		

Scale: Full size.

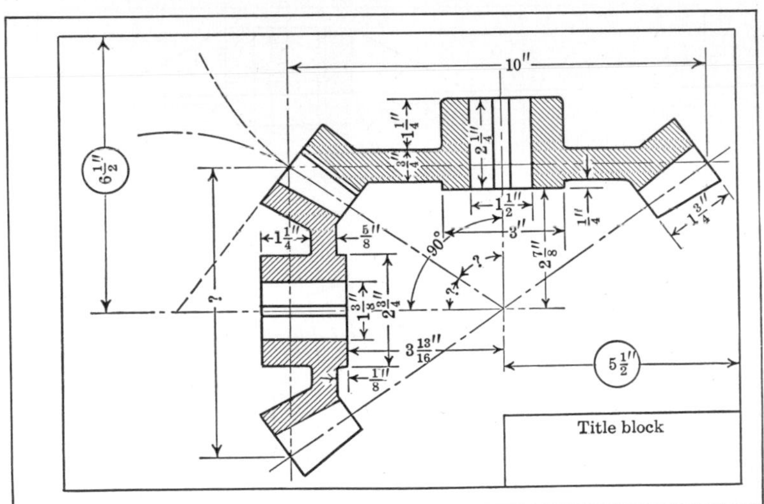

PLATE 22.

PROBLEM 27

Crown gear and pinion

Make a drawing of a crown gear and pinion in section, as illustrated in Plate 23. The involute teeth have standard 20° involute proportions, no backlash being provided. The diametral pitch is 2.

Show the tooth forms on the developments of normal cones at both ends of the teeth, constructing the profiles by the generating principle of Art. 8·17.

Tabulate pitch diameters, numbers of teeth, diametral pitch, circular pitch, angle between shafts, pitch angles, and diameters of blanks.

Data:

Angular velocity ratio	6:10	Bore of pinion hub	$1\frac{3}{16}$ in.
Pitch diameter of gear	10 in.	Keyways	$\frac{3}{8} \times \frac{3}{16}$ in.
Bore of gear hub	$1\frac{7}{16}$ in.		

Scale: Full size.

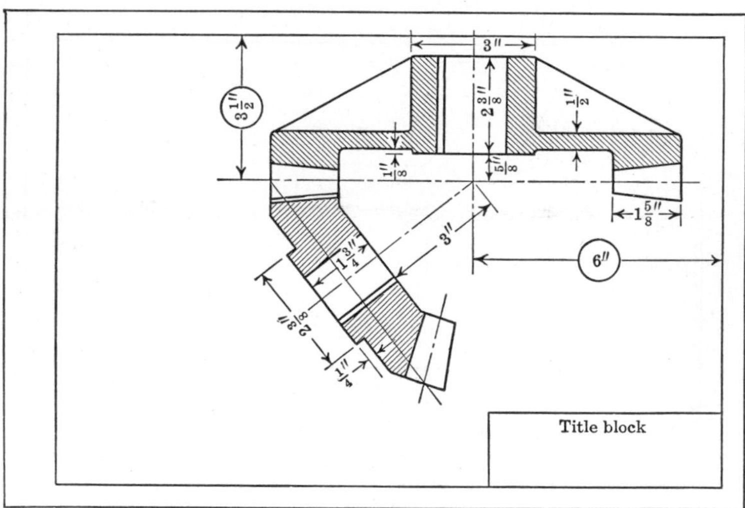

PLATE 23.

PROBLEM 28

Worm and worm wheel

(See Plate 24.)

Make a drawing of a worm and worm wheel with involute teeth, for a velocity ratio of 26 to 1.

Data:

Worm: Steel, case-hardened, $14\frac{1}{2}°$ involute proportions, single right-hand thread, outside diameter $2\frac{3}{4}$ in., bore $\frac{15}{16}$ in., keyway $\frac{1}{4} \times \frac{1}{8}$ in.

Worm wheel: Bronze, face angle 60°, bore $1\frac{7}{16}$ in., circular pitch 0.8125 in., keyway $\frac{3}{8} \times \frac{3}{16}$ in.

Dimension drawing fully, using decimals for the distance between centers, the throat diameter, the throat radius of the wheel, and the root diameter of the worm wheel.

Scale: Full size.

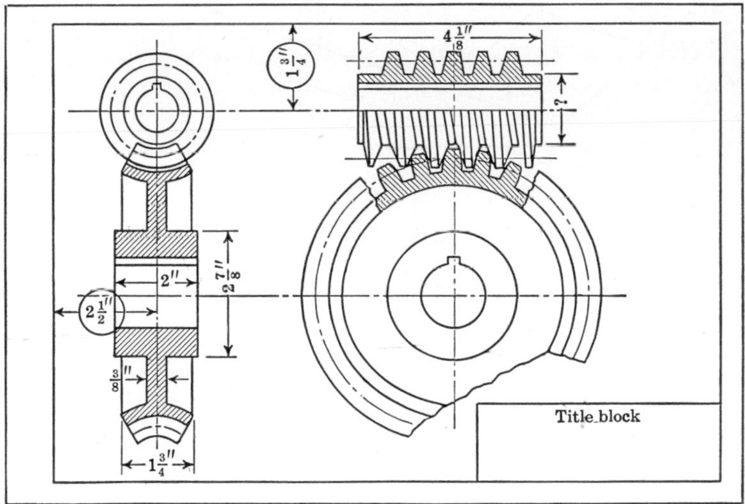

PLATE 24.

PROBLEM 29

The pantograph

1. Draw the two forms of the pantograph shown in Plate 25.

2. In the upper figure, move the tracing point *P* to other positions *Q*, *R*, *S*, *T*, *U*, located at uniform intervals around the circumference of a circle $1\frac{1}{2}$ in. in diameter. Find the corresponding positions of the copying point *V*.

3. In the lower figure, move the tracing point *A* to points *B*, *C*, *D*, *E*, *F*, located on a triangle of the form shown in the plate. Find the corresponding positions of the copying point *G*.

4. For both pantographs, find the ratio of magnification.

Scale: Full size.

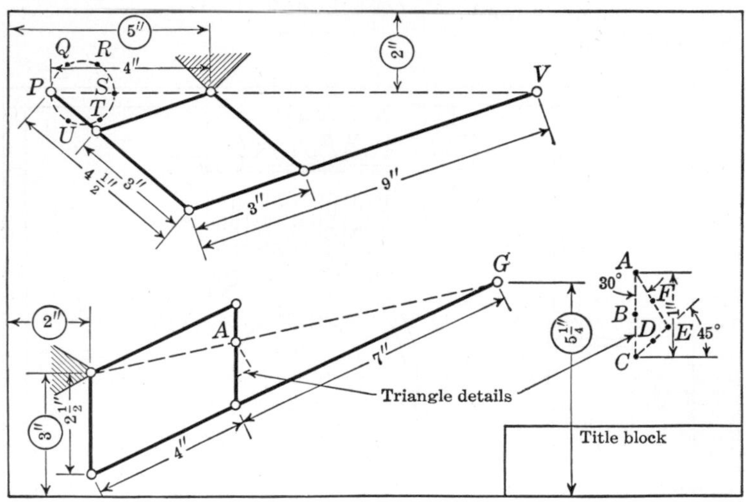

PLATE 25.

Index